HUMBER PERSPECTIVES

A REGION THROUGH THE AGES

Hull University Press

HUMBER PERSPECTIVES

A REGION THROUGH THE AGES

Edited by

S. Ellis

School of Geography and Earth Resources, and Institute of Estuarine and Coastal Studies, University of Hull

and

D.R. Crowther

St Edmundsbury Museums Service, Bury St Edmunds

HULL UNIVERSITY PRESS
1990

© Hull University Press

British Library Cataloguing in Publication Data

Humber Perspectives : a region through the ages.
1. Humberside, history
I. Ellis, S. (Stephen) II. Crowther, D.R.
942.8'3

ISBN O-85958-484-4

All rights reserved. No part of this publication may be reproduced in any form or by any means, electronic, mechanical, photocopy, recording or otherwise, in accordance with the provisions of the Copyright Act 1956 (as amended), without the prior permission of the Hull University Press.

Phototypeset in 11 on 12 pt Times and printed by the Central Print Unit, the University of Hull and bound by Khromatec.

Frontispiece. The upper photograph shows the Duke of York (later King George VI) at the laying of the foundation stone of the University College of Hull on 28 April 1928. The lower photograph, taken in 1963, shows the excavation by E.V. Wright (far right) of the third Bronze Age boat to be discovered on the Humber foreshore at North Ferriby; the first craft was discovered in 1937 and the second in 1940.

Contents

Preface		xi
Acknowledgements		xiii
List of contributors		xiv
Note to readers		xvi

1 Introduction   1
 S. Ellis and D.R. Crowther

Part I   ENVIRONMENTAL SETTING

2 Geology and relief   13
 J.A. Catt

3 Soils   29
 S. Ellis

4 Vegetational history   43
 J.R. Flenley

5 The Humber estuary   54
 J.S. Pethick

Part II   EARLY WETLAND EXPLOITATION

6 An East Yorkshire retrospective   71
 E.V. Wright

7 The Holderness meres: stratigraphy, archaeology and environment   89
 D.D. Gilbertson

8 The upper Hull valley: archaeology under threat   102
 J. Dent

9	Early boats of the Humber basin S. McGrail	109
10	Recent work on the archaeological and palaeoenvironmental context of the Ferriby boats P.C. Buckland, C.J. Beal and S.V.E. Heal	131
11	The archaeology of the Holme-on-Spalding-Moor landscape P. Halkon	147
12	Faxfleet 'B', a Romano-British site near Broomfleet B. Sitch	158
13	The topography and archaeology of Redcliff D. Crowther, S. Willis and J. Creighton	172
14	The Humber frontier in the first century AD J. Creighton	182
15	Exploitation of the alluvium of the lower Hull valley in the Roman period P. Didsbury	199

Part III URBAN ORIGINS AND DEVELOPMENT

16	The archaeology of the Grimsby-Cleethorpes area P.J. Wise	213
17	The historical development of Grimsby and Cleethorpes R.W. Ambler	227
18	The geographical shaping of Hull from pre-industrial to modern times M.T. Wild	250

19	The archaeology of Beverley *D.H. Evans*	269
20	Post-medieval Beverley *D. Neave*	283
21	The small towns of south Humberside *R.W. Ambler*	293
22	Market towns of the Humber north bank, 1700-1850 *M.K. Noble*	307
23	The rise and decline of Goole as a Humber port *J.D. Porteous*	321
24	The development of Scunthorpe *D.C.D. Pocock*	332

Part IV THE EMERGING REGION

25	Iron Age and Romano-British settlement in the southern Vale of York and beyond: some problems in perspective *M. Millett*	347
26	The Humber and its people during the medieval period *G.C. Knowles*	357
27	Rural population and land use in Humberside from the sixteenth to early nineteenth centuries *D. Neave and S. Neave*	373
28	Population change and settlement geography in the Humber region, 1801 to present *M.T. Wild*	388

29	The history of the Humber crossing *J. North*	406
30	Development of the Humber region during the nineteenth and twentieth centuries *J. North*	422

Index 437

Preface

The last two years have marked two important local anniversaries - the sixtieth anniversary of the founding of the University College of Hull in 1928, and the fiftieth anniversary of the discovery in 1937 of the first of the 'Ferriby boats', Bronze Age plank-built boats so far unique to the Humber estuary and therefore of international archaeological significance. These events have heralded over half a century of effort and enquiry aimed at providing a fuller understanding of the Humber region through time, so today we can see the area as one of considerable physical, cultural and economic variety, developed over several millennia.

To celebrate the Ferriby boats anniversary, a Day School was held on 19 September 1987, organised by the Council for British Archaeology Group 4 (Yorkshire and Humberside) in conjunction with the School of Adult and Continuing Education at the University of Hull, with, as its central theme, the origin, development and impact of the Humber on social and landscape change since late glacial times. In order to commemorate this event in a more permanent manner, however, and also to celebrate its own, closely coincident sixtieth anniversary, the University of Hull agreed to publish the present volume of papers developing this theme.

The Humber region is a product of natural and cultural processes requiring interpretation through geology, biology, archaeology, history, geography and other related disciplines; this volume offers such a multidisciplinary approach, unavailable hitherto. Thirty-one authors were initially invited to contribute, of which six were unable to do so, although two of these were able to be replaced by the kind agreement of alternative contributors. The resulting thirty chapters therefore represent the efforts of twenty-seven authors (excluding the editors) from a variety of institutions both local and further afield. To all concerned we offer our sincere thanks, both for their willingness to participate in this venture and for ensuring that the submission of none of the manuscripts was excessively delayed.

We are also extremely grateful to Alan Harris, Martin Millett, John North and Trevor Wild for acting as referees for certain contributions. Thanks are also due to Jean Smith and Joyce Bellamy of Hull University Press for their advice and assistance, Keith Scurr and Mark

Daddy for their drawing of many of the diagrams herein, John Garner for photographic work, and Joyce Bell, Jayne Karlsen, Karen Keating, Anne Lamb, Dorothy Soulsby and Margaret Tutty for typing and secretarial support.

S. Ellis and D.R. Crowther
September 1989

Acknowledgements

The following organisations have kindly granted permission for the reproduction of copyright and photographic material: Academic Press (Figs 23.1, 23.2, 23.3); School of Geography and Earth Resources, University of Hull (Figs 3.4, 30.1); Grimsby Evening Telegraph (Fig. 17.7); Hull Museums (Figs 6.1, 6.4, 9.2, 9.4, 9.8); Humberside Archaeology Unit (Fig. 16.4); Hutton Press (Fig. 22.6); National Maritime Museum (Figs 9.5, 9.6, 9.7, 9.9); National Westminster Bank (Fig. 17.6); Nottingham Museums (Fig. 9.3); Quaternary Research Association (Fig. 4.3); Sir Douglas Fox & Partners (Fig. 29.4); Welholme Galleries (Fig. 16.3).

List of contributors

R.W. Ambler — School of Adult and Continuing Education, University of Hull, Hull.
C.J. Beal — Department of Geography, University of Birmingham, Birmingham.
P.C. Buckland — Department of Archaeology and Prehistory, University of Sheffield, Sheffield.
J.A. Catt — Rothamsted Experimental Station, Harpenden.
J. Creighton — Department of Archaeology, University of Durham, Durham.
D.R. Crowther — St Edmundsbury Museums Service, The Clock Museum, Angel Corner, Bury St Edmunds.
J. Dent — Humberside Archaeology Unit, Property Services Department, Humberside County Council, County Hall, Beverley.
P. Didsbury — Humberside Archaeology Unit, Property Services Department, Humberside County Council, County Hall, Beverley.
S. Ellis — School of Geography and Earth Resources, University of Hull, Hull.
D.H. Evans — Humberside Archaeology Unit, Property Services Department, Humberside County Council, County Hall, Beverley.
J.R. Flenley — Department of Geography, Massey University, Palmerston North, North Island, New Zealand.
D.D. Gilbertson — Department of Archaeology and Prehistory, University of Sheffield, Sheffield.
P. Halkon — 35 Queensway, Cottingham, Near Hull.
S.V.E. Heal — Devon House, South Molton Street, Chulmleigh, Devon.
G.C. Knowles — Humberside County Libraries, Central Library, Albion Street, Hull.
S. McGrail — Institute of Archaeology, University of Oxford, Oxford.
M. Millett — Department of Archaeology, University of Durham, Durham.
D. Neave — School of Adult and Continuing Education,

S. Neave	University of Hull, Hull. School of Adult and Continuing Education, University of Hull, Hull.
M.K. Noble	Humberside College of Higher Education, Hull.
J. North	School of Geography and Earth Resources, University of Hull, Hull.
J.S. Pethick	School of Geography and Earth Resources, University of Hull, Hull.
D.C.D. Pocock	Department of Geography, University of Durham, Durham.
J.D. Porteous	Department of Geography, University of Victoria, Victoria, British Columbia, Canada.
B. Sitch	Hull City Museums and Art Galleries, Queen Victoria Square, Hull.
M.T. Wild	School of Geography and Earth Resources, University of Hull, Hull.
S. Willis	Department of Archaeology, University of Durham, Durham.
P.J. Wise	Warwickshire Museum, Market Place, Warwick.
E.V. Wright	Hall Place, Wycombe End, Beaconsfield.

Note to readers

Place names have been referred to, where possible, in the form in which they appear on the most recent Ordnance Survey maps. Dates are given in years AD, BC and BP (before present); uncalibrated radiocarbon dates are shown as radiocarbon years a.d., b.c. and b.p.

1

Introduction

S. Ellis and D.R. Crowther

It is now sixty years since the first academic year of the University College of Hull, following the laying of the foundation stone of the College by the Duke of York (later King George VI) on 28 April 1928. It is also fifty years since the discovery by the brothers E.V. and C.W. Wright of the first of the 'Ferriby boats' on the Humber foreshore in September 1937, an event of international archaeological significance. Ten years ago, celebration of the former occasion as the University's fiftieth anniversary saw the publication of the institution's history (Bamford 1978). Its sixtieth anniversary was therefore considered a timely occasion on which to produce another celebratory publication, and, in view of the close coincidence of this event with a major anniversary of the Ferriby boats discoveries, a dual celebration appeared appropriate. The present publication is therefore based on a characteristic which these events share - the furthering of our understanding of the physical, cultural and economic development of the Humber region.

This region has attracted the attention of scholars for well over a century and, indeed, this publication follows closely the appearances of two edited volumes relating to the area and published by Hull University during the past two years (Symes 1987, Jones 1988); the former examines the nature of Humberside in the 1980s from a geographical perspective while the latter provides an introductory background to the natural and human environments of the Humber estuary. However, although some of the themes in both of these works are common to those of this volume, the present collection of papers is seen as complementary rather than duplicative, in that it sets these issues in a broader context, both temporally and spatially. Its wide-ranging, multidisciplinary approach includes contributions in fields as diverse as maritime archaeology and social history, palaeoecology and economic geography, and geology and demography, all of which are assembled herein as a record of our present state of knowledge.

Any attempt to delimit rigidly the Humber region is obviously unrealistic, since its boundaries will vary according to the nature of the investigation, be it of the physical or human environment, and the time period involved. For the purposes of this volume, however, the region can be loosely defined as the area adjacent to the Humber estuary and the lower reaches of its tributaries. On this basis its boundary can be considered as a line running approximately from Bridlington, through Driffield, Pocklington, Selby, Thorne, Gainsborough and Market Rasen, to Mablethorpe (Fig. 1.1). The area circumscribed therefore comprises predominantly pre-1974 northern Lincolnshire and the East Riding of Yorkshire, although much of it now lies within the county of Humberside.

Combining perspectives from so many disciplines that cover so many issues is no easy task. Our approach is a thematic one, dividing the volume into four major sections, within which are chapters dealing briefly with specific topics, written by subject specialists and arranged on a broadly chronological basis. Numerous references will, it is hoped, take the reader unfamiliar with, for example, geology, archaeology or economic history, to other reading, perhaps for the first time. On the subject of references, it should be noted that the Harvard system has been adopted because this was used by the majority of contributors, although it is freely acknowledged that certain authors preferred a numerical system, as indeed will some readers, particularly for archival sources. However, since references to such material are rarely extensive, they have been incorporated, perhaps unusually but hopefully unobtrusively, within the main body of the text.

Part I presents an introduction to the natural environment of the region, providing a background against which the cultural and

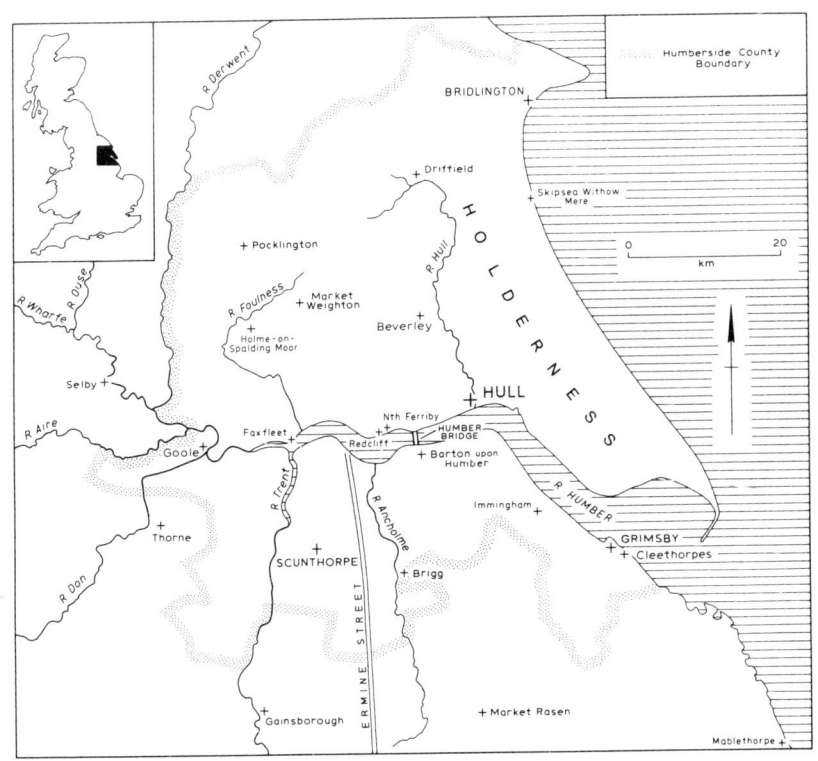

Fig. 1.1. The Humber region: location map.

economic developments in Parts II, III and IV can be set. In the first chapter John Catt outlines the major geological and relief characteristics of the area, from which may be seen the contrast between the relatively simple bedrock sequence upon which has been superimposed a more complex series of sediments deposited during the most recent period of geological time, the Quaternary. The varying geology and relief have given rise to a variety of soil conditions, which Steve Ellis discusses in the following chapter along with the important influences of human activity upon them. Such activity, along with climatic variations, has also had a substantial impact on vegetation, whose history is then examined by John Flenley. Part I concludes with John Pethick's summary of the past and predicted future development of the Humber estuary, the predictions possessing important implications for future activities, both archaeological and socio-economic, within the area.

Part II examines the early exploitation of the wetlands of the Humber region, focusing on a number of recently completed or ongoing archaeological investigations. An historical context for this research is provided by Ted Wright's retrospective of the archaeology of the Humber north bank, a personal account following the development of archaeology in this region since his childhood in the 1920s, set against the background of his own Ferriby boat discoveries. Dave Gilbertson then focuses attention on the wetlands of Holderness, and in particular the former Skipsea Withow Mere. This has produced archaeological and palaeoenvironmental evidence for human exploitation of this area since the end of the last ice age, showing that the landscape offered a resource-rich colonisation route for plants, animals and people from continental Europe to the emerging British Isles. Moving slightly westwards to the upper Hull valley, John Dent discusses the archaeology of an area which has yielded material ranging from Mesolithic to late Saxon times, but one in which the preservation of such material is currently under threat due to present and proposed quarrying and drainage activity.

There follows a report by Sean McGrail on the early vessels discovered in the Humber basin since the eighteenth century, some of which date back to the Bronze Age. This shows that the region's contribution to maritime archaeology is not only of national but of international importance. The Humber foreshore, at the location of the boat discoveries at North Ferriby, is then examined by Paul Buckland, Carl Beal and Veryan Heal. Timbers exposed on the foreshore since the time of the boat finds have provided further evidence for the function of the site, while preservation of animal and plant remains within the estuarine sediments has allowed a reconstruction of its ecology.

There then follows a series of investigations of Iron Age and Romano-British settlement and economic activity around the upper half of the estuary. First Peter Halkon provides evidence for iron and pottery manufacture around Holme-on-Spalding-Moor and the use of the River Foulness, which formerly connected with a large estuarine inlet of the Humber, as a trading route. Bryan Sitch then examines pottery and lead ingot evidence from Faxfleet, located at the mouth of this former inlet, from which he concludes that a 'staging post' for vessels travelling along the Humber existed here between the first and third centuries AD. Moving slightly downstream to Redcliff, Dave Crowther, Steve Willis and John Creighton report on the excavation of a site which imported goods from the Roman World during the first century AD when the Humber lay on the Imperial frontier. The effects of the Roman army's move northwards across the estuary around AD 70 are then examined from a south bank perspective by John Creighton, on the basis of coinage and brooch distribution. This illustrates the fluctuating fortunes of south bank settlements in relation to the establishment of Ermine Street and associated trade routes across the Humber. Moving further downstream still, Peter Didsbury concludes Part II by providing evidence for occupation and exploitation of the alluvium of the lower Hull valley in the late Iron Age and Romano-British periods, during which time this area formed a tidal estuarine inlet of the Humber.

Part III concentrates on the region's urban origins and development. Philip Wise begins by presenting archaeological evidence for settlement in the Grimsby-Cleethorpes area from the Neolithic to medieval periods. This theme is continued and extended to the present day by Rod Ambler, who contrasts Grimsby's growth as a major Humber port with the relatively recent development of Cleethorpes as a seaside resort. Moving to the north bank of the estuary, Trevor Wild then investigates the historical geography of Hull from medieval to modern times, based extensively on the many historical plans which exist of the city. The coverage includes maritime-related development adjacent to the Humber and River Hull, and also an examination of the widespread growth of suburbia 'inland' during the nineteenth and twentieth centuries. This is followed by two contributions on the development of Beverley, first by Dave Evans' report based largely on its Saxon and medieval archaeology, and then by David Neave's review of the town's expansion during post-medieval times, following its initial decline at the beginning of this period.

The following two chapters examine the growth of market towns both north and south of the Humber. Rod Ambler recognises the importance of waterway communications in the development of Barton, Brigg and Immingham on the south bank, while Margaret Noble stresses the importance of both natural and artificial waterways in the expansion of north-bank towns such as Beverley, Driffield, Selby, Pocklington and Market Weighton. Doug Porteous and

Douglas Pocock conclude Part III by providing an interesting contrast between the histories of Goole and Scunthorpe, both very 'young' towns compared with those previously examined, the former owing its development exclusively to its establishment as a port and the latter solely to its location upon mineral deposits.

Part IV concludes the volume by examining the way in which the Humber region has emerged through time, concentrating primarily on settlement and economic activity. In Martin Millett's discussion of social and settlement evolution in the Iron Age and Romano-British periods, the Humber is seen both as a boundary and route of access in political and cultural terms. He concludes that the Iron Age inhabitants lacked focal nucleated settlements, in contrast to those of southern Britain, and that their Romanisation appears to have presented few difficulties, with Roman military attention being focused on the area to the west of the estuary. Chris Knowles then reviews the development of the region in medieval times. This shows that once again the Humber and its tributaries formed an important communications network, both in the early Anglo-Scandinavian conflicts and the subsequent settlement and economic exploitation of the region.

This is followed by David and Susan Neave's discussion of the history of rural parts of the region from the sixteenth to early nineteenth centuries, concentrating on agriculture, manufacturing industry, population and settlement. Over this period agricultural improvements and changes in the pattern of land ownership created the rural landscape with which we are familiar today, while population fluctuations can be related to both these factors, in addition to national changes in birth and death rates. Trevor Wild continues the theme of population and settlement, for both rural and urban areas of the region, from the time of the first national census in 1801 up to the present day. The pattern is seen to be predominantly one of urban growth and rural depopulation, although this trend has altered to some extent in recent years with the expansion of commuter villages around the region's major urban centres.

In the final two chapters John North examines the economic development of the Humber region during the nineteenth and twentieth centuries, with particular reference to the role of the estuary. This is achieved firstly by presenting a short history of the attempts to construct a permanent estuarine crossing, which culminated in the opening of the road bridge in 1982, and secondly by discussion of regional economic development against the backcloth of both land and water communications. Both chapters illustrate the contrasting linking and dividing roles of the Humber, themes which appear throughout this volume, and the problems of the region's geographical location within a national context.

Throughout the volume there emerges a picture of the Humber through time as a catalyst for change, be it social, economic or political. The natural constraints of the Humber and its environs have both shaped, and in turn been shaped by, the communities who have exploited their surroundings for thousands of years and who continue to do so today. However, in a story as wide-ranging as this, there are inevitable gaps in the telling. As Table 1.1 shows, some time periods and areas have received greater coverage than others (the chapters of Part I have been omitted due to the different nature of their temporal coverage). The south bank is under-represented, and coverage of pre-Iron Age and Anglo-Saxon settlement is limited, although such gaps are being filled, and it is encouraging that new archaeological excavations at Wood Hall in North Yorkshire and Sutton Common in South Yorkshire are providing fresh evidence for early wetland exploitation in the much neglected west and south of the region. However, for many aspects of environmental and archaeological research, time is not on our side. In the face of widespread destruction of the region's wetlands, a project to assess their archaeological and palaeoenvironmental wealth is shortly to be undertaken by the Universities of Hull, Sheffield, York and Durham, the county Archaeological Units in Humberside, North Yorkshire and South Yorkshire, Hull Museums and English Heritage, in a unique venture of collaboration cutting across disciplinary and institutional boundaries.

This volume should be read in the same spirit. Reviewing recent work and looking to the future, it underlines the need for an interdisciplinary approach to a region and its people through time. In the years to come, closer collaboration between workers, professional and amateur alike, can only benefit our understanding, appreciation and indeed our enjoyment of a region focused on one of the great estuaries of England.

Table 1.1. Distribution of chapters according to time period and location.

Chapter number	Stone Age	Bronze Age	Iron Age	Romano-British	Anglo-Saxon	Medieval	Post-medieval	North bank	South bank
Part II									
6	X	X	X	X	X	X		X	
7	X							X	
8	X	X	X	X	X			X	
9		X	X		X		X	X	X
10		X						X	
11			X	X		X		X	
12				X				X	
13				X				X	
14			X	X					X
15			X	X				X	
Part III									
16	X	X	X	X	X	X			X
17						X	X		X
18						X	X	X	
19				X	X	X		X	
20							X	X	
21						X	X		X
22							X	X	
23							X		X
24							X		X
Part IV									
25			X	X				X	X
26						X		X	X
27							X	X	X
28							X	X	X
29							X	X	X
30							X	X	X

References

Bamford, T.W. (1978). *The University of Hull: the first fifty years.* Oxford University Press for the University of Hull, Oxford.

Jones, N.V. (ed.) (1988). *A Dynamic Estuary: man, nature and the Humber.* Hull University Press, Hull.

Symes, D.G. (ed.) (1987). *Humberside in the Eighties.* Department of Geography, University of Hull.

Part I
ENVIRONMENTAL SETTING

2

Geology and relief

J. A. Catt

Introduction

The Humber originates on the eastern side of the Vale of York by the confluence of the Ouse and Trent, and flows eastwards through a broad gap in the escarpment of the Yorkshire and Lincolnshire Wolds, between North and South Ferriby (Fig. 2.1). On the eastern side of the escarpment it is joined at Kingston upon Hull by the River Hull, which drains the lowland area of Holderness to the north. It then turns southeastwards to flow between southeast Holderness and the low-lying Lincolnshire Marsh, and finally enters the North Sea between Spurn Point and Grimsby. Throughout this distance of approximately 60 km the river is never less than 1 km wide, and after the first 3 km it is between 2 and 10 km wide, so it really qualifies as an estuary for the whole of its length. Although this course traverses an area of no great relief, it does pass through one of great geological diversity. This is best examined on the basis of a two-fold distinction, namely the older, Mesozoic rock types which form the bedrock foundations of the area, and the younger, Quaternary sediments which form a blanket over the bedrock in almost all parts of the region.

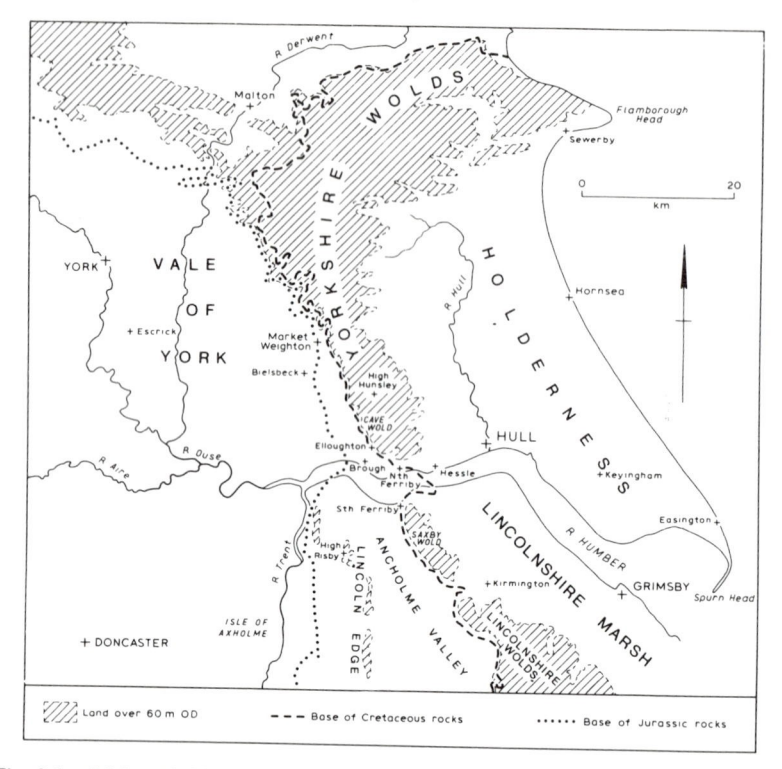

Fig. 2.1. Main relief features of the Humber region, and location of sites mentioned in the text.

Mesozoic geology

Most of the Vale of York, the Lincolnshire Marsh and Holderness lie below the +15 m contour, so the Chalk escarpment, rising to over 160 m at Cave Wold and High Hunsley a short distance north of the Humber, and to over 100 m at Saxby Wold to the south, is much the most prominent landscape feature of the area. North of the river the Chalk forms the Yorkshire Wolds, which extend northwards almost to Malton, then eastwards to Flamborough Head (Fig. 2.1). South of the Humber it forms the Lincolnshire Wolds. These never rise quite as high as their equivalent in Yorkshire, and their steep west-facing scarp slope is offset a few kilometres to the west compared with that of the Yorkshire Wolds immediately north of the Humber. The offset probably results from a minor east-west anticlinal fold beneath the

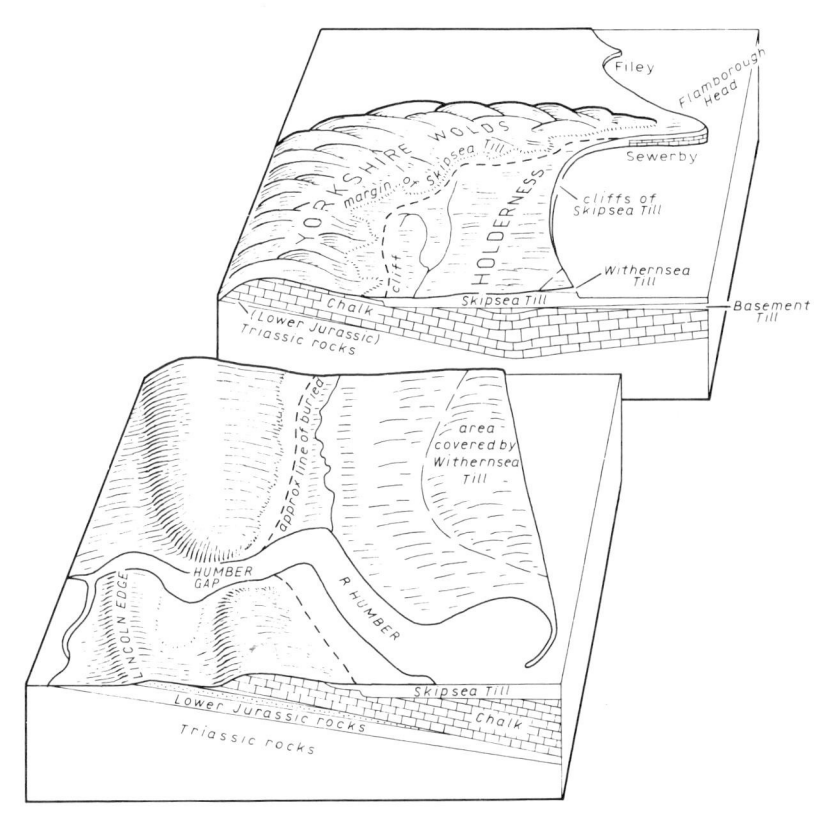

Fig.2.2. Block diagram to show the geological structure of the region.

bed of the Humber, with several westnorthwest-eastsoutheast faults downthrowing to the south on the northern limb of the anticline between Elloughton and North Ferriby. Shattering and weakening of the Chalk along the faults and fold crest may also explain why such a large valley has been formed through the escarpment at this particular point.

The inverted L-shape of the Yorkshire Wolds results from gentle folding of the Chalk during the Tertiary period, to form a shallow syncline with a northwest-southeast axis plunging to the southeast (Fig. 2.2). The western limb of this syncline dips at 2-4° to the east, and forms both the north-south section of the Yorkshire Wolds stretching northwards from the Humber, and the Lincolnshire Wolds south of the river. Eastwards the Chalk dips beneath an increasing thickness of Quaternary glacial deposits in Holderness and the Lincolnshire Marsh.

To the west of the Wolds, rocks older than the Chalk appear at the surface (Fig. 2.2). Beneath most of the Vale of York, Triassic rocks underlie glacial deposits or glacial lake sediments, although the Isle of Axholme, rising to 40 m, is one of several areas in which Mesozoic rocks crop out at the surface. On the eastern side of the Vale there are narrow north-south outcrops of Jurassic rocks (mudstones, limestones and sandstones) and of Cretaceous deposits older than the Chalk (Carstone and Red Chalk). Table 2.1 summarises this sequence of Mesozoic strata; de Boer *et al.* (1958) gave detailed descriptions of individual beds.

To the north of the Humber the Jurassic outcrop is narrow and forms nothing more than a bench at the foot of the Yorkshire Wolds scarp slope, but to the south the rocks thicken to form the Lincoln Edge escarpment, which rises to over 70 m near High Risby and is separated from the Lincolnshire Wolds escarpment by the Ancholme valley. The Jurassic and lower Cretaceous outcrops are narrowest and the deposits thinnest in the Market Weighton area, where a block of the earth's crust was uplifted throughout the Jurassic and early Cretaceous (Kent 1955), so that the area was either land or beneath very shallow sea. This meant that less sediment was deposited than in areas to the north and south where the water was deeper; also, when the block was close to or even above sea level, earlier deposits were removed by erosion. Measurements of gravity over the Market Weighton block suggest that the uplift resulted from intrusion of granite deep in the crust (Kent 1980).

In the centre of the plunging syncline beneath Holderness the Chalk reaches a total thickness of approximately 500 m, but only the lowest 230-50 m occur in the Lincolnshire Wolds and southern part of the Yorkshire Wolds. Most of the Chalk is a fine-grained, fairly hard, pure, white limestone containing more than 98% calcium carbonate, though the lowest 25-30 m are less pure, the middle part of the sequence contains bands of flint nodules, and thin beds of grey or greenish clay or marl occur sporadically throughout. The lowest part (the Ferriby Chalk Formation of the Cenomanian Stage) thins slightly over the Market Weighton block, but higher parts of the Chalk are not affected by it. This is because sea level rose during the late

Table 2.1. *Sequence of Mesozoic and later Quaternary deposits in the Humber region.*

Quaternary stages	Tentative dating (years before present)	Main deposits
Holocene	10 000 to 0	River alluvium, peat, mere deposits
Loch Lomond Stadial	11 000 to 10 000	Windblown sands
Dimlington Stadial	26 000 to 13 000	Withernsea Till
		Skipsea Till, Ferriby moraine and Lake Humber deposits
		Loess of Wolds
		Moss silts at Dimlington
Early Devensian	116 000 to 26 000	Hessle beach deposits
Ipswichian interglacial	128 000 to 116 000	Sewerby beach deposits
Wolstonian	186 000 to 128 000	Basement Till at Sewerby and Dimlington
Ilfordian interglacial	245 000 to 186 000	Bielsbeck Farm deposits
Hoxnian interglacial	339 000 to 303 000	Kirmington estuarine interglacial deposits
Anglian	478 000 to 423 000	Glacial deposits beneath Kirmington interglacial

Mesozoic stages	Periods	Main deposits
Campanian		Flamborough Chalk Formation (Upper Chalk)
Santonian		
Coniacian		Burnham Chalk Formation (Upper Chalk)
Turonian	Upper Cretaceous	Welton Chalk Formation (Middle Chalk)
Cenomanian		Ferriby Chalk Formation (Lower Chalk)
Albian		Red Chalk
		Carstone
Kimmeridgian		Ancholme Clay
Corallian		
Oxfordian	Upper Jurassic	
Callovian		Kellaways Sands and Sandstone
		Cornbrash
Bathonian	Middle Jurassic	Upper Estuarine Sands and Mudstones
Bajocian		Lincolnshire Limestone
Whitbian		Coleby Mudstones
Pliensbachian	Lower Jurassic	
Sinemurian	(=Lias)	Frodingham Ironstone
Hettangian		Scunthorpe Mudstones
	Triassic	Penarth Group (=Rhaetic)
		Mercia Mudstone (=Keuper Marl)

Cretaceous, so that the depth of water over the block was greatly increased compared with Jurassic and early Cretaceous times. Electron microscope studies of the Chalk show that it is composed mainly of calcite crystals (coccoliths) a few microns across, which originally formed ring-shaped aggregates (coccospheres) secreted by unicellular algae living in the Chalk sea.

There are no Tertiary or early Quaternary deposits known anywhere in the Humber region. It is possible that early Tertiary beds once existed above the Chalk and have been completely eroded away, because they are known from the floor of the central North Sea. However, the character of the Tertiary sediments beneath the sea suggests that the coastline during the Tertiary lay at least 70 km east of the present coast, therefore it is unlikely that thick Tertiary marine sediments ever extended as far west as the present coast (Kent 1980). During the Tertiary and early Quaternary periods the region was probably uplifted above the sea, tilted to the east and eroded mainly by streams. On higher parts of the Yorkshire Wolds various remnants of old erosion surfaces have been recognised (e.g. Lewin 1969), some of which may be as old as Tertiary, though most are probably of early Quaternary age.

Quaternary geology

Later Quaternary deposits are very extensive over both the Chalk and older rocks in the Humber region; most of them resulted from glaciation, but there are also several fossiliferous deposits dating from warmer, interglacial periods (Table 2.1). It is now known that there were about thirteen quite long cold periods during the last million years, and glaciers may have invaded parts of the region during any of these. However, there is firm evidence for only three glaciations of the area. The most recent resulted in the majority of the Quaternary deposits in Holderness and the Vale of York, and has been dated by the radiocarbon method to between 18 000 and 13 000 years ago (Penny *et al.* 1969, Beckett 1981). This period, the first part of the Late Devensian stage of the Quaternary, is termed the Dimlington Stadial (Rose 1985). It is named after a site (Dimlington Farm) near Easington in southeast Holderness, where the glacial sediments (boulder clay or till, and gravel) are over 30 m thick, and are underlain by lacustrine silts containing arctic moss remains dated to 18 240-18 500 years ago. An earlier glaciation resulted in a thick till (the Basement Till) lying between the Chalk and the moss-containing lacustrine deposits at Dimlington (Catt and Penny 1966). The exact date of this glaciation has not yet been determined, but it was probably about 140 000 years ago during the cold period known as the Wolstonian. The earliest definite glaciation mainly affected areas south of the Humber and probably occurred about 450 000 years ago.

During the Dimlington Stadial, ice approached the Humber from two different directions, north and northeast (Fig. 2.3). Ice from the north (the Vale of York glacier) had come mainly from the Lake District and southwest Scotland, crossing the Pennines by way of the Stainmore Gap between the Vale of Eden and Teesdale. Ice from the northeast was on the western margin of a large lobe filling the western part of the North Sea basin; this lobe had originated partly from the Stainmore ice stream (which divided to pass either side of the Cleveland Hills) and partly from ice spreading eastwards across southeast Scotland and Northumberland, and then moving southwards down the coast. At this time the North Sea area was largely dry land because, with so much water held in continental ice sheets over Europe and North America, the sea had fallen as low as 160 m below its present level (OD).

The edge of the North Sea ice sheet reached to a height of at least 60 m OD on the eastern side of the Yorkshire and Lincolnshire Wolds, and consequently blocked the Humber Gap. As ice had already blocked the northern part of the Vale of York as well, an extensive lake, known as Lake Humber, was impounded in the low-lying parts of the Vale of York (Fig. 2.3). The Vale of York glacier partly floated on the lake, and consequently surged or advanced unusually quickly southwards to form a tongue-shaped mass extending as far south as the area between Doncaster and the Isle of Axholme (Gaunt 1976). However, this advanced position of the ice margin was short-lived, and it soon retreated northwards to a more stable position at Escrick, where the ice deposited an arcuate ridge of till.

The water level in Lake Humber initially stood for a short while at 33 m OD, and patches of beach gravel were deposited at this height in various parts of the Vale of York, including the foot of the west-facing scarp of the Wolds on either side of the Humber. Later the level fell to 8-14 m OD, and several metres of laminated clays accumulated

20　　　　　　　　　　*Humber Perspectives*

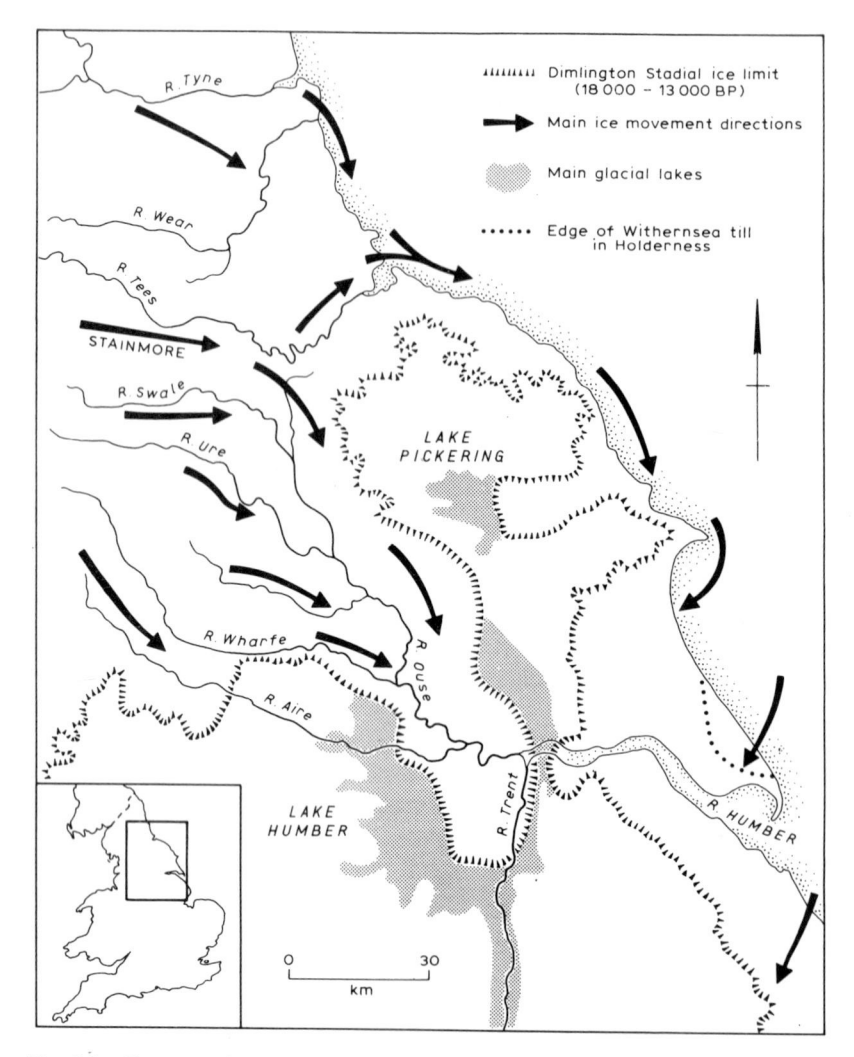

Fig. 2.3. Features of the Dimlington Stadial glaciation (based on British Geological Survey maps, Gaunt 1976, Madgett and Catt 1978).

over large areas of the lake floor. When the lake dried up completely, a network of streams draining towards the Humber developed across the exposed surface of the lake clays. Apart from a few minor changes of course, these streams developed into the present rivers of the Vale of York (Gaunt 1981).

The different levels of Lake Humber were probably determined by the ice plug in the Humber Gap, and later by the morainic ridge of till deposited across the gap by the glacier. Sections throughout this ridge can be seen on either side of the Humber at North and South Ferriby (Crowther 1987). However, the ridge does not mark the furthest limit of the North Sea ice, because till extends westwards beyond it into the Vale of York almost as far as Brough, and also southwards for a few kilometres into the Ancholme valley (Fig. 2.3). This means that the margins of the Vale of York and North Sea glaciers were no more than 6 km apart in what is now the uppermost part of the Humber, though they may not have reached here at exactly the same time.

Because the North Sea ice reached Holderness by two different routes, it deposited two slightly different tills (Madgett and Catt 1978). The lower of these, known as the Skipsea Till (= Drab Clay of Bisat 1939), extends throughout Holderness and the Lincolnshire Marsh, forms the core of the Ferriby moraine ridge, and thins to a feather edge on the eastern slopes of the Wolds. The upper Withernsea Till (= Purple Clay of Bisat 1939) occurs only in an arcuate area in southeast Holderness (Figs 2.2 and 2.3); it is visible in the coastal cliffs between Hornsea and Easington, and extends inland as far as Keyingham (i.e. a maximum of approximately 10 km). In Holderness the Skipsea and Withernsea Tills can be distinguished by colour, particle size distribution, carbonate content, the mineralogy of 16-63 μm and 63-250 μm fractions, and the assemblages of erratic stones brought from various areas by the ice (Madgett and Catt 1978). The uppermost 5 m of till were originally distinguished as a third unit known as the Hessle Clay (Wood and Rome 1868), but Madgett and Catt showed that this is merely the weathered upper part of whichever Dimlington Stadial till happens to occur at the surface.

On the southern side of Flamborough Head the cliff section at Sewerby exposes deposits associated with an ancient cliff (Lamplugh 1891) buried by the Skipsea Till. Beach shingle occurring at the foot of the buried cliff contains fossilized bones of three large mammals hippopotamus, elephant and rhinoceros (Boylan 1967) - which are a clear indication in England and Wales of deposits dating from a warm Quaternary period between 128 000 and 116 000 years ago (the last or Ipswichian interglacial). Traced laterally across the foreshore at Sewerby, the beach shingle transgresses from the Chalk onto a weathered surface of the Basement Till, thus showing that the

Basement Till is older than the last interglacial (Catt and Penny 1966). The buried cliff extends beneath the Skipsea Till around the eastern foot of the Wolds at the western margin of Holderness and the Lincolnshire Marsh (Fig. 2.2). At Hessle, where it intersects the northern bank of the Humber, the associated deposits contain a different assemblage of fossils from those at Sewerby; these indicate somewhat colder conditions than the last interglacial, and probably date from some period between 116 000 years ago and the arrival of the glacier in the Dimlington Stadial (Boylan 1967).

Other important fossiliferous Quaternary deposits in the region occur at Bielsbeck Farm, about 4 km southsouthwest of Market Weighton, and at Kirmington on the Lincolnshire Wolds. The Bielsbeck deposit was originally studied in the 1820s, and yielded a different assemblage of mammalian remains from those found at Sewerby and Hessle (Vernon Harcourt 1829). Its relationship to the glacial sequences of Holderness and the Vale of York is unknown, but the mammalian assemblage suggests it dates from an earlier interglacial than Sewerby (Boylan 1977), possibly one between 245 000 and 186 000 years ago, and known provisionally as the Ilfordian from a site at Ilford in Essex. The deposits at Kirmington lie in a deeply incised valley, which probably originated as a south bank tributary of the Humber cut during a Quaternary cold period when the sea level was very low. The site is close to the limit of the Dimlington Stadial ice sheet, and the sequence is capped by a thin, weathered layer of Skipsea Till. This overlies a coarse beach shingle, in which Palaeolithic flint implements of the Acheulian and Clactonian industries have been found (Boylan 1966). Beneath this bed are about 9 m of silts, peat and sands, which contain fossil pollen assemblages (Watts 1959) indicating that the deposits accumulated in an estuary during a yet earlier interglacial (the Hoxnian), which probably dates from 339 000 to 303 000 years ago. Sea level must have risen considerably between incision of the channel and deposition of the estuarine silts, because these sediments occur up to 22.5 m OD and would have accumulated close to the contemporary sea level. A borehole through the estuarine deposits indicated glacial sediments in the base of the channel (Stather 1905); as these are probably pre-Hoxnian in age, they must be older than the Basement Till at Dimlington and Sewerby, and may be equivalent to tills occurring in south Lincolnshire and East Anglia which were probably deposited in a cold period between 478 000 and 423 000 years ago (the Anglian Stage).

Just before the Dimlington Stadial glaciers reached their maximum between 18 000 and 13 000 years ago, silt was blown from glacial outwash plains on the North Sea floor and deposited over the Wolds as a layer of loess up to 1 m thick (Catt et al. 1974). Because the climate was then extremely cold and the exposed Chalk was susceptible to frost-shattering, the loess was mixed during deposition with small angular fragments of chalk and flint. Much of this mixture, known locally as Chalky Grut (= Grit, or possibly Grout as it was once quarried for mortar), has been eroded from steeper slopes on the Wolds or weathered to a brown silty clay on the more stable plateau surfaces. However, accumulations remain in the heads and floors of many Wold valleys, and a thin layer is often preserved beneath the Skipsea Till (e.g. at Sewerby).

During cold stages of the Quaternary, such as the Dimlington Stadial, land surfaces not covered by glaciers (i.e. periglacial areas) were frozen to a considerable depth for long periods. In warm summer months the uppermost 0.5-1.0 m of this impermeable permafrost zone often thawed, to form a mobile, active layer saturated with water, which could flow downhill even on very gentle slopes. This downslope movement of frost-shattered rock and other loose material *en masse,* known as gelifluction, was the main process responsible for eroding the Chalky Grut from the Wolds, and over long periods it probably produced the rounded, rolling relief of the Wolds. Frequently the amount of meltwater from snow and ground ice exceeded that required for gelifluction, and torrential streams flowed along the Wolds valleys, scouring out previous valley floor accumulations of gelifluction deposits and deepening the valleys considerably (Reid 1887). Most of the Wolds valleys were shaped mainly by these processes during Quaternary cold periods, though some were excavated partly by glacial meltwater flowing away from the edge of the North Sea ice (de Boer 1944, de Boer et al. 1958). The valleys are now dry, and are scarcely modified by contemporary processes because there is no permafrost to make the chalk impermeable; most precipitation consequently infiltrates directly into fissures in the rock, and percolates down to the ground-water table deep below the ground surface. However, occasional storms (Foster 1978) and rapid thaws of snow (Cole 1887) still produce brief floods which can result in some valley-side erosion.

Other effects of ground freezing during cold periods of the Quaternary were the heaving of stones upwards through the soil, the thermal contraction of ground to form polygonal patterns of cracks, and the sinking of dense materials into less dense parts of the saturated active layer above permafrost. The last of these processes, known as cryoturbation, is thought to be responsible for flask-shaped intrusions of loess or thin till into the top of the underlying frost-shattered chalk. The polygonal cracks also became infilled with loess, and were often elongated and streaked downslope by gelifluction, thus forming parallel stripes of alternating thick and thin layers of loess over chalk (Evans 1976, Ellis 1981).

A further process in cold periods was the erosion, blowing and redeposition of sand by the wind. This occurred at times when there was little precipitation, so that the ground surface was dry and unprotected by vegetation. Extensive deposits of aeolian sands (often termed coversands) accumulated during the final cold episode of the Late Devensian (the Loch Lomond Stadial between approximately 10 000 and 11 000 years ago) in north Lincolnshire (Buckland 1982) and parts of the Vale of York (Matthews 1970). The Lincolnshire coversands seem to have been blown from the west, possibly from the Trent valley, as they are banked against the small west-facing scarps formed by the harder Jurassic and Cretaceous rocks, and also become finer eastwards.

When the Dimlington Stadial glaciers melted, the newly exposed surface of till and glacial gravel was rather irregular, with elongate moraine ridges extending approximately transverse to the direction of ice movement, hummocks and enclosed hollows. Topographic differences resulting from such features have been noted by Valentin (1957), Straw (1969) and others, and have led to suggestions either that there was more than one glacial advance during the Devensian, or that some areas remained unglaciated throughout this period. In Holderness, for example, the relief features are more prominent in the east, where they have been referred to as 'young morainic topography' (e.g. Fig. 4.1 this volume), suggesting a more recent ice advance than that which occurred in the west. There is, however, no stratigraphic support for more than the single ice advance of the Dimlington Stadial; the less marked relief of western Holderness can therefore be attributed to natural variation of the till surface, and perhaps also to partial burial of the western areas of till by the subsequent deposition of alluvium and peat, particularly in the Hull valley.

Many of the enclosed hollows in the till surface are probably kettle-holes, which originated by slow melting and collapse of buried blocks of ice. Water often accumulated in the hollows to form small lakes or meres, in which clays and peats have subsequently been deposited. These mere deposits often contain human artefacts, pollen and other plant remains, which provide useful evidence for changes in the surrounding vegetation and the activities of early man in the area (Flenley, Gilbertson this volume). The earliest mere deposits date from about 13 000 years ago, and record a sequence of quite rapid climatic changes leading to a more stable warm period (the Holocene or Flandrian) commencing approximately 10 000 years ago and lasting to the present day.

Because the sea level was still very low in the early Holocene, rivers such as the Humber and Hull incised quite deep channels across the glacial deposits (Gaunt and Tooley 1974, Pethick this volume). By about 5000 years ago the sea was approaching its present level, and incision was replaced by natural accumulation of peat and fine silty or clayey alluvium along the river valleys (Gaunt 1981). More recently, man has influenced Holocene fluvial action by redirecting river courses (Gaunt 1975), by draining meres and other low-lying areas to improve the land for agriculture (Sheppard 1957, 1958, 1966) and by encouraging deposition of alluvium by the procedure of warping (Ellis this volume).

References

Bisat, W.S. (1939). The relationship of the " Basement Clays" of Dimlington, Bridlington and Filey Bays. *The Naturalist*, 133-5 and 161-8.

Boylan, P.J. (1966). The Pleistocene deposits of Kirmington, Lincolnshire. *Mercian Geologist* **1**, 339-50.

Boylan, P.J. (1967). The Pleistocene Mammalia of the Sewerby-Hessle buried cliff. *Proceedings of the Yorkshire Geological Society* **36**, 115-25.

Boylan, P.J. (1977). *The Ice Age in Yorkshire and Humberside*. The

Yorkshire Museum, York.
Buckland, P. (1982). The coversands of north Lincolnshire and the Vale of York. In: *Papers in Earth Sciences, Lovatt Lectures* (ed. B.H. Adlam, C.R. Fenn and L. Morris) pp. 143-78. GeoAbstracts, Norwich.
Catt, J.A. and Penny, L.F. (1966). The Pleistocene deposits of Holderness, East Yorkshire. *Proceedings of the Yorkshire Geological Society* **35**, 375-420.
Catt, J.A., Weir, A.H. and Madgett, P.A. (1974). The loess of eastern Yorkshire and Lincolnshire. *Proceedings of the Yorkshire Geological Society* **40**, 23-39.
Cole, E.M. (1887). Note on dry valleys in the Chalk. *Proceedings of the Yorkshire Geological Society* **9**, 343-6.
Crowther, D.R. (1987). Sediments and archaeology of the Humber foreshore. In: *East Yorkshire Field Guide* (ed. S. Ellis) pp. 99-105. Quaternary Research Association, Cambridge.
de Boer, G. (1944). A system of glacier lakes in the Yorkshire Wolds. *Proceedings of the Yorkshire Geological Society* **25**, 223-33.
de Boer, G., Neale, J.W. and Penny, L.F. (1958). A guide to the geology of the area between Market Weighton and the Humber. *Proceedings of the Yorkshire Geological Society* **31**, 157-209.
Ellis, S. (1981). Patterned ground at Wharram Percy, North Yorkshire: its origin and palaeoenvironmental implications. In: *The Quaternary in Britain* (ed. J. Neale and J. Flenley) pp. 98-107. Pergamon Press, Oxford.
Evans, R. (1976). Observations on a stripe pattern. *Biuletyn Peryglacjalny* **25**, 9-22.
Foster, S.W. (1978). An example of gullying on arable land on the Yorkshire Wolds. *Naturalist* **103**, 157-61.
Gaunt, G.D. (1975). The artificial nature of the River Don north of Thorne, Yorkshire. *Yorkshire Archaeological Journal* **47**, 15-21.
Gaunt, G.D. (1976). The Devensian maximum ice limit in the Vale of York. *Proceedings of the Yorkshire Geological Society* **40**, 631-7.
Gaunt, G.D. (1981). Quaternary history of the southern part of the Vale of York. In: *The Quaternary in Britain* (ed. J. Neale and J. Flenley) pp. 82-97. Pergamon Press, Oxford.

Gaunt, G.D. and Tooley, M.J. (1974). Evidence for Flandrian sea-level changes in the Humber estuary and adjacent areas. *Bulletin of the Geological Survey of Great Britain* **48**, 25-41.

Kent, P. (1955). The Market Weighton structure. *Proceedings of the Yorkshire Geological Society* **30**, 197-227.

Kent, P. (1980). *British Regional Geology: Eastern England from the Tees to The Wash.* Institute of Geological Science, HMSO, London.

Lamplugh, G.W. (1891). Final report of the committee, ..., appointed for the purpose of investigating an ancient sea-beach near Bridlington Quay. *Report of the British Association for the Advancement of Science* (1890), 375-7.

Lewin, J. (1969). *The Yorkshire Wolds: a study in geomorphology,* University of Hull Occasional Papers in Geography No. 11. University of Hull Publications, Hull.

Madgett, P.A. and Catt, J.A. (1978). Petrography, stratigraphy and weathering of Late Pleistocene tills in East Yorkshire, Lincolnshire and north Norfolk. *Proceedings of the Yorkshire Geological Society* **42**, 55-108.

Matthews, B. (1970). Age and origin of aeolian sand in the Vale of York. *Nature* **227**, 1234-6.

Penny, L.F., Coope, G.R. and Catt, J.A. (1969). Age and insect fauna of the Dimlington Silts, East Yorkshire. *Nature* **224**, 65-7.

Reid, C. (1887). On the origin of dry chalk valleys and of coombe rock. *Quarterly Journal of the Geological Society of London* **43**, 364-73.

Rose, J. (1985). The Dimlington Stadial/Dimlington Chronozone: a proposal for naming the main glacial episode of the Late Devensian in Britain. *Boreas* **14**, 225-30.

Sheppard, J.A. (1957). The medieval meres of Holderness. *Transactions of the Institute of British Geographers* **23**, 75-86.

Sheppard, J.A. (1958). *The Draining of the Hull Valley.* East Yorkshire Local History Society, York.

Sheppard, J.A. (1966). *The Draining of the Marshlands of South Holderness and the Vale of York.* East Yorkshire Local History Society, York.

Stather, J.W. (1905). Investigation of the fossiliferous drift deposits at Kirmington, Lincolnshire and at various localities in the East

Riding of Yorkshire. Report of the committee ... *Report of the British Association for the Advancement of Science* (1904), 272-4.

Straw, A. (1969). Pleistocene events in Lincolnshire: a survey and revised nomenclature. *Transactions of the Lincolnshire Naturalists' Union* **18**, 85-98.

Valentin, H. (1957). Glazialmorphologische Untersuchungen in Ostengland. *Abhandlungen der Geographische Institut der Freien Universitat, Berlin* **4**, 1-86.

Vernon Harcourt, W. (1829). On the discovery of fossil bones in a marl pit near North Cliff. *Philosophical Magazine* Series 2 **6**, 225-32.

Watts, W.A. (1959). Pollen spectra from the interglacial deposits at Kirmington, Lincolnshire. *Proceedings of the Yorkshire Geological Society* **32**, 145-51.

Wood, S.V. and Rome, J.L. (1868). On the glacial and postglacial structure of Lincolnshire and south-east Yorkshire. *Quarterly Journal of the Geological Society of London* **24**, 146-84.

3

Soils

S. Ellis

Introduction

The Humber region possesses a wide variety of soils which have developed as a response to natural factors such as parent material (geology), relief, climate and vegetation (Jenny 1941), and also anthropogenic factors related mainly to agriculture. This chapter examines the distribution of soil types, their principal characteristics, the way in which they have been modified by human activity and their present agricultural status. In doing so, it will provide a background to the important role which soil conditions have played in determining landuse patterns throughout history and prehistory.

Soil type distribution

The Soil Survey of England and Wales has mapped and described a number of areas around the Humber in some detail (e.g. Matthews 1971, Bullock 1974, Furness and King 1978, 1986, King and Bradley 1987), although the majority of the region has been mapped only at a 1:250 000 scale (Soil Survey of England and Wales 1983, Jarvis *et al.* 1984). Figure 3.1 is a simplified soil map based on this work, from which it can be seen that eight major soil types occur within the region.

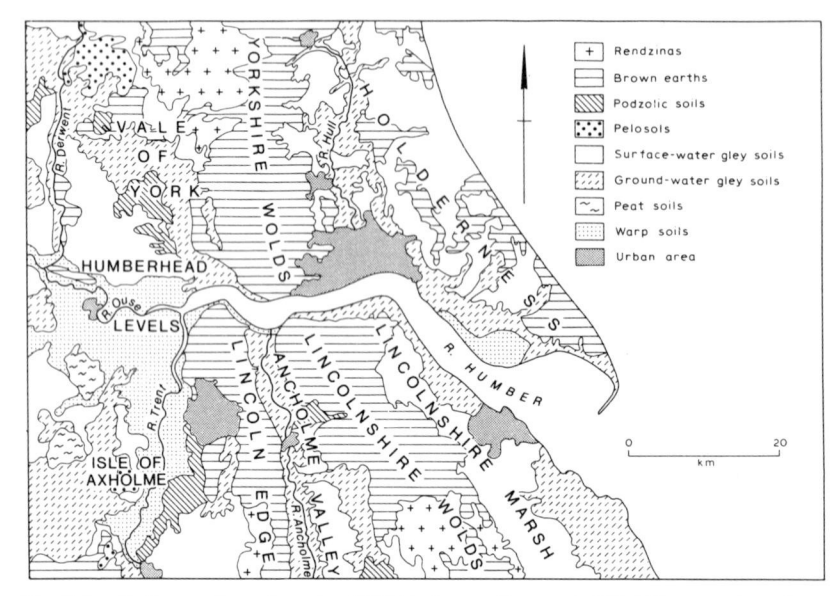

Fig. 3.1. Soil map (based on the 1983 Ordnance Survey 1:250 000 map of the Soil Survey of England and Wales with the permission of the Controller of Her Majesty's Stationery Office, Crown copyright reserved).

Although the distribution pattern is complex, many of the soil types occur in units which run broadly north-south, in association with the major geological and physiographic components of the region (cf. Catt this volume). This indicates that parent material, relief and drainage have exerted an important influence on soil formation. In contrast, climatic variation within the area is slight, and of little significance in soil developmental terms. The influence of vegetation on the soils relates largely to human activity, to be examined later in this chapter. The soil types characteristic of each physiographic unit are summarised in Table 3.1, along with their parent materials, relief and drainage conditions. The latter relate to natural conditions, although it is important to note that the drainage of many soils has been improved artificially, as discussed later. Details of the system used to classify the soil types are given in Avery (1980), while their principal characteristics are described below.

Table 3.1. Summary of soil conditions in each physiographic unit.

Physiographic unit	Principal soil types	Principal parent materials	Relief	Predominant drainage
Holderness	Browth earths Surface-water gleys Ground-water gleys Warp soils	Till Alluvium	Flat to gentle slopes	Poor to moderate
Lincolnshire Marsh	Surface-water gleys Ground-water gleys	Till Alluvium	Flat to gentle slopes	Poor
Yorkshire and Lincolnshire Wolds	Rendzinas Brown earths	Aeolian deposits over chalk	Gentle to steep slopes	Moderate to good
Ancholme valley	Ground-water gleys	Alluvium	Flat	Poor
Lincoln Edge	Rendzinas Brown earths	Aeolian deposits Sandstone and limestone	Gentle to steep slopes	Moderate to good
Vale of York	Brown earths Podzolic soils Pelosols Surface-water gleys Ground-water gleys	Till Glacial outwash Aeolian sand Lake deposits Alluvium Marls and clays	Flat to gentle slopes	Poor to moderate
Humberhead Levels	Surface-water gleys Ground-water gleys Peat soils Warp soils	Lake Deposits Alluvium	Flat	Poor to moderate
Isle of Axholme	Pelosols	Marls	Gentle slopes	Poor to moderate

Soil type characteristics

Rendzinas

The main characteristics of these soils are their calcareous nature, which relates to their high chalk or limestone content, and their shallowness (less than 30 cm deep). They occur on the Yorkshire and Lincolnshire Wolds and the Lincoln Edge, are found on a wide variety of slopes and are freely drained and fertile. On the Wolds, in areas which support permanent grassland, the soils possess an organic-rich topsoil and are known as humic rendzinas of the Icknield series; many of these areas have, however, been subjected to arable farming over the past few decades, as a result of which their organic contents have declined and the soils have changed to brown rendzinas of the Andover series (Furness et al. 1982).

Brown earths

These soils are developed on a variety of parent materials and occur throughout the region, mainly on gentle to moderate slopes. They range from poorly to freely drained, are generally deeper than rendzinas, may be either calcareous or non-calcareous, depending on the parent material, and their fertility is moderate to good. On the Yorkshire and Lincolnshire Wolds they grade into rendzinas where the soil cover becomes thinner, often as a result of downslope soil movement (Newsome 1985, Furness and King 1986). This has occurred due to gelifluction operating under the periglacial conditions of the Dimlington Stadial (Catt this volume), and also Flandrian soil erosion resulting from agriculture, to be discussed later.

The texture of the Wolds soils also reflects a periglacial legacy, as do the various patterns which the soils exhibit. Textures often show a high silt or sand component, derived from aeolian material deposited over the chalk during the cold, dry conditions of the Dimlington and Loch Lomond Stadials, while soil patterns relate to variations in the depth of soil overlying the weathered chalk, which result from cryoturbation and gelifluction during periglacial conditions (Catt this volume). Large-scale patterns are best seen from aerial photographs (Williams 1964, Evans 1976), while small-scale features have been encountered during archaeological excavations (Manby 1976, Ellis 1981).

Podzolic soils
These are developed on sandy parent materials, often of an aeolian origin, and occur mainly in restricted areas of the Vale of York and eastern Trent and Ancholme valleys. They are acid, nutrient-deficient soils, characterised by the downwashing of organic matter and/or iron and aluminium, and are consequently of limited agricultural value unless improved artificially by chemical additives. In low-lying areas the soils often experience waterlogging in their lower parts and are therefore of the gley-podzol variety (Bullock 1974, Furness and King 1978).

Pelosols
These are clayey soils occurring where Jurassic clays and Triassic marls outcrop in the Vale of York and Isle of Axholme. They occupy mainly flat to gently sloping terrain and, although fertile, their high clay content causes drainage problems; they can become waterlogged, making harvesting difficult, but can also suffer from drought during dry periods owing to the development of large fissures which allow rapid penetration of rainfall and little wetting of the upper parts of the soil. They therefore require careful agricultural management.

Surface-water gley soils
These occur commonly throughout the low-lying areas on a variety of parent materials. They are found on flat to gently sloping terrain and are characterised by seasonal saturation resulting from the accumulation of near-surface water derived either from rainfall or lateral ground-water flow in the upper soil layers.

Ground-water gley soils
These occur on similar parent materials and in similar topographic situations to surface-water gleys, but differ in that their poor drainage results from the presence of a ground-water table close to the surface. Both soil types are often found on till, glaciolacustrine deposits and alluvium, whose high clay contents contribute to their poorly drained nature. This results in the presence of either grey/brown mottles relating to periodic saturation, with iron occurring in both reduced and oxidized forms, or totally grey zones of permanent saturation in which all the iron is in a reduced form due to a lack of oxygen. Both ground-water and surface-water gleys are potentially fertile, but

require artificial drainage for successful arable use. Some alluvial soils, however, become very acid following drainage and are therefore of limited potential.

Peat soils
These occur in the Humberhead Levels where organic matter, mainly *Sphagnum* moss, has accumulated under waterlogged, anaerobic conditions. They are therefore organic-rich and poorly drained. Their agricultural value is extremely limited without drainage and fertiliser application, although some of the peat is extracted commercially.

Warp soils
These are classified as gleyic brown calcareous alluvial soils by the Soil Survey of England and Wales and form an important soil type in the Humberhead Levels; similar soils also occur around Sunk Island in southern Holderness. Warp soils are largely man-made and will be discussed in more detail later in this chapter.

Human influences

Soil erosion
The earliest human influences on the soils relate to deforestation associated with the development of agriculture. Although there is evidence that woodland clearance may have started as early as 8-9000 years BP on the Yorkshire Wolds, the major onset of deforestation in much of the region occurred after about 5000 years BP (Flenley this volume), and it was this removal of the protective woodland cover, often followed by ploughing, which gave rise to soil erosion. Such erosion is evidenced from the former meres of Holderness, where their sediments show inputs of soil washed from adjacent areas following woodland clearance (Gilbertson this volume). A similar situation occurred at Willow Garth on the Yorkshire Wolds, where soil moved downslope into the river and was then deposited over peat from around 2100 b.p. onwards (Bush and Ellis 1987). Excavation of dry valley deposits on the Wolds has also indicated soil erosion, where charcoal fragments occurring to a depth of 1.2 m below the surface are thought to relate to vegetation clearance and their subsequent incorporation in the valley floor sediments as a result of

soil movement downslope (Foster 1985).

Evidence for early soil erosion is also seen on upland areas of the Yorkshire Wolds, for example at Hutton Plantation near Thwing, where soils of a brown earth type are buried beneath a Bronze Age earthwork, whereas the adjacent modern soils are of the thinner rendzina type. This indicates the loss of 20-30 cm of topsoil since earthwork construction, as a result of woodland clearance and/or arable farming. Tentative evidence for even earlier soil erosion has been reported from a nearby soil buried beneath the Neolithic Kilham Long Barrow (Manby 1976).

Present-day soil erosion has also been reported on the Wolds, resulting from heavy rainfall on unvegetated arable soils; this can cause sheet wash, and gullying due to the concentration of water flow along furrows (Foster 1978). Although no time scale is given, it has been suggested that the shallow grey rendzinas of the Upton series may have developed entirely as a result of erosion of the organic-rich humic rendzinas of the Icknield series, following their cultivation (Furness et al. 1982).

In addition to the soils of Holderness and the Wolds, those of the Vale of York have been subject to erosion, but in this instance by wind. Unlike the previous areas, however, little is known of the history of erosion, except that some of the sandy parent materials themselves originated as aeolian deposits around 10-11 000 years ago, and that subsequent erosion probably occurred as a result of Anglian and medieval forest clearance (Matthews 1970). Wind erosion still occurs, and fine sand particles of 0.06-0.20 mm size are particularly susceptible to this process (Matthews 1971, Furness and King 1978). The Humberhead Levels also show evidence of soil erosion, based on alluvial sedimentary sequences; from archaeological and palaeoecological investigation it appears that the erosion, by perhaps both water and wind, dates to late Roman or early post-Roman times and was initiated by changes in cultivation practices (Buckland and Sadler 1985).

Drainage and reclamation

In their natural state, many of the low-lying areas suffer from poor drainage, but since medieval times they have been subject to extensive drainage improvement procedures (e.g. Sheppard 1958, 1966, Knowles, and Neave and Neave this volume). These have included the cutting of new drainage channels, enlarging and diverting of existing watercourses, construction of embankments and sluices and installation of pumps, powered initially by wind. As a result of this activity many of the lowland soils are now under intensive cultivation.

Large areas of low-lying land have also been improved by warping. This is a term applied locally to the accumulation of sediment on areas adjacent to the Humber and lower Ouse and Trent due to flooding at high tide and deposition of the sediment from the water as it subsequently drains away (Heathcote 1951). Although this process has occurred naturally for several millennia, artificial warping was conducted from the mid eighteenth to mid twentieth centuries by means of a 'warping drain' which conveyed water at a controlled speed, via sluices, between 'call banks' into an embanked area; the water was then allowed to drain away via a series of 'return drains', thereby depositing its sediment in a layer of uniform thickness within the embankments (Fig. 3.2). By this method the rate of sediment accumulation approached 1 m per year under optimum conditions, and the texture of the material deposited ranged from fine sand to clay, depending on the speed of water movement. The warping process was undertaken during fine, dry weather between spring and autumn, with spring tides at the equinoxes being considered the most suitable. Extremely cold or windy conditions were unsuitable due to the potential damage to wet embankments by frost, waves or unexpectedly high tides, and the blockage of sluices by ice. Natural flooding of the rivers was also considered unsuitable due to the danger of erosion of the artificially accumulated deposits.

When warping was completed, the land was allowed to dry and was then sown with grass varieties and used for stock grazing, which assisted in consolidation of the sediment. This was followed by division of the warpland into fields, drainage and crop rotation. It was important not to finish warping during the summer, since at this time of year the low river conditions would increase the salinity of the warp soils, and leaching of salts to a safe depth would only be slight due to lower rainfall; hence summer warping was completed in the autumn in order to leave the soils in a less saline condition.

A slightly different practice from warping has been conducted in the area of Sunk Island in southern Holderness, where, since the second half of the seventeenth century, land has been reclaimed from

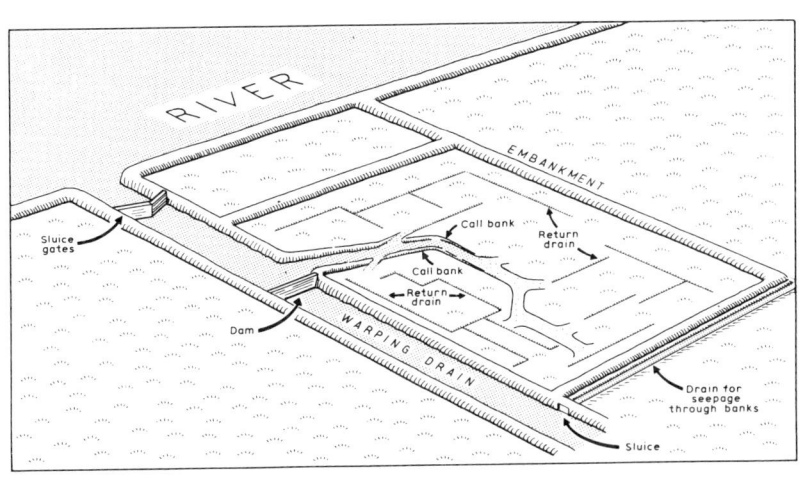

Fig. 3.2. View of a warping compartment (based on Heathcote 1951).

the Humber by the construction of a series of embankments which have allowed the natural accretion of estuarine sediments (Sheppard 1966, de Boer 1978).

Present soil conditions

Today many of the region's soils are of great agricultural value. The majority of parent materials produce soils of moderate to high fertility (see above), and the relief of the area generally presents few obstacles to modern farming practices. Historically, the principal constraint was poor drainage of the low-lying areas, but drainage improvement and warping over the past few centuries have greatly reduced this problem. Climatic conditions also make the region's soils agriculturally attractive. Mean annual temperatures vary with altitude, from around 8 to 10°C, and median accumulated temperature above 0°C for the period January to June ranges from 1250 day-degrees on the high Wolds to over 1400 day-degrees in the low-lying areas. The latter is one of the highest figures in northern England (Jarvis *et al.* 1984), and there is therefore relatively high heat energy available for plant growth. The area also receives low rainfall in relation to much of northern England, with mean annual totals ranging from 600-700 mm in the low-lying parts, rising to 800 mm on

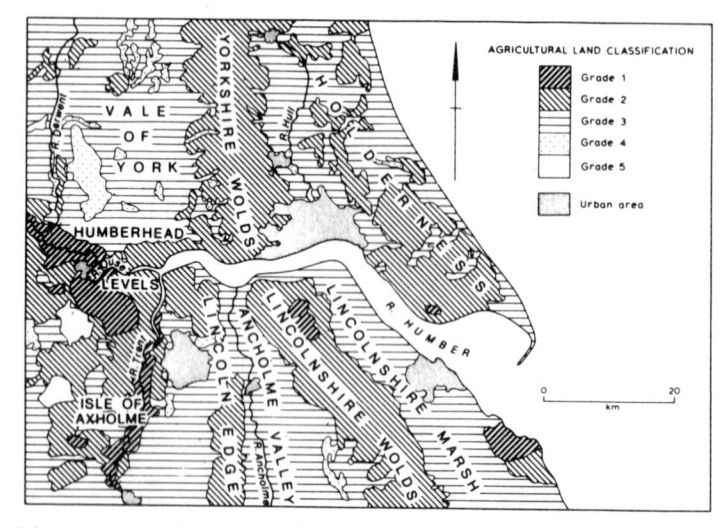

Fig. 3.3. Agricultural land classification map (based on the 1977 Ordnance Survey 1:250 000 maps of the Ministry of Agriculture, Fisheries and Food with the permission of the Controller of Her Majesty's Stationery Office, Crown copyright reserved).

the Yorkshire Wolds. Consequently, with a median field capacity period in the order of 125-200 days, the soils are accessible for long periods. The main climatic problems from an agricultural viewpoint are the long, cold winters and cold springs often experienced in the higher areas, and the mean accumulated maximum potential soil moisture deficit, ranging from 125 mm on the high Wolds to over 175 mm close to the Humber, which can give rise to droughtiness.

The region now possesses some soils of the highest quality, being classified as Grade 1 or 2 according to the Ministry of Agriculture, Fisheries and Food (1977) agricultural land classification system (Fig. 3.3). These categories represent land with no, or only minor, limitations to agricultural use, which is therefore usually arable. This is found in the warplands, around the Isle of Axholme, on the Lincoln Edge, throughout much of the Wolds and on the better drained areas of Holderness and the Lincolnshire Marsh. Many of the remaining areas are classified as Grade 3; these impose moderate limitations on agricultural use due to soil, relief or drainage conditions, but as a result of fertiliser application and improved drainage they are, nevertheless, able to be extensively devoted to arable farming. Grade

Soils 39

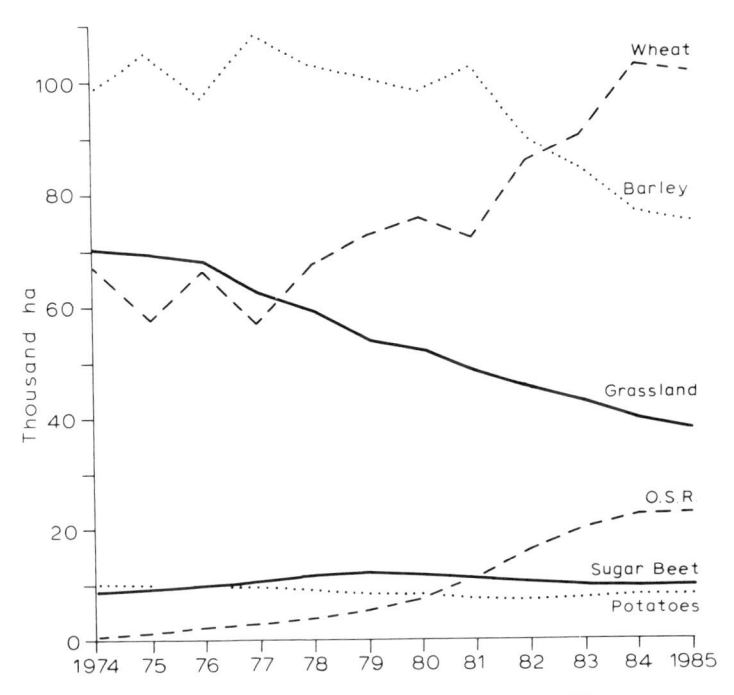

Fig. 3.4. Humberside land use trends, 1974-85 (from Symes 1987).

4 or 5 land, which imposes severe or very severe limitations, occurs only in limited areas, in particular on river flood plains and in the southern Vale of York, where problems relate to waterlogging, on the peat soils of Thorne and Hatfield Moors, and on steep slopes of the Wolds which, along with shallow soils, inhibit arable farming.

At the present time arable crops account for a massive 83% of agricultural land use in Humberside, with cereals being dominant (Symes 1987). Since the mid 1970s much temporary and permanent grassland has been ploughed up and converted to arable land, while, of the arable crops, wheat and oil seed rape have seen the most marked increase in area (Fig. 3.4). Ploughing out of grassland, often associated in low-lying areas (both within the region and elsewhere) with improved drainage, is causing serious degradation of organic material within the soils, including that of an archaeological and palaeoecological nature; clearly, this makes the recovery of such material a matter of some urgency (Schadla-Hall 1987, Dent this volume).

Acknowledgement

Mr S.J. King of the Soil Survey of England and Wales is gratefully acknowledged for his comments on the manuscript.

References

Avery, B.W. (1980). *Soil Classification for England and Wales (Higher Categories)*, Soil Survey Technical Monograph No. 14. Rothamsted, Harpenden.

Buckland, P.C. and Sadler, J. (1985). The nature of late Flandrian alluviation in the Humberhead Levels. *East Midland Geographer* 8, 239-51.

Bullock, P. (1974). *Soils in Yorkshire III, Sheets SE 64/74 (Escrick/Barmby Moor)*, Soil Survey Record No. 16. Rothamsted, Harpenden.

Bush, M.B. and Ellis, S. (1987). The sedimentological and vegetational history of Willow Garth. In: *East Yorkshire Field Guide* (ed. S. Ellis) pp. 42-52. Quaternary Research Association, Cambridge.

de Boer, G. (1978). Holderness and its coastal features. In: *North Humberside Introductory Themes* (ed. D.G. Symes) pp. 69-76. Department of Geography, University of Hull.

Ellis, S. (1981). Patterned ground at Wharram Percy, North Yorkshire: its origin and palaeoenvironmental implications. In: *The Quaternary in Britain* (ed. J. Neale and J. Flenley) pp. 98-107. Pergamon Press, Oxford.

Evans, R. (1976). Observations on a stripe pattern. *Biuletyn Peryglacjalny* 25, 9-22.

Foster, S.W. (1978). An example of gullying on arable land on the Yorkshire Wolds. *Naturalist* 103, 157-61.

Foster, S.W. (1985). The Late Glacial and Early Post Glacial History of the Vale of Pickering and Northern Yorkshire Wolds. Ph.D. thesis, University of Hull.

Furness, R.R. and King, S.J. (1978). *Soils in North Yorkshire IV, Sheet SE 63/73 (Selby)*, Soil Survey Record No. 56. Rothamsted, Harpenden.

Furness, R.R. and King, S.J. (1986). *Soils in Humberside II. Sheet*

SE 85 (Fridaythorpe), Soil Survey Record No. 97. Rothamsted, Harpenden.

Furness, R.R., Jarvis, R.A. and King, S.J. (1982). Soils and land use on the Yorkshire Wolds. *Proceedings of the North of England Soils Discussion Group* **18**, 1-21.

Heathcote, W.R. (1951). A soil survey on warpland in Yorkshire. *Journal of Soil Science* **2**, 144-62.

Jarvis, R.A., Bendelow, V.C., Bradley, R.I., Carroll, D.M., Furness, R.R., Kilgour, I.N.L. and King, S.J. (1984). *Soils and their Use in Northern England*, Soil Survey Bulletin No. 10. Rothamsted, Harpenden.

Jenny, H. (1941). *Factors of Soil Formation: a system of quantitative pedology*. McGraw-Hill, London.

King, S.J. and Bradley, R.I. (1987). *Soils of the Market Weighton District*, Memoirs of the Soil Survey of Great Britain. Rothamsted, Harpenden.

Manby, T.G. (1976) . The excavation of the Kilham Long Barrow, East Riding of Yorkshire. *Proceedings of the Prehistoric Society* **42**, 111-59.

Matthews, B. (1970). Age and origin of aeolian sand in the Vale of York. *Nature* **227**, 1234-6.

Matthews, B. (1971). *Soils in Yorkshire I, Sheet SE 65 (York East)*, Soil Survey Record No. 6. Rothamsted, Harpenden.

Ministry of Agriculture, Fisheries and Food (1977). *1:250 000 Series Agricultural Land Classification of England and Wales*. HMSO, London.

Newsome, D. (1985). An Investigation of Pedogenesis on the Yorkshire Wolds, Northeast England. M.Sc. thesis, University of Hull.

Schadla-Hall, R.T. (1987). Early man in the eastern Vale of Pickering. In: *East Yorkshire Field Guide* (ed. S. Ellis) pp. 22-30. Quaternary Research Association, Cambridge.

Sheppard, J.A. (1958). *The Draining of the Hull Valley*. East Yorkshire Local History Society, York.

Sheppard, J.A. (1966). *The Draining of the Marshlands of South Holderness and the Vale of York*. East Yorkshire Local History Society, York.

Soil Survey of England and Wales (1983). *Soils of England and Wales, Sheet 1, Northern England*. Ordnance Survey,

Southampton.
Symes, D.G. (1987). Agriculture. In: *Humberside in the Eighties* (ed. D.G. Symes) pp. 9-22. Department of Geography, University of Hull.
Williams, R.B.G. (1964). Fossil patterned ground in eastern England. *Biuletyn Peryglacjalny* **14**, 337-49.

4

Vegetational history

J.R. Flenley

Introduction

It is possible to reconstruct the vegetational history of a region by a variety of methods. Some of these, based on extrapolation from what is known of former climates and soils, are rather speculative. Others, based on fossil remains of former animals of many groups - vertebrates, molluscs, beetles etc. - are, when the ecology of the animal species is known and is restricted, of greater value. By far the most direct and satisfactory technique, however, is that based on fossil remains of plants themselves. These may be seeds, fruit, leaves, wood etc., the so-called macro-fossils. Alternatively, micro-fossils, especially pollen grains, may be used. Both these groups are best preserved in anaerobic situations such as lakes or bogs, and the Humber region is, for the most part, well provided with such locations. Macro-fossils have the advantage of indicating that the plant from which they originated probably grew close by. On the other hand, they emphasise the floras of wetlands at the expense of well-drained habitats. Pollen grains, by contrast, may be carried through the air considerable distances; they therefore give a regional picture, but the precise origin of the grains may be uncertain.

The pre-Devensian (before c. 100 000 years BP)

Almost nothing is known of the vegetation during the Pliocene period, but it was probably, as elsewhere in Britain and Europe, a forest containing not only our native British trees but also a number of others now not native here - *Sequoia* (redwood), *Tsuga* (hemlock), *Pterocarya*, *Abies* (fir), *Picea* (spruce) etc. (Godwin 1975). The ensuing Quaternary period was characterised by repeated ice ages (Catt this volume) which drove the forests southward and replaced them with tundra vegetation or, in the more severe cases, with ice sheets. The warmer interglacial periods provide the first direct evidence of the vegetation of the Humber region. At Kirmington on the Lincolnshire Wolds, Watts (1959) found pollen evidence of a forest vegetation including *Abies* and *Picea* as well as our present natives, from a period about 300 000 years ago (the Hoxnian interglacial). What may be a later interglacial (the Ipswichian), about 125 000 years ago, is evidenced at Speeton, at the southern end of Filey Bay, where West (1969) found sparse pollen of our native species plus *Picea*. Also present was *Carpinus* (hornbeam), which today probably does not occur as a native north of Norfolk.

The Devensian (100 000-10 000 years BP)

The maximum extent of Devensian (Dimlington Stadial) ice was reached about 18 000 years ago, at which time it covered much of the lowland area of the region and dammed the Humber, creating a vast lake in the Vale of York (Catt this volume). The Yorkshire and Lincolnshire Wolds do not appear to have been ice-covered, probably because of low precipitation at the time, and presumably bore some sort of tundra vegetation. Unfortunately, however, we have no direct evidence of this.

The retreat of the ice began about 15 000 BP, leaving the glacial deposits of Holderness and the Lincolnshire Marsh pock-marked with innumerable depressions which became lakes and ponds. Evidence for the former existence of over seventy such water bodies in Holderness was collected by Sheppard (1956) (Fig. 4.1). Only Hornsea Mere survives, though many others were drained comparatively recently (Sheppard 1957). Their stratified deposits

Vegetational history

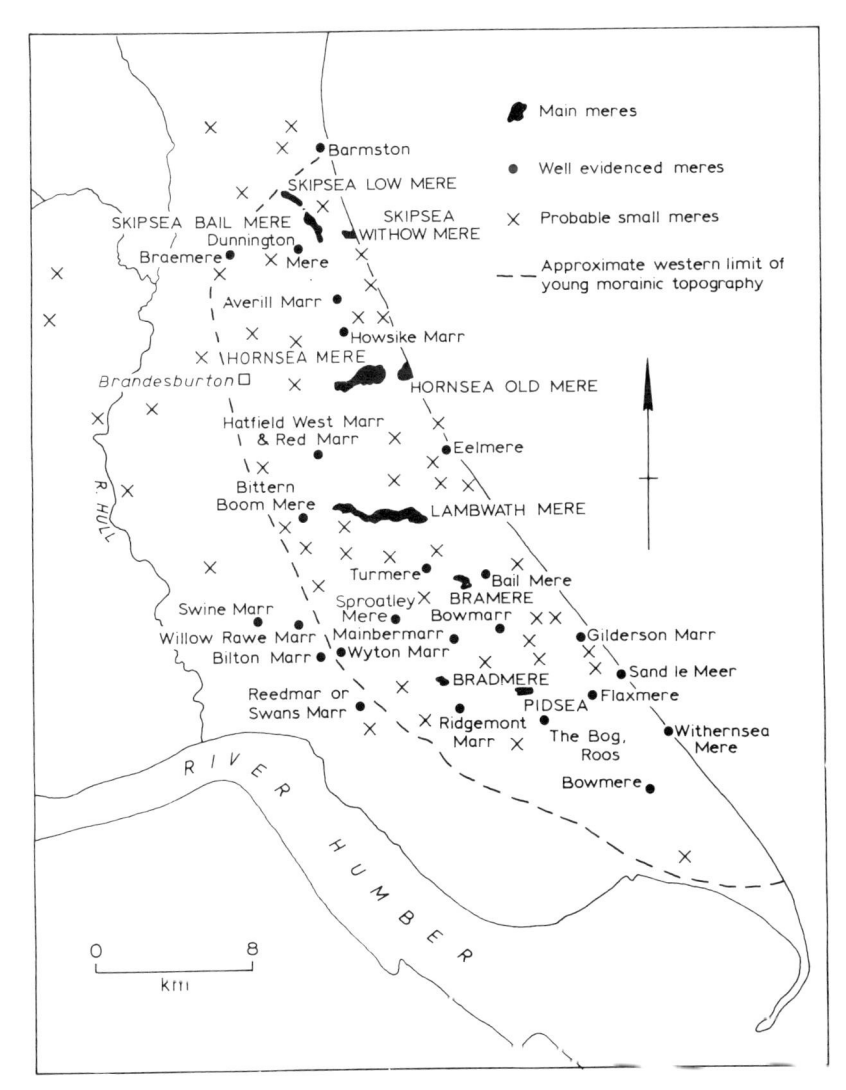

Fig. 4.1. The ancient meres of Holderness (after Sheppard 1956).

provide invaluable record books from which, with skill and care, we may read the history of Holderness.

The till deposits were originally rich in chalk, so it is not surprising that the initial vegetation, although tundra-like, also contained plants characteristic of alkaline soils. Grasses and sedges dominated, but plants like the rock rose (*Helianthemum*) and the meadow rue (*Thalictrum*) were also present. This and other early phases are well demonstrated in the pollen record from The Bog, Roos (Fig. 4.1), produced by Beckett (1981) (Fig. 4.2).

The improvement in climate was not steady, but was interrupted at least once and probably twice. The evidence for this is partly in the stratigraphy, which shows oscillations from organic deposits (indicating temperate conditions) to mineral deposits (indicating cold and/or dry conditions). The first of these temporary setbacks occurred just above a radiocarbon date of $13\ 045 \pm 270$ b.p. at Roos. At this time there was a rise of pollen of *Hippophae* (sea buckthorn). This is surprising, for *Hippophae* is a coastal shrub at present, and the coast was a very long way from Roos at that time. It is known to occur inland, however, but only in dry, well-drained situations. Perhaps, therefore, this indicates a period of cold and very dry climate. Soon (*c.* 12 000 BP) the climate was once again suitable for a wide range of herbs and shrubs, including the dwarf birch (*Betula nana*). This is the period known as the Windermere Interstadial. Even the tree birch (*Betula*) was present, forming perhaps a patchy woodland. At Willow Garth, in the Great Wold Valley of the northern Yorkshire Wolds, Bush and Hall (1987) found stem-wood of *Alnus* (alder) at this time; this is one of the earliest occurrences of alder in Britain after the ice age.

Around 11 000 BP a second climatic cooling set in, this time a very severe one (the Loch Lomond Stadial). There was a renewal of glacial activity in the mountains of Britain, and trees disappeared from the Humber region. At The Bog, Roos, and many other sites in Holderness (Flenley 1987), as well as at Aby Grange in the southern Lincolnshire Marsh (Suggate and West 1959), sediments changed from organic mud to inorganic clay. At Roos this contained macrofossils of *Fontinalis antipyretica,* an aquatic moss. Clearly the lake still existed, but conditions were apparently too cold for tree growth. The pollen record reverted to plants of open ground, such as *Rumex acetosa* (sorrel) and *Artemisia*, probably *A. norvegica* (wormwood). Abundant pine (*Pinus*) pollen at this time was probably wind-blown from southern England. The coldest phase lasted *c.* 500 years, but it was 10 000 BP before the vegetation showed much sign of recovery.

Vegetational history

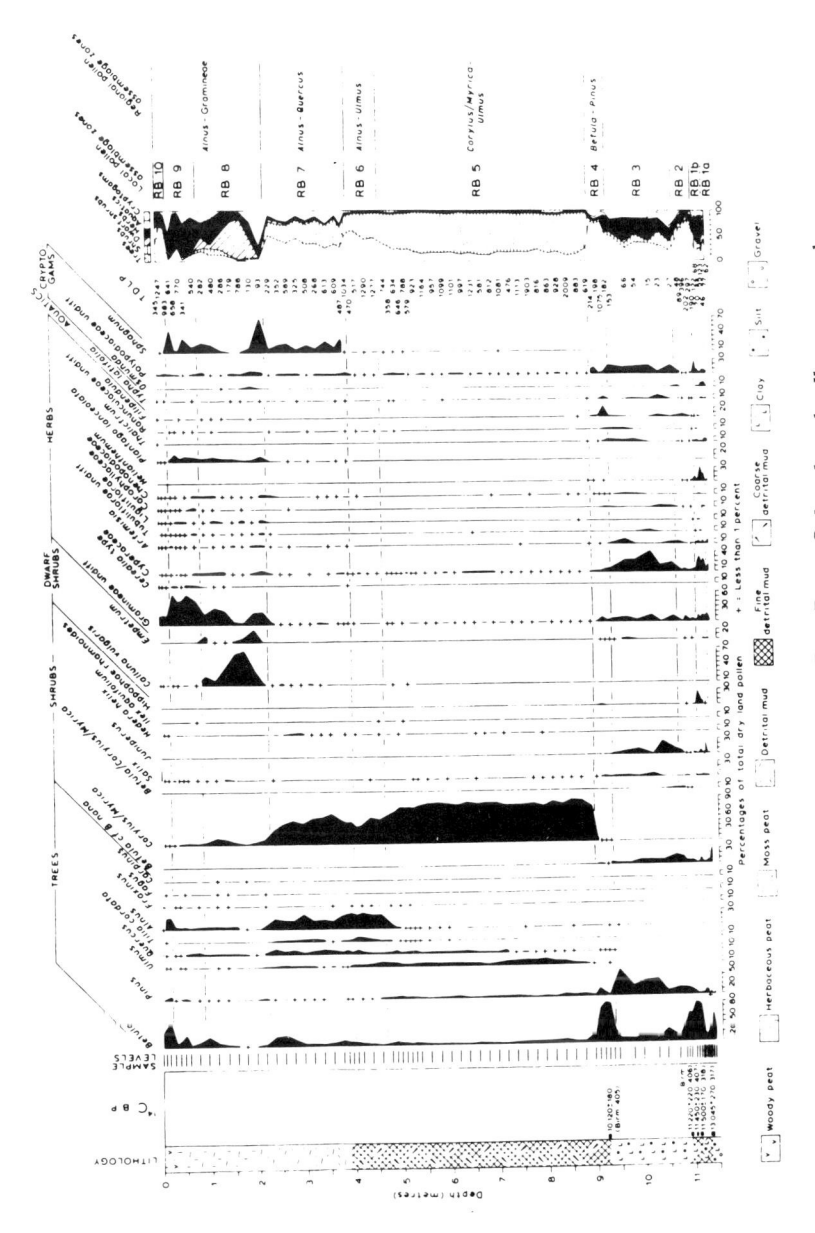

Fig. 4.2. Pollen diagram from The Bog, Roos. Only selected pollen taxa are shown. Recalculated and redrawn from Beckett (1981).

The early Holocene (10 000-5000 years BP)

The rapidly improving climate of the post-glacial (Holocene or Flandrian) period led to the swift immigration of trees from refugia in southern England or on the continent. Birch (*Betula*) was the first to dominate the landscape, forming closed-canopy woodland which shaded out many of the previously abundant herbs. This was soon followed by pine (*Pinus*) and then by the mixed broadleaf trees and shrubs - hazel (*Corylus*), elm (*Ulmus*), oak (*Quercus*), alder (*Alnus*) and lime (*Tilia*). The successive arrival of these trees was formerly taken to imply a progressive amelioration of the climate. While this may be partially true, it is also relevant to note that birch and pine are often pioneer trees, partly because of the mobility endowed by their winged seeds, and partly because of their tolerance of fresh soils. Oak and hazel on the other hand, with their heavy acorns and nuts, may be expected to be slower migrators, and prefer well-developed brown earth soils. It is therefore possible that conditions were uniformly warm at this time, and that the sequence of trees is simply related to rates of migration, or to rates of maturation of soils.

People of the Mesolithic culture were certainly present in the region during this period. They had the ability to cut down trees with stone axes, as indicated by the felled oak tree found in the mere deposits at Sproatley in Holderness (Fig. 4.1), and dated to around 6300 b.p. (Flenley 1987). Similar felling was clearly seen in the excavations of similar date at Star Carr, immediately north of the Yorkshire Wolds in the eastern Vale of Pickering (Walker and Godwin 1954), but there is no evidence in pollen diagrams from Holderness that these efforts had any significant effects on the vegetation at large. Rather, a continuous, dense forest cover is indicated, with perhaps a slight suggestion of temporary forest reduction at Sproatley (Flenley 1987).

The story from the Yorkshire Wolds is somewhat different. Waterlogged deposits are naturally lacking on the porous chalk substratum, so preservation of plant fossils is generally poor and records are therefore difficult to obtain. Fortunately, however, in the Great Wold Valley the shallow deposit at Willow Garth proves to cover much of the Holocene period (Bush 1986, Bush and Ellis 1987, Bush and Flenley 1987) (Fig. 4.3). The vegetational record suggests that although the rise of *Betula* commenced as in Holderness, it was

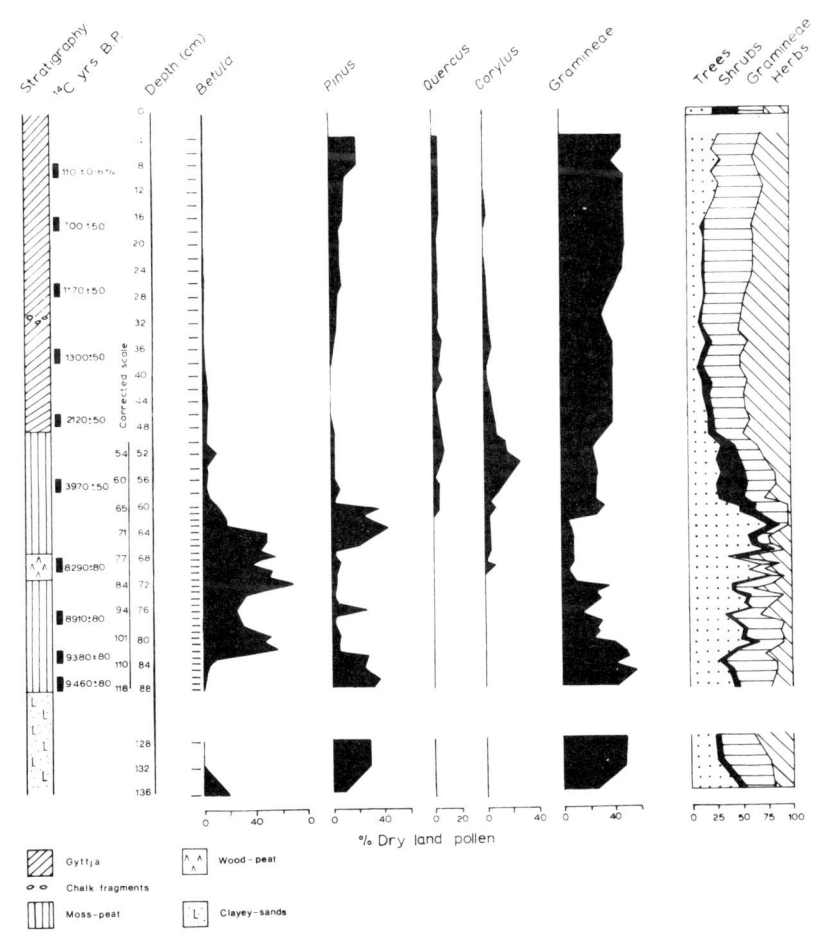

Fig. 4.3. Pollen diagram from Willow Garth (from Bush and Ellis 1987). Only selected pollen taxa are shown. The corrected depth scale adjusts for compression of the 50-118 cm section of the core during sampling.

interrupted once the tree pollen percentage reached about 75%. Thus grasses and other herbs, for example *Helianthemum* (rock rose), were able to persist. Even *Teucrium botrys* (cut-leaved germander), a species now found only on the southern chalk, was recognisable by its distinctive pollen. The presence of open grassland is confirmed by the remains of beetles and molluscs characteristic of this habitat (Bush 1986). Unfortunately there is then a hiatus in the record, from about 7000 to 4000 BP, so we cannot tell whether these grasslands were the direct progenitor of the chalk grassland which we know and value today, but there is a strong supposition that they were.

The exact cause of this persistence of open grassland on the chalk is difficult to ascertain. Certainly trees will grow and form closed woodland on even the thinnest of chalk soils today, and woodland, because of its greater height, will always tend to shade out grassland. The surviving chalk grasslands today are maintained by grazing, either by rabbits or by domestic stock, and when this activity ceases, they degenerate rapidly into hawthorn scrub and eventually woodland. Whether wild or domesticated grazing animals were sufficiently numerous at *c*. 8000 BP to prevent and even reverse the spread of forest is unknown. An alternative possibility is that a drier or colder climate inhibited tree growth, but there is no independent evidence for this. Other possibilities involve the direct activity of man. There is insufficient charcoal in the sediments to imply burning on a grand scale, but chopping might have been practised, perhaps for the benefit of stock in winter. A few pollen grains of possible attribution to cereals occur, but these are presumed to be of wild varieties, so to argue for the emergence of arable farming this early would be highly speculative.

The late Holocene (5000 years BP to present)

The second half of the post-glacial period is ushered in by the arrival of Neolithic farmers with their improved technology for forest clearance. The start of this phase in the Roos pollen record, at about 5000 BP, is marked by the well-known decline of *Ulmus* (elm) (Fig. 4.2). This decline is widespread in Britain and western Europe and is almost synchronous everywhere. Possible explanations include an attack of Dutch elm disease, a climatic decline and the impact of man, perhaps especially by lopping trees to provide winter feed for stock. This practice may still be observed in Switzerland, southeast Europe and northern India. It is difficult to decide between these possible explanations, however, although the attack of Dutch elm disease in recent years brings the plausibility of that explanation forcibly to mind. The extent of actual forest clearance by Neolithic man seems to have been rather limited in Holderness. No doubt the dense oak forest was difficult to clear with stone tools, and the heavy, clay soils were difficult to work with wooden ploughs.

On the lighter chalk soils with their perhaps less dense forests, things seem to have gone differently. By the time the Willow Garth record resumes, at *c.* 4000 BP, the Wolds had been very largely cleared. Pollen grains of grasses were then abundant, along with those of pastoral weeds such as *Plantago lanceolata*. Undoubted pollen of cereals is also present, however, so it is evident that a mixed pastoral and arable type of farming was practised.

In the immediately following Bronze Age the Wolds continued to be intensively used, for the pollen record shows no sign of forest recovery. In the wetter lowlands some inroads were now being made on the forest, and dwelling-platforms were established in a number of the northern Holderness meres (Smith 1911). Associated with these, in time and place, the distinctive pollen grains of *Trapa natans* (the water chestnut) have been found (Flenley *et al.* 1975). That the species was indeed growing locally was confirmed later by E. Smith's (unpublished) discovery of the fruit spines in the same deposits. *Trapa* does not occur at present nearer than central France, and in order for it to have fruited successfully a summer temperature about 2°C warmer than now would probably have been necessary. The fruits of *Trapa* are widely used as food, for humans and pigs, and it is interesting to speculate that the inhabitants of the dwelling-platforms may have been using them in the same way (Flenley and Maloney 1976).

With the advent of the Iron Age, the stronger plough then available made possible the use of the heavy lowland soils. The resulting clearance of forest in Holderness is beautifully demonstrated in the Roos pollen diagram, where tree pollen is dramatically replaced by a wide range of herbaceous types (Fig. 4.2), again suggesting mixed farming. However, this did not apparently lead to a reduction in pressure on the vegetation of the Wolds, which continued to support mixed agriculture, with further decline of forest cover.

Probably the last parts of the region to be used intensively by man were the wet valley bottoms and the marshlands adjacent to the Humber. There is place-name and documentary evidence that drainage of the Hull valley marshes and southern Vale of York commenced in medieval times, while the salt marshes of Sunk Island in southern Holderness were reclaimed more recently (Sheppard

1958, 1966). The same evidence confirms that several of the Holderness meres were in existence throughout this time, and many were drained only in the nineteenth century (Sheppard 1957).

The twentieth century has seen accelerating change. There has been a general replacement on the eastern side of the country of mixed pastoral and arable farming by pure arable farming, with stock kept only in special units (Symes and Marsden 1978, Symes 1987). Along with the extensive use of herbicides and the removal of hedgerows, this has greatly reduced the available habitat in many areas. The net result has been a severe diminution in the area of semi-natural vegetation. Many once common wild flowers are now rare, and there have been parallel reductions in the populations of birds, mammals, butterflies and other species.

We are about to witness yet further changes in the vegetation as European Community surpluses force a re-thinking of agricultural economies. Perhaps more woodland will be planted; perhaps some wetlands will be re-flooded. This will be one further stage in a process of continuous change in the vegetation of the Humber region, which has already occurred for many thousands of years.

References

Beckett, S.C. (1981). Pollen diagrams from Holderness, North Humberside. *Journal of Biogeography* **8**, 177-98.

Bush, M.B. (1986). The Late Quaternary Palaeoecological History of the Great Wold Valley. Ph.D. thesis, University of Hull.

Bush, M.B. and Ellis, S. (1987). The sedimentological and vegetational history of Willow Garth. In: *East Yorkshire Field Guide* (ed. S. Ellis) pp. 42-52. Quaternary Research Association, Cambridge.

Bush, M.B. and Flenley, J.R. (1987). The age of the British chalk grassland. *Nature* **329**, 434-6.

Bush, M.B. and Hall, A.R. (1987). Flandrian *Alnus*: expansion or immigration? *Journal of Biogeography* **14**, 479-81.

Flenley, J.R. (1987). The meres of Holderness. In: *East Yorkshire Field Guide* (ed. S. Ellis) pp. 73-81. Quaternary Research Association, Cambridge.

Flenley, J.R. and Maloney, B.K. (1976). Reply to a comment by P.A.

Tallantire. *Nature* **261**, 347.
Flenley, J.R., Maloney, B.K., Ford, D. and Hallam, G. (1975). *Trapa natans* in the British Flandrian. *Nature* **257**, 39-41.
Godwin, H. (1975). *The History of the British Flora*. 2nd ed., Cambridge University Press, Cambridge.
Sheppard, J.A. (1956). The Draining of the Marshlands of East Yorkshire. Ph.D. thesis, University of Hull.
Sheppard, J.A. (1957). The medieval meres of Holderness. *Transactions of the Institute of British Geographers* **23**, 75-86.
Sheppard, J.A. (1958). *The Draining of the Hull Valley*. East Yorkshire Local History Society, York.
Sheppard, J.A. (1966). *The Draining of the Marshlands of South Holderness and the Vale of York*. East Yorkshire Local History Society, York.
Smith, R.A. (1911). Lake-dwellings in Holderness. *Archaeologia* **62**, 593-610.
Suggate, R.P. and West, R.G. (1959). On the extent of the Last Glaciation in eastern England. *Proceedings of the Royal Society of London Series B* **150**, 263-83.
Symes, D.G. (1987). Agriculture. In: *Humberside in the Eighties* (ed. D.G. Symes) pp. 9-22. Department of Geography, University of Hull.
Symes, D.G. and Marsden, T.K. (1978). Recent developments in agriculture on North Humberside. In: *North Humberside Introductory Themes* (ed. D.G. Symes) pp. 31-41. Department of Geography, University of Hull.
Walker, D. and Godwin, H. (1954). Lake stratigraphy, pollen analysis and vegetational history. In: *Excavations at Star Carr* (ed. J.G.D. Clark) pp. 25-69. Cambridge University Press, London.
Watts, W.A. (1959). Pollen spectra from the interglacial deposits at Kirmington, Lincolnshire. *Proceedings of the Yorkshire Geological Society* **32**, 145-51.
West, R.G. (1969). A note on pollen analyses from the Speeton Shell Bed. *Proceedings of the Geologists' Association* **80**, 217-18.

5
The Humber estuary
J.S. Pethick

Introduction

The Humber is generally regarded as the type example of the macro-tidal estuary. It has a maximum tidal range of 7.2 m, a marked tidal asymmetry, a long flared outline and a well-mixed saline intrusion. Yet, despite these classic features, in detail the Humber is as idiosyncratic as any other large-scale landform; its history throughout the Quaternary has provided it with some exceptional features, while engineering works in the estuary over the past few hundred years have done much to give it its present unique form and dynamics. This chapter examines briefly the physical characteristics of the estuary, its Quaternary history and future development.

Physical characteristics

The Humber is one of the largest estuaries of the United Kingdom. It has a maximum width of 14 km at the mouth and its tidal length at present is 120 km on the River Trent and 140 km on the River Ouse (Fig. 5.1), although these limits are governed by the presence of tidal locks in both cases. Channel depth at high water exceeds 18 m in the outer estuary. The freshwater drainage area of the estuary covers 24 240 square kilometres, approximately one-fifth of the area of

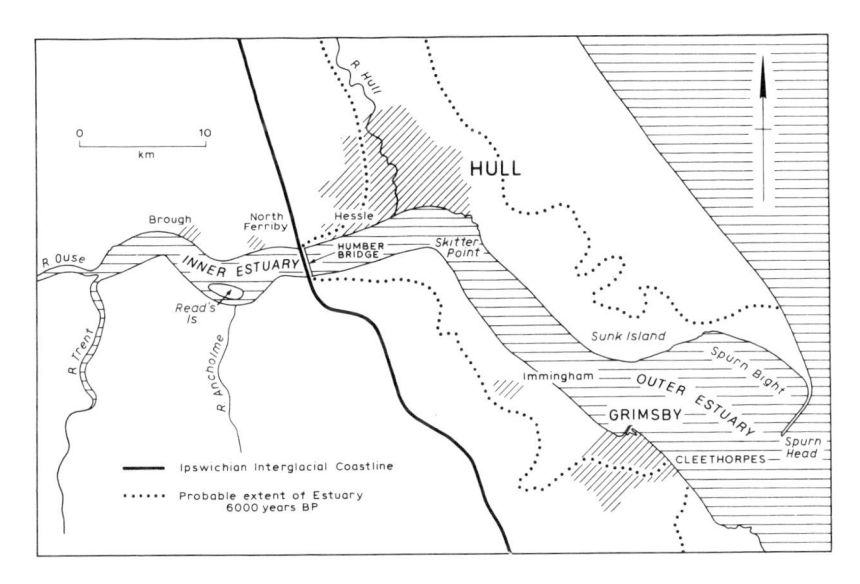

Fig. 5.1. The Humber estuary.

England, extending to Birmingham in the south, the Pennine watershed in the west and Swaledale in the north. This enormous drainage area contributes over 13 million cubic metres of water to the estuary each day, yet this volume is small compared to the 160 million cubic metres of tidal flow - the tidal prism - which passes the mouth of the estuary during each tide.

Although the Humber is generally regarded as a well-mixed estuary with no marked discontinuity between the fresh and saline waters, nevertheless there is a slight vertical halocline, or salinity gradient, in the outer estuary whose maximum range is 5 g/l at Immingham. More interesting is the presence of a horizontal halocline across the width of the estuary. The salinity of the surface waters, for example, across the estuary at Immingham varies from 29 g/l in the south to 32 g/l in the north. This slight halocline is probably caused by the influence of the Coriolis Force, resulting from the Earth's rotation, so that the saline intrusion is forced along the northern bank of the estuary while the freshwater river input follows the southern bank. One important implication of this is that the heavily contaminated waters from the industrial areas of the hinterland tend to flow to the south in the estuary, while the cleaner North Sea water inputs flow to the north, a situation which is exemplified by the range of water quality in the Humber as measured by the Water Authorities (Edwards *et al.* 1987).

The increasing asymmetry of the tidal wave as it passes into the Humber is a classic macro-tidal estuary phenomenon. The almost sinusoidal tidal curve at Spurn has both flood and ebb times of 6.25 hours, but by the time the tide reaches Brough this has been distorted to give a 4.5 hour flood and an 8 hour ebb. The result of this asymmetry is to create higher flood than ebb velocities, an imbalance accentuated by the strong residual current caused by the saline intrusion. The dominant flood currents mean that there tends to be a net input of sediments from the North Sea into the Humber, which accounts for the high suspended sediment concentrations in the estuary and the rapid accretion rates experienced in many of the inter-tidal areas. Concentrations of 2000 p.p.m. are common in the estuary during the winter (Fig. 5.2), a concentration which would be equivalent to a total suspended load of over 3 million tonnes at any one time. This net input of sediments means that the Humber is gradually decreasing in volume. Navigation charts over the past 100 years indicate that this decrease is caused mainly by a reduction in channel width, averaging 14% over the period 1851-1966 (Wilkinson *et al.* 1973).

The saline intrusion into the Humber reaches some 45 km inland, approximately to the position of the Humber Bridge. This means that the turbidity maximum of the estuary lies in this reach, so that maximum sediment concentrations are experienced here (Fig. 5.2). As a consequence, deposition rates in both the sub-tidal channel and the inter-tidal zone are extremely high here, and channel swings caused by this deposition are frequent. One outcome of this is that bank erosion and deposition phases rapidly succeed each other at this location as the channel swings towards the bank or away from it (Pethick 1987); the implications to navigation, shore installations and indeed archaeology are obvious enough.

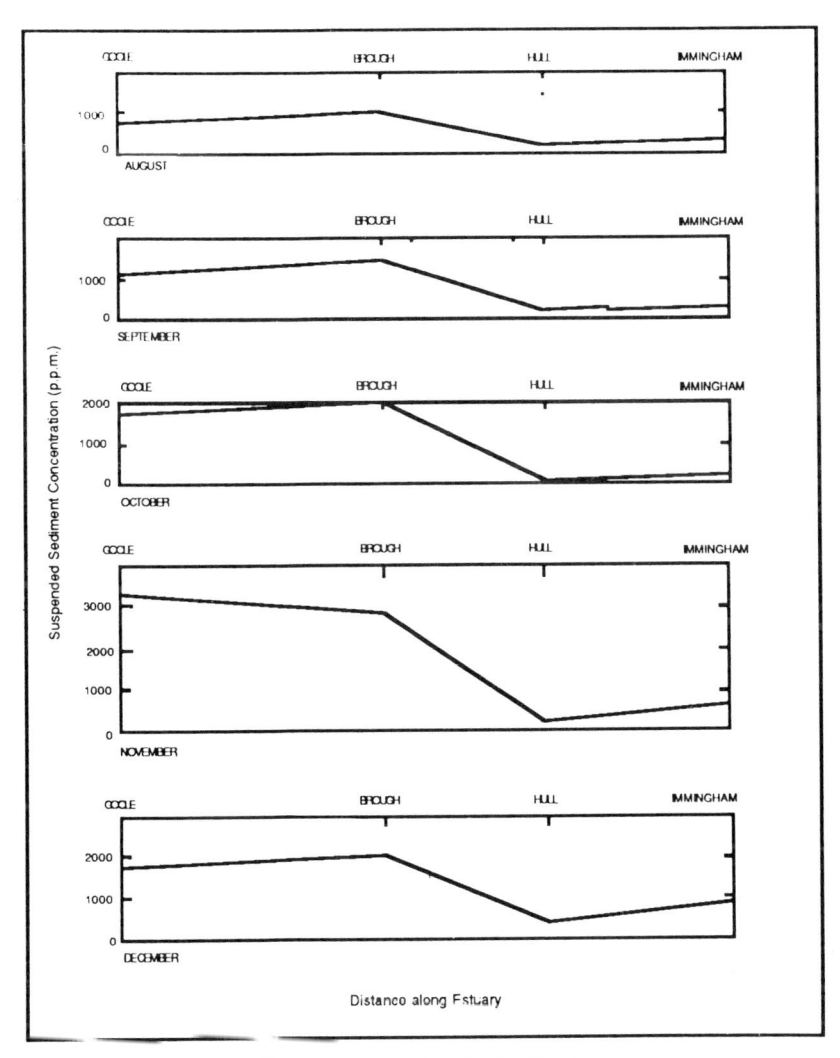

Fig. 5.2. Suspended sediment concentrations in the Humber.

Quaternary history

Such changes in the estuary as those mentioned above need to be viewed not as a compendium of isolated facts but in the context of the overall functioning of the estuary. One way in which this may be achieved is by considering the theoretical development of the estuary towards a steady state or equilibrium form and then comparing observed form and changes in it with this theoretical optimum. An extensive literature on the subject of the 'ideal' or steady state estuary concludes that it will possess an exponential decline in width inland, constant depth and velocity, and equal energy expenditure along its length (e.g. Langbein 1963, McDowell and O'Connor 1977). Consideration of these factors in the Humber reveals some interesting discrepancies between theoretical ideal and observed form. The energy distribution in the estuary, for example, is complex. Figure 5.3 indicates that although it remains fairly constant for the first 40 km inland, as predicted for the 'ideal' estuary, it then plunges dramatically by an order of magnitude over the next 10-20 km, attaining a new approximately constant value over the inland 50 km channel reach.

It is interesting that the dramatic decrease in energy expenditure in the Humber occurs in that reach of the estuary marked by the Humber Bridge. Seawards of the Bridge the high energy output seems to indicate that tidal dynamics and estuarine morphology are not in adjustment, while landwards a more efficient morphology is indicated. Consideration of the Quaternary history of the estuary provides an explanation for this division. The coastline during the Ipswichian interglacial period is marked by a buried cliff line running approximately north-south along the eastern edge of the Yorkshire and Lincolnshire Wolds (Catt this volume). Figure 5.1 shows that this coastline would have crossed the present Humber at the exact position of the Humber Bridge, and indeed recent roadworks on the northern approach road to the Bridge revealed the chalk cliff of this coast. Thus during the Ipswichian period, say between 128 000 and 116 000 years BP, the Humber estuary would have entered the North Sea some 45 km westwards of its present mouth at Spurn. During this period, and the ensuing cold phase of the Early and Middle Devensian (116 000 to 26 000 BP), a considerable degree of adjustment between tidal processes and morphology would have taken place, so that this inner estuary may be regarded as relatively mature. This Ipswichian Humber may, of course, have existed in previous interglacial periods so that 100 000 years must be regarded as its minimum age at the onset of the Late Devensian (Dimlington Stadial) glaciation around 26 000 BP.

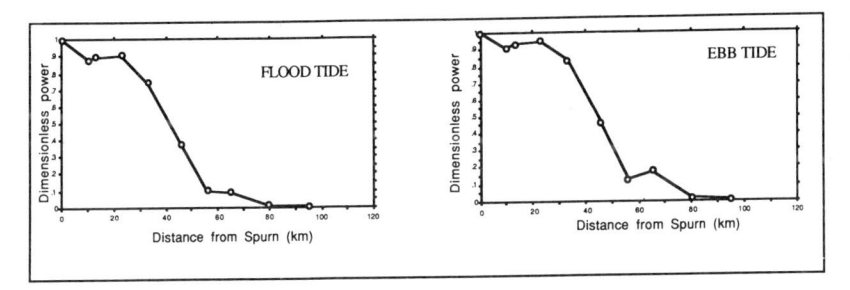

Fig. 5.3. Power expenditure in the Humber.

In marked contrast to the maturity of the inner estuary, the outer 45 km reach of the Humber can only have been in existence for the past 3000 or 4000 years, that is since the present sea level was established during the Flandrian transgression (Gaunt and Tooley 1974). This extension to the Ipswichian estuary has been formed in the glacial tills of the Dimlington Stadial which constitute Holderness (Catt this volume). As deglaciation proceeded in Holderness, the fluvial discharges from the Ouse and Trent cut across these tills, forming a deep channel within a wide shallow valley (Gaunt 1981). The northeasterly retreat of the ice front was temporarily halted along what is now the northern shore of the Humber, forming the Sutton moraine and forcing the river discharge to flow southeast, thus creating the marked bend in the estuary marked by Skitter Point (Straw and Clayton 1979). As sea level rose, this wide valley became flooded, forming a proto-Humber; sedimentation was extremely rapid in the inter-tidal area and the estuary width had halved by 2000 BP. The depth of the central estuary channel, however, did not shoal appreciably, the underlying chalk being exposed in the present-day channel in several places (Hull 1969). The inner estuary would not, of course, have escaped major modification during the Devensian and Flandrian periods. It seems likely that most of the inter-tidal sediments laid down during the Ipswichian interglacial would have been stripped from the channel during the Devensian cold period and that these would have been replaced by younger deposits as the Flandrian sea level flooded the inner estuary (Gaunt and Tooley 1974). Thus the only section of the Humber which would not have been affected by Flandrian inter-tidal deposition would have been the short reach between Brough and Hessle, where the channel cuts through the chalk and extensive inter-tidal deposits were never present.

The large tidal prism in the wide outer Humber during the early Flandrian would have meant a very high energy expenditure which rapidly decreased as sedimentation proceeded. The disparity between this outer section and the efficient inner estuary would have been great at this stage, but would have decreased as the tidal prism was reduced in the outer section. Thus the Quaternary history of the Humber provides an explanation for the observed differences in the present estuary, the demarcation between the two sections lying, coincidentally, almost exactly at the position of the Humber Bridge, where the Ipswichian coastline marks the mouth of the inner channel.

The morphological changes in the Humber described above have been initiated by the dramatic changes in sea level experienced during the Devensian and Flandrian periods. During the Quaternary the lowest sea level attained appears to have been 150 m below its present level at about 20 000 to 25 000 BP (Carter 1988). The onset of warmer conditions meant that sea level was beginning to rise rapidly by 13 000 BP and evidence from the Humber suggests that it had risen to -18 m OD by 8000 BP (Gaunt and Tooley 1974). During this period the Ouse and Trent incised deeply into the sediments of the inner Humber, producing a channel whose base lies at -20 m OD in the Vale of York (Gaunt et al. 1971, Gaunt 1981), while in the outer estuary a deep channel was incised into the glacial tills. Evidence from a bore hole at the Market Place in Hull indicates that sea level had risen by 6890 100 years b.p. to give low tide at ± 9.15 m OD (Gaunt and Tooley 1974). This is corroborated by evidence from a site on Spurn showing that at 6270 180 years b.p. high tide stood at ± 2.40 m OD (Gaunt and Tooley 1974), indicating a tidal range of 6.75 m, equivalent to that of the present day. Approximate present-day sea level was first established around 3000 years BP, as indicated by the date of a sample of *Alnus* wood found beneath one of the Bronze Age boats embedded in estuarine deposits at North Ferriby. The date for the wood is 3120 105 years b.p. (Gaunt and Tooley 1974) and it was found at ± 0.27 to ± 0.87 m OD. The subsequent behaviour of sea level in the Humber is uncertain, although Gaunt and Tooley (1974) have recognised two periods in which a rise in sea level took place, one

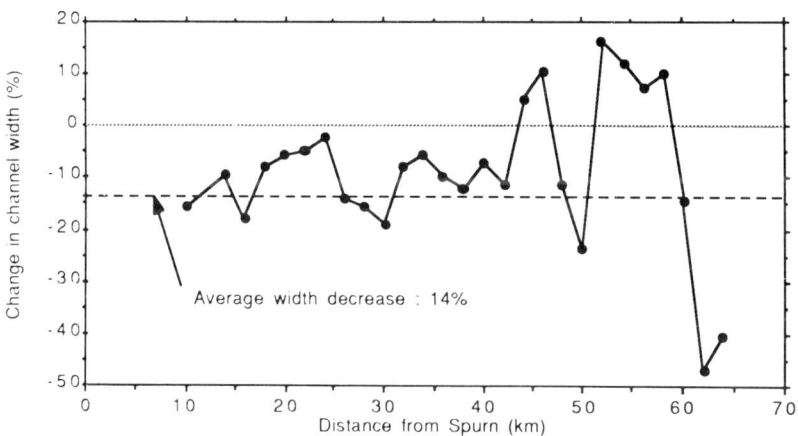

Fig. 5.4. Percentage width changes in the Humber, 1851-1966 (data from Wilkinson et al. 1973).

culminating at about 2000 BP and a later rise between the first and fourth centuries AD.

Future development

The disparity between the inner and outer sections of the Humber has been reduced considerably since the establishment of present sea level at around 3000 BP by inter-tidal sedimentation, but this process is by no means complete. The future development of the estuary must be towards further tidal prism reduction between Spurn and the Humber Bridge, involving a considerable decrease in channel width. This decrease in width is occurring at the present time, as shown by measurements over the past 100 years (Fig. 5.4). An overall reduction of 14% of the width in the outer estuary has occurred in this period and an even greater relative reduction has taken place in the inner section, although it should be noted that these are percentage changes rather than absolute figures. It is interesting to note that the Humber Bridge section is characterised by a net increase in channel width during this period, a change which probably reflects the adjustment in energy levels between the two channel sections on either side.

Since the width of an estuary is the most sensitive of its morphological characteristics, it is useful to examine in more detail the relationship between the present width of the Humber and that necessary to produce the ideal or equilibrium conditions discussed above. Many authors have suggested that the equilibrium form will be an exponential decay in width inland (e.g. Pillsbury 1939, Ippen and Harleman 1966, Wright *et al.* 1973, McDowell and O'Connor 1977). Ippen and Harleman (1966) have provided a mathematical expression for this exponential form which allows the prediction of channel width if the width at the mouth is fixed. In the case of the Humber, however, this is not possible since it is to be expected that the mouth width will change considerably in the future. Instead it is possible to use the width of the present channel at the Humber Bridge as a fixed section, since here the chalk escarpment constrains the channel, as mentioned above. Using this as the base for calculations, it is possible to construct a theoretical width plot for the equilibrium Humber.

Figure 5.5 shows this theoretical plot and a comparison with the present-day morphology, from which three interesting points emerge. First, the width of the mouth of the Humber is seen to be several kilometres greater at present than that predicted for an equilibrium estuary, implying that future deposition will cause this section to narrow. If merely the direction, rather than the magnitude, of this prediction is accepted it implies that Spurn Bight is a stable feature which will increase in size over time. Second, there are two sections in the outer estuary in which the discrepancy between observed and predicted widths implies an increase in channel width in the future - Sunk Island and Skitter Point. Land reclamation at Sunk Island (Sheppard 1966) has caused a constriction in the channel which is now narrower than that needed for equilibrium. The result is that the estuary will attempt to widen along this section, and indeed erosion here is presently occurring on both sides of the channel. At Skitter Point the marked bend in the Humber, caused by the retreat of the Dimlington Stadial ice, means that higher energy demands are placed on the tidal flow. The narrower channel satisfies this requirement so that, unless the Skitter Point bend is removed by erosion or deposition, which seems unlikely, the channel will probably remain as a negative anomaly on the width plot at this point. Third, the agreement between the predicted and observed width curves from the Humber Bridge inland is in accordance with the concept of a more mature inner estuary, as outlined above. The one exception to this is the reach centred around Read's Island. Here the present channel is

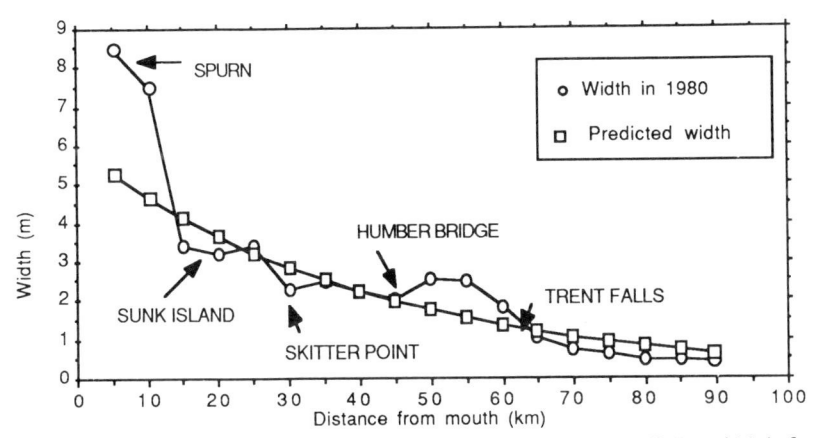

Fig. 5.5. Predicted and actual widths of the Humber (above Trent Falls, width is for the Trent and Ouse combined).

wider than predicted, probably due to the presence of the tributary valley of the River Ancholme, and it is to be expected that the present rapid deposition in this area will eventually remove the positive anomaly.

The future development of the Humber estuary depends to a very large extent on the changes which may take place in the relative sea level. At the present time predictions of a rapidly rising sea level over the next 100 years or so are being based on the so-called 'Greenhouse Effect' - the increase in global temperatures due to the release of carbon dioxide from burning fossil fuels (e.g. Clark and Primus 1987). Although detailed predictions for the Humber itself are not available, the work of Tooley and Shennan (1987) on the neighbouring Tees estuary suggests a worst case prediction of a 3.45 m rise in sea level by AD 2100, while the most conservative estimate puts the rise at 0.55 m by that year. Although the predictions are in fact for an exponential increase in sea level, the average rate of sea level rise over the next 100 years under these two models is a worst case of 27.6 mm per year and a conservative estimate of 4.4 mm per year. It is interesting to compare these estimates with the observed relative sea level changes that have taken place in the Humber over the present century. This may be achieved using the tidal records from Immingham, which is a Standard Tidal Port. Figure 5.6 shows the extreme water levels recorded here in each year since 1920 with a best fit regression line to the data. The gradient of the line indicates

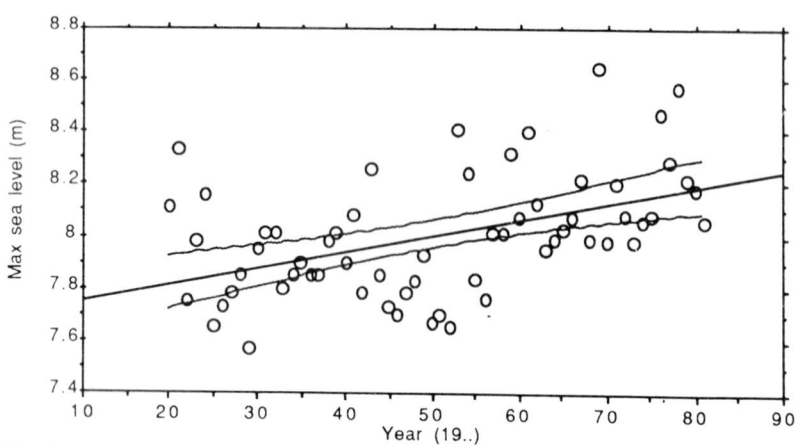

Fig. 5.6. Best fit regression line (with 95% confidence limits) to extreme water levels, Immingham tide gauge, 1920-82.

that the extreme water level at Immingham has been rising by 7 mm per year over the past 62 years, considerably more than the conservative prediction of 4.4 mm per year for the Tees estuary over the next century. Although use of the extreme annual water levels in this calculation must be treated with some caution, since they include the effects of changes in storm frequency and magnitude and changes in local bathymetry, the results do indicate that by AD 2100 the mean sea level in the Humber will stand at 4.99 m OD if the present trend continues. Since large areas of the reclaimed marshland bordering the Humber - including the city of Hull - have surface levels close to 3.0 m OD, the future possibility of severe flooding must be faced unless coastal defences are raised to accommodate the expected increase in sea level.

There are two other implications of the rise in sea level for the Humber, less obvious than the possibility of flooding but both requiring serious consideration. First, the amplitude of the tide will be modified, together with the speed of propagation of the tide and its asymmetry. This will have profound effects on the morphology of the estuary channel, the rate of deposition and erosion within the channel and the movement of suspended materials by the tide, including the movements of effluents. Second, wave action within the mouth of the Humber will be altered. The pattern of wave refraction is entirely dependent upon water depths, and a change in refraction will mean that sensitive areas such as Spurn Point, Donna Nook and the shores of Spurn Bight and the Grimsby to Cleethorpes sands will suffer extensive changes. These changes in the dynamics of the estuary will alter profoundly the long-term stable state of the estuary, so that prediction of morphological change using past measurements will no longer be possible. This conclusion is particularly relevant to the feasibility studies, now proceeding, for the construction of a Humber Barrage. The proposed structure would be sited immediately west of Immingham and would be a tidal barrage, that is allowing tidal movement across the barrier but capable of closing in extreme conditions. Such a structure is one answer to the problems which will be faced in the estuary should sea level begin to rise by the amount predicted; the alternative would be to raise sea defences by an appropriate height along the entire estuarine coastline. However, feasibility studies for a barrage must be based upon present-day estuarine dynamics, and the possibility of major changes in tidal regimes, current velocities and sediment loads caused by sea level change introduces a complex unknown into these calculations.

Conclusions

The Humber is presented here as an estuary which has undergone fundamental changes over the past 10 000 years, changes which are reflected in the present-day dynamic status of the estuary. It is possible to predict the medium-term future behaviour of the estuary using an assumption of a steady state end point, and such predictions may be evaluated by reference to the behaviour of the estuary over the past 100 years during which accurate records have been taken. Such predictive models are of the utmost importance for efficient management of the estuary, whether this be for shipping, industrial activity on the banks or wildlife conservation. They also possess implications for the destruction of archaeological material and planning of rescue excavations.

The possibility of a dramatic change in sea level over the next 100 years may, however, fundamentally alter the conclusions from such predictive models, based, as they are, on boundary conditions imposed by a relatively slow rise in sea level over the past 2000 years. Data presented by Shennan (1988) for sites on the east coast - the Fens, Norfolk Broads and Thames estuary - indicate that over the past

2000 years sea level has risen by 2.78 m, 2.88 m and 3.23 m respectively. Thus the worst case predictions for the next 100 years of a rise of 3.45 m (Tooley and Shennan 1987) is greater than the total rise in sea level over the past 2000 years, a situation which may preclude the use of short-term historical analogues in the verification of any estuarine models. What is clear is that the present morphology and dynamics of the Humber are about to undergo a major transformation and that our future use of the estuary may therefore be very different from that of the past.

References

Carter, R.W.G. (1988). *Coastal Environments*. Academic Press, London.
Clark, J.A. and Primus, J.A. (1987). Sea level changes resulting from future retreat of ice sheets: an effect of CO_2 warming of the climate. In: *Sea Level Changes* (ed. M.J. Tooley and I. Shennan) pp. 356-70. Blackwell, Oxford.
Edwards, A.M.C., Freestone, R. and Urqhart, C. (1987). *The Water Quality of the Humber Estuary 1986*. Humber Estuary Committee, Hull.
Gaunt, G.D. (1981). Quaternary history of the southern part of the Vale of York. In: *The Quaternary in Britain* (ed. J. Neale and J. Flenley) pp. 82-97. Pergamon Press, Oxford.
Gaunt, G.D. and Tooley, M.J. (1974). Evidence for Flandrian sea-level changes in the Humber estuary and adjacent areas. *Bulletin of the Geological Survey of Great Britain* **48**, 25-41.
Gaunt, G.D., Jarvis R.A. and Matthews, B. (1971). The Late Weichselian sequence in the Vale of York. *Proceedings of the Yorkshire Geological Society* **38**, 281-4.
Hull, J.H. (1969). *Cruise Report Humber Investigations 1968*, Institute of Geological Sciences Report 69/3. Institute of Geological Sciences, London.
Ippen, A.T. and Harleman, D.R.F. (1966). Tidal dynamics in estuaries. In: *Estuary and Coastline Hydrodynamics* (ed. A.T. Ippen) pp. 493-545. McGraw-Hill, New York.
Langbein, W.B. (1963). The hydraulic geometry of a shallow estuary. *International Association of Scientific Hydrology* **8**, 84-94.

McDowell, D.M. and O'Connor, B.A. (1977). *Hydraulic Behaviour of Estuaries.* Macmillan, London.

Pethick, J.S. (1987). *The Humber Estuary,* Estuarine and Brackish Waters Association Bulletin 47. Woods and Woods, Norwich.

Pillsbury, G.B. (1939). *Tidal Hydraulics,* US Army Corps of Engineers Professional Paper 34. Washington.

Shennan, I. (1988). *Sea Level Changes in The Wash.* Nature Conservancy Council, London.

Sheppard, J.A. (1966). *The Draining of the Marshlands of South Holderness and the Vale of York.* East Yorkshire Local History Society, York.

Straw, A. and Clayton, K.M. (1979). *Eastern and Central England.* Methuen, London.

Tooley, M.J. and Shennan, I. (eds) (1987). *Sea Level Changes.* Blackwell, Oxford.

Wilkinson, H.R., de Boer, G. and Thunder, A. (1973). *A Cartographic Analysis of the Changing Bed of the Humber,* University of Hull Department of Geography Miscellaneous Series 14. University of Hull.

Wright, L.D., Coleman, J.M. and Thom, B.G. (1973) Processes of channel development in a high-tide range environment: Cambridge Gulf-Ord River Delta, W. Australia. *Journal of Geology* **81**, 15-41.

Part II
EARLY WETLAND EXPLOITATION

6

An East Yorkshire retrospective

E.V. Wright

Introduction

My discovery of the first of the three Ferriby Bronze Age boats in September 1937 was a turning point in my own life, and perhaps it might be said, also for maritime archaeology in this country (Greenhill 1976). In accepting the invitation to contribute to this volume with a retrospective, I should therefore like to repeat the story of the find, and also review some of the more important local archaeological events which led up to and followed from it.

My brother and I were singularly fortunate when we were growing up in the East Riding for the opportunities available for original investigation in the fields of geology and archaeology, and for the help readily accessible to amateurs from individuals and local institutions. In our family the pursuit of natural history had been an accepted norm during our childhood, and our early interests were in insects and fossils, with the emphasis very much on collecting. Increasingly, however, fossils took over as our prime pursuit and by the early 1930s we had begun to lay the foundations of what was to become a major collection of the remains of Cretaceous invertebrates from Yorkshire and elsewhere in Britain. Our mentor and guide in the early years had been Tom Sheppard (Fig. 6.1), who was always ready to introduce us to unfamiliar exposures. One of the sparks which

Fig. 6.1. Tom Sheppard (second from left) on the Humber foreshore at South Ferriby with members of the Hull Geological Society around 1930.

helped to kindle our parallel interest in archaeology was a trip with Sheppard to South Ferriby, his birthplace, where Romano-British sherds were to be had from the foreshore and the low cliff bordering it.

Searching for fossils and antiquities having become second nature to us, it was inevitable that we should look to our own doorstep at North Ferriby (Fig. 6.2), where the Humber bank provided ample scope for collecting within a mile's walk from our home. It was in the school holidays in the winter of 1930/31 that Sheppard told us about the observation by another Ferriby resident, the eminent geologist W.S. Bisat, of the effects of the shift in the deep-water channel from the south to the north side of the estuary in the previous October. This had washed away the seemingly permanent mantle of warp extending out over the foreshore to reveal, from Welton nearly to Hessle, an uninterrupted platform of till running down to low water. This was overlaid at each end by peat and estuarine silty clay, the latter readily distinguishable from the more recent warp. The

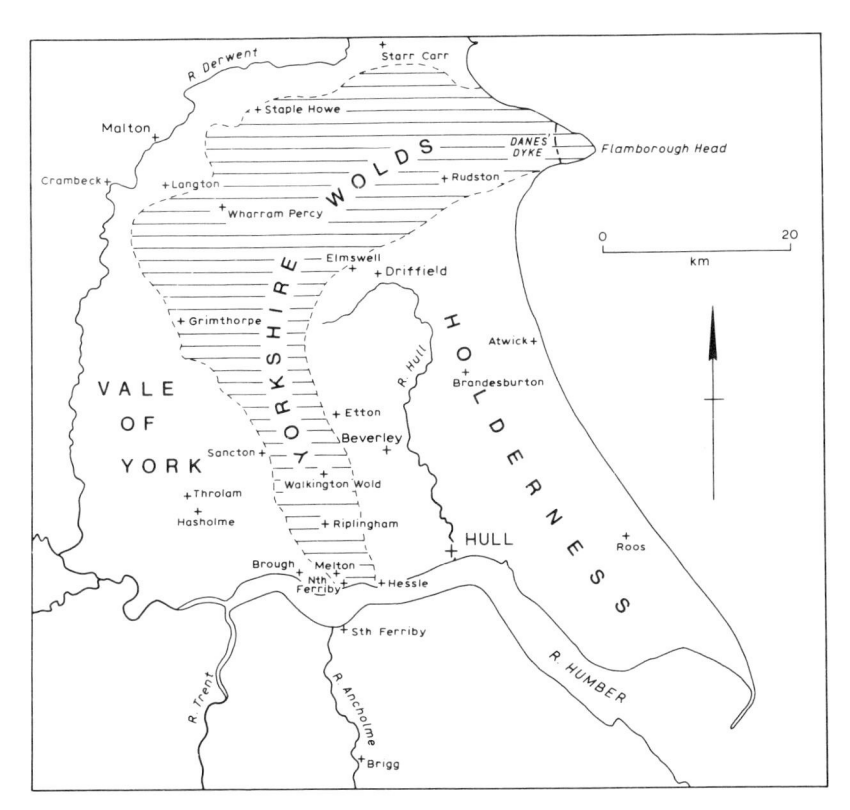

Fig. 6.2. Location map.

deposit at the Welton end had been noted 35 years earlier by J.W. Stather, matched by a similar exposure at South Ferriby (Stather 1896); this surely was the site of the so-called 'coracle' reported by Sheppard (1926). The exposure at North Ferriby, however, was previously unrecorded (Bisat 1932). From 1931 onwards my brother and I began our regular examination of the peat and clays, initially collecting plant and insect remains, molluscs and mammalian bones, and these formed the subject for our first publication (Wright and Wright 1933). Increasingly, however, we began to find in both the Welton and Ferriby deposits artefacts in the form of sharpened stakes and structures of interlaced roundwood rods which we categorised as 'hurdles'. Our searching was sufficiently thorough and frequent for it to be no accident when, in September 1937, I came upon the projecting ends of three stout oak planks and immediately recognised them as belonging to an ancient boat (Fig. 6.3). Excavations and further discoveries nearby followed before, during and after the Second World War, and indeed still continue to this day (Crowther 1987a, Buckland *et al.* this volume).

Our regular visits to the river bank also led from 1932 onwards to the recovery of potsherds just below the topsoil at intervals along the low cliff cut in glacial deposits between Ferriby and Melton, known locally as Redcliff. The pottery ranged from very coarse hand-made vessels to a wide variety of fine, wheel-turned wares to which were added a couple of bronze brooches and some poorly preserved ironwork. This assemblage was first identified as of first century AD date by Mary Kitson Clark and included in her gazetteer (Kitson Clark 1935). We were lucky, therefore, to have near our home a site accessible at high water to add to the two inter-tidal ones, all three of which were suited to regular observation and yielded a steady accumulation of finds.

The great names of East Riding archaeology in those days were still Greenwell and Mortimer. Although *British Barrows* had been published over 50 years earlier (Greenwell 1877) and *Forty Years Researches* (Mortimer 1905) for half as long, it was then one of the tenets of faith for local archaeologists that the subject remained under their domination. The result was a bias towards the fruits of excavation of funerary monuments, a bias which perhaps lingers to this day for the Wolds at least.

Archaeology in the 1920s and 30s

My first relevant memory is of the occasion of the British Association's Hull Meeting in 1922. It might well be asked how this could be so for a child of four, and the answer is that my family accommodated two visiting professors for the duration of the meeting, one of whom was the unforgettable D'Arcy Thompson and the other Stanley Gardner. The multi-talented D'Arcy (he held chairs in both classics and zoology) was the epitome of the traditional professorial figure, with a great flowing beard and a booming voice, and his repeated utterance 'You are wrong, Stanley Gardner, you are wrong!' became a byword in the family. This, however, is by the way and no

An East Yorkshire retrospective 75

Fig. 6.3. Ferriby boat 1, August 1946.

more than an attempt to establish my credentials for commenting on events in 1922!

In preparation for the Meeting, Sheppard edited the astonishingly compendious *Handbook* (Sheppard 1922) which *inter alia* from his pen included four chapters of archaeological notes on prehistoric, Roman, Anglo-Saxon and Danish topics. Earthworks, with Danes' Dyke to the fore, were given adequate emphasis, and there was also a useful summary on Boynton's excavations of the Holderness lake-dwellings which had been adequately published by Smith (1911). Sheppard, however, did not refer to any relics earlier than Neolithic, and it was at this meeting that he first challenged publicly the authenticity of William Morfitt's Maglemosian harpoon heads (Gilbertson this volume) which were confirmed as genuine later in the same year by a Cambridge committee (Clark and Godwin 1956). Perhaps it was prejudice against Morfitt which also led to omission of any reference to the so-called 'pit dwellings' found by him at Atwick, which had also been published before World War 1 (Greenwell and Gatty 1910). Curiously, Sheppard also omitted any mention of two of the most spectacular prehistoric objects in the Hull Museum, on both of which he had himself published notes, the Roos boat-model (Sheppard 1901) and the Brigg Dugout (Sheppard 1910). The four chapters are otherwise a fair introduction to the archaeology of the neighbourhood as then known.

The funerary bias, the 'Greenwell-Mortimer syndrome' perhaps, received further impetus when in 1929, nearly 10 years after its acquisition by Sheppard for Hull, the Mortimer Collection was put on display in the rooms previously used as the municipal art gallery. Here the public's 'morbid taste for bones', to borrow the title of a popular historical novel, could be given free rein, although rows of skulls remained an incongruous back-drop for the balls and other social functions which continued to be held there! However, the original Municipal Museum at Albion Street still drew visitors to see such treasures as the great logboat from Brigg, suspended from the ceiling of the main hall (Fig. 6.4). Sheppard was always a little coy about how he acquired it from Mr V. Cary-Elwes, the Lord of the Manor, who had established his legal claim against the Brigg Gasworks Company.

Another important addition to the local archaeological record came with Burchell's (1930) publication of his discovery of Palaeolithic

Fig. 6.4. The Brigg logboat on display in the original Municipal Museum at Albion Street, Hull.

implements in the drifts of Flamborough Head and the Holderness gravels. However, as with the Mesolithic harpoons, Sheppard remained sceptical, this time of Burchell's attribution of them to the Palaeolithic or even of their human manufacture. By 1930, therefore, while the records of archaeological discoveries in the Humber region were both extensive and varied, ranging over all periods from the Palaeolithic onwards, there was a lack of modern excavated evidence.

Change, however, was on the way, stimulated by the appearance of a stronger academic influence originating from the newly founded Hull University College. The two individuals most active in this direction were the physicist L.S. Palmer and the historian F.W. Brooks, and it was largely the latter's influence on the Local History Committee which was behind the initiative to explore the Romano-British site at Brough. I well remember cycling over to witness the opening of Philip Corder's first trial trench there in August 1933, and thereafter participating from time to time in the five-year programme of excavations which, along with Corder's earlier work at Malton, Crambeck, Langton and Throlam, laid reliable foundations for the study of the Roman period in the East Riding. Alas, I was not present on the day in 1937 when Bertie Gott found and then delicately exposed the inscribed slab which provided confirmation of the identification of *Petuaria* and its status as a *vicus* in the Antonine period (Corder 1934, 1935, Corder and Romans 1936-8).

After the five seasons at Brough, during which Maurice Barley joined the University staff in the Department of Extramural Studies and became an active force in local archaeology, Corder's next enterprise was to carry forward A.L. Congreve's work at Elmswell. This yielded traces of occupation from the early Iron Age to the Anglo-Saxon period (Corder 1940), but was crowned by the discovery of the superb Celtic panel of repoussé bronze surmounted by its strip of champlevé enamel-work, which added to Hull Museums' store of archaeological treasures (Corder and Hawkes 1940). Before the Elmswell team dispersed, we were able to carry out a week's trial-trenching of the Redcliff site at North Ferriby which added to the range of imported pottery and brooches, but provided nothing significant by way of evidence for structures (Corder *et al.* 1939). During this week Corder, Barley, Congreve, Romans, my brother and I spent one day carrying out the fourth and, up to that time, most ambitious excavation on Boat 1, which added greatly to our knowledge of the find but still not enough for a reliable interpretation (Wright and Wright 1939).

An account of archaeological activity in the East Riding in the decade before the Second World War would be incomplete without mention of Mary Kitson Clark's admirable *Gazetteer of Roman Remains in East Yorkshire* (1935) and the successive excavations of the Rudston Villa, both under the aegis of the Yorkshire Archaeological Society and its Malton Committee (Richmond 1933, Woodward and Steer 1934-7). A convenient summary of the work immediately preceding the war is contained in *The History of the East Riding of Yorkshire,* prepared as an accompaniment to the Exhibition of Local History by the Hull University College Local History Committee (1939). The geographical background is described by Palmer and the prehistoric periods by Sheppard, still holding manfully to his contention that 'no trace of Palaeolithic man has yet been found in all Yorkshire'. Kitson Clark does justice to the Roman scene and Barley to the Anglo-Saxon rural development. The work is rounded off by contributions from Brooks and Foot Walker, and is a valuable complement to the wider ranging synthesis by Elgee and Elgee (1933).

Developments in the 1940s and 50s

For most of us the war years meant exile from our home pursuits, but leave from the services provided opportunities for observation and occasional rescue work at Ferriby. It was on such an occasion in November 1940 that I came upon the projecting end of another great oak plank (Boat 2) to the west of the 1937 find. During the next few days I was able to establish that Boat 2 was represented by much of the keel-plank, with the rest absent, but what there was present displayed generally better preserved details than those we had by then seen of Boat 1. In 1941 my brother rescued some of the eastern end of Boat 1, which was in danger of being washed away, and deposited it at Hull Museum where, with the Brigg Dugout, it was destroyed in the disastrous fire of 1942. Another casualty was our strange forked timber from the Ferriby site (Fig. 6.5), subsequently interpreted as the side-frame of a beach-capstan (Wright 1986).

What I believe to be the most significant archaeological developments in and around the neighbourhood during the decade following the end of the Second World War were, in chronological order, our own work at North Ferriby in 1946 (Wright and Wright 1947), Clark's and others' at Star Carr from 1947 to 1951 (Clark 1954), Brewster's at Staple Howe from 1950 onwards (Brewster 1963), which also performed the long-needed service of publishing the early Iron Age pottery from Holderness, and the identification of a Maglemosian site at Brandesburton in 1953 (Clark and Godwin 1956). For lack of resources, the influence of Hull Museum was less than it had been before the war, and leadership was largely assumed by the Local History Committee of the University, which sprouted an Excavation Sub-Committee whose purpose was to maintain momentum in fieldwork. This we did at a variety of locations and with varied success, but I am ashamed to say that the record of publication of results is notable for its absence. However, we did at least stimulate interest and in some cases pave the way for better organised and better reported excavation later. What was needed was an injection of professional leadership and guidance to supplement

Fig. 6.5. The forked timber on the North Ferriby foreshore, 1938. The ruler is opened to a length of 1 ft.

amateur enthusiasm at a time when the archaeological discipline was itself the subject of rapid technical development. This was, for example, the period when absolute dating by radiocarbon assay was being introduced (Libby 1955). The first determination for the East Riding of which I am aware was on some Ferriby timber (2700 ± 150 years b.p. BM 58); this faced me with the dramatic possibility that the boats were made in the Bronze Age, rather than the early Iron Age as I had previously deduced (Wright 1960).

I remember paying a visit to Oxford about this time in order to recruit graduates for the company of Reckitt and Colman for whom I worked. At lunch I found myself sitting next to Christopher Hawkes, and I asked him what he thought I ought to do to improve the technical quality of archaeological investigations in the area. His reply was words to the effect that I should persuade my industrial friends to endow a chair in archaeology at Hull University, which had progressed from University College to full University status at an impressive ceremony in 1954. I am afraid that I took no initiative in this direction, however, having little faith in the willingness of the local magnates to finance an art or science viewed as of little practical value. By the same token, I recall at the opening of the 1966 exhibition of Recent Archaeological Discoveries (Bartlett 1966) at the Hull City Hall talking to a veteran among the city fathers and being told that he could not understand what 'them dook-eggs' saw in archaeology. I think he meant 'egg-heads', but the message was clear enough!

Professionally led excavations in the 1950s reflected the improved funding of archaeology by the Ministry of Works and other institutions, with priority usually having been given to rescue work ahead of building development and road works. Examples from this period are the identification of the first late Bronze Age/early Iron Age hill fort in the East Riding at Grimthorpe (Stead 1968), further work at Brough/*Petuaria* which notably rounded off Corder's pre-war results (Wacher 1960, 1969), and the excavation of the medieval lost village at Riplingham (Wacher 1966). Rather outside our area, but nonetheless influential, there was also the long-running Wharram Percy project. From 1959 onwards, one of our most important classes of prehistoric monument, the Iron Age 'square barrow' cemetery, received from Ian Stead the modern and expert treatment it had long merited, culminating in his monograph *The La T`ene Cultures of Eastern Yorkshire* (1965).

Our last exercise under the Excavation Sub-Committee resulted from the location of the Anglo-Saxon cemetery at Sancton by that eagle-eyed fieldwalker, Jack Taylor. Several seasons of work (1954-8) yielded much information and some 240 properly provenanced urns or fragments to add to the large number discovered in the nineteenth century and dispersed as far afield as the USA and New Zealand. This new material, together with what could be traced of the earlier finds, was eventually and amply published in the most ambitious issue in the whole of the Hull Museum Publications series, No. 218 (Myres and Southern 1973); the significance of the Sancton cemetery has now been placed in its proper context by Myres (1986).

The last three decades

The neighbourhood still lacked a firm local base in archaeology, but this was remedied when, in 1959, the city fathers of Hull appointed a qualified archaeologist, John Bartlett, to succeed J.B. Fay as Director of Museums. Under his influence it was not long before the Museum regained the place it had had in Sheppard's day as the prime focus for archaeological activity, a position I am happy to say it still retains. My association with Bartlett was a close and fruitful one, and with him I enjoyed much active fieldwork and the stimulus of the two societies in the forming of which he was the moving spirit - the East Riding Archaeological Society in 1969 with W.J. Varley as its first chairman, and the Hull Museums Society in 1968. The Hull Museum Publications series was revived and I can remember the great pride Bartlett took in the first new issue, No. 214 in 1963, after a gap of 22 years since Sheppard's last on Bronze Age implements in 1941, the year of his retirement. Earlier in the same year, I found the third boat-fragment at Ferriby (Fig. 6.6), and the speed with which a rescue campaign was mounted is evidence enough for the drive by then available; it was little more than a month from first discovery to consignment of the planks to freshwater holding tanks behind Wilberforce House in High Street. Once again the urge for prompt publication inculcated into anyone practising in these parts came into play. I managed to record the find by working during lunch-hours through the ensuing summer, and had an account into print the following year (Wright and Churchill 1965).

There is insufficient space to enumerate all the ventures in which I was lucky enough to participate before leaving East Yorkshire in 1970, but one which sticks in my mind is the Walkington Wold excavations of 1967-9. This was the most ambitious field exercise of the East Riding Archaeological Society up to that time, and proved to be an interesting and difficult campaign on a much disturbed, multi-period site, comprehensively reported in Bartlett and Mackey (1973). My strongest memory is the arrival of a much excited John Bartlett at my house in Walkington one Saturday afternoon, bursting to tell someone about the Bronze Age gold bracelet which he produced from the customary tobacco tin in his pocket. It had its first weighing on our kitchen scales!

Those were exciting and educational days, and no account should

Fig. 6.6. Ferriby boat 3 in 1963.

omit the efforts of Bill Varley who, by his own admission, used to move from one teaching post to another so that he could pursue his archaeological interests. To him we owe the first modern investigation of the Holderness crannogs, or lake-dwellings (Varley 1968), and valuable work on medieval sites at Beverley and Etton among others. Greater use was also being made at this time of aerial photographs, and this led to the identification of the first henge-monument from the East Riding, Maiden's Grave near Rudston, excavated by the Museum with reinforcements from the East Riding Archaeological Society (McInnes 1964). The area round Driffield had in the late 1950s begun to yield increasing evidence for settlement sites of the late Neolithic with overlapping Beaker influences, and this development, largely initiated by the Granthams and extended and published by T.G. Manby (e.g. Manby 1958, 1974), has led to the present situation that the Neolithic/Bronze Age transition in East Yorkshire is now better documented than any other period before the early Iron Age.

Since leaving the East Riding I have to my regret not kept as closely in touch with the whole range of archaeological activity as I should have wished. Through the 1970s I felt it my duty to secure and order the Ferriby boat records as a prelude to full-scale publication. I had become a trustee of the National Maritime Museum in 1972, with a clear mission to support the development of an archaeological facility in the museum which soon emerged as the Archaeological Research Centre, now alas disbanded for lack of resources. Participation in the series of conferences and seminars mounted by the museum provided a ready means of better educating myself and maintaining a steady flow of publication of successive aspects of the Ferriby story (Wright 1976, 1978, 1984, 1985). This was refreshed by regular inspections of the site which inevitably yielded further finds, some of which have illuminated the constructional processes, fastenings especially. More recently, the projected definitive work has taken shape and a first draft is with a publisher, albeit still requiring much detailed attention before it can appear in print. The Archaeological Research Centre's own programmes have embraced two excavations within our compass - the relocation and re-excavation of the Brigg Raft (McGrail 1981, this volume), and several seasons of digging on the Ferriby site, which have added to the dating evidence (McGrail 1983) and provided a basis for much more complete investigation of the environmental background than Churchill's summary work in 1963 (Buckland *et al.* this volume). Happily, the Centre was also able to provide some support for the excavation and recording of the Hasholme logboat in 1984 (McGrail this volume); this will make a worthy replacement for the lost Brigg Dugout as the flagship of British logboats.

To round off this chapter I should like to return to two of my own pet sites, the Welton foreshore and Ferriby Redcliff. Successive visits had shown that both were at increasing risk from erosion and, in the latter case, pillaging also. I felt a personal responsibility for each, but lacked the resources at 200 miles distance to do more than watch and occasionally salve any significant artefacts exposed by water or weather. After several years of abortive attempts to interest potentially capable authorities in tackling these sites, no-one was more relieved than I when David Crowther set up his programme for their professional investigation using the resources of Hull Museum and the East Riding Archaeological Society. Already there are preliminary findings in print (Crowther 1987 a, b, Crowther *et al.* this volume), and I look to the day when these two previously neglected projects, in whose beginning I had a pioneering hand half a century ago, are the subject of the full publication which their significance merits.

I hope that this review will demonstrate that the flourishing practice of archaeology in the Humber region in the past fifty years can be seen to have dealt adequately with as wide a range of opportunities and challenges as exist in any part of Britain. I am grateful for the chances that have come my way to participate in, and contribute to, the process, and for being invited to share my memories with you.

References

Bartlett, J.E. (1966). *Recent Archaeological Discoveries*, Hull Museum Publications 216. Hull Museum, Hull.

Bartlett, J.E. and Mackey R.W. (1973). Walkington Wold excavations 1967-1969. *East Riding Archaeologist* 1, 1-100.

Bisat, W.S. (1932). Glacial and post-glacial sections on the Humber shore at North Ferriby. *Transactions of the Hull Geological Society* 7, 83-95.

Brewster, T.C.M. (1963). *The Excavation of Staple Howe*. East Riding Archaeological Research Committee, Scarborough.

Burchell, J.P.T. (1930). Upper and Lower Palaeolithic man in East Yorkshire. *Proceedings of the Prehistoric Society of East Anglia* 6, 226-33.

Clark, J.G.D. (1954). *Excavations at Star Carr*. Cambridge University Press, London.

Clark, J.G.D. and Godwin, H. (1956). A Maglemosian site at Brandesburton, Holderness, Yorkshire. *Proceedings of the Prehistoric Society* 22, 6-22.

Corder, P. (1934 & 1935). *Excavations at the Roman Fort at Brough-on-Humber*. Hull University College Local History Committee, Hull.

Corder, P. (1940). *Excavations at Elmswell, East Yorkshire, 1938*, Hull Museum Publications 207. Hull Museum, Hull.

Corder P. and Hawkes, C.F.C. (1940). A panel of Celtic ornament from Elmswell, East Yorkshire. *Antiquaries Journal* 20, 338-57.

Corder, P. and Romans, T. (1936-8). *Excavations at the Roman Fort at Brough-on-Humber.* Hull University College Local History Committee, Hull.

Corder, P., Wright, C.W. and Wright, E.V. (1939). The pre-Roman settlement of the Parisi at North Ferriby. *The Naturalist* **1**, 237-43.

Crowther, D.R. (1987a). Sediments and archaeology of the Humber foreshore. In: *East Yorkshire Field Guide* (ed. S. Ellis) pp. 99-105. Quaternary Research Association, Cambridge.

Crowther, D.R. (1987b). Redcliff. *Current Archaeology* **104**, 284-5.

Elgee, F. and Elgee, H.W. (1933). *The Archaeology of Yorkshire.* Methuen, London.

Greenhill, B.J. (1976). *Archaeology of the Boat.* A. and C. Black, London.

Greenwell, W. (1877). *British Barrows.* Clarendon Press, Oxford.

Greenwell, W. and Gatty, R.A. (1910). The pit-dwellings at Holderness. *Man* **48**, 86-90.

Hull University College Local History Committee (1939). *The History of the East Riding of Yorkshire.* Hull University College Local History Committee, Hull.

Kitson Clark, M. (1935). *A Gazetteer of Roman Remains in East Yorkshire,* Roman Malton and District Reports 5, Scarborough.

Libby, W.F. (1955). *Radiocarbon Dating.* Chicago University Press, Chicago.

Manby, T.G. (1958). A Neolithic site at Craike Hill, Garton Slack. *Antiquaries Journal* **38**, 223-36.

Manby, T.G. (1974). *Grooved Ware Sites in Yorkshire and the North of England,* British Archaeological Reports (British Series) 9. British Archaeological Reports, Oxford.

McGrail, S. (ed.) (1981). *The Brigg 'Raft' and Her Prehistoric Environment,* National Maritime Museum Archaeological Series 6, British Archaeological Reports (British Series) 89. British Archaeological Reports, Oxford.

McGrail, S. (1983). The interpretation of archaeological evidence for maritime structures. In: *Sea Studies* (ed. P. Annis) pp. 33-46. National Maritime Museum, Greenwich.

McInnes, I.J. (1964). A class II henge in the East Riding of Yorkshire. *Antiquity* **38**, 218-19.

Mortimer, J.R. (1905). *Forty Years Researches in British and Saxon Burial Mounds of East Yorkshire*. A. Brown, Hull.
Myres, J.N.L. (1986). *The English Settlements*. Clarendon Press, Oxford.
Myres, J.N.L. and Southern, W.H. (1973). *The Anglo-Saxon Cremation Cemetery at Sancton, East Yorkshire*, Hull Museum Publications 218. Hull Museum, Hull.
Richmond, I.A. (1933). *The Roman Pavements at Rudston, East Riding*, Roman Malton and District Reports 6, Scarborough.
Sheppard, T. (1901). *Notes on the Ancient Model of a Boat found at Roos in Holderness*, Hull Museum Publications 4. Hull Museum, Hull.
Sheppard, T. (1910). *The Prehistoric Boat from Brigg*, Hull Museum Publications 73. Hull Museum, Hull.
Sheppard, T. (ed.) (1922). *Handbook to Hull and the East Riding of Yorkshire*, British Association for the Advancement of Science. A. Brown, Hull.
Sheppard, T. (1926). Roman remains in North Lincolnshire. *Transactions of the East Riding Antiquarian Society* **25**, 170-4.
Smith, R.A. (1911). Lake-dwellings in Holderness, Yorkshire. *Archaeologia* **62**, 593-610.
Stather, J.W. (1896). Drifts of the Humber gap. *Proceedings of the Yorkshire Geological and Polytechnic Society* **13**, 210-20.
Stead, I.M. (1965). *The La T`ene Cultures of Eastern Yorkshire*. Yorkshire Philosophical Society, York.
Stead, I.M. (1968). An Iron Age hillfort at Grimthorpe, Yorkshire, England. *Proceedings of the Prehistoric Society* **34**, 148-90.
Varley, W.J. (1968). Barmston and the Holderness crannogs. *East Riding Archaeologist* **1**, 11-26.
Wacher, J.S. (1960). Petuaria: new evidence for the Roman town and its earlier fort. *Antiquaries Journal* **40**, 58-64.
Wacher, J.S. (1966). Excavations at Riplingham, East Yorkshire, 1956-7. *Yorkshire Archaeological Journal* **41**, 608-69.
Wacher, J.S. (1969). *Excavations at Brough-on-Humber, 1958-61*, Research Report 25. Society of Antiquaries, London.
Woodward, A.M. and Steer, K.A. (1934-7). Rudston Roman villa. Interim reports in *Yorkshire Archaeological Journal*.
Wright, C.W. and Wright, E.V. (1933). Some notes on the Holocene

deposits at North Ferriby. *The Naturalist,* 210-12.
Wright, C.W. and Wright E.V. (1939). Submerged boat at North Ferriby. *Antiquity* **13**, 349-53.
Wright, E.V. (1960). The North Ferriby boat - radiocarbon dating. *Proceedings of the Prehistoric Society* **26**, 351.
Wright, E.V. (1976). *The North Ferriby Boats: a guidebook,* National Maritime Museum Monograph 23. National Maritime Museum, Greenwich.
Wright, E.V. (1978). Artefacts from the boat-site at North Ferriby. *Proceedings of the Prehistoric Society* **44**, 187-202.
Wright, E.V. (1984). Practical experiments in boat-stitching. In: *Aspects of Maritime Archaeology and Ethnology* (ed. S. McGrail) pp. 57-84. National Maritime Museum, Greenwich.
Wright, E.V. (1985). The North Ferriby Boats - a revised basis for reconstruction. In: *Sewn Plank Boats,* National Maritime Museum Archaeological Series 10 (ed. S. McGrail and E. Kentley) pp. 105-44. British Archaeological Reports, Oxford.
Wright, E.V. (1986). A Bronze Age beach-capstan? *Oxford Journal of Archaeology* **5**, 309-21.
Wright, E.V. and Churchill, D.M. (1965). The boats from North Ferriby, Yorkshire, England. *Proceedings of the Prehistoric Society* **31**, 1-24.
Wright, E.V. and Wright, C.W. (1947). Prehistoric boats from North Ferriby, East Yorkshire. *Proceedings of the Prehistoric Society* **13**, 114-38.

7

The Holderness meres: stratigraphy, archaeology and environment

D.D. Gilbertson

Introduction

It may be a surprise to the casual observer of the Holderness landscape to discover the extent to which the rather flat, often bleak and prairie-like condition of modern Holderness is quite unlike the complex mosaics of lakes, islands, marshes and woodland that were such rich resources of wildlife, food, wood and water in earlier historic and prehistoric times. The palaeogeographic reconstruction by Sheppard (1956, 1957) provides a conservative estimate of the number of meres known or suspected to have existed in the medieval period (Fig. 4.1 this volume), and if the data in Sheppard (1912) concerning those meres and villages believed to have been lost through coastal erosion since medieval times are included, at least another four or five notable water bodies can be added to the map. However, as a result of siltation, artificial drainage and coastal erosion, Hornsea Mere is now the sole survivor.

The former meres are located on the Skipsea or Withernsea Tills, which were deposited by the ice sheet of the Dimlington Stadial some 13-18 000 years ago (Catt this volume). They may have developed as a result of the melting of large bodies of ice within the till to produce kettle holes, water accumulating in the depressions on an uneven surface of the till, or drainage impedance by eskers left by the ice sheet. Valentin (1957) suggested that east-west elongate lake basins such as Hornsea or Lambwath Mere might represent the sites of former, pre-till valleys draining eastwards and eroded into the underlying Chalk bedrock. Local modifications to the shape and extent of meres have probably been caused in historical times by the excavation of lake basin peats and perhaps even the quarrying of clays from the tills.

It is important to recognise that in the period of time from the decay of the Dimlington Stadial ice sheet to the inundation of the land to the east by the incoming North Sea in the mid Holocene (Gaunt and Tooley 1974), the complex wetland landscape of Holderness was only the western outpost of a similar landscape which stretched across to continental Europe. On the other hand, the vast majority of these former lake basins are likely to have been enclosed and isolated from each other. Streams are rare in Holderness, and it was not until the construction of drains and canals in medieval times that it became possible to travel by small boat inland from Barmston and then down the River Hull, and hence to distinguish the 'Isle of Holderness' as described by Sheppard (1912).

As a result of the extensive coastal erosion of eastern Holderness, it is possible to examine in vertical section a remarkable series of lake deposits, fossils and artefacts which together illustrate the fascinating and complex history of the meres. The components of this history cover a period of approximately 13 000 years and include ice sheet decay, climatic change, the invasion and colonisation of the area by diverse assemblages of plants, animals and people, soil development and erosion, changes in lake dimensions, chemistry and modes of sedimentation, and the spread and changing impacts of deforestation and agriculture. This chapter aims briefly to review some of these aspects on the basis of the evidence which has been obtained primarily from the coastal exposures of the deposits of the former Skipsea Withow Mere (National Grid Reference TA 184547, Fig. 4.1 this volume).

Later prehistory

Probably the best exposures of late prehistoric mere deposits in

Holderness were those recorded by Thomas Boynton, a Drainage Commissioner, who observed oak piles and bones at West Furze and Round Hill, Ulrome (TA 161556) in 1880 after clearing the Skipsea branch of the Barmston Drain. Shortly afterwards he carried out a pioneering series of small excavations in and around Skipsea, during the course of which he observed peat layers interbedded with freshwater, shelly, calcareous marls. The results of his work were later reported by Smith (1911). The most interesting points were the discoveries, in the upper levels of these wetlands, of a human skull, oak piles and wooden structures which he described, in the tradition of the time, as 'crannogs', most of which were broadly attributed to the Bronze Age and Iron Age. This is much the same picture as that advanced subsequently by Sheppard (1912) and Varley (1968).

At present the evidence available is insufficient to decide whether there is any regional pattern or general significance in the alternations between peat and marl sedimentation in the isolated lake basins, or whether or not they have significance for our understanding of the impacts of the developing and intensifying agriculture of the times upon soil erosion, and hence the chemical character of the former lake waters and the deposits accumulating within them. The roles of the oak piles and other wooden structures are equally unclear. The limited evidence from recent unpublished coastal exposures in the lake margin deposits of the former Skipsea Withow Mere indicates the presence of wooden platforms built of long poles laid horizontally on the water-washed surface of a lake margin and held in place with pegs. Overall, the structures appear to be parts of platforms associated with the exploitation of the lake and edge of the fringing marsh and alder/oak carr.

However, other timbers from these Skipsea Withow Mere deposits, which are reported in Gilbertson (1984a, b), have indicated a different aspect of ancient human ecological activity. Figure 7.1 shows an 'elbow' or 'heel of coppicing'. The abrupt right-angle bend is the result of 'lopping' a thick branch from a tree that has been deliberately managed (coppiced) in order to provide timber of required dimensions, perhaps for building or platform construction. At approximately the same level in these deposits there occurred thinner rods with zig-zag fractures caused by pushing the wood, when green, into a peat surface, only for it to meet a harder object at depth and then buckle. One carved stake or rod of alder, also at this level,

Fig. 7.1. An 'elbow' or 'heel of coppicing' approximately 4500 years old, suggesting early Neolithic management of alder carr occurred at the margins of the former Skipsea Withow Mere. The rod is 30 cm long.

was radiocarbon dated to around 4770 years ago.

These finds indicate not only the exploitation of wetland and woodland, but also the management of woodland at the edge of a mere in order to utilise a valued biological resource. The radiocarbon date places the carved alder rod clearly in the early Neolithic, and the managed and worked wood with which it was associated, among the earliest Neolithic wooden structures so far found in the British Isles; for example, the date lies well within the range of radiocarbon dates for similar finds in the very old Sweet Track of the Somerset Levels (Coles 1979, Morgan 1979, 1987).

The pollen analytical studies reported in Gilbertson (1984a), Beckett (1981) and Flenley (1987, this volume) indicate forest clearance and farming were underway in Holderness at this time. At Skipsea Withow Mere a radiocarbon date from the top of the lake margin/carr peat deposits suggests that both the scale and intensity of soil erosion consequent upon prehistoric farming were such that this sector of the former lake margin was being buried in colluvium, caused by accelerated soil erosion, by about 4500 years ago. However, whether or not this date is too old as a result of a 'hard-water error' caused by carbonate-rich runoff from the surrounding chalk-rich tills is not known. Elsewhere in Holderness the burial of lake margin deposits in agriculturally-derived colluvium in late prehistoric or even historic time is widely suspected, but not always securely dated. It is likely to have occurred at many places at different times, depending upon the particular land use

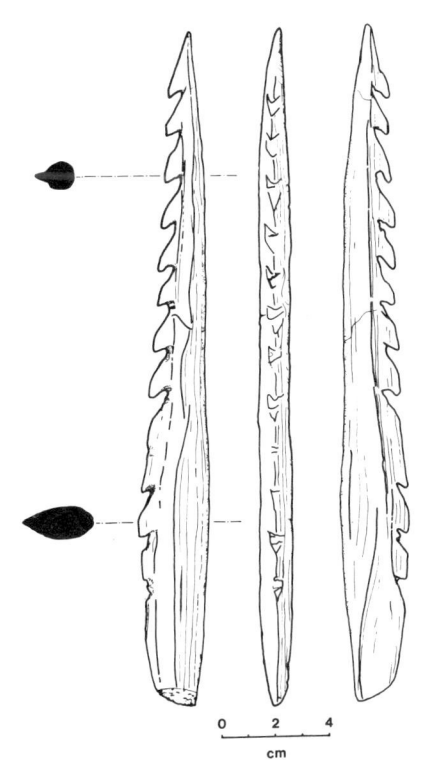

Fig. 7.2. The barbed bone point taken from Skipsea Withow Mere by Mr B. Morfitt in 1903 (redrawn from Clark and Godwin 1956).

and topographic circumstances of the location, and this agent remains a principal cause of the loss of many Holderness meres.

Early Mesolithic

The area from Skipsea Withow Mere to Brandesburton (Fig. 4.1 this volume) has yielded a fascinating series of barbed 'harpoon' points made of bone (Fig. 7.2), flints and flint blades (e.g. Armstrong 1922, 1923a, b, c, Read *et al.* 1923, Sheppard 1923, Godwin and Godwin 1933, Clark and Godwin 1956, Davis-King 1980, Gilbertson 1984a). Some of these were found on, or were 'associated with', the higher gravel ridges of eskers which overlook the lowlands and meres of

Holderness, while others, such as those from Skipsea Withow described by Armstrong, were found in the mere deposits. The bone points contrast with those made of antler which characterise the well-known barbed points from the wetland site of Star Carr, some 35 km to the northwest in the Vale of Pickering (Clark 1954, Schadla-Hall 1987).

The Skipsea bone harpoons were the subject of great controversy which developed between Thomas Sheppard, Director of Hull Municipal Museums, and A. Leslie Armstrong, a similarly formidable, but amateur, archaeologist based in Sheffield. Sheppard thought the harpoons were frauds - the work of the 'beach-combing' Morfitt family who had informed Armstrong that the harpoons were recovered by them from just below the complete skeleton of a giant elk (*Megaceros giganteus*) embedded within the base of the peats, or within the lake silts and clays beneath the peats, which were exposed at Skipsea Withow. In a letter to Mr Hazzledine Warren (a notable archaeologist and geologist of the time) dated 17 September 1929, Sheppard wrote 'The Maglemose harpoons were made by Mr B. Morfitt in the presence of his sister who was spending the weekend with Mrs Sheppard and I and told us how it was done.' However, there have now been sufficient *in situ* finds of bone points and flint blades in and around the Holderness meres to suggest that the controversial Armstrong/Morfitt finds were genuine, and it is therefore likely that the Morfitts were enjoying a joke at the expense of Mr and Mrs Sheppard. The later and pioneering pollen analytical dating studies by Godwin and Godwin (1933), promoted by Armstrong, indicated that the source clays could not be later than Pollen Zone IV (see Godwin 1975) and might be earlier. However, as a result of a confusion that arose in the primary and secondary literature concerning the sites, the lake silts and clays from the Skipsea Withow Mere, together with their associated Mesolithic remains, giant elk etc., all became referred in the literature to the mid Holocene rather than to the Late Devensian/early Holocene (see Gilbertson 1984a for a full discussion).

In recent years research has indicated the quality of the geological and palaeoecological record concerning the Late Devensian and early Holocene records that can be obtained from the Holderness meres, a record which clarifies several questions concerning the antiquity and environmental contexts of the controversial finds mentioned above.

A borehole in the mere deposits at The Bog, Roos (Fig. 4.1 this volume) by Beckett (1981) yielded a 2-5 cm thick layer of organic mud which was radiocarbon dated to around 13 000 years ago. This is the oldest date yet known for mere infill deposits that accumulated on the Late Devensian (Dimlington Stadial) till of Holderness shortly after the ice sheet had melted. Boreholes at Skipsea Bail Mere and Flaxmere, as well as at Roos, also yielded organic muds suggestive of the milder Late Devensian period known as the Windermere Interstadial, which lasted from approximately 12-11 000 years ago; the associated pollen indicate a landscape of tree birch and dwarf birch with sedge and herbs (Beckett 1981, Flenley 1987, this volume). The final period of the Late Devensian, the Loch Lomond Stadial lasting from around 11-10 000 years ago, was one of marked climatic severity, with small cirque glacier development occurring in the mountain regions of Britain. The evidence from the Holderness mere cores reveals that this was followed by a rapid climatic improvement, beginning about 10 200 years ago, which ushered in the milder conditions and woodland development of the present Holocene period (Flenley 1987, this volume).

However, recent studies carried out in the cliff exposures of the deposits of Skipsea Withow Mere have been able to put much new detail on the picture of change outlined above, for two principal and related reasons. First, these deposits, like those examined previously at this site by Armstrong and Godwin, are essentially lake *margin* deposits, and they therefore record in detail the manifold changes in the positions and state of the ancient shoreline. Thus the evidence complements that from isolated boreholes from the more central areas of former meres. Second, at the coastal exposures it is possible to examine a 100 m long section through the deposits, a feature which leads to a better scale and quality of evidence than that available from core samples. Full details of the studies are given in Gilbertson (1984a).

A significant part of the earliest history of this mere is represented by the exposures at its northern and southern margins. The till surface on the northern side is readily recognised as the interface between vertically-cracked and non-cracked deposits, the latter containing large stones (Fig. 7.3). This surface shows evidence of weathering, slumping and the development of gley soils, all dating from the period immediately after deglaciation. Above this lie the

Fig. 7.3. The exposure at the northern margin of Skipsea Withow Mere.

earliest lake deposits. Initially these exhibit pronounced textural couplets, which probably reflect seasonal freezing and thawing of the lake. The lake then became increasingly biologically-rich and eutrophic, features aided by the input of mineral-rich runoff from the surrounding till. Eventually the waters became sufficiently lime-rich for carbonate precipitation to occur, commencing in Figure 7.3 at the level marked by the trowel point; the layers of white precipitate are particularly clear immediately above the trowel.

A fine Mesolithic blade (the 'Skipsea blade') was recovered from the stratigraphic equivalent of these deposits in 1978. The stratigraphic and palaeoecological evidence described in Gilbertson (1984a) indicates that these deposits date from the period shortly after deglaciation, during the equivalent of Pollen Zone I (Godwin 1975). This indicates that the Skipsea blade was made by some of the very earliest human colonisers of the British deglacial landscape.

The Late Devensian sequence is continued in the exposures at the southern side of the site. Windermere Interstadial deposits representative of the Pollen Zone II of Godwin (1975) have yet to be located at Skipsea Withow, but those of the Loch Lomond Stadial

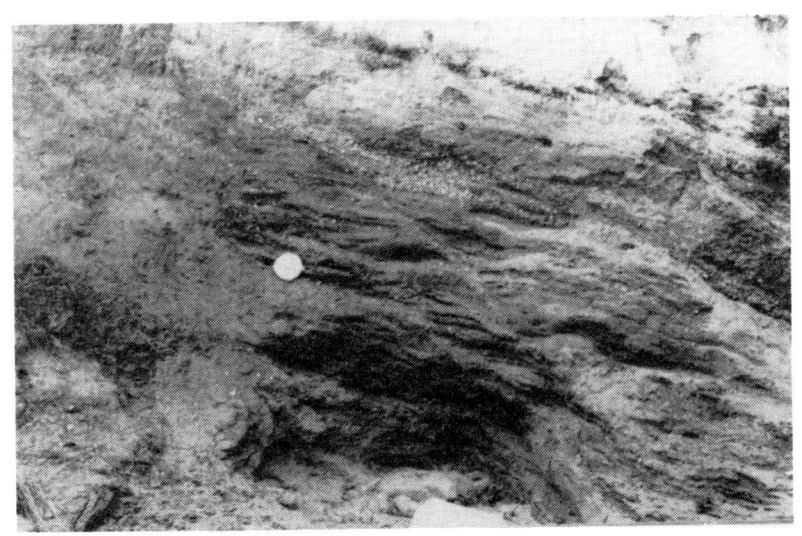

Fig. 7.4. The exposure at the southern margin of Skipsea Withow Mere.

(Pollen Zone III) are present, and indicate a series of very local, but important, geomorphic events. While the north bank appears to have remained essentially stable, the south bank was characterised by slides and slumps of gravel into the lake from the adjacent till. In Figure 7.4 these are clearly seen overlying the tape which rests upon relatively undisturbed lake muds. The gravels also incorporate, and are interbedded with, ancient soils and lake margin sediment surfaces, which are rich in plant macrofossils and molluscan remains. These reveal that, although the pollen of tree birch was rare at the time, tree birches were growing around the lake margin; a branch of a tree birch yielded a radiocarbon date of around 10 440 years ago. During this period slumping and faulting were common and are clearly seen affecting the gravels and interbedded lake sediments and soils in Figure 7.4. Such features are rarely observed in Quaternary mere deposits and offer fresh insight into the landscape and geomorphic processes of the Loch Lomond Stadial.

The final stages in this brief cold episode are represented by the base of the peat seen in Figure 7.3 above the trowel. The surface is clearly erosional, and the white/grey laminations of the lake muds are here a distinct orange/brown and lacking in molluscan fossils as a result of sub-aerial weathering of the exposed surface of the lake muds. This erosion surface marks a major change in the size and status of the lake. The lake level appears to have dropped by at least 8 m, if not more, and further episodes of small-scale faulting occurred. The climatic or other reasons for this major hydrological change are not known, but in general terms it corresponds with the start of the Holocene period. An episode of marked aridity may be involved; on the other hand, the arrival of a rich tree flora may have had the effect of pumping much water out of the soil. This episode may have great archaeological significance, since some degree of reworking and concentration of artefacts, as well as of materials such as natural flints and other pebbles, could be expected on this new land surface. Indeed, it corresponds with the find spot descriptions and appears to match some of the sedimentary associations of Armstrong's flints, elks and bone harpoons.

Radiocarbon dating of peats from near the base of the organic lake muds overlying the inorganic Late Devensian muds indicates that by about 9880 years ago a biologically-rich lake in a fully temperate interglacial (Holocene) forested landscape had come into existence and its waters reached to heights of 5-6 m above the modern beach level.

Conclusions

The most recent generation of studies of the Holderness meres, by the good fortune of being able to inspect the evidence both from deep cores in the centres of several meres (Flenley 1987, this volume), and the complex of deposits that accumulated at the margin of one lake, has been able to provide important information concerning the chronology, life and times of prehistoric peoples. The well-attested deforestation and agricultural activity of the Neolithic period appears to have been accompanied by the exploitation of the lakes and the management of wetland woodland resources; this continued into the Bronze and Iron Ages.

Mesolithic activity occurred around several lakes at least, as well as on the drier gravel ridges overlooking them. The remains of bone harpoons and blades at Skipsea Withow Mere appear to be related to an episode of reduced water levels, which may also have brought about the reworking and mixing of artefacts. Even in the cold episode at the end of the Late Devensian stage, tree birch, pine and many other species were growing in the area. The lakes appear likely to have experienced notable changes in size, chemistry, sedimentation, biological activity and colonisation after their initiation in the period immediately post-dating the decay of the Dimlington Stadial ice sheet. If the evidence from Skipsea Withow Mere is correctly interpreted, then people were among the very earliest of the colonisers of the evolving landscape of Holderness.

Acknowledgements

This synthesis is based upon the combined researches of undergraduate and postgraduate students at the Universities of Sheffield and Hull, and the contributions of Drs D.J. Briggs, J.R. Flenley, S.J. Gale, C.O. Hunt, D.A. Harkness, R.D.S. Jenkinson, P.A. Mellars, V.R. Switsur, C.M. Williams, Miss A.M. Blackham and Messrs H.K. Kenward, N.M. Thew and D.A. Woodall, to all of whom the author is indebted.

References

Armstrong, A.L. (1922). Two East Yorkshire bone harpoons. *Man* **75**, 130-2.
Armstrong, A.L. (1923a). Further evidence of Maglemose culture in East Yorkshire. *Man* **83**, 135-8.
Armstrong, A.L. (1923b). The Maglemose remains of Holderness and their Baltic counterparts. *Proceedings of the Prehistoric Society of East Anglia* **4**, 57-70.
Armstrong, A.L. (1923c). On two bone points from Hornsea, East Yorkshire. *Man* **83**, 49-50.
Beckett, S.C. (1981). Pollen diagrams from Holderness, North Humberside. *Journal of Biogeography* **8**, 177-98.
Clark, J.G.D. (ed.) (1954). *Excavations at Star Carr*. Cambridge University Press, London.
Clark, J.G.D. and Godwin, H. (1956). A Maglemosian site at Brandesburton, Holderness, Yorkshire. *Proceedings of the*

Prehistoric Society **22**, 6-22.
Coles, J.M. (1979). Radiocarbon dates: third list. *Somerset Levels Papers* **5**, 101.
Davis-King, S. (1980). A note on new barbed points from Brandesburton, North Humberside. *Archaeological Journal* **137**, 22-6.
Flenley, J.R. (1987). The meres of Holderness. In: *East Yorkshire Field Guide* (ed. S. Ellis) pp. 73-81. Quaternary Research Association, Cambridge.
Gaunt, G.D. and Tooley, M.J. (1974). Evidence for Flandrian sea-level changes in the Humber estuary and adjacent areas. *Bulletin of the Geological Survey of Great Britain* **48**, 25-41.
Gilbertson, D.D. (1984a). *Late Quaternary Environments and Man in Holderness*, British Archaeological Reports (British Series) 134. British Archaeological Reports, Oxford.
Gilbertson, D.D. (1984b). Early Neolithic utilisation and management of alder carr at Skipsea Withow mere, Holderness. *Yorkshire Archaeological Journal* **56**, 17-22.
Godwin, H. (1975). *The History of the British Flora*. 2nd ed., Cambridge University Press, Cambridge.
Godwin, H. and Godwin, M.E. (1933). British Maglemose harpoon sites. *Antiquity* **7**, 36-48.
Morgan, R.A. (1979). Tree-ring studies in the Somerset Levels: floating oak tree-ring chronologies from trackways and their radiocarbon dating. *Somerset Levels Papers* **5**, 98-100.
Morgan, R.A. (1987). Dendrochronological Studies of Prehistoric Trackways in the Somerset Levels. Ph.D. thesis, University of Sheffield.
Read, C.H., Woodward, A.S. and Kendall, P.F. (1923). On two bone harpoons from Hornsea, East Yorkshire. *Man* **31**, 49-50.
Schadla-Hall, R.T. (1987). Early man in the eastern Vale of Pickering. In: *East Yorkshire Field Guide* (ed. S. Ellis) pp. 22-30. Quaternary Research Association, Cambridge.
Sheppard, J.A. (1956). The Draining of the Marshlands of East Yorkshire. Ph.D. thesis, University of Hull.
Sheppard, J.A. (1957). The medieval meres of Holderness. *Transactions of the Institute of British Geographers* **23**, 75-86.
Sheppard, T. (1912). *The Lost Towns of the Yorkshire Coast*. Brown,

London.
Sheppard, T. (1923). The Maglemose harpoons. *Naturalist*, 169-79.
Smith, R.A. (1911). Lake-dwellings in Holderness, Yorkshire. *Archaeologia* **62**, 593-610.
Valentin, H. (1957). Glazialmorphologische Untersuchungen in Ostengland. *Abhandlungen der Geographische Institut der Freien Universitat, Berlin* **4**, 1-86.
Varley, W.J. (1968). Barmston and the Holderness crannogs. *East Riding Archaeologist* **1**, 11-26.

8

The upper Hull valley: archaeology under threat

J. Dent

Introduction

The area of study is bounded on the north and west by the gradually rising ground of the Yorkshire Wolds. Here drainage is subterranean, and streams only surface where the slopes merge with the low-lying floor of the Hull valley. To the east streams feed the River Hull from the undulating glacial deposits of Holderness, while the southern limits of the area are marked by a string of low ridges which extend like stepping stones across the valley from Beverley eastwards, and which carry the main A1035 through Tickton and Routh (Fig. 8.1). These ridges represent the main historic crossing point over the marshy floor of the Hull valley, and their existence has held back water on their northern side to create carrs and meres which, in the case of Leven Carrs, remained undrained until the eighteenth century. Higher up the valley the mere of Rotsea still survives as a place name, and a number of farms or hamlets with the suffix 'holme' preserve the Anglo-Scandinavian word for an island in a marsh.

The earliest human activity detected in the region extends back to the end of the Late Devensian stage (*c.* 10 000 years ago), following the melting of the Dimlington Stadial ice sheet. At this time low sea levels allowed a dry passage to continental Europe, and the ability of hunter-gatherer groups to make the crossing is reflected by harpoons from the region. Indeed, northern Holderness was the first place in

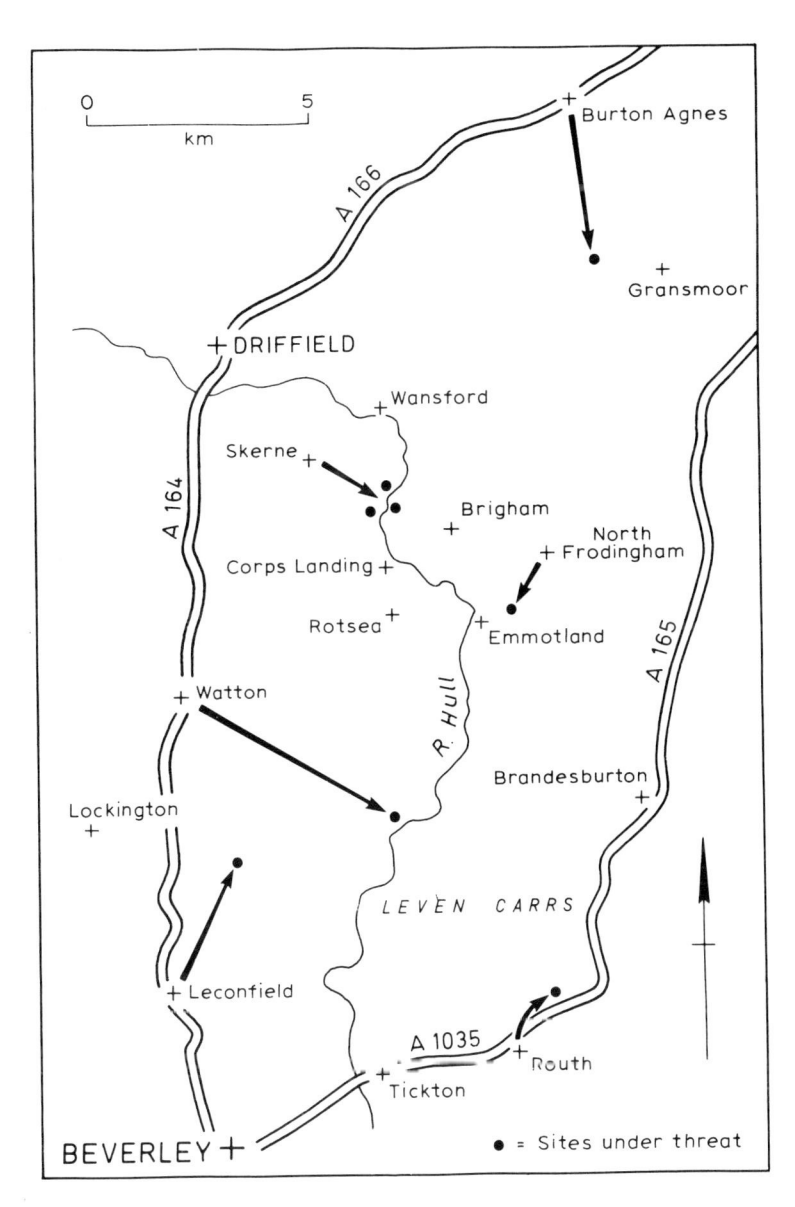

Fig. 8.1. The upper Hull valley.

Britain where these artefacts, named after the Danish site of Maglemose, were found (Gilbertson this volume). The severance of the land link with the continent during the Mesolithic period created difficulties for subsequent immigrants, but East Yorkshire is particularly well provided with evidence of the later prehistoric period, best known from the remains on the Wolds, and evidence of human settlement continues through to the present day.

In the upper Hull valley dry locations for settlements tended to be restricted to sand and gravel ridges or islands within marshland, but the streams, meres and open marshes also played an important role as sources of food and raw materials. Archaeological remains from the wetland areas can be extremely well preserved, but exposure of organic matter to air through drainage or disturbance leads to rapid deterioration. Ancient sites must have been destroyed virtually wherever any gravel working has taken place in the region, from the partial destruction of the monastic grange at Barf Hill, Lockington (so long ago that the quarry is now itself an archaeological feature) to the twentieth century large-scale extractions on the eastern side of the valley from Burton Agnes to Routh, but particularly centred on Brandesburton. Drainage in the valley is a constant problem, and the construction of large lagoons at Tophill Low pumping station, and fish farms at Skerne and Wansford, further limit the areas where well preserved organic remains can be expected to survive. Cultivation also takes its toll, at the same time as it brings to light new evidence of sites, as for example at Wilfholme, Watton, where evidence of ancient tree felling has recently been observed.

Past fieldwork

In the nineteenth century the renowned J.R. Mortimer concentrated his efforts on upstanding barrows of the Wolds, but his contemporary, T. Boynton, a drainage engineer, had ample opportunity to observe archaeological remains in the wetlands during the extensive reclamations of the 1880s. He recorded the well preserved 'lake dwellings' at Skipsea, Ulrome, Barmston and Burton Agnes, which were published for him by R.A. Smith (1911). W. J. Varley followed up one of these sites at Barmston, where he excavated in 1960/61 and obtained radiocarbon dates in the tenth and eleventh centuries BC

(Varley 1968). No work has been done on the other sites, although ten years earlier, at Thornham Hill, C.N. and G.E. Grantham excavated part of a mid first millennium BC settlement, adjacent to the Burton Agnes site, which was subsequently destroyed by a gravel quarry (Brewster 1963, Loughlin and Miller 1979).

Extensive activity in the region during prehistory is also attested by fieldwork which the Granthams carried out, particularly at Emmotland, Brigham, Corps Landing and Gransmoor, and by chance finds, some of which must represent votive deposits in meres or river channels in later prehistory (Loughlin and Miller 1979, Manby 1980). J.G.D. Clark's work at Brandesburton showed how important the water courses of the region were to Mesolithic hunters, and that the original harpoons are not so rare as was once thought (Clark and Godwin 1956). Clark's work at Brandesburton is complemented by that of Gilbertson and others at Skipsea Withow Mere, where the first harpoon point was discovered in 1903 (Gilbertson 1984, this volume).

Recent fieldwork by the writer, centred on the river at Skerne, incorporated additional information from Snakeholme, Wansford. A late Saxon wharf or possible bridge abutment, dated by a ninth/tenth century sword, was discovered during the excavation of fish lagoons at Cleaves Farm, Skerne, and two sets of Roman ditches came to light at the same time, one at Cleaves Farm and the other at adjacent Copper Hall Farm (Dent 1983). The Saxon site was sealed by a layer of calcareous alluvial clay 0.6 to 0.7 m thick, and at the base of the clay A. Hulse (unpublished) found traces of marine diatoms. This suggests that exceptional circumstances forced sea water a considerable distance up the Hull valley at a time when this clay was being deposited. An historical context for this event could be one of the periods when Spurn Point was temporarily eroded, perhaps in the fourteenth century (de Boer 1978). Support for this date comes from fragments of brick and pottery, not earlier than the fourteenth century, which were found beneath this clay at Cleaves Farm and at Snakeholme, Wansford. If this clay does represent late medieval and post-medieval flooding it provides a useful *terminus ante quem* for anything sealed beneath it wherever it occurs. The bricks sealed by alluvium were in river gravels and presumably represent ballast dropped overboard to lighten boats. The recent work contrasts with earlier finds which by and large tended to be prehistoric in date. The medieval use of waterways, and the settlements, both secular and monastic, which they linked are topics for future research.

Sites under threat

Deposits in the upper Hull valley temporarily offer good opportunities for the recovery of archaeological information, but these opportunities will not last indefinitely. Due to threatened quarrying, drainage or other disturbances these deposits will soon disappear or dry out. They are to be found at a number of sites.

The first is at Routh, Low Farm (National Grid Reference TA 098438), located where the only guaranteed crossing of the Hull valley existed until the eighteenth century. Quarrying on a large scale will destroy the interface between the dry gravel ridge and the lake bed of Leven Carrs. This is one of the few unquarried gravel deposits along a lake margin in an area known to have been a Mesolithic hunting ground (Clark and Godwin 1956). In the later Bronze Age the waters of the lakes attracted offerings of five bronze swords, as well as smaller objects (Manby 1980). Secondly, at Burton Agnes, Thornham Hill (TA 112598), proposed extension of the quarry into an area with overlying peat deposits threatens to remove the contemporary environmental evidence for the settlement excavated by the Granthams, who also found pottery in the peats.

Other important sites are at Skerne, Cleaves Farm and Copper Hall Farm (TA 058541 to TA 065547), where, from two fish farm lagoons, the writer recorded well preserved evidence of Romano-British and late Saxon occupation (Dent 1983), as mentioned above. The lagoons also give a rare opportunity to map out old river courses and to distinguish peat deposits of different ages, but these are drying out with the effect of newly cut channels through them.

At Watton, Wilfholme Landing (TA 064475), recent drainage improvements brought to light a series of split bog oaks with axe marks and a late Bronze Age spearhead was found nearby. This presents a rare opportunity to examine what could be a buried trackway, or an area of prehistoric forestry, before drainage operations dry the site out or shrink the peat so that the plough cuts away buried horizons.

At Leconfield alterations to the course of Aike Beck (TA 02804657) will require a cut through an existing earthwork adjacent to scheduled monument no. 56, an Iron Age barrow, one of two on the site (Loughlin and Miller 1979). The ditch of the earthwork and the adjacent flood plain of the stream offer excellent opportunities for the recovery of contemporary environmental and possible artefactual data.

Finally, North Frodingham, Coneygarth Hill Farm (TA 091519), deserves study. In the 1920s a Ewart Park type bronze sword was found in peat at the foot of the gravel holme or hillock where the farm stands. Many bog oaks have since been brought to the surface by the plough, and continued shrinkage of the peat brings deeper buried surfaces within its reach, thereby increasing their chances of destruction.

Although planning consent was given in 1987, the Routh and Burton Agnes gravel quarries will work a phased programme over a number of years. The drainage operations at Aike Beck will be carried out as soon as the Yorkshire Water Authority can arrange a programme. Other drainage works, already carried out, are now drying the peat to the detriment of the organic remains therein. A similar situation has been reported immediately to the north of the Yorkshire Wolds in the eastern Vale of Pickering, resulting in a substantial loss of archaeological material over the last 30 years (Schadla-Hall 1987).

The future

Although each of the sites listed above could individually justify a research and rescue project of their own, future work in the short term might best be spent in rapid evaluation. Through a programme of limited fieldwork, it would be possible to (a) date peat deposits at different localities within the study area and assess the chronological range of their deposition, (b) identify common depositional horizons across the study area, (c) reconstruct the environmental history of the chosen sites and trace environmental horizons between sites and (d) identify evidence of human activity and relate this to its historical and environmental context. From such work it might then be possible to outline the potential of the wetlands in this region and to provide a sound basis for future fieldwork in an area where archaeological material is constantly under threat.

References

Brewster, T.C.M. (1963). *The Excavation of Staple Howe.* East Riding Archaeological Research Committee, Winteringham.

Clark, J.G.D. and Godwin, H. (1956). A Maglemosian site at Brandesburton, Holderness, Yorkshire. *Proceedings of the Prehistoric Society* **22**, 6-22.

de Boer, G. (1978). Holderness and its coastal features. In: *North Humberside Introductory Themes* (ed. D.G. Symes) pp. 69-76. Department of Geography, University of Hull.

Dent, J.S. (1983). Skerne. *Current Archaeology* **91**, 251-3.

Gilbertson, D.D. (1984). *Late Quaternary Environments and Man in Holderness,* British Archaeological Reports (British Series) 134. British Archaeological Reports, Oxford.

Loughlin, N. and Miller, K.R. (1979). *A Survey of Archaeological Sites in Humberside.* Humberside Libraries and Amenities, Hull.

Manby, T.G. (1980). Bronze Age settlement in Eastern Yorkshire. In: *Settlement and Society in the British Later Bronze Age* (eds J. Barrett and R. Bradley) pp. 307-70, British Archaeological Reports (British Series) 83. British Archaeological Reports, Oxford.

Schadla-Hall, R.T. (1987). Early man in the eastern Vale of Pickering. In: *East Yorkshire Field Guide* (ed. S. Ellis) pp. 22-30. Quaternary Research Association, Cambridge.

Smith, R.A. (1911). Lake-dwellings in Holderness, Yorkshire. *Archaeologia* **62**, 593-610.

Varley, W.J. (1968). Barmston and the Holderness crannogs. *East Riding Archaeologist* **1**, 11-26.

9

Early boats of the Humber basin

S. McGrail

Introduction

Of the five prehistoric plank boats known in northwest Europe, four are from the Humber basin. In fact, the oldest plank boats in the world, outside Egypt, are from a site at North Ferriby on the foreshore of the Humber north bank. In addition, several important logboats (dugout canoes) have been excavated in this region, adding much to our knowledge of early boatbuilding and use. Thus the Humber and its tributaries are of great importance to maritime archaeology, as they provide the greater part of the direct evidence for early boats and boatmanship in northwest Europe.

Boat finds have been reported from or near almost every major river of the Humber basin, and also from former meres in Holderness. Not all of the boats have survived, however, and some of the reports on the lost finds are inadequate. Of those that do survive, two may not be boats at all, and others which undoubtedly are boats are not well dated. The doubtful and poorly documented finds will be mentioned only briefly in this chapter, while the well provenanced and well reported boats will be discussed in more detail.

Fig. 9.1. Boat finds from the Humber basin. 1 Hull, 2 Roos Carr, 3 Owthorne, 4 Hornsea, 5 South Holme, 6 Marton, 7 Stanley Ferry, 8 Chapel Flat Dyke, 9 Hulton Abbey, 10 Burton-on-Trent, 11 Clifton, 12 Holme-Pierrepont, 13 East Ferry, 14 Scotter, 15 Appleby, 16 Brigg, 17 North Ferriby, 18 Hasholme.

The finds

Individual boat finds from the Humber basin are described below, starting at the River Hull and progressing anti-clockwise around this vast river system (Fig. 9.1).

Hull

This logboat of pine, now in Hull Museums, was found early this century in alluvial silt when foundations were being prepared for a new Guildhall. Sheppard (1912) considered that this small boat, some 2.59 m in length, 0.50 m in breadth and 0.25 m in height of sides, should be dated to the sixteenth century AD.

Early boats of the Humber basin 111

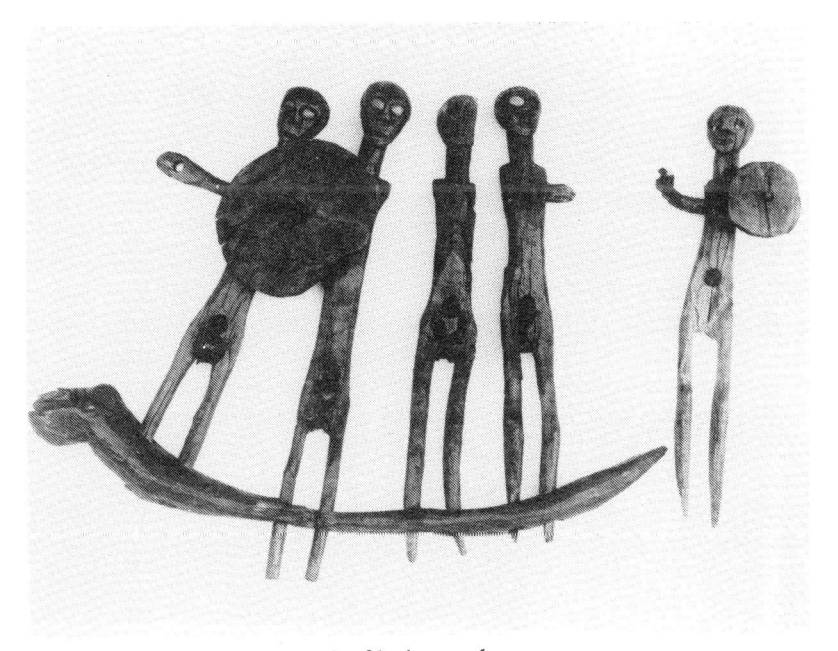

Fig. 9.2. The Roos Carr models of logboat and crew.

Roos Carr
This model, probably of a logboat, was discovered in the wetlands between Roos and Halsham in 1836 (Poulson 1841, Sheppard 1901, 1902) and is now at Hull Museums. It is *c.* 50 cm in length and associated with models of armed men (Fig. 9.2). One end of the boat has the form of an animal's head with holes for quartz eyes; this feature may be compared with a similarly shaped head with eye sockets on the first/second century BC (SRR-403) logboat from Loch Arthur/Lotus, Kirkudbright, now in the National Museum of Scotland. Piggott and Daniel (1951) considered that the Roos Carr models may be late Bronze Age because of the circular shields carried by the men, and this has recently been supported by a radiocarbon date of 2460 ± 70 b.p. (OXA-1718) (B. Coles pers. comm.). Although this model gives an early example of the use of *oculi* (eyes) on boats and suggests that such boats were sometimes used in warfare, it reveals little about the constructional details and performance of prehistoric logboats.

Owthorne

Two logboats are reported to have been found near Withernsea, one in 1715 and the other in 1785 (Poulson 1841, Trollope 1872), but neither has survived and there may indeed have been only one find. It seems likely that they were used on the mere formerly in these parts (Fig. 4.1 this volume), but their age is unknown.

Hornsea

A small logboat is said to have been found at Hornsea in the nineteenth century (Sheppard 1910). This boat was also probably used on the mere, but has not survived and is of unknown age.

South Holme

This undated vessel was found in 1869 in the Derwent valley near Malton (McGrail 1978), and possibly survives as an unmarked object in the Yorkshire Museum, York. It is small, 2.13 x 0.91 m, and not certain that it is a logboat; it may be some other type of hewn-out vessel such as a trough or coffin.

Marton

This boat was found in 1797 in the valley of the River Ouse near Boroughbridge, but was subsequently destroyed (Smith 1852). The bottom of the boat had been perforated with holes to make a fish well, and it is not clear whether this was a logboat or a plank boat.

Stanley Ferry

This logboat was found in the bed of the River Calder during excavations for an aquaduct in 1838 (Bowman 1855). The remains, which have been much restored and added to, are now in the Yorkshire Museum, York. A radiocarbon date (HAR-2835) suggests that the boat was in use during the early eleventh century AD. It formerly measured *c.* 5.41 x 1.03 x 0.33 m and originally had eleven treenail-fastened ribs which probably supported thwarts. With a relatively broad beam, flared transverse sections, and stabilisers, this boat would have had the stability to carry passengers sitting on the thwarts. It therefore seems likely that this was a ferry for crossing the River Calder, propelled by paddles or poles at the bow and stern, or hauled along a rope fastened to strong points on the banks (McGrail 1981a).

Chapel Flat Dyke

This fragment, *c.* 3.15 m in length, was found in 1963 in the valley of the River Don near Rotherham (Ramm 1965, Radley 1966) and is now in the Sheffield Museum. It has been radiocarbon dated to the mid second millennium BC (BM-213). However, as this fragment of a hollowed log has no other features, it cannot be unambiguously identified as part of a logboat.

Hulton Abbey

This hewn-out oak artefact was found in 1930, when drains were being laid in a former bed of the River Trent in Stoke-on-Trent (Pape 1931). It measures *c.* 2.25 x 1.24 x 0.60 m and is now in Hanley Museum. Although the bottom is flat and the sides and ends are vertical, such a box-like shape does not preclude the possibility that this is a boat, as plank boats of this general shape are known today (McGrail 1978, 1985); it may have been used on the nearby fish ponds of the abbey at Hulton. If it is a boat, it would have been capable of carrying a load of up to *c.* 350 kg, propelled by one man with a pole or paddle. The artefact has not yet been dated, although a sample (Q-1397) has been at the Godwin Laboratory, University of Cambridge, for radiocarbon assay since 1975.

Burton-on-Trent

This logboat was found in a gravel pit near Burton-on-Trent in 1963, but was subsequently destroyed before it could be recorded (McGrail 1978).

Clifton

Three logboats were found in 1938 during dredging of the River Trent near Nottingham. Two were recovered and are now in the Castle Muscum, Nottingham (Philips 1941), but have not yet been dated, although samples (Q-1374, 1375) have been at the Godwin Laboratory since 1975. Each boat is fashioned from a whole oak log, has a generally rectangular transverse section, and tapers in plan, with the parent log, towards the bow. The boats have similar dimensions, Clifton 1 being *c.* 8.55 x 0.76 x 0.36 m and Clifton 2 *c.* 9.25 x 0.76 x 0.38 m. They both have moss-caulked transoms fitted at the stern, and a series of seven shallow ridges across the bottom of the boat (Fig. 9.3). Fitted transoms are common in large oak logboats, and it

Fig. 9.3. Logboats Clifton 1 and 2, viewed from their sterns. Part of the transom can be seen at the stern of the boat on the right.

seems likely that this way of making the stern watertight was used when the parent log was found to have a rotten core (heart rot) in its lower bole (McGrail 1978). The ridges, which are integral with the bottom of the boat, are less easily explained (McGrail 1978), but they may have supported loose bottom boards to keep cargo and crew clear of any water in the bilges.

The boats could each have carried a crew of eight to ten kneeling paddlers, or two paddlers and 350 to 500 kg of cargo. As they were so similar, it is possible that they could have been operated as a pair, side by side, thus increasing both load capacity and stability (McGrail 1978). However, no obvious way of linking these boats securely together is apparent from the surviving remains.

Holme-Pierrepont
Three large oak logboats were found in 1967 during gravel extraction from a former course of the River Trent (MacCormick 1968). The boats were subsequently excavated and, after being recorded, were re-buried under sand on a site near Nottingham. Boat 1 has been radiocarbon dated to *c.* 230 b.c. (Birm-132), and the others may be of a similar date. All three boats were damaged during gravel extraction and were incomplete and fragmented when recovered. There are some significant differences between the published drawings and the text which can only be resolved by re-examination of the remains. Boat 1 was *c.* 7 x 0.95 x 0.55 m, boat 2 *c.* 5.31 x 0.85 x 0.65 m and boat 3 *c.* 10 x 1.25 x 0.65 m. Boat 3 had a fitted transom stern, otherwise the ends seem to have been integral. Boats 1 and 3 had transverse timbers (beam-ties) fitted across their stern to prevent the log from opening out or splitting.

East Ferry and Scotter
Nineteenth century reports indicate that two logboats were found near the River Trent in the vicinity of Gainsborough, one in 1810 and the other in 1811 (McGrail 1978), but there may have been only one find. The East Ferry boat was said to measure 12.19 x 1.22 x 0.91 m and the Scotter boat 16.15 x 1.22 m, but no remains survive.

Appleby
This logboat was recovered during dredging in the Old River Ancholme near Appleby in 1943 and is now in Scunthorpe Museum (Dudley 1943). It has been radiocarbon dated to *c.* 1100 b.c. (Q-80), and on this evidence is the oldest logboat from England so far dated. A further sample (Q-1462) has been at the Godwin Laboratory since 1975. The boat was fragmented and incomplete when found, the remains measuring *c.* 8 x 1.35 m. At the stern there was a transverse groove for a fitted transom.

Brigg
During the 1880s there were three important archaeological finds near

the River Ancholme at Brigg (Wylie 1884, McGrail 1978, 1981b). In 1884 a timber causeway (trackway) was exposed on an east-west alignment some 250 m south of where the New River Ancholme meets the Old River Ancholme, northwest of Brigg. During excavations for the Brigg Gas Works in 1886, some 600 m southeast of this junction, a large logboat was exposed near the Old River Ancholme (Fig. 9.4), and in 1888 the wooden remains known as the Brigg 'raft' were encountered during the digging of brick clay, some 120 m north of the causeway site (McGrail 1981b fig. 1.1.1).

After its initial display in Brigg, the logboat was exhibited in the original Municipal Museum in Hull (Fig. 6.4 this volume) until it was destroyed by fire in 1942. It was made from an enormous oak log, exceeding 14.78 m in length and with a lower girth of 5.90 m and an upper girth of 5.40 m; its impressive dimensions inspired an early observer to break into verse *(Yorkshire Weekly Post* 29 May 1909):

AN ARCHAEOLOGICAL LYRIC

The discovery we note of a prehistoric boat -
It is said to be the finest that exists;
All will readily admit that the subject is most fit
To be studied by the Archaeologists.

They will tell us what 'twas for, whether used for peace or war,
Also if propelled by oars or sails or not;
If 'twas once a battleship, or conveyed a pleasure trip,
Say a prehistoric Dreadnought or a yacht.

'Tis of most stupendous strength, nearly fifty feet in length,
And it's hewn from a single trunk of oak;
Well, the prehistoric man, who this piece of work could plan,
Must have had some brains to guide him, stroke by stroke.

Some are proud of their descent, and on heraldry intent,
Talk of coats-of-arms, shield, crest and motto trite,
And of genealogy, but can they produce a "tree"
Like the one this ancient vessel brings to light?

'Tis not likely that again 'twill be launched upon the main,

Early boats of the Humber basin

Fig. 9.4. The Brigg logboat after recovery in 1886.

There to cleave the briny billows with its prow;
For it's reached the place we know, where the good antiques go
And is landed in the Hull Museum now.

LEODIENSIAN

At the stern of the boat a two-piece transom was fitted in a groove caulked with moss. There were holes through the side abaft and forward of the transom in which beam-ties were probably fitted, although such timbers were not found on excavation. Forward of the transom were longitudinal shelves projecting into the boat just below the top of the sides; these are very similar to those found in the Hasholme logboat (see below) and were probably where a decking was fitted for the steersmen. Also in common with the Hasholme boat, there was a series of 50 mm diameter horizontal holes just below the sheerline. It is difficult to determine their function, but they may have been used during construction to hold the sides together until the transom and beam-ties were fitted. Shelves or knees near the bows may be interpreted as supports for a deck where a bowman sometimes stood with a pole or paddle to steer the boat clear of hazards in rock-strewn or shoal waters. On each side of the bow, large knot holes had been fitted with wooden bosses, presumably to give the impression of eyes or *oculi*.

A sample of wood has been radiocarbon dated to *c.* 834 b.c. (Q-78), although it is not known from where in the boat the sample was taken. The felling date of the tree could have been considerably later than the radiocarbon date if the sample came from near the centre of the log. Calibration of the date to convert it from radiocarbon years to calendar years would, on the other hand, tend to give a date earlier by say 200 to 300 years. Thus this boat may have been in use in the early first millennium BC, although the possibility also exists that it is only a few centuries older than the Hasholme boat, which has been dated more precisely by dendrochronology to *c.* 300 BC (see below).

In an earlier assessment of the performance of this logboat, I had come to the conclusion that she was best suited to carry a full complement of men or high-density cargo such as stone or iron; low-density materials such as timber, grain, meat or peat seemed to result in the boat having insufficient transverse stability (McGrail 1978). It is now clear, however, that some of the parameters used in these early calculations were not appropriate (McGrail 1988); larger logboats, such as Brigg, were penalised by the selection of very deep drafts as the standard for assessment. A better method is to assess the boats loaded to drafts at defined fractions of the total side height of the hull. When these criteria are used, the Brigg logboat has a much better theoretical performance, and can carry all types of loads, including low-density ones, down to a draft of 0.60 m (i.e. 60% of side height) and beyond. Some typical results are set out in Table 9.1, along with the corresponding data for the Hasholme logboat.

The flat-bottomed Brigg 'raft' (not a raft but a plank boat) was first described and drawn by Thropp (1887), the Lincolnshire County Surveyor. After about five months of exposure, part of the 'raft' was lifted, but, of this, only a very minor fragment survived in Lincoln Museum and the remainder was re-covered with clay. E.V. Wright realised the importance of this find during his work on the Ferriby boats (see below), and encouraged the National Maritime Museum to re-locate the remains. This was done in 1973 and the 'raft' was re-excavated the following year (McGrail 1981b). The remains, about three-fifths of the bottom planking and part of one of the lowest side strakes, are now in the reserve collection at Greenwich. The boat has

Table 9.1. Theoretical load-carrying performance of the logboats from Brigg and Hasholme.

Boat	Description	Draft (m)	Free-board (m)	(1) %	(2) Dead-weight (kg)	(3) Dead-weight coefficient
Brigg	Light displacement (2809 kg)	0.25	0.75	25	-	-
Hasholme	Light displacement (4398 kg)	0.38	0.87	30	-	-
Brigg	Maximum men (2 plus 22)	0.35	0.65	35	1440	0.34
Hasholme	Maximum men (2 plus 18)	0.46	0.79	37	1200	0.21
Brigg	5 men plus 5891 kg peat (4)	0.60	0.40	60	6191	0.69
Hasholme	5 men plus 5502 kg peat (4)	0.75	0.50	60	5802	0.57

Notes:
1. Ratio of draft to maximum height of sides expressed as a percentage. It is considered that the 60% values are best for comparison of boats as cargo carriers (McGrail 1988).
2. Weight of cargo and crew.
3. Deadweight/Displacement. A measure of ability of boats to carry cargo, in particular high-density loads.
4. Alternatively, materials or greater bulk density (e.g. grain, meat, timber, iron or stone) may be carried, resulting in increased stability.

also been radiocarbon dated to *c.* 650 b.c. (Q-1199, 1200, 1255-61).

The five oak bottom planks of this boat were linked by transverse oak timbers which passed through holes in cleats, which were an integral part of each plank (Fig. 9.5). The planks were also sewn together by continuous zig-zag stitching of willow withies over a caulking of moss capped by longitudinal laths of hazel along each seam. The boat had at least two side strakes sewn to the outer bottom planks at a near-vertical angle. The ends did not survive and must therefore be more conjectural; the minimum hypothesis is that these were also vertical (McGrail 1985). The overall dimensions of the boat were 12.20 x 2.27 x 0.34 m (two side strakes) or 0.55 m (three side strakes).

Environmental evidence recovered in 1974 demonstrates that the 'raft' was deposited at a time of local sea level maximum, just to the west of the main channel of the River Ancholme, which was then a tidal arm of the Humber estuary. The 'raft' was probably used as a ferry, paddled or poled across estuarine waters between the Lincoln Edge to the west of the Ancholme valley and the Lincolnshire Wolds to the east. She was operated from mud flats on the edge of the estuarine channel, possibly from a hard of light timbers, where animals, people and goods could be embarked. At her landing place

Fig. 9.5. A 1:10 reconstruction model of the Brigg 'raft'. The parts outlined in white represent elements excavated in 1974.

the 'raft' would have been run aground for disembarkation of cargo and crew; during this grounding the transverse timbers wedged within their cleats would maintain the relative positions of the five bottom planks and thus prevent excess stress on the sewn fastenings.

The Brigg 'raft' had a good cargo capacity (McGrail 1985), and examples of loads which could be carried in conditions of adequate stability are given in Table 9.2, for two heights of side. With a two-strake side, 1.54 tonnes could be carried at a draft of 0.25 m; this is equivalent to say 25 men or 10 men and 18 sheep. With a three-strake side, 7.16 tonnes would be possible, equivalent to 20 men and 100 sheep.

At some stage, the use of the 'raft' as a boat became impracticable or uneconomic and she was moored on the mud flats and used as part of an approach causeway to the estuarine channel, with one end on relatively dry ground and the other end floating in the channel where boats could be moored. As the local sea level fell from a maximum at c. 650 b.c. and the Brigg region became non-tidal, the 'raft' settled into a reed bed and was covered by sediments from upstream.

North Ferriby
Of great significance to the development of maritime archaeology in

this country, and indeed in northwest Europe, was the discovery by E.V. and C.W. Wright in 1937 of the remains of a sewn plank boat (Fig. 6.3 this volume) on the inter-tidal foreshore of the Humber at North Ferriby. A second boat was subsequently found and both were excavated in 1946; a third boat fragment (Fig. 6.6 this volume) was excavated in 1963 (Wright 1976, 1985, this volume). Samples from these boats have been radiocarbon dated to *c.* 1500 b.c. (Q-715, 836, 837, 1197, 1217, BM-58), and further samples (Q-1198, 1218-20, 1551-4) have been at the Godwin Laboratory since 1975. All three boats are now in the reserve collection of the National Maritime Museum, boat 3 being on loan from Hull Museums. The drawings and photographic record compiled by E.V. Wright in the mud of the Ferriby foreshore, in most difficult circumstances, and afterwards in the museums at Hull and Greenwich make a matchless archive, documenting the boats' structure and enabling deductions to be made about their size and shape.

Most remains survive from boat 1 which, when excavated, consisted of the greater part of the bottom of the boat (*c.* 13 m out of a conjectural 15.4 m) and part of one side strake. The oak planking was fastened by individual stitches (rather than the continuous sewing of the Brigg 'raft') of yew withies, over a caulking of moss and longitudinal oak laths. The three bottom planks were also connected by transverse timbers wedged within cleats on the planking. As in the Brigg 'raft', these timbers helped to maintain the bottom planks in a constant relationship, thereby reducing the stress on the fastenings, and they could also be used to re-align the planking for re-stitching after periodic dismantling, for which there is much ethnographic evidence (McGrail 1981b).

The ends of the boat were given an upward curve by external shaping and hollowing out of the ends of the central bottom plank (plank-keel). The lowest side strake was fashioned at its end to give curves in two dimensions to form the beginnings of the bow and the turn of the bilge. Bevels of varying cross-section were worked along the lower edge of this strake so that it fitted *within* a rabbet in the edge of the outer bottom plank, but *enveloped* the edge of the plank-keel where it met it towards the end of the boat. Such joints were not only designed to be watertight when packed with moss and lashed over a lath, but also ensured that the outer portions of the fastening stitch would not be scuffed and damaged when the boat was beached.

Table 9.2. Theoretical cargo capacities of the plank boats from North Ferriby and Brigg.

Boat	Draft (m)	Freeboard (m)	(1) %	(1) Deadweight (kg)	(1) Deadweight coefficient
Ferriby 1	0.30	0.36	45	3000	0.54
	0.40	0.26	61	5500	0.52
Brigg 2	0.25 (2)	0.09	74	1540	0.23
	0.46 (3)	0.09	84	7160	0.57

Notes: 1. See notes 1, 2 and 3 in Table 9.1.
2. Side height of 0.34 m.
3. Side height of 0.55 m.

The lowest and second side strakes had bevels along their adjacent edges to form an edged half-lap joint. The workmanship required to fashion these bottom and side joints was of a very high standard indeed.

The Ferriby boats were incomplete when found and no doubt had been distorted during the 3500 years they were buried. To obtain some idea of their performance it is necessary to reconstruct, in a theoretical manner, the original form of a complete boat. Several reconstructions are compatible with the excavated evidence (e.g. Wright 1976 figs 15-19), although not all are necessarily compatible with the boatbuilding technology known to have been used in second millennium BC northwest Europe. Wright has recently published (1985) a re-assessment of his excavation records, together with revised reconstruction drawings, work which has been welcomed and is now being evaluated. Of other reconstructions, the most likely seems to be the 'minimum solution' (Fig. 9.6). This boat has a generally flat bottom and two flared side strakes. The ends are closed by watertight transoms or bulkheads, the planking providing a fairing to the ends of the boat beyond the transoms. Internal support to this shell is given by three composite frames set into projections from the bottom planks and lashed to the planking. Conjectural crossbeams notched over the top strakes provide further support to the sides and could have been used as thwarts by crew and passengers. A variant reconstruction incorporates a third 'strake' of hide, rather than timber, thereby adding to the freeboard and cargo-carrying capacity with minimal additional weight penalty.

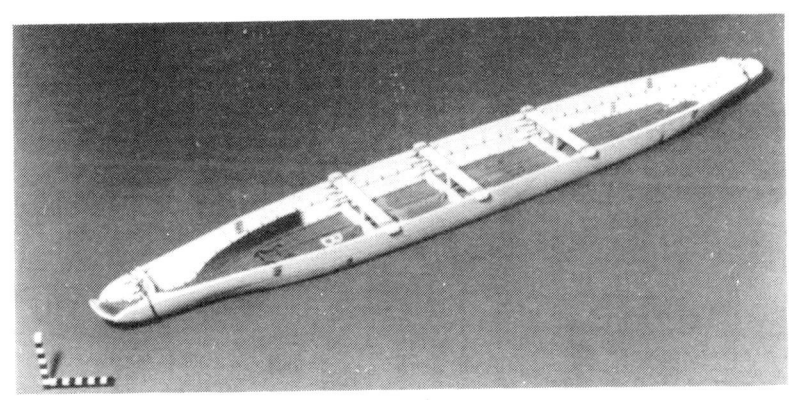

Fig. 9.6. A 1:10 reconstruction model of Ferriby boat 1 based on drawings compiled by John Coates from information supplied by E.V. Wright. The black parts represent those elements excavated; white parts are conjectural.

The three Ferriby boats were more suitable for rivers and estuaries than the sea. As ferries across the Humber and along its tributaries, they would have been propelled and steered by paddles, or by poles in the shallows. Examples of the sort of loads they could have carried in conditions of adequate transverse stability are given in Table 9.2.

Hasholme
In July 1984 what was thought to be a buried tree ('bog oak') was encountered by a machine laying field drains at Hasholme Hall, near Holme-on-Spalding-Moor. Pieces dragged from the path of the machine were subsequently identified as parts of a logboat of some size and complexity, and an excavation (Fig. 9.7) was carried out by a team from the University of Durham, the National Maritime Museum and the East Riding Archaeological Society, under the general auspices of Hull Museums (Millett and McGrail 1987). After many of the fragments had been re-assembled at Greenwich and the boat had been recorded, the remains were transported to Hull where they are now displayed in the Archaeology Museum (Fig. 9.8). A dendrochronological date of 322-277 BC has been obtained for the felling of the tree from which the main part of this boat was built.

The parent oak of this boat must have been over 12.58 m in length, with a lower girth of 5.40 m and a girth at 11 m of 5.22 m. Such a tree could have weighed 28 tonnes and would have been 800 years or more old when felled. Trees over *c.* 300 years of age have invariably developed heart rot, starting at the butt end. The Hasholme oak was

Fig. 9.7. The Hasholme logboat during excavation.

Fig. 9.8. The Hasholme boat under wax sprays in the Boatlab at the Archaeology Museum, Hull, August 1988.

so old that this rot had spread to the top of the bole, therefore, when the boat was built, hollowing out the inside became that much easier. On the other hand, the open ends had to be closed by some means to make the boat watertight. The woodworking techniques used to solve these and other boatbuilding problems in this craft are among the most advanced yet seen in the Iron Age of northwest Europe (McGrail 1987a).

The stern was closed by the insertion into a groove of a single-piece transom of oak (Fig. 9.9) which was then tightly wedged so that caulking was evidently unnecessary. A transverse beam-tie driven through holes in the boat's sides abaft the transom impinged on a U-shaped protrusion and forced the transom downwards and outwards into its groove. A second beam-tie was fastened to the sides on top of the transom, holding it down and clamping the sides of the boat together. A third beam-tie of similar form was fitted *c.* 1 m further forward. There are two large holes through the transom, above and outboard of the U-shape, which were probably used during the building of the boat when the transom, weighing 60 to 75 kg, had to

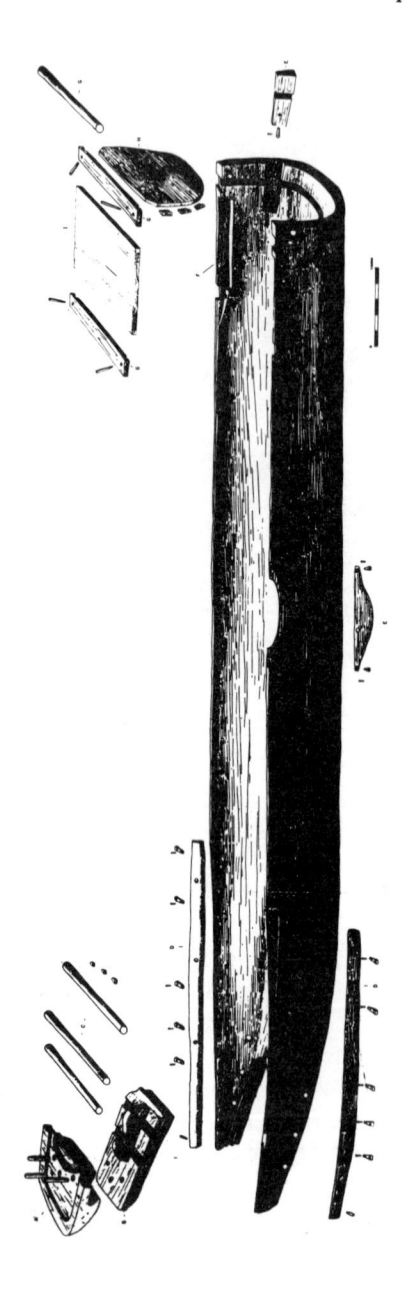

Fig. 9.9. An exploded diagram of the Hasholme boat as reconstructed. A upper bow with treenails, B lower bow, C transverse timbers and wedges, D washstrakes with treenails locked by keys, E repairs with treenails locked by keys, F shelves, G beam-ties with treenails, H transom with wedges, I conjectural decking.

be lifted above the boat and then lowered into its groove. Before the transom was fitted, a repair block had to be fastened to the hull, held in position by its dovetailed shape and by a horizontal treenail locked in by a key inboard. A further repair patch had to be fitted to the port side.

The forward end of the boat was closed by a two-part bow. The lower bow rested on ledges worked in the parent log, and was held in position by two transverse timbers wedged within cleats which were integral with the lower bow timber; this is reminiscent of the cleats and transverse timbers of the Ferriby boats. A third transverse timber aft of the lower bow also helped to hold the sides of the boat together. The upper bow enveloped the leading edges of the lower bow and the boat's sides, and was fastened by three vertical treenails, thereby locking all elements together at the forward end of the boat.

The parent log of the boat had a taper which increased somewhat over the upper (i.e. forward) four metres, and to compensate for this, and thus maintain the boat's freeboard at the bows, washstrakes were added to the top of the sides. These oak planks were fastened to the main hull by horizontal treenails which were locked inboard by vertical keys or cotters (pegs driven through holes in the protruding treenails). This is the earliest known use of this technique in northwest European boatbuilding. On the starboard side of the bows outboard (and also probably on the fragmented port bow), just below the washstrake, a semi-circular groove was worked into the hull, a further example of *oculi*.

Near the stern, between the second and third beam-ties, horizontal shelves had been worked inside the hull *c.* 0.15 m from the top edge. It is thought likely that a loose decking was fitted here, on which two steersmen stood so that they could see over the crew and cargo. The upper bow had an elegant platform worked on its upper surface, on which a bow steersman could stand or kneel to steer the boat clear of hazards in rocky or shoal waters.

At the time the boat was in use, the area where she was found was a tidal creek which joined the Humber between the present-day sites of Faxfleet and Brough (Halkon this volume). It seems likely that she was lost when carrying a cargo of timber, and possibly joints of meat, towards a landing place on mud flats to the north of this creek. She was able to carry a sizeable crew of paddlers or a range of cargo; examples of her cargo capacity are given in Table 9.1. In her cargo role, propelled by say five paddlers, she may have achieved 3 kt, and with a full crew of twenty paddlers she probably had a maximum speed of 5 kt. With a good beam measurement at the waterline, the boat had more than adequate stability for use on inland waters and on the middle reaches of the Humber estuary in relatively calm conditions, although it is unlikely that she was used at sea.

Conclusion

It must be borne in mind that this small group of finds (a maximum of twenty-six, all of them logboats or plank boats and spread over a period of almost 3000 years) is not necessarily representative of the range of water transport in use in early times in the Humber basin. It is conceivable that boats of hide, and rafts of logs and of reed bundles were used on inland waters from the Mesolithic period onwards (McGrail 1987b), but evidence for them has not survived or has not yet been recognised. There are, however, two intriguing reports which may indicate finds of these types of water transport. The editor of de la Pryme's diary (Jackson 1870 p. 65) recorded that ' a very primitive "raft" fastened together with wooden pegs' had been found at Greenhoe, Yaddlethorpe, near Scunthorpe, and Sheppard (1926) noted that a 'coracle-type vessel' containing a skeleton had been found at South Ferriby near the mouth of the River Ancholme and was possibly of Roman date. Neither find survives.

References

Bowman, W. (1855). *Reliquiae Antiquae Eboracenses.* Leeds.

Dudley, H.E. (1943). One-tree boat at Appleby, Lincolnshire. *Antiquity* **17**, 156-61.

Jackson, C. (ed.) (1870). *The Diary of Abraham de la Pryme, the Yorkshire Antiquary.* Surtees Society, Durham.

MacCormick, A.G. (1968). Three dugout canoes and a wheel from Holme Pierrepont, Nottinghamshire. *Transactions of the Thoroton Society* **72**, 14-31.

McGrail, S. (1978). *Logboats of England and Wales,* National Maritime Museum Archaeological Series 2, British

Archaeological Reports (British Series) 51. British Archaeological Reports, Oxford.

McGrail, S. (1981a). A medieval logboat from the River Calder at Stanley Ferry, Wakefield, Yorkshire. *Medieval Archaeology* 25, 160-4.

McGrail, S. (ed.) (1981b). *The Brigg 'Raft' and Her Prehistoric Environment*, National Maritime Museum Archaeological Series 6, British Archaeological Reports (British Series) 89. British Archaeological Reports, Oxford.

McGrail, S. (1985). Brigg 'raft' - problems in reconstruction and in the assessment of performance. In: *Sewn Plank Boats*, National Maritime Museum Archaeological Series 10, British Archaeological Reports S276 (ed. S. McGrail and E. Kentley) pp. 165-94. British Archaeological Reports, Oxford.

McGrail, S. (1987a). Early boatbuilding techniques in Britain and Ireland - dating technological change. *International Journal of Nautical Archaeology* 16, 343-54.

McGrail, S. (1987b) *Ancient Boats in N W Europe: the archaeology of water transport to AD 1500*. Longman, London.

McGrail, S. (1988). Assessing the performance of an ancient boat - the Hasholme logboat. *Oxford Journal of Archaeology* 7, 35-46.

Millett, M. and McGrail, S. (1987). The archaeology of the Hasholme logboat. *Archaeological Journal* 144, 69-155.

Pape, T. (1931). Canoe from Stoke-on-Trent. *Antiquaries Journal* 11, 162-3.

Phillips, C.W. (1941). Some recent finds from the Trent near Nottingham. *Antiquaries Journal* 21, 133-43.

Piggott, S. and Daniel, G.E. (1951). *Picture Book of Ancient British Art*. Cambridge.

Poulson, G. (1841). *History and Antiquities of the Seigniory of Holderness*, Vol. 2, Hull.

Radley, J. (ed.) (1966). Yorkshire Archaeological Register 1966. *Yorkshire Archaeological Journal* 42, 1-9.

Ramm, H.G. (1965). Yorkshire Archaeological Register 1965. *Yorkshire Archaeological Journal* 41, 315-17.

Sheppard, T. (1901). Notes on the ancient model of a boat, and warrior crew, found at Roos, in Holderness. *East Riding Antiquarian Society Transactions* 9, 62-74.

Sheppard, T. (1902). Additional note on the Roos Carr Images. *East Riding Antiquarian Society Transactions* **10**, 76-9.

Sheppard, T. (1910). Prehistoric boat from Brigg. *Transactions of the East Riding Antiquarian Society* **17**, 33-60.

Sheppard, T. (1912). *Some Glimpses of Old Hull*, Hull Museum Publications 89. Hull Museum, Hull.

Sheppard, T. (1926). Roman remains in North Lincolnshire. *East Riding Antiquarian Society Transactions* **25**, 170-4.

Smith, H.E. (1852). *Reliquae Isurianae*.

Thropp, J. (1887). An ancient 'raft' found at Brigg, Lincolnshire. *Associated Architectural Societies Reports and Papers* **19** part 1, 95-7.

Trollope, E. (1872). *Sleaford and the Wapentakes of Flaxwell and Aswardham*. London.

Wright, E.V. (1976). *The North Ferriby Boats: a guidebook*. National Maritime Museum Monograph 23. National Maritime Museum, Greenwich.

Wright, E.V. (1985). The North Ferriby Boats - a revised basis for reconstruction. In: *Sewn Plank Boats*, National Maritime Museum Archaeological Series 10, British Archaeological Reports S276 (ed. S. McGrail and E. Kentley) pp. 105-44. British Archaeological Reports, Oxford.

Wylie, W.M. (1884). A note by A. Atkinson on the Brigg trackway. *Proceedings of the Society of Antiquaries NS* **10**, 110-15.

10

Recent work on the archaeological and palaeoenvironmental context of the Ferriby boats

P.C. Buckland, C.J. Beal and S.V.E. Heal

Introduction

Since the discovery of three Bronze Age boats in the sediments of the Humber foreshore at North Ferriby (Wright this volume), tidal erosion has continued to expose archaeological material in stratigraphically similar deposits, suggesting considerable human activity in this area at that time. In addition to revealing the remains of maritime activities, however, such erosion is also removing them, and it is only by frequent and systematic examination of the foreshore that at least a proportion may be recovered. Although work of this nature has been somewhat sporadic, a number of exposed artefacts have been recovered (Wright 1976, 1978), and excavation around the original boat locations has also yielded evidence of structures (McGrail 1983, Heal 1986). In addition, stratigraphic and palaeoecological analyses have been undertaken in order to set the finds within a broader environmental context.

Recent archaeological discoveries

Between 1978 and 1980 excavations at the boat site (Fig. 10.1)

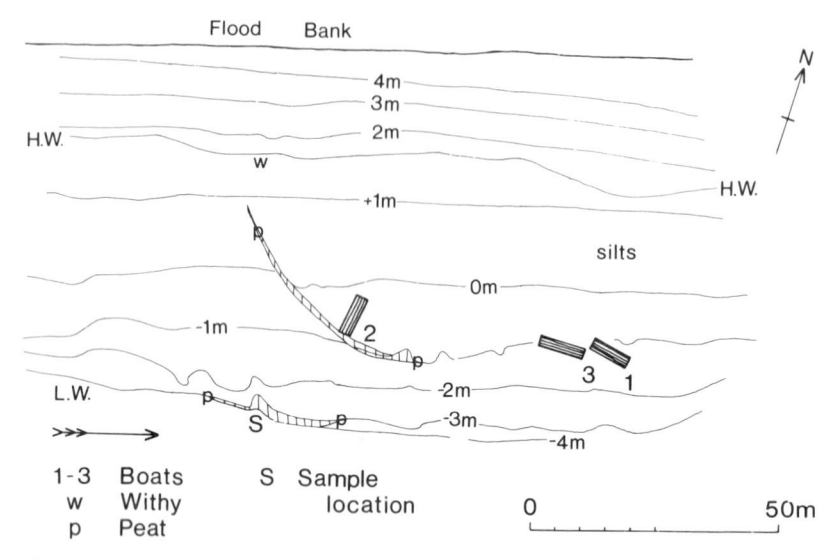

Fig. 10.1. Plan of the North Ferriby boat site.

revealed scatters of roundwood, comprising oak (*Quercus*), willow (*Salix*) and birch (*Betula*), 30-40 cm below the present surface (McGrail 1983, Heal 1986). Much of the wood lay approximately horizontally and was aligned up the slope of the foreshore. However, there were also some vertically positioned fragments whose human origin was indicated by their worked lower ends. Radiocarbon dates range from 1590 to 1200 b.c., suggesting that the wood is broadly contemporaneous with the Ferriby boats. Similar structures have also recently been discovered approximately 1 km upstream on the foreshore near Melton, from which radiocarbon dates of around 1000 b.c. have been obtained (Crowther 1987).

In 1982 a pilot survey of the Ferriby boat site yielded horizontal and vertical roundwood, along with wood chips and a rim and shoulder sherd of later Iron Age pottery. Subsequent visits to the site have recorded a number of wooden artefacts, including twisted hazel (*Corylus*) withies.

Although more radiocarbon dates are required to confirm association of the evidence, the axe-cut wood chips, withies and apparently deliberate dismantling of the boats, along with their repair and modification (Wright 1985), all suggest that this was a boat building and repairing site at which cut stems of oak, willow and birch were laid, without any cohesive structure but occasionally stabilised by vertical pegs, in order to provide a better footing on the soft and slippery foreshore surface.

Palaeoecological sampling

The sediments of the Humber estuary are hardly ideal for palaeoenvironmental investigation. The shifting patterns of distributaries which affect the modern channels (Wilkinson *et al.* 1973) are likely to have been equally active in the past, and the resulting cut and fill is frequently difficult to detect in the uniformly coloured silty clay deposits. At the Ferriby boat site sampling is further complicated by the extensive disturbance of the sediments during attempts to lift the boats (Wright 1976). However, the survival of a piece of timber from beneath boat 2 *in situ* sealed a suitable context, and a sample (Sample 1) was recovered for macrofossil analysis from immediately beneath this (Fig. 10.1).

The sediments in the area of boat 2 had been relatively less disturbed during the attempts to lift the boat, and three samples for pollen spectra were obtained to compare with a diagram prepared from a monolith through the full sequence of organic sediments. As the site of the boat finds lay between -0.5 m and -1.0 m OD, well below modern high tide level, it proved impractical to excavate a pit immediately beneath the site of boat 2 and the monolith was therefore taken from an erosion scar (exposing the full succession down to the underlying till) some 25 m to the south of this boat (Fig. 10.1). As Wright and Wright (1947) had found, it is virtually impossible to distinguish any divisions in the stratigraphy in which the boats lay, and the possibility remains that the two localities are of slightly differing ages. However, further samples, taken as a vertical column through the silts to the underlying peat (Samples 2-4), immediately adjacent to the monolith taken for palynological study, were remarkably consistent in their macrofossil content and these did not differ significantly from those from Sample 1 from beneath boat 2; these therefore combine to suggest little variation in the overall palaeoenvironment in the period around the abandonment of the boats.

Stratigraphy

Throughout much of the estuary, deposits are characterised by interdigitating, discontinuous beds of peat and poorly sorted clay-silts, the latter usually referred to, in its more recent phases, as the Humber Warp (Versey 1939, Ellis this volume). Wright and Churchill (1965 p. 9) described the sequence exposed at low water on the North Ferriby foreshore as '1 to 2 ft (0.35-0.70 m) of estuarine clay overlying an eroded alder-lime fen-wood peat of variable thickness, formed in hollows of an underlying chalky boulder clay'. The continued erosion of the small cliff created by tidal scour at low water suggests that the peat in fact fills shallow channels in the underlying till, and an augered transect during the course of the present study has confirmed this sequence to close to the modern floodbank. Some 150 m west of the boat site a similar channel contains a marl and tuffaceous marl beneath the peat (Wright and Wright 1933) and a more reddish, 'oxidised' alluvium overlies this. While the latter may relate to the phase of late Roman or early medieval erosion of soils noted in the Humberhead Levels (Buckland and Sadler 1985), the basal Flandrian sediments should extend the sequence back considerably before the period of the boat's deposition. They appear similar to the deposits examined by Preece and Robinson (1984) in the Ancholme valley on the south side of the Humber upstream from South Ferriby, and Smith (1958) recorded a similarly variable succession in the lower Ancholme valley around South Ferriby.

Although correlation can only be regarded as tentative, the inception of peat growth must be related to rising base level consequent upon sea level approaching that of the present day from around 5000 years ago (Tooley 1978). Wright and Churchill (1965) noted that the contact between the peat and overlying clay-silts was erosional, with considerable wear to the surface of the exposed large tree trunks in the top of the peat. Elsewhere, however, the transition to clay-silt warp deposition appears more gradual and at the main sample locality, only a few metres from the site of boat 2 (Fig. 10.1), the section shows no trace of erosion. Profiles through the deposits also show considerable variation in thickness, but Table 10.1 gives an indication of a typical section.

Table 10.1. Section through deposits exposed at low water at North Ferriby, September 1978.

Depth (m)	Description
0-0.36	Dark olive grey (Munsell no. 5Y 3/2) poorly sorted clay-silt with some sand and scattered, unidentifiable plant debris; occasional gasteropods and bivalves occur in the deposit, some of the latter in life positions.
0.36-0.78	Very woody detrital peat with complete tree trunks and some *in situ* stools. Dark reddish brown (5YR 2.5/2) darkening on exposure to air.
>1.02	Dark greyish brown (10YR 4/2) clay with chalk and other erratics (till).

Macrofossil analysis

While seeds had to be recovered by sorting the entire organic residue under a binocular microscope, insect remains could be concentrated by the use of the paraffin (kerosene) flotation technique devised by Coope and Osborne (1968). Flotation also recovered foraminifera and ostracoda. Few seeds were recovered; Sample 1 produced two of *Ranunculus scleranthus* (the celery-leaved buttercup), and the float from Sample 4 a few *Juncus* (rush) seeds. The invertebrate fauna, however, was much more extensive (Table 10.2) and allows a more detailed picture of the boat environment to be reconstructed.

The consistent indications of the insect faunas, particularly the more diverse sample from beneath the wood below boat 2 (Sample 1), strongly reinforce the picture of estuarine conditions, to the extent that the evidence from the foraminifera and previously identified mollusca (Wright and Churchill 1965) becomes secondary. The small ground beetle *Bembidion normannum* occurs in three out of the four samples. Lindroth (1974) noted that it is exclusively a sea-shore species and, in Sample 1, it is joined by congener *B. fumigatum*, which is also usually found near the sea, amongst wet plant debris in marshland with a clayey substrate (Lindroth 1949, 1974). *Dromius linearis*, whilst not a halophile, is also a seaside species, although as a predator which climbs the vegetation its usual habitat is further from the open mudflats than the species of *Bembidion*. There are few water beetles in the deposits, but the majority of these are further

Table 10.2. Insect remains from North Ferriby.

	Sample 1 (Boat 2)	Sample 2 (0-50 mm)	Sample 3 (50-100 mm)	Sample 4 (100-150 mm)
Insecta				
Dermaptera				
Forficulidae				
*Forficula (?) auricularia L.	2	-	-	-
Coleoptera				
Carabidae				
Trechus secalis (Payk.)	-	-	1	-
Bembidion quadripustulatum Serv.	1	-	-	-
* B. fumiguatum Duft.	1	-	-	-
* B. normannum Dej.	2	-	1	2
* Pterostichus niger (Sch.)	1	-	-	-
* Agonum moestum (Duft.)	1	-	-	-
Agonum sp.	1	-	-	1
* Dromius linearis (Ol.)	1	-	-	-
Dytiscidae				
Ilybius sp.	1	-	-	-
Hydrophilidae				
Helophorus grandis Ill.	1	-	-	-
Helophorus sp. (small)	1	1	-	-
Cercyon sp.	-	-	1	-
Paracymus aeneus (Germ.)	1	-	-	-
Hydraenidae				
* Ochthebius auriculatus Rey	18	-	7	-
* O. dilatatus Steph.	7	-	-	19
O. minimus (F.)	5	-	1	-
Ochthebius spp.	-	1	6	-
Hydraena testacea Curt.	1	-	-	-
Hydraena sp.	1	-	-	-
Limnebius truncatellus (Thun.)/ papposus Muls.	1	-	-	-
Staphylinidae				
* Metopsia retusa (Steph.)	-	-	-	1
* Anotylus nitidulus (Grav.)	1	-	-	-
Stenus spp.	2	-	-	2
Heterothops sp.	2	-	-	-
Tachinus marginellus (F.)	1	-	-	-
Aleochara sp.	1	-	-	-
Aleocharinae indet.	7	1	-	2
Pselaphidae				
Bryaxis (?) bulbifer (Reich.)	1	-	-	-
* Brachygluta helferi (Sch.)	2	-	2	3
Geotrupidae				
Geotrupes sp.	1	-	-	-
Scarabaeidae				
Aphodius sp.	1	-	-	-
Onthophagus ovatus (L.)	-	1	-	-
Phyllopertha horticola (L.)	-	-	-	2
Scirtidae				
Cyphon sp.	1	-	-	-
indet.	1	-	-	-
Heteroceridae				
Heterocerus flexuosus Steph.	2	-	-	1
H (?) flexuosus Steph.	4	-	-	-
Heterocerus sp.	-	-	1	-

	Sample 1 (Boat 2)	Sample 2 (0-50 mm)	Sample 3 (50-100 mm)	Sample 4 (100-150 mm)
Elateridae				
Agriotes (?) *sordidus* Ill.	1	-	-	-
Cantharidae				
* *Cantharis rufa* L.	1	-	-	-
* *C. thoracica* (Ol.)	1	-	-	-
Rhagonycha lutea (Mull.)	1	-	-	-
Cryptophagidae				
Atomaria sp.	1	-	-	-
Lathridiidae				
Corticariinae indet.	-	1	-	-
Scraptiidae				
Anaspis sp.	1	-	-	-
Cerambycidae				
Gracilia minuta (F.)	1	-	-	-
Chrysomelidae				
* *Macroplea* (?) *mutica* (F.)	1	-	-	-
* *Chrysolina staphylaea* (L.)	1	-	-	-
Chaetocnema spp.	1	-	-	-
Attelabidae				
Rhynchites aeneovirens (Marsh.)	1	-	-	-
Apionidae				
Apion sp.	1	-	-	-
Curculionidae				
* *Phyllobius viridiaeris* (Laich.)	1	-	-	-
Ceutorhynchus sp.	3	-	-	-
Phytobius sp.	1	-	-	-
Limnobaris pilistriata (Steph.)	1	2	3	7
Rhynchaenus sp.	1	-	-	-
Scolytidae				
Scolytus sp.	-	-	-	1
Hemiptera				
Saldidae				
Salda sp.	2	-	-	-
Chaetoscirta sp.	3	-	1	-
Homoptera				
indet.	---------------------- not counted ----------------------			
Hymenoptera				
Formicidae				
Lasius sp.	17	-	-	-
Myrmica sp.	6	-	2	2
Diptera				
Bibionidae				
Dilophus sp.	1	-	-	-
Orthoptera				
indet.	-	-	-	1
Mollusca				
Bivalvia				
Tellinaciae				
Macoma balthica (L.)	4 (valves)	-	-	-
Foraminifera				
indet.	---------------------- not counted ----------------------			

indicators of estuarine conditions.

The most frequent identifiable insects in all samples are species of *Ochthebius*. Of the three identified, two, *O. auriculatus* and *O. dilatatus*, are halophiles (Lohse 1971), the former being an obligate salt-marsh beetle, while the latter is also recorded from stagnant freshwater (Balfour-Browne 1958). The faunal list also includes four other coastal species - *Brachygluta helferi, Heterocerus flexuosus, Cantharis rufa* and *Macroplea mutica*. The large number of ants beneath the boat (Sample 1) at first appeared unusual until D.S. Ranwell (pers. comm.) pointed out that he had observed both *Lasius* and *Myrmica* species foraging upon estuarine mudflats, surviving the tide by trapping air between setae and body.

The generalised nature of much of the available literature on collections of modern insects makes comparison with fossil death assemblages particularly difficult. The work of Hincks *et al.* (1952) on the fauna of Spurn provides records of many of the species found fossil, and there are additional records by Thornley and Wallace (1908-13) from the south side of the Humber; species with such relatively recent records are indicated in Table 10.2 with asterisks. The nature of individual habitat associations, however, often remains obscure and the fragmentation of once continuous habitats by embankment of the channel, pollution and urban development further compounds the problems. Nevertheless, the insect evidence is sufficient to narrow down the picture of the palaeoenvironment more closely.

The paucity of phytophages suggests that the boats lay below the vegetated zone of the foreshore, on the open mudflats, some way below contemporary high tide. This would accord with the virtual absence of identifiable plant macrofossils and it is tempting to see the declining numbers of the weevil *Limnobaris pilistriata*, which is recorded from a wide range of aquatic reeds and sedges, including *Juncus*, with which it is associated in Sample 4, as a result of progressive onlap, moving the high tide line further inland beyond the sampling locality. Such a hypothesis is supported by examination of the faunas from the fen peat beneath the silts, where the rising water table and move to more estuarine conditions is evident. An augered profile from the low tide-scoured bluff at -4.0 m OD to the base of the modern flood bank at 1.5 m OD shows that the estuarine clay-silts are continuous, overlying channels eroded into the underlying chalky till and infilled initially with a fen peat.

This may seem an excellent situation for accurate estimation of contemporary sea level. The boats, at between -0.5 and -1.0 m OD, on the palaeoecological evidence must have lain between -0.5 and -2.0 m below average tidal maximum and the cluster of radiocarbon dates around 1350 b.p. provides a chronological framework, which has already been used in the construction of a sea level curve for the estuary (Gaunt and Tooley 1974). North Ferriby, however, lies some 45 km from the modern mouth of the Humber, and the configuration of the outlet makes considerable differences to the nature of the tidal regime (Wilkinson *et al.* 1973). The rate of coastal retreat in Holderness and the cycle of construction and destruction of spits and gravel bars around the Humber mouth (de Boer 1964) indicate that, during the second millennium BC, Ferriby is likely to have been many kilometres further inland. Gerrard *et al.* (1984) have recently warned against the dangers of extrapolation of regional sea level figures from constricted localities and the Ferriby data, without comparative adequately dated contemporary faunas closer to the present mouth of the Humber, can only be used on a local correlative basis.

The predominantly stenotopic nature of the Ferriby insect assemblages provides little evidence for the wider environment. There is little trace of the activities of the people associated with the boats. Jackson (1947) recorded bones of cattle, sheep, pig, horse and red and roe deer from the 'grey clay', but their stratigraphic position remains doubtful. Sample 1, beneath boat 2, produced a single molar of *Bos*. Four dung beetles, including the now relatively local *Onthophagus ovatus*, occur in the samples but such might be expected as part of the background fauna. The small longhorn beetle *Gracilia minuta* is often synanthropic, usually in items of wickerwork (Kaufmann 1948). Kaufmann also noted *G. minuta* from bramble and loganberry canes. The Ferriby example may have come from willow or other trees close to the locality, on which the weevil *Phyllobius virideueris* could also have lived, but the large number of minor structures in the sediments, constructed of roundwood, partly of willow (see above), provides a more immediate source for the animal.

Pollen analysis

The pollen spectra are based upon a minimum total count of 150 grains of tree pollen, including Coryloid, and the diagram (Fig. 10.2) is constructed on the basis of percentage total tree pollen. The profile through the full succession will be discussed first, and the spectra from beneath boat 2 will then be considered in relation to this.

The base of the profile, immediately above the underlying till, is notable for the high percentages of tree pollen in relation to total pollen. This implies a well-wooded landscape and the consistently high, if declining, values for *Tilia* suggest that lime was the dominant tree in the forest, a suggestion supported by the presence of macrofossils in the peat (Wright and Churchill 1965). Although Smith (1958) was initially inclined to discount high *Tilia* values at the nearby site of Brigg as being the result of differential preservation, a number of other diagrams, including that recently published by Turner (1987) from the Hasholme boat site, some 20 km upstream of North Ferriby, show similarly high percentages. Greig (1982) has reassessed the evidence for lime in northern Europe as a whole and concluded that the tree formed a major component of the pre-clearance forest canopy, an argument supported by the high frequency of the lime-feeding bark beetle *Ernoporus caucasicus* in third millennium BC deposits in the Humberhead Levels (Buckland 1979).

As *Tilia* values decline in the Ferriby diagram, those for *Quercus* (oak) rise and this change is accompanied by a massive rise in the percentage of Gramineae (grasses). As Turner (1962) has shown, the fall in lime pollen frequency is clearly anthropogenic and it is possible that limewoods were being felled and replaced by grassland. The accompanying rise in pollen of the Chenopodiaceae and the appearance of *Triglochin*, however, suggest that the changes reflect increasing marine influence. That inception of peat growth relates to rising sea level is indicated towards the base of the diagram by the appearance of grains of *Plantago maritima/coronopus* and *Limonium*, both of which are likely to have grown close to estuarine conditions. The massive rise in Gramineae pollen, therefore, may relate to the expansion of estuarine reed swamps as the low-lying ground around the Humber was progressively inundated.

Although elsewhere along the section the contact between peat and overlying silts is clearly erosional (Wright and Churchill 1965), the

The context of the Ferriby boats 141

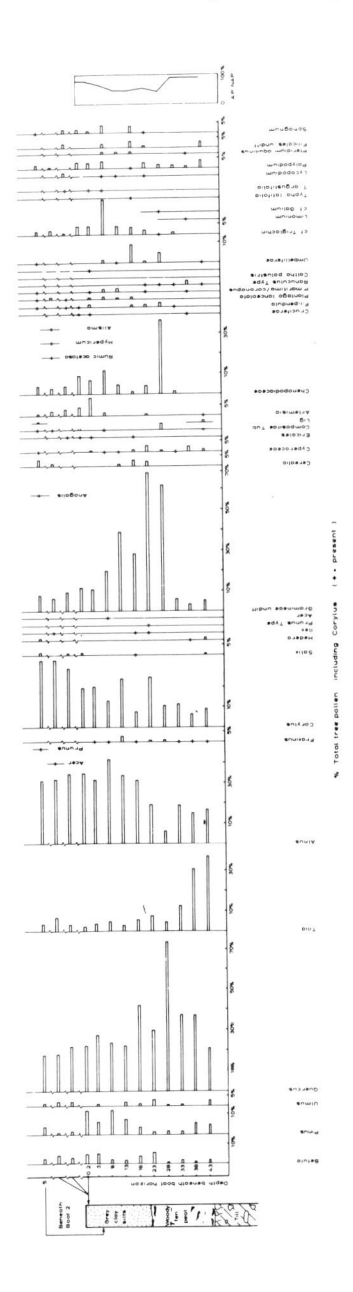

Fig. 10.2. North Ferriby pollen diagram.

transition at the diagram locality appears gradual and the pollen sequence reflects no major changes. The Coryloid component, as at Roos in Holderness (Beckett 1981) probably largely hazel, shows a marked, if temporary, decline and this is accompanied by the first clear indicators of cultivation in the area, with both *Plantago lanceolata* and cereal-type pollen making a significant contribution to the pollen rain. While the fluctuations in the hazel curve may reflect woodland management (cf. Turner 1987), it should be noted that the Cerealia counts may include a number of wetland grasses. *Pteridium* spores also appear at this horizon and it is possible that bracken was expanding into areas of clearance on the lighter, more acid soils, provided by the podzolisation of soils on the Late Devensian blown sand deposits to the west (Buckland 1982).

Despite this putative evidence for human activity, the landscape appears to remain essentially forested, the uppermost samples registering between 62% and 84% arboreal pollen. This may reflect wet oak and alder woods fringing the estuary, land which it would be of little value to attempt to farm without drainage, and a habitat which has now virtually disappeared from the Humber. This screening of the farmlands from the estuary by carrs, with the large local input of non-arboreal pollen from the plants of the salt marsh and estuary, effectively reduces the value of the diagram for examining the regional picture and correlation with other work. The rising alder and grass spectra, however, clearly place the upper part of the succession in Beckett's (1981) *Alnus*/Gramineae regional pollen assemblage zone.

The continuing, if declining, trace of lime implies that the top of the sequence pre-dates the final *Tilia* decline, which, although shown to be diachronous, has been dated at Thorne Moor, some 25 km to the southwest, at around 1300 b.p. (Turner 1962). Turner's main *Tilia* decline must also lie within the period covered by the Ferriby diagram, probably towards the top of the peat, and her Thorne dates of around 3000 b.p. for this event provide some indication of the probable age of the lower part of the Ferriby succession. In conventional archaeological terms, therefore, the Ferriby sediments appear to span the greater part of the Bronze Age.

Despite the reservations about the extent of cut and fill which may have taken place before the deposition of the boats, the three pollen spectra from beneath the plinth from which boat 2 was recovered are relatively consistent and can be matched with the evidence from the upper part of the profile through the full succession, as well as with that obtained by Allison and Godwin (1947) from near boat 1. Variation is slight, but the boat samples provide slightly stronger evidence for cultivation, with not only cereal-type and plantain pollen but also single grains of *Rumex acetosa* (sorrel) and *Anagalis* (pimpernel), both likely to be associated with disturbed ground.

Conclusions

Palaeoecological evidence suggests that the Ferriby boats were abandoned and dismantled on saline mudflats below contemporary high tide level, beyond the zone of any extensively vegetated salt marsh. On stratigraphic grounds, noted by Wright and Churchill (1965), it seems probable that the boats lay in a shallow creek or runnel in the foreshore. The inter-tidal mudflats were backed by estuarine vegetation, giving way to wet, oak-alder carr beyond. Although both the archaeology and palaeoecology provide evidence for the activities of man, both in the presence of domestic stock and the palynological record of his impact upon the wider landscape, the immediate area was still essentially wooded, with lime, elm and pine still forming a part of the forest canopy. The more recent impact of man upon the Humber has removed such gradual intergrades between habitats from its landscapes and several of the invertebrates survive only as disjunct fragments of former communities in temporary refuges from development and pollution.

It is clear that foreshore environments of the Humber possess great archaeological and palaeoecological potential. That the majority of archaeological finds from the foreshore date to the mid second millennium BC may reflect particularly intense activity at that time, but it is probable that it simply represents recent erosion by the river of contemporary deposits, later levels having already been lost. Whether there are Neolithic and earlier finds yet to be revealed in the vicinity or at similar locations elsewhere remains to be seen, but, in view of the fact that these areas are continually under the threat of erosion, it is vital that both their detailed, systematic and casual but more regular inspection be continued.

Acknowledgements

The palynological research was supported by a grant to the Department of Geography, University of Birmingham, from the National Maritime Museum. Sampling and survey work in 1980 and 1983 was assisted by D.R. Ingram, P. Larkham and A. Moss. The authors are also grateful for the assistance of K.J. Edwards and J.R.A. Greig with the palynological aspects of the project, and D.D. Gilbertson with the mollusca. G.R. Coope and P.J. Osborne provided entomological expertise and J. Squirrel identified the plant macrofossils.

References

Allison, J. and Godwin, H. (1947). Appendix B. Report on plant material associated with the Ferriby boats. *Proceedings of the Prehistoric Society* **13**, 138.

Balfour-Browne, F. (1958). *British Water Beetles, III.* Ray Society, London.

Beckett, S.C. (1981). Pollen diagrams from Holderness, North Humberside. *Journal of Biogeography* **8**, 177-98.

Buckland, P.C. (1979). *Thorne Moors: a palaeoecological study of a Bronze Age site,* University of Birmingham Department of Geography Occasional Paper 8. Birmingham.

Buckland, P.C. (1982). The cover sands of north Lincolnshire and the Vale of York. In: *Papers in Earth Sciences, Lovatt Lectures* (ed. B.H. Adlam, C.R. Fenn and L. Morris) pp. 143-78. GeoAbstracts, Norwich.

Buckland, P.C. and Sadler, J. (1985). The nature of late Flandrian alluviation in the Humberhead Levels. *East Midland Geographer* **8**, 239-51.

Coope, G.R. and Osborne, P.J. (1968). Report on the coleopterous fauna of the Roman well at Barnsley Park, Gloucestershire. *Transactions of the Bristol and Gloucestershire Archaeological Society* **86**, 84-7.

Crowther, D.R. (1987). Sediments and archaeology of the Humber foreshore. In: *East Yorkshire Field Guide* (ed. S. Ellis) pp. 99-105. Quaternary Research Association, Cambridge.

de Boer, G. (1964). Spurn Head: its history and evolution. *Transactions of the Institute of British Geographers* **34**, 71-89.
Gaunt, G.D. and Tooley, M.J. (1974). Evidence for Flandrian sea-level changes in the Humber estuary and adjacent areas. *Bulletin of the Geological Survey of Great Britain* **48**, 25-41.
Gerrard, A.J., Adlam, B. and Morris, B. (1984). Holocene coastal changes - methodological problems. *Quaternary Newsletter* **44**, 7-14.
Greig, J.R.A. (1982). Past and present lime woods of Europe. In: *Archaeological Aspects of Woodland Ecology* (ed. M. Bell and S. Limbrey) pp. 23-55. British Archaeological Reports, Oxford.
Heal, S.V.E. (1986). Recent work at North Ferriby, North Humberside, England. *Proceedings of the Prehistoric Society* **52**, 317-19.
Hincks, W.D., Shaw, S. and Steel, W.O. (1952). The entomology of Spurn Peninsula. 7-9. Coleoptera. *Naturalist* **843**, 169-76.
Jackson, J.W. (1947). Appendix C. Report on animal remains from North Ferriby, E. Yorks. *Proceedings of the Prehistoric Society* **13**, 138.
Kaufmann, R.R.V. (1948). Notes on the distribution of the British longicorn coleoptera. *Entomologist's Monthly Magazine* **84**, 66-85.
Lindroth, C.H. (1949). *Die Fennoskandinavischen Carabidae. Eine Tiergeographische Studie.* Meddelanden fram Göteborgs Musei Zoologiska Avdeln, Göteborg.
Lindroth, C.H. (1974). *Carabidae,* Handbooks for the Identification of British Insects, IV, 2. Royal Entomological Society of London, London.
Lohse, G.A. (1971). Hydraenidae. In: *Die Käfer Mitteleuropas, 3* (ed. K.W. Harde and G.A. Lohse) pp. 95-125. Goecke & Evers, Krefeld.
McGrail, S. (1983). The interpretation of archaeological evidence for maritime structures. In: *Sea Studies* (ed. P.G.W. Annis) pp. 33-46. National Maritime Museum, London.
Preece, R.C. and Robinson, J.E. (1984). Late Devensian and Flandrian environmental history of the Ancholme Valley, Lincolnshire: Molluscan and ostracod evidence. *Journal of*

Biogeography **11**, 319-52.
Smith, A.G. (1958). Post-glacial deposits in south Yorkshire and north Lincolnshire. *New Phytologist* **57**, 19-49.
Thornley, A. and Wallace, W. (1908-13). Lincolnshire Coleoptera. *Transactions of the Lincolnshire Naturalists' Union* (1908) 274-88, (1909) 119-46, (1910) 220-7, (1911) 245-89, (1912) 38-58, (1913) 115-49.
Tooley, M.J. (1978). *Sea-level Changes in North-West England during the Flandrian Stage.* Oxford University Press, Oxford.
Turner, J. (1962). The Tilia decline: an anthropogenic interpretation. *New Phytologist* **61**, 328-41.
Turner, J. (1987). The pollen analysis. *Archaeological Journal* **144**, 85-8.
Versey, H.C. (1939). The Humber warp. *Proceedings of the Leeds Philosophical Society* **3**, 553-6.
Wilkinson, H.R., de Boer, G. and Thunder, A. (1973). *A Cartographic Analysis of the Changing Bed of the Humber,* University of Hull Department of Geography Miscellaneous Series 14. University of Hull.
Wright, C.W. and Wright, E.V. (1933). Some notes on the Holocene deposits at North Ferriby. *Naturalist*, 210-12.
Wright, E.V. (1976). *The North Ferriby Boats: a guidebook,* National Maritime Museum Monograph 23. National Maritime Museum, Greenwich.
Wright, E.V. (1978). Artefacts from the boatsite at North Ferriby, Humberside, England. *Proceedings of the Prehistoric Society* **44**, 187-202.
Wright, E.V. (1985). North Ferriby boats - a revised basis for reconstruction. In: *Sewn Plank Boats* (ed. S. McGrail and E. Kentley) pp. 105-44. British Archaeological Reports, Oxford.
Wright, E.V. and Churchill, D.M. (1965). The boats from North Ferriby, Yorkshire, England. *Proceedings of the Prehistoric Society* **31**, 1-24.
Wright, E.V. and Wright, C.W. (1947). Prehistoric boats from North Ferriby, East Yorkshire. *Proceedings of the Prehistoric Society* **13**, 114-38.

11

The archaeology of the Holme-on-Spalding-Moor landscape

P. Halkon

Introduction

Romano-British pottery has been recorded in the Holme-on-Spalding-Moor area since last century, with excavations having been carried out at Throlam (Corder 1930) and Hasholme (Hicks and Wilson 1975). In 1980 systematic fieldwork was begun by the writer and members of the East Riding Archaeological Society, mainly concentrated around Bursea and Hasholme. Prehistoric flints and Romano-British pottery sherds and iron slag where found to be concentrated on the ridges of aeolian sand bordering the River Foulness (Halkon 1983); this showed that Romano-British settlement and industry were considerably more extensive than previously supposed. In 1983 the survey area was expanded to an 8 x 8 km landscape block with its corners at National Grid References SE 7732, 7740, 8540 and 8532 (Fig. 11.1), and the writer joined forces with Martin Millett of Durham University, with a view to linking systematic fieldwalking, aimed at relating sites to soils and water courses, with research and some rescue excavation at key sites (Halkon 1987, Millett and Halkon 1988). The aim of this chapter is to set the archaeology of the Holme-on-Spalding-Moor landscape, with its extensive Iron Age and Romano-British settlement and

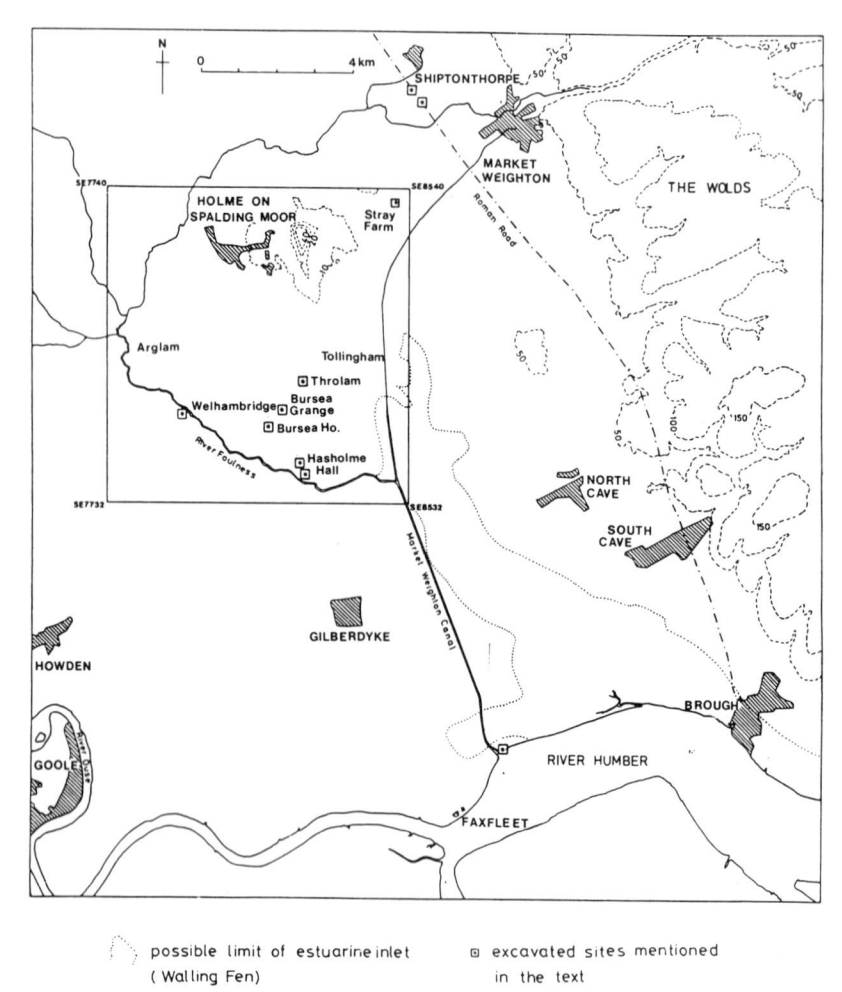

Fig. 11.1. Location of the Holme-on-Spalding-Moor landscape block.

industry, and its medieval pottery kilns, in the wider context of the Humber basin.

Topography

Holme-on-Spalding-Moor appears in the Domesday Book as 'Holm', an island in the marshland (Jensen 1972). Church Hill, an inlier of Triassic Keuper Marl, dominates the landscape to the north of the study area, and the flatness of the remainder is interrupted only by the ridges of aeolian sand which rarely rise above 8 m OD. Underneath and between the ridges is the glacio-lacustrine clay of the former Lake Humber (Catt this volume), and it was this which provided the raw material for Romano-British and medieval potters.

To the south lies Wallingfen, now farmland, dissected by many drainage ditches, but once a large saltmarsh extending northwards from the Humber (Sheppard 1966). Study of soil maps and recent research (Millett and McGrail 1987) shows that the Wallingfen was previously an estuarine inlet of the Humber (Fig. 11.1). Running into this was a dendritic creek system, the course of which can be detected from soil maps and aerial photographs as bands of alluvium on either side of the River Foulness, itself now straightened and canalised, but once meandering and bordered by marshland (Halkon 1987).

It has been possible to propose a reconstruction of the pre-Market Weighton canal (1772) river system (Halkon 1987), and the discovery of the Iron Age logboat at Hasholme by the writer and Martin Millett, and its subsequent excavation and recovery, have thus provided dating evidence for the creek system in which it sank (McGrail and Millett 1985, Millett and McGrail 1987, McGrail this volume). Archaeological and place-name evidence, for example Bursea - the byre of the lake (Smith 1937) - suggests that another section of this creek system remained open into the Middle Ages and beyond (Halkon 1987); the discovery and excavation of a medieval bridge at Stray Farm (SE 845397) in 1986 suggest that this relict tributary of the River Foulness had been crossed at this period (Millett and Halkon 1987).

The modern landscape around Holme-on-Spalding-Moor is largely the creation of artificial drainage and embankment, without which much of the low-lying areas would be flooded. It is therefore difficult, in an area of such localised topographic variation, to make a generalised statement about the effect on this area of flooding in the Humber estuary and its accompanying river systems in former times, although it is likely that minor changes in climate and/or sea level could have made significant differences to settlement potential (cf. Sitch this volume). Research does, however, suggest that the sandy ridges supporting podzols and brown soils of the Holme Moor and

Naburn series (Furness and King 1978) formed the most suitable land for settlement and agriculture, due to their superior drainage qualities as compared with the peat and clay soils of the landscape block. Although abundant water made conditions difficult, it did provide a resource for settlement and industry, and a means of communication to the Humber and beyond.

The Iron Age

Although little Iron Age pottery has been found during fieldwalking, probably due to its friable nature, aerial photography shows extensive crop marks of enclosures, droveways, hut circles and field systems, which can be typologically dated to this period. The excavation in 1986 of one of the most prominent of these features, a large hut circle within a rectilinear double-ditched enclosure, has reinforced this dating (Millett and Halkon 1987).

A feature of the area long-noticed by local farmers is the presence of large amounts of iron slag, or 'nosmun' as it is locally known. During fieldwalking, forty-nine sites with iron slag were found, seventeen of which showed major concentrations suggestive of large-scale manufacture (Fig. 11.2). Romano-British pottery, ubiquitous elsewhere in the landscape block, was only present on two of these sites (Halkon 1987). In an excavation of an iron manufacturing site at Moore's Farm, Welhambridge, 5388 kg of slag were recovered, but not a single sherd of pottery was found. However, very similar material was found at North Cave in Iron Age contexts, and further excavation at Bursea House has now confirmed that iron manufacture was being carried out in the Iron Age in the Holme area. In 1987 large pieces of slag were found in a shallow gully, possibly associated with a building, with the greater part of a wheel-thrown Belgic type vessel, very similar to those found at Dragonby, near Scunthorpe, and dated to the last years of the first century BC (May 1970). Almost identical sherds have been found in recent years by J. Dent at Brantingham and by P. Didsbury at Risby. The Bursea find therefore suggests trading contact of some form along the same creek system in which the Hasholme boat sank; it is noticeable that the majority of the major iron manufacturing sites were close to the creek system (Fig. 11.2), especially at Welhambridge, Bursea and Wholsea, suggesting

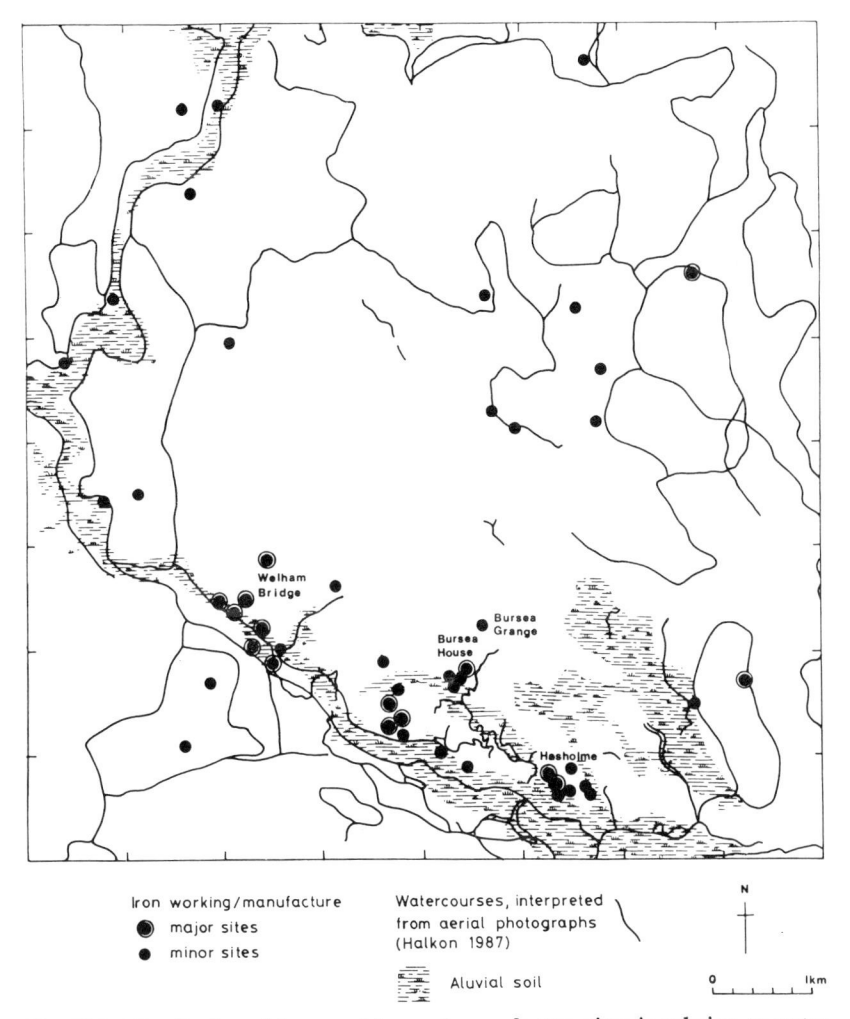

Fig. 11.2. Distribution of iron working and manufacture sites in relation to water courses of the Holme-on-Spalding-Moor area.

that water was used for the transportation of raw materials and finished products.

The origin of raw materials for the iron industry is a matter of some debate. It was previously thought that local siderite ores, extracted from the sand, or even bog ores were utilised (Halkon 1983). Gregory (1982) suggests that the hard iron pan which forms the upper levels of the Greensand on the Norfolk Fen edge was likely to have been smelted in the Romano-British period. However, A. Aspinall (pers. comm.) considers that the use of ores from sand layers or bog ores is unlikely in the Holme area and that ores from Scunthorpe or South Cave could have been used which were more productive. If this was the case, siting the iron smelting centres near the river system would have made good sense. Alternatively, it could be that the large amount of non-magnetic slag present on some sites is symptomatic of the exploitation of poor quality local ores extracted from the sand or peat on the creek margins (J. Evans pers. comm.). This would further explain the coincidence of sites close to the waterways.

It is likely that by the end of the Iron Age much of the available dry land in the Holme area was exploited for pastoral and arable agriculture, as shown by the presence of droveways and enclosures appearing as crop marks, and by environmental evidence; preliminary examination of samples of excavated deposits from the Iron Age settlement at Bursea Grange and the Romano-British kiln site at Bursea House showed that cereals had been cultivated near both locations (Halkon 1987). Some woodland did remain, however, and it is likely that this was managed as a fuel for furnace-based industries; preliminary examination of carbonised wood in the flue of a Romano-British pottery kiln at Bursea House has shown evidence of coppicing. Along with the creek system leading into the tidal inlet of the Humber, the basic infrastructure was therefore present for Romano-British expansion.

Romano-British industry and settlement

Pottery production appears to have begun on a large scale in the later second and early third centuries AD, reaching its height in the later fourth century (Evans 1985, Halkon 1987, Sitch this volume). During the survey, which included the study of museum collections and sites and monuments records, and fieldwalking, a total of 106 Romano-British sites were located, including thirty-seven with evidence for pottery manufacture (Fig. 11.3). Iron manufacture also took place on some of these, for example at Hasholme Hall, where a smelting furnace and anvil were found (Hicks and Wilson 1975, Halkon 1987).

The Holme-on-Spalding-Moor landscape

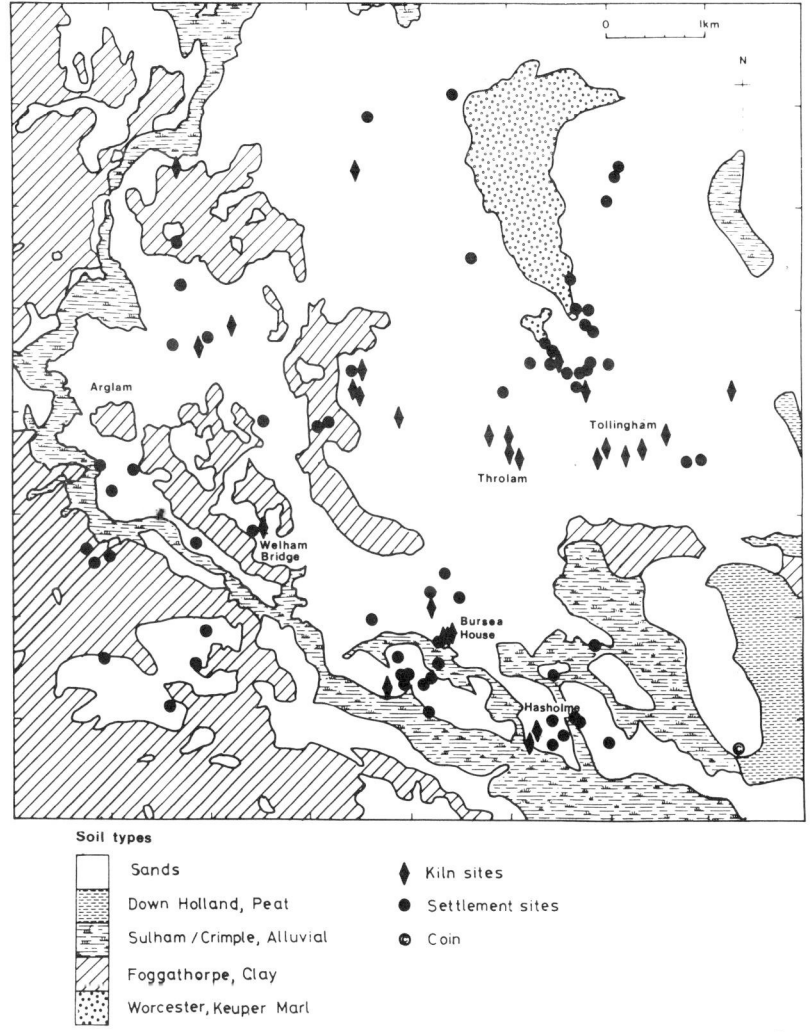

Fig. 11.3. Distribution of Romano-British kiln and settlement sites on the soils of the Holme-on-Spalding-Moor area.

Some of these Romano-British sites had Iron Age predecessors, for example at Hasholme and Bursea, and it has been possible to define a broad chronology for the sites based on pottery fabric and form analysis. The sandy ridges closest to the creek system appear to have been exploited first, with the major centre of pottery production moving to the Throlam/Tollingham area in the later fourth century.

In the third century AD the production of Dalesware type pottery and the form of kilns (Swan 1984) suggest links with north Lincolnshire, and the presence of large quantities of Holme products at Brough (Wacher 1969) and Faxfleet (Sitch this volume), which were situated on either side of the tidal inlet of the Humber, also suggests trade along the creek system during the Roman period. The presence of late Roman pottery shows that the Holme area remained occupied, and was not subject to any total marine innundation as has been previously suggested (Eagles 1979).

Romano-British industry and settlement appeared to cluster around the present hamlets of Bursea, Hasholme, Arglam, Welhambridge, Tollingham and Throlam, but it is as yet unknown whether there was any continuity between Romano-British sites and these hamlets; this coincidence may simply be caused by the same settlement constraints being present in both periods. In 1986, however, a blue glass bead of Anglian age was found during fieldwalking at The Homelands (SE 804383), on a site with both Roman and medieval industry and settlement.

The medieval pottery industry

In 1944-5 a medieval kiln was excavated by E. Greenfield near Kiln Garth (Mayes and Hayfield 1980). The pottery was later identified as being Humber Ware type and its production dated from the later fourteenth to early sixteenth century AD. In 1986 a large amount of medieval wasters was recovered nearby at The Homelands (SE 804383), indicating the presence of more kilns. A further kiln site was discovered in 1987 at Runner End, and yet another, about 500 m to the north, at Brandywells. Several large sacks of pottery were recovered from each site.

Although work on these new discoveries has only just commenced, it is becoming clear that medieval pottery manufacture was of a much larger extent than hitherto supposed. It is likely that the finished products, like their Roman predecessors, were transported along the River Foulness to the Humber, in much the same way as the products of the Newport and Broomfleet brickworks from the 1770s to this century were carried along the Market Weighton Canal, thence to

Hull, York and beyond (Duckham 1972, Reader 1972).

Conclusions

Through a programme of systematic survey and selective excavation in the area of Holme-on-Spalding-Moor, it has been possible to throw light on a dynamic industrial past which contrasts dramatically with the rural landscape of today. The availability of raw materials, an efficient network of rivers and roads, and easily accessible markets on the Humber and beyond were all important factors in the industrial development of Holme and its environs. The comparatively large quantity of sherds associated with pottery production discovered in this area has provided a medium through which the archaeologist can observe these economic and cultural changes. The use of the Humber and its tributaries, however, provides a point of continuity in this seemingly changing story.

Acknowledgements

Thanks must be given to all the farmers who allowed fieldwalking and excavation to take place on their land, to Dr M. Millett and the joint excavation teams from the University of Durham Department of Archaeology and the East Riding Archaeological Society and to all those who took part in fieldwalking. Thanks are also due to S. King and R. Furness of the Soil Survey of England and Wales, and to D. Riley and T. Betts of the National Monuments Record and the Royal Commission on Historical Monuments for their assistance with aerial photographs. The maps for this chapter were drawn by Dr H. Halkon.

References

Corder, P. (1930). *The Roman Pottery at Throlam, Holme on Spalding Moor, East Yorkshire,* Roman Malton and District Report 3. Yorkshire Archaeological Society Roman Antiquities Committee, Hull.

Duckham, B.F. (1972). *The Inland Waterways of East Yorkshire*

1700-1900. East Yorkshire Local History Society, York.
Eagles, B.N. (1979). *The Anglo-Saxon Settlement of Humberside*, British Archaeological Reports (British Series) 68. British Archaeological Reports, Oxford.
Evans, J. (1985). Aspects of Later Roman Pottery Assemblages in Northern England. Ph.D. thesis, University of Bradford.
Gregory, T. (1982). Romano-British settlement in West Norfolk and the Norfolk Fen edge. In: *The Romano-British Countryside*, British Archaeological Reports (British Series) 103 (ed. D. Miles) pp. 351-66. British Archaeological Reports, Oxford.
Halkon, P. (1983). Investigations into the Romano-British industries of Holme on Spalding Moor, East Yorkshire. *East Riding Archaeologist* 7, 15-24.
Halkon, P. (1987). Aspects of the Romano-British Landscape around Holme on Spalding Moor, East Yorkshire. M.A. thesis, University of Durham.
Hicks, J. and Wilson, J. (1975). The Romano-British kilns at Hasholme. *East Riding Archaeologist* 2, 49-70.
Jensen, G. (1972). *Scandinavian Settlement Names in Yorkshire*. Akademisk Forlag, Copenhagen.
May, J. (1970). Dragonby: an interim report on excavations of an Iron Age and Romano-British site near Scunthorpe, Lincolnshire. *Antiquaries Journal* 50, 222-45.
Mayes, P. and Hayfield, C. (1980). A late medieval kiln at Holme on Spalding Moor, East Yorkshire. *East Riding Archaeologist* 6, 99-110.
McGrail, S. and Millett, M. (1985). The Hasholme logboat. *Antiquity* 59, 117-20.
Millett, M. and Halkon, P. (1987). Excavations at Shiptonthorpe, Stray Farm and Bursea Grange, East Yorkshire, 1986. *Universities of Durham and Newcastle upon Tyne Archaeological Reports 1986*, 46-7.
Millett, M. and Halkon, P. (1988). Landscape and economy: recent fieldwork and excavation around Holme on Spalding Moor. In: *Recent Research in Roman Yorkshire*, British Archaeological Reports (British Series) 193 (ed. J. Price and P.R. Wilson) pp. 37-47. British Archaeological Reports, Oxford.
Millett, M. and McGrail, S. (1987). The archaeology of the

Hasholme logboat. *Archaeological Journal* **144**, 69-155.
Reader, E.M. (1972). *Broomfleet and Faxfleet - two townships through two thousand years*. Ebor Press, York.
Sheppard, J.A. (1966). *The Draining of the Marshlands of South Holderness and the Vale of York*. East Yorkshire Local History Society, York.
Smith, A.H. (1937). *The Place Names of the East Riding of Yorkshire and York*. English Place Name Society, Cambridge.
Swan, V.G. (1984). *The Pottery Kilns of Roman Britain*. Royal Commission on Historical Monuments, London.
Wacher, J.S. (1969). *Excavations at Brough-on-Humber, 1958-61*, Research Report 25. Society of Antiquaries, London.

12

Faxfleet 'B', a Romano-British site near Broomfleet

B. Sitch

Introduction

In autumn 1967 quarrying by contractors working for the Yorkshire Ouse and Hull Water Authority uncovered Romano-British remains close to Market Weighton Lock near Broomfleet (National Grid Reference SE 87472573) (Fig. 12.1). The Water Authority had purchased land to use as a borrow pit or quarry for the excavation of material to reinforce the flood embankment of the Humber. However, the discovery of considerable quantities of Romano-British pottery, building materials and a lead ingot with an inscription was not reported by workmen, and the site (now known as Faxfleet 'B') would have gone completely unnoticed were it not for a watching brief by members of the East Riding Archaeological Society. The stretch of the Humber between Faxfleet and Broomfleet had first attracted archaeological interest in 1962, when high tides and strong winds revealed features on the Humber foreshore at Faxfleet 'A', to the west of Market Weighton Lock (SE 87402565) (Fig. 12.1).

In October 1967 a small 'rescue' excavation was organised under the direction of John Bartlett, then Director of Hull City Museums. A large quantity of soil had already been removed from the borrow pit, so the work of the excavation team was limited to collecting unstratified material from the spoil heaps left by the contractors and recording exposed features. A series of ditches, gullies and pits,

Faxfleet 'B', a Romano-British site

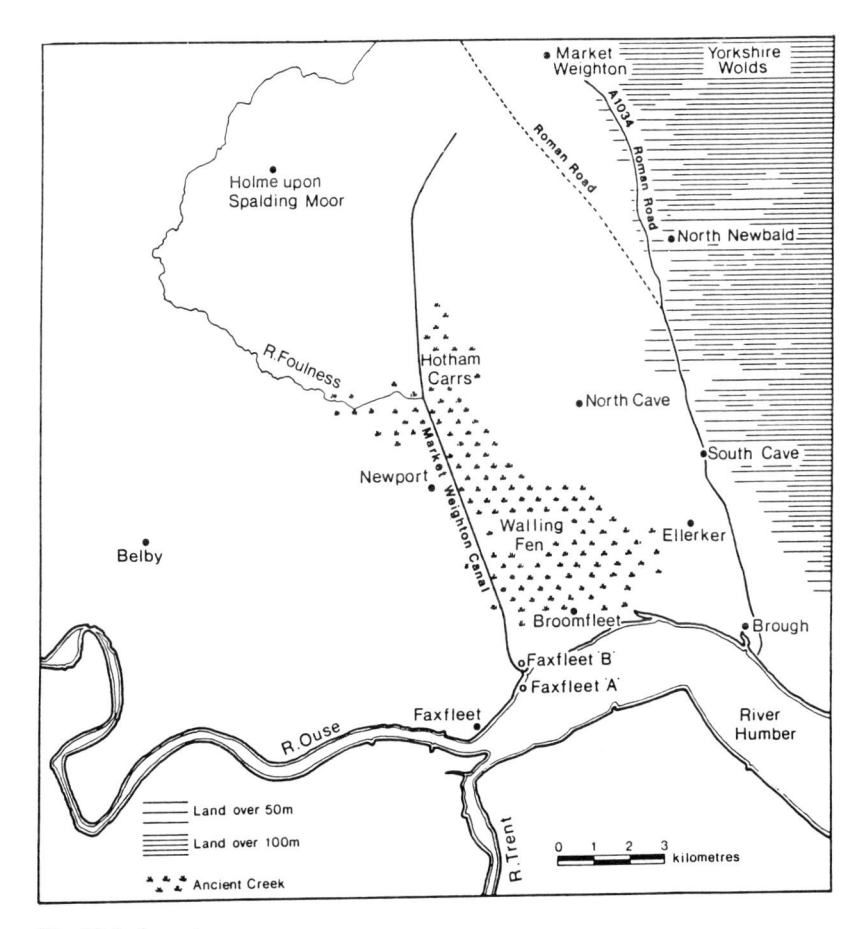

Fig. 12.1. Location map.

numbered B1 to B15 by the excavators, was recorded (Figs 12.2 and 12.3), but there were no structural features. Large quantities of samian, Nene Valley colour-coated ware, Dales ware and miscellaneous greywares were recovered, but bad weather and the rising water level in the borrow pit put an end to further excavation in spring 1968. Brief reports of the Faxfleet 'B' discoveries were published (Bartlett 1967, 1968, Wilson 1968), but no post-excavation work was undertaken until that of the present author (Sitch 1987), a summary of which forms the basis of this chapter.

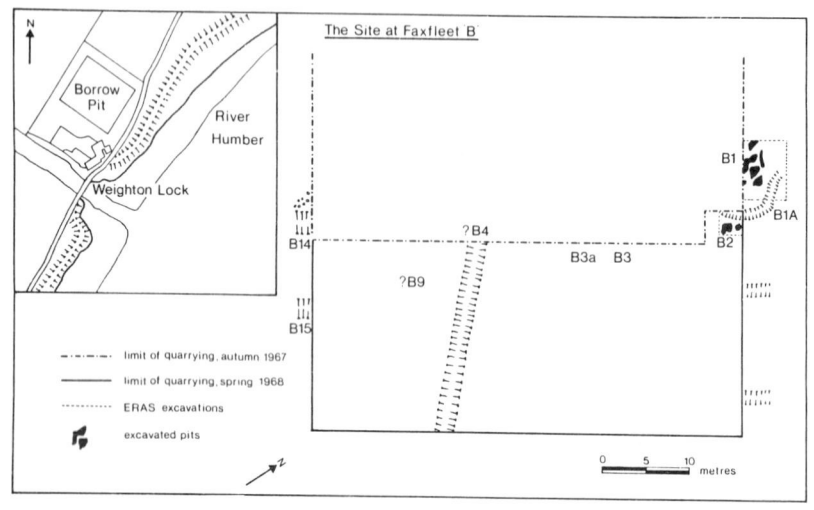

Fig. 12.2. Site plan of Faxfleet 'B'.

Situation and settlement

Situated on the threshold of the Vale of York, at the focal point of the tributary river systems of the Humber estuary, Faxfleet 'B' lies on an important natural trade route which provides access to the north of England and the Midlands. Drainage, however, has always been a problem in this landscape. Indeed, before the extensive drainage schemes of the medieval period (Sheppard 1966) and the cutting of the Market Weighton Canal in the eighteenth century, the area at the head of the Humber estuary was exceedingly wet and is thought to have formed a tidal inlet comparable to The Wash (Duckham 1967). Environmental evidence from soil maps and the excavation of the Iron Age Hasholme logboat (Millett and McGrail 1987) indicates that there was an estuarine inlet running from the Humber towards Holme-on-Spalding-Moor (Fig. 12.1). Faxfleet 'B' occupies marginally higher ground and the site may have been an island or part of a peninsula on the western shore of this inlet (Evans 1985).

The proximity of marine, freshwater and terrestrial habitats must have provided an extremely rich natural resource. Hunting, fishing

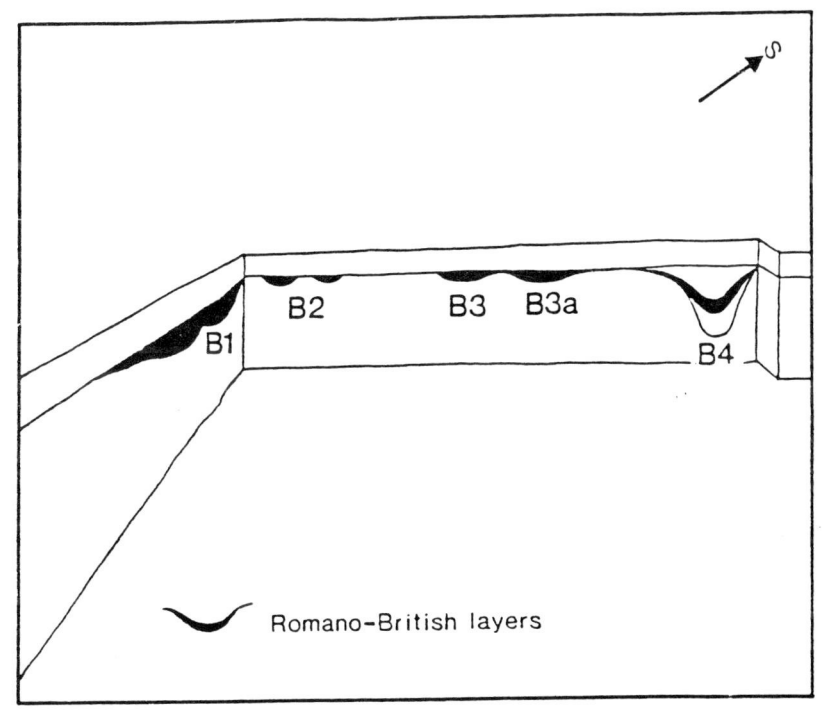

Fig. 12.3. The borrow pit features (unpublished sketch by J. Bartlett).

and gathering activities probably played an important part in the lives of the inhabitants of Faxfleet 'B', since marsh and fen provide an excellent habitat for wildfowl, while rushes, sedges and peat could have provided building materials and fuel. The estuary would have provided fish, crustaceans and edible plants such as salicornia; the latter could also be used to provide potash for glass making, and a glass-making site has recently been identified near Holme-on-Spalding-Moor at SE 81303368 (Halkon 1987).

Direct evidence for structures at Faxfleet is very limited. Sections of some of the features can be seen in Bartlett's rough sketch of the southern face of the pit (Fig. 12.3), and plans of the excavated features B1, B2 and B1A could conceal the location of a round-house with a circular eavesdrip gulley (Fig. 12.2). Unfortunately, accurate recording was hindered by appalling conditions in the pit, but the discovery of wattle and daub seems to confirm that there was domestic occupation here.

A strong case for settlement of the lower reaches of the Hull valley in the late Iron Age and early Romano-British period has been made by Didsbury (this volume), and much of the evidence cited is equally pertinent to the site at Faxfleet 'B'. Although more research must be done on the Faxfleet 'A' pottery assemblage, initial occupation of this site can be related to a similar phase of exploitation of marginal land made viable by marine regression. There is late first century AD samian and glass from Faxfleet 'B', but the archaeological evidence suggests that the main phase of occupation began in the late second century AD. The location of Faxfleet 'B' on higher ground than Faxfleet 'A' suggests that rising sea levels in the estuary were causing concern (Radley and Simms 1970). Faxfleet 'B' was probably abandoned in the fourth century AD when the marine transgression Lytham IX (Gaunt and Tooley 1974) was approaching its maximum extent; contemporary parallel ditches B14 and B15 in close proximity to each other (Fig. 12.2) indicate that drainage was a problem. However, a transgression involving cataclysmic flooding need not be envisaged because relatively small changes in sea level, by raising the ground-water level, would severely restrict the settlement potential of low-lying areas.

The pottery

Over 1800 sherds weighing 52 kg were examined, following a system developed by Evans (1985). The assemblage was quantified by sherd weight, sherd number, minimum number of rims and minimum number of vessels. Quantification of the Faxfleet 'B' assemblage by sherd weight supports the conclusions of Evans' (1985) study of the production and distribution of the pottery kilns of northern England. A little over 20% of the assemblage came from the continent or from native British kilns outside the Humber region. Samian represents nearly 5% of the assemblage and Hartley and Dickinson (unpublished) concluded that there was an intensive phase of occupation at Faxfleet 'B' at c. AD 160-200, although there is a significant quantity of Trajanic-Hadrianic (AD 98-138) samian. If Faxfleet 'B' really was a small port on an important trade route between northern England and the continent, the paucity of samian may reflect a comparatively low level of activity on the site.

The other imported wares on the site (over 5%) include Northern Gaulish jars and pinched rim flagons, Moselkeramik, a Rhineland mortarium and sherds from a Spanish Dressel 20 amphora. All of these can be dated to the late second and third centuries AD. Bayard (1980) dated the Northern Gaulish greyware jar with double-lipped rim and waist cordon (Fig. 12.4) to between *c.* AD 200 and 275/6; Northern Gaulish jars and flagons were also found in third century contexts at the New Wharf in London (Dyson 1986). The discovery of Northern Gaulish vessels at Faxfleet 'B' complements the marked bias in distribution of these wares along the eastern coast. Richardson and Tyers (1983) suggested that this pattern may be the result of trans-shipment through London and other Thames estuary ports along the trade routes of the east coast in the direction of the northern frontier. The Moselkeramik is only present in very small quantities in the Faxfleet 'B' assemblage, and has been dated to between AD 180 and 250 in Britain (Richardson and Tyers 1983). Rhineland mortaria were also found at Brough (Fig. 12.1) (Wacher 1969), and have been dated to the late second and third centuries AD (Dyson 1986).

Native British wares from kilns outside the Humberside region represent over 10% of the Faxfleet 'B' assemblage. Nene Valley colour-coated wares account for 8% of the assemblage. This percentage compares favourably with figures from Castleford - 6.5% by sherd number (Evans 1985) - and indicates that water transport played an important role in the distribution of these wares. Black-burnished wares account for just over 2% of the Faxfleet 'B' assemblage, which is perhaps surprisingly low given the location of kilns in the Thames estuary, the important trade route along the east coast and the presence of ports such as Brough on the Humber (Williams 1977). However, Evans (1985) concluded that social constraints operated on the distribution of pottery in East Yorkshire, with considerable reluctance to accept goods, other than specialist products such as samian, mortaria and amphorae, from outside the *civitas* boundaries. Although these constraints might be expected to break down in the vicinity of a port, it would appear that there was little market for Black-burnished wares at Faxfleet 'B'. It is interesting to note the presence at the site of a small number of micaceous Black-burnished tripod bowls (Fig. 12.4). These types were found in early to mid third century AD contexts at New Wharf in

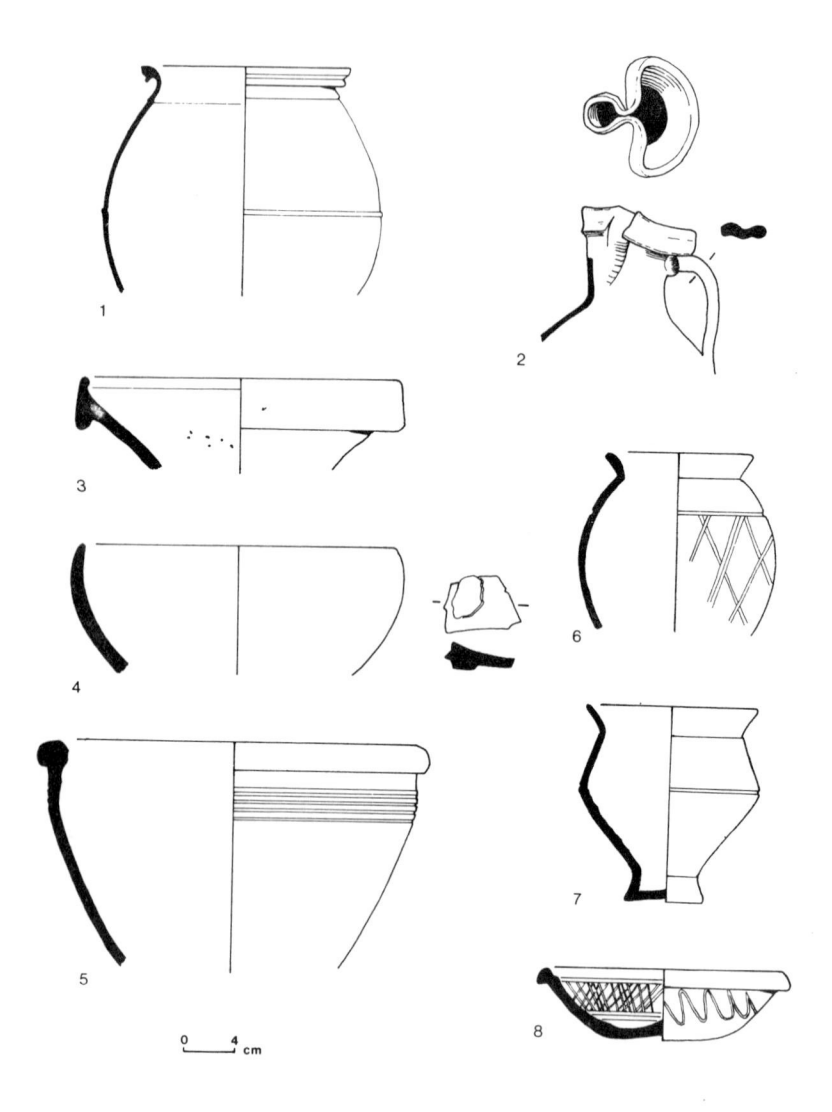

Fig. 12.4. Romano-British pottery from Faxfleet 'B'. 1 Northern Gaulish jar, 2 Northern Gaulish flagon, 3 Rheinland mortarium, 4 Black-burnished tripod bowl, 5 South Yorkshire bowl, 6 Holme-on-Spalding-Moor jar, 7 Holme-on-Spalding-Moor carinated bowl, 8 Roxby Form H dish.

London (Dyson 1986).

Holme-on-Spalding-Moor supplied the largest percentage of the Faxfleet pottery (over 32%), with carinated bowls and jars (Fig. 12.4) being some of the commonest forms. This figure compares favourably with those of Evans (1985) for Brough, where Holme-on-Spalding-Moor fabrics represent one-quarter of the pottery found in the early to mid third century AD, and is consistent with the fact that Brough and Faxfleet 'B' lay on opposite shores of an estuarine inlet in this period (Fig. 12.1) (Halkon 1987, this volume). The discovery and excavation of the Hasholme logboat in a former branch of the River Foulness confirms that the inlet and its tributaries were used for water transport (Millett and McGrail 1987).

Dales ware represents 8% of the Faxfleet 'B' assemblage. Loughlin (1977) suggested the area between Burton Stather and Alkborough, opposite Faxfleet on the south bank, as a likely centre of production. Dales ware was dated to AD 280-340 in northern England (Gillam 1957 type 157), but at Winterton on the south bank it was being used shortly after AD 200 (Stead 1976), while Evans (1985) noted a small supply of Dales ware at Brough dating to the early to mid third century AD.

Crambeck greywares represent 3% of the assemblage. The dating of these wares was recently reassessed by Evans, and production could have started in the last quarter of the third century AD. Their low percentage at Faxfleet 'B' suggests that the site was abandoned some time before mass production began in *c*. AD 370.

Roxby fabrics also represent about 3% of the Faxfleet 'B' assemblage. The vessels found are mostly Roxby Form H dishes (Fig. 12.4) and Form E jars. A Form H dish was found in the primary fill of the ditch at Greylees Avenue in Hull (Crowther and Didsbury 1985), a context which was dated to shortly before AD 180 (Didsbury pers. comm.), and at Brough this form occurs in Flavian to Antonine (AD 71-161) contexts (Stead 1976). Of the other kilns in the area, Parisian ware was represented by a single sherd, and there were several sherds from a South Yorkshire greyware wide-mouthed bowl (Fig. 12.4).

Quantification of the Faxfleet 'B' assemblage has therefore revealed that a significant proportion of the pottery was imported or was shipped over long distances from kilns in Britain, although the bulk of the pottery came from local kilns. The relatively small percentage of exotic fabrics probably represents occasional trade, rather than the regular commercial activities associated with a port.

The lead ingot

The discovery of a lead ingot was instrumental in bringing the site at Faxfleet 'B' to the attention of John Bartlett and the East Riding Archaeological Society. The moulded inscription on the base of the ingot (as cast) poses no problem of expansion and interpretation: SOCIOR(VM) LVT(VDARENSIVM) BR(ITANNICVM) EX ARG(ENTARIIS) or 'product of the Lutudarensian partners: British lead from the lead-silver mines (Bartlett 1968).

Over eighty Roman lead ingots have been found in Britain (Liversidge 1968), and of these, twenty-nine can be attributed with confidence to the Derbyshire lead mines. The largest concentration of Derbyshire ingots outside the Ashbourne/Matlock/Wirksworth area is to be found in the immediate vicinity of Brough, where ten have been found since the early eighteenth century (Table 12.1). These ingots indicate that the Humber was an important trade route between Derbyshire and the continent in Roman times (Bartlett 1968). The lead ingots were probably transported downriver in shallow-draughted boats and then transferred to sea-going vessels at Brough (Kitson Clark 1941). The upper reaches of the Humber must have presented a considerable hazard, since even today with sophisticated aids the upper Humber is one of the most difficult stretches of water in the country to navigate (Storey 1971). An altar, dedicated by Minucius Audens, *gubernator* (river pilot) of the Sixth Legion at York, supports this contention (Collingwood and Wright 1965, Roman Inscriptions of Britain number 653).

Wacher (1969) suggested that the Brough ingots were part of a limited consignment for use by the Parisi, or part of the stock of a ship repair yard. How they were lost is a matter of conjecture; given the number of ingots found near the line of a Roman road (Fig. 12.1) or near a former harbour, it would appear that losses in transit were inevitable, but whether this represents pilferage, accidental loss or even the deliberate lightening of loads is impossible to say.

The Faxfleet 'B' ingot cannot be dated with any certainty because the moulded inscription simply refers to the *societas Lutudarensis*, the

Table 12.1. Lead ingots found in the vicinity of Brough.

No.	Provenance	Find date	Inscription and remarks	Weight (kg)	Reference
1	Brough	Early 18th C.	BREXARC	?	Horsley (1732)
2	South Cave	1890	C. IVL. PROTI. BRIT. LVT. EX. ARG Incomplete	61.2	Hall (1892)
3	Belby	1910	SOCIOR LF BR EX ARG	51 approx.	Wright (1941)
4	Brough	1940	C.IVL. PROTI. BRIT. LVT. EX. ARG. Incomplete	86.3	Smythe (1940) Wright (1941)
5	Brough	1940	C. IVL. PROTI. BRIT. LVT. EX. ARG.	86.9	"
6	Brough	1940	C. IVL. PROTI. BRIT. LVT. EX. ARG.	89.0	"
7	Brough	1940	SOC. LVT. BRIT. EX. ARG.	87.7	"
8	Brough	1940	Rough casting, no inscription	36.6	"
9	Ellerker	1957	SOC. LVT. BRIT. EX. ARG.	79.5	Richmond (1958)
10	Broomfleet	1967	SOCIOR LVT BR. EX. ARG	79.4	Bartlett (1967)

company of associates involved in lead mining at Lutudarum, somewhere in or around Derbyshire (Monet-Lane 1976). However, a late first to early second century AD date can be suggested. The earlier of these dates depends upon the identification of the lessee Ti.Cl.Tr., who is attested on Lutudarum ingots from Matlock (Page 1905) and Pulborough (Way 1859) with an individual whose initials Ti.Cl.Trif. were cold-stamped on four ingots from the Mendips in the reign of the emperor Vespasian (AD 69-79) (Cockerton 1952). The later date is based on the fact that the Matlock and Pulborough ingots use the formula LVT.BR.EX.ARG., suggesting that they pre-date the imposition of direct imperial control on lead mining, resumed by the emperor Hadrian (AD 117-138); ingots of Hadrian's reign refer to *metalli Lutudares* rather than *societates* (Page 1905). Although the evidence leaves a great deal to be desired, it would appear that the Faxfleet 'B' ingot dates to *c.* AD 70-120. This conclusion is apparently confirmed by the evidence of the hoard of ingots discovered at Brough in 1940 (Table 12.1 nos. 4-8). Number 7 has a very similar inscription to that of the Faxfleet 'B' ingot, and is presumably contemporary with ingot numbers 4, 5 and 6 of C. Iulius

Protus (dated to the first century AD on epigraphic grounds). It is also significant that a small quantity of Trajanic-Hadrianic (AD 98-138) samian and predominantly first-second century AD glass was found at Faxfleet 'B'.

Conclusions

The ceramic evidence suggests that Faxfleet 'B' was occupied in the late first century AD, but the main phase of occupation occurred in the late second and third centuries AD. The site's function is less clear. There is no evidence for a fort or villa. The suggestion that it was a small port has received the widest currency (e.g. Wacher 1969, Reader 1972, Ramm 1978), but there is no archaeological evidence of port facilities such as river frontage. Neither is there any evidence of the dumping of goods damaged in transit or during storage. It is interesting, however, that two pottery bases stacked one inside the other were found at Faxfleet 'A', and one of these vessels, a rusticated jar, had apparently not been used (J. Leonard pers. comm.). A study of the Faxfleet 'A' pottery assemblage could therefore prove very informative. The quantification analysis of the Faxfleet 'B' assemblage revealed a considerable amount of imported pottery, but this need not imply a wide-ranging network of trading contacts. The pottery could have reached the site via a chain of transactions as part of a mixed cargo trans-shipped from an east coast port.

Duckham (1967) pointed out that, before the advent of steam and later the diesel engine, shipping depended on the flood tides to move upriver because it was impossible to sail against the ebb tide. A number of safe anchorages would therefore have been required so that shipping could await a suitable tide. Since many tides would be needed to travel upriver, Faxfleet 'B' could have been a 'staging post' in a Humber itinerary. In view of the modest nature of the Broomfleet borrow pit features and the marginal location of the site, perhaps Faxfleet 'B' was a small riverside settlement rather than a small port. The site certainly did benefit from the important trade route along the Humber, but the exotic pottery, the lead ingot and a fragment of Andernach-Niedermendig quern stone could just as easily indicate sporadic trade with passing vessels as opposed to a regular commerce.

Acknowledgements

The study of the Faxfleet 'B' assemblage was conducted at the University of Durham Department of Archaeology for an MA dissertation under the supervision of Dr M. Millett, with the support of a British Academy State Studentship.

References

Bartlett, J. (1967). A Roman pig of lead from Broomfleet, East Yorkshire. *Derbyshire Archaeological Journal* **87**, 167-8.

Bartlett, J. (1968). A pig of lead and other finds from Broomfleet, East Yorkshire. *Kingston upon Hull Museums Bulletin* **1**, 2-6.

Bayard, D. (1980). La commercialisation de la ceramique commune a Amiens du milieu du II e. a la fin du III e. siecle apres J.C. *Cahiers Archaeologiques de Picardie* **7**, 147-209.

Cockerton, R.W.P. (1952). Roman pigs of lead from Derbyshire- recent dating evidence from the Mendips. *Derbyshire Archaeological Journal* **79**, 88-96.

Collingwood, R.G. and Wright, R.P. (1965). *The Roman Inscriptions of Britain Vol. 1*. Oxford University Press, Oxford.

Crowther, D.R. and Didsbury, P. (1985). Excavation of a Romano-British ditch at Greylees Avenue, Hull. *CBA Forum 1984-85*, 11-16.

Duckham, B.F. (1967). *The Yorkshire Ouse: the history of a river navigation*. David and Charles, Newton Abbot.

Dyson, T. (ed.) (1986). *The Roman Quay at St. Magnus House, London*. Museum of London and the London and Middlesex Archaeological Society, London.

Evans, J. (1985). Aspects of Later Roman Pottery Assemblages in Northern England. Ph.D. thesis, University of Bradford.

Gaunt, G.D. and Tooley M.J. (1974). Evidence for Flandrian sea-level changes in the Humber Estuary. *Bulletin of the Geological Survey of Great Britain* **48**, 25-41.

Gillam, J.P. (1957). *Types of Roman Coarse Pottery Vessels in Northern Britain*. Society of Antiquaries of Newcastle upon Tyne, Gateshead.

Halkon, A.P.M. (1987). Aspects of the Romano-British Landscape

around Holme on Spalding Moor, East Yorkshire. M.A. thesis, University of Durham.
Hall, J.G. (1892). *A History of South Cave.* Edwin Ombler, Hull.
Horsley, J. (1732). *Britannia Romana.* Reprinted 1974, Graham, Newcastle upon Tyne.
Kitson Clark, M. (1941). Brough on Humber. *Yorkshire Archaeological Journal* **35**, 223.
Liversidge, J. (1968). *Britain in the Roman Empire.* Routledge and Kegan Paul, London.
Loughlin, N. (1977). Dales ware: a contribution to the study of Roman coarse pottery. In: *Pottery and Early Commerce* (ed. D.P.S. Peacock, pp. 85-146. Academic Press, London.
Millett, M. and McGrail, S. (1987). The archaeology of the Hasholme logboat. *Archaeological Journal* **144**, 69-155.
Monet-Lane, H.C. (1976). *The Romans in Derbyshire.* Veritas Publications, Chesterfield.
Page, W. (ed.) (1905). *The Victoria County Histories of England: a history of Derbyshire.* Archibald Constable and Co. Ltd, London.
Radley, J. and Simms, C. (1970). *Yorkshire Flooding - some effects on man and nature.* Ebor Press, York.
Ramm, H. (1978). *The Parisi.* Duckworth, London.
Reader, E.M. (1972). *Broomfleet and Faxfleet: two townships through 2000 years.* Ebor Press, York.
Richardson, B. and Tyers, P.A. (1984). North Gaulish pottery in Britain. *Britannia* **15**, 133-41.
Richmond, I.A. (1958). Roman Britain in 1957 - No. 12, Ellerker, Yorkshire. *Journal of Roman Studies* **48**, 152.
Sheppard, J.A. (1966). *The Draining of the Marshlands of South Holderness and the Vale of York.* East Yorkshire Local History Society, York.
Sitch, B.J. (1987). Faxfleet B, a Romano-British Site near Broomfleet, North Humberside. M.A. thesis, University of Durham.
Smythe, J.A. (1940). Roman pigs of lead from Brough. *Transactions of the Newcomen Society* **20**, 139.
Stead, I.M. (1976). *Excavations at Winterton Roman Villa,* Department of the Environment Archaeological Reports No. 9. HMSO, London.

Storey, A. (1971). *Pilotage and Navigational Aids of the River Humber (1512-1908)*. Ridings Publishing Co., Driffield.
Wacher, J.S. (1969). *Excavations at Brough-on-Humber, 1958-61*, Research Report 25. Society of Antiquaries, London.
Way, A. (1859). Enumeration of blocks of lead and tin discovered in Great Britain. *Archaeological Journal* **16**, 22-40.
Williams, D.F. (1977). The Romano-British Black-Burnished industry: an essay on characterisation by heavy mineral analysis. In: *Pottery and Early Commerce* (ed. D.P.S. Peacock) pp. 163-220. Academic Press, London.
Wilson, D.R. (ed.) (1968). Roman Britain in 1967 - No. 31, Broomfleet. *Journal of Roman Studies* **58**, 210.
Wright, R.P. (ed.) (1941). Roman Britain in 1940 - No. 17, Belby, Howden, Yorkshire. *Journal of Roman Studies* **31**, 146.

13

The topography and archaeology of Redcliff

D. Crowther, S. Willis and J. Creighton

Topographic setting

Redcliff is the name given to a stretch of coastline on the north bank of the Humber, west of North Ferriby (National Grid Reference SE 980250). It is readily distinguishable, for it rises abruptly from an otherwise flat riverside, and runs as a low cliff for 0.8 km. As an upstanding body of land at the water's edge it is an anomaly, and is matched on the south bank by a similar formation at South Ferriby. Both are positioned in that constricted portion of the estuary known as the Humber Gap, cut through the chalk escarpment of the Yorkshire and Lincolnshire Wolds, and represent the remnants of a morainic ridge that impounded the glacial Lake Humber in the Late Devensian (Crowther 1987a, Catt this volume).

To each side of the Redcliff eminence are depressions in the till formed by early post-glacial drainage. As sea level rose through the Flandrian period (Gaunt and Tooley 1974), freshwater back-up in these channels led to peat formation and extensive tree mortality. Further increases in sea level through time led to the deposition of estuarine clay-silts, indicating conditions no longer conducive to peat growth and a tidal flow with considerable alluvial carrying capacity. Exposures of these deposits on the inter-tidal foreshore up and downstream of Redcliff were first described in detail after 1930 (Bisat 1932), when a major shift in the main tidal channel of the Humber scoured the foreshore of all later overburdens and heralded the beginning of an interest in foreshore investigations at this location that continues to this day (Wright and Buckland *et al.* this volume).

Whether peat or clay-silts, water is the common agent in the formation of surface deposits both upstream and downstream of Redcliff. Redcliff alone stands out in the vicinity as a body of landscape that has not been subject to diurnal or seasonal inundation by the tidal waters of the Humber. This is especially important in the context of later prehistory, when the landscapes around the main tideway were not embanked, drained or warped (Ellis this volume), and were thus at the mercy of a fluctuating water table that may have been predictable, but was altogether uncontrollable.

Previous archaeological investigations

Redcliff is ideally located for people wishing to exploit the resources and opportunities offered by the Humber, while maintaining easy access to the upland hinterland of the Yorkshire Wolds and their dryland margins. In this regard it is not unique - the area of what is now Brough provided a highly advantageous combination of lines of communication - but is nevertheless exceptional enough for it to have been a focus for human settlement and activity in the past.

By the Bronze Age, human activity within a kilometre or so of the waterside was on such a scale that structural remains of tracks or platforms, as well as boats, have been discovered in the foreshore deposits around Redcliff (Crowther 1987a, Wright and Buckland *et al.* this volume), showing how the mudflats could be utilised at low tide. At Melton, where a hurdle-on-rail platform or trackway dating to around 1000 b.c. was excavated (Crowther 1987a), evidence for more than one rebuild was found, with a laid timber surface separated from one above by alluvial clays, suggesting that maintenance and making good of access tracks or 'hards' for boats was necessary in such a changeable and uncontrollable environment.

In 1932 a series of archaeological features was recorded in the cliff face at Redcliff, containing material somewhat later than the activities recorded on the foreshore. The presence of imported wheelmade pottery of late Iron Age date indicated that material was coming into the area from far afield. Subsequent excavations confirmed a site linked with exotic imported goods dating from around the mid first century AD. The intriguing possibility was offered that here, at a time when the Roman Empire had reached a line between the Bristol Channel and the Humber estuary, a native trading station was doing business with the Roman World (Corder and Davies Pryce 1938, Corder *et al.* 1939).

No further serious fieldwork was undertaken at Redcliff for the following half century, though a steady flow of stray finds from the vicinity, including Iron Age silver coins, came to the attention of museum staff at Hull. Aspects of this assemblage have been discussed elsewhere (Crowther and Didsbury 1988). Whilst the significance of Redcliff to the period had been widely recognised (Cunliffe 1974, May 1976), it was not until the 1980s that any modern assessment of the site and its setting through fieldwork was attempted.

Current fieldwork

Following a programme of erosion monitoring as part of a project of archaeological assessment of the vicinity, excavation and related survey work in the arable field behind Redcliff began in 1986. Like the work of the Wright brothers fifty years earlier, it was the exposure of features in the eroding cliff face which has influenced the operation of the project, efforts concentrating on the area known to contain earthfast features most directly under threat. The background and initial work has been described elsewhere (Crowther 1987b, Crowther and Didsbury 1988).

In addition to rigorous topsoil sampling for phosphate data and finds distributions, a close-interval contour survey across the field surface, cliff face and foreshore was conducted. Using computer mapping of the values across the survey area, an oblique view of the mapped micro-topography of the cliff, and field behind, can be constructed (Fig. 13.1). The top of the Redcliff eminence forms a wide ridge, running northwest-southeast across the middle of the field, corresponding with a capping of fluvial gravels. To the east of this ridge, settlement and activity of an as yet unknown extent has been examined through small-scale excavation.

In 1986 a hand-cut excavation slot in the southeast corner of the

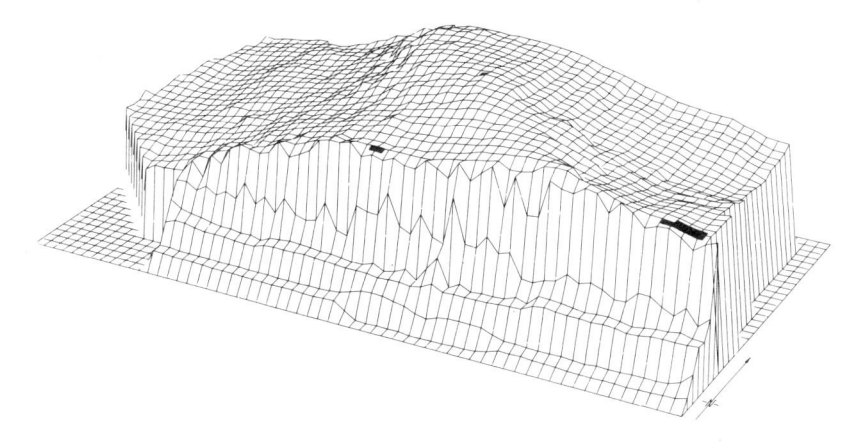

Fig. 13.1. The microtopography of Redcliff (oblique view looking northwest). Grid squares = 10 m x 10 m.

field, directly behind exposed features in the cliff face, revealed evidence for activity in the first century AD around a cobbled surface cut into the subsoil. Excavations in 1987 extended the area in order to evaluate and interpret these features more fully. A provisional interpretation of the sequence of activity within the excavated area is summarised in Figure 13.2, which presents the excavated features according to their stratigraphic positions within the chronology of the site.

The major feature of the site is a linear one, aligned approximately northwest-southeast, cut into the slope of the natural subsoil. To the southeast, and downslope, it originally opened out onto a laid surface of cobbles. This surface, sitting directly on natural sands and silts, appears to extend around each side of a protruberance in the natural sand, with the latter effectively dividing the cobbles into a Y shape. The linear feature which meets this area was subsequently modified. This alteration saw the revettment of one side of the feature (and probably the other) together with the consolidation of its base which was then covered with a carefully laid cobble surface.

Cut features of a linear form are, for the archaeologist, generally 'clear-cut' in every sense. Ditches, whether for drainage or land demarcation, have been dug for as long as people have settled and divided up their surroundings. Redcliff in this regard is no exception,

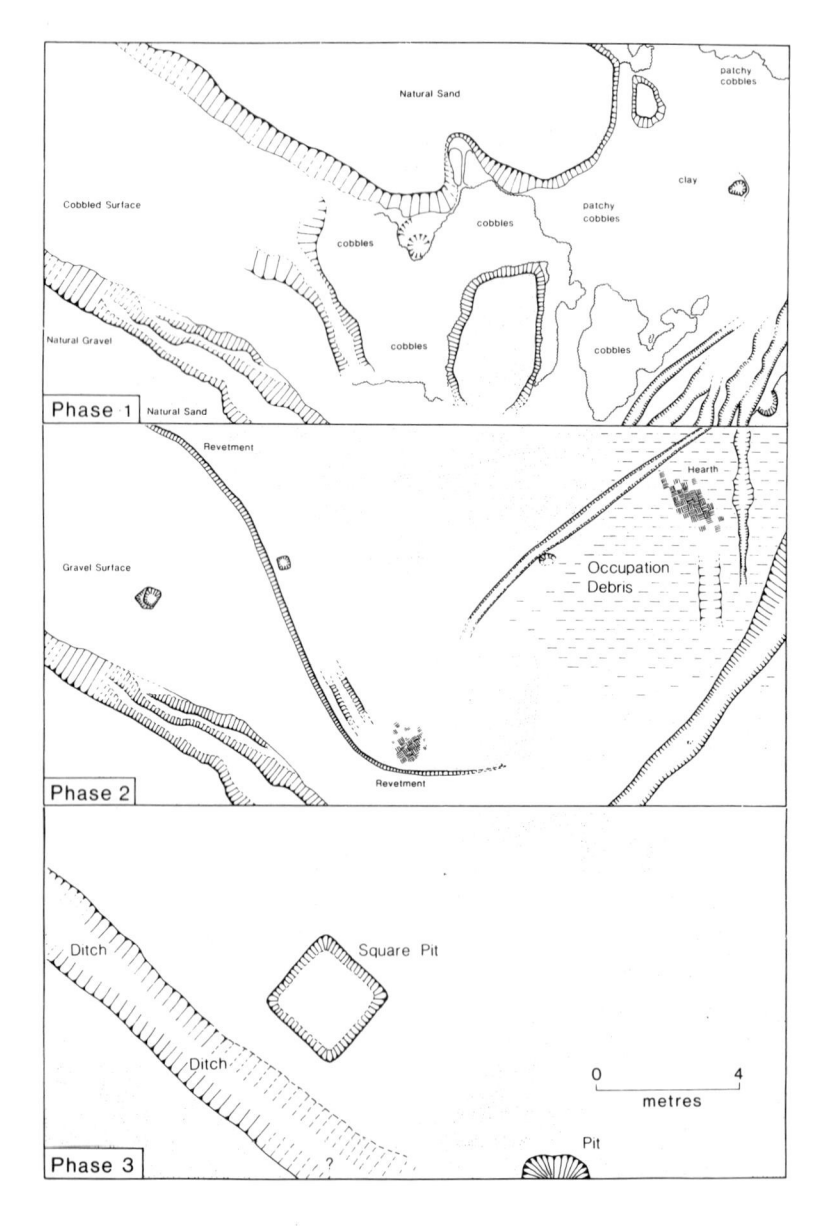

Fig. 13.2. Excavated features at Redcliff; a provisional phasing of the 1987 evidence.

but this particular feature may be. After the exposure of only a metre or two in 1986, it had appeared to be a conventional ditch, but the cobbling and revetting of this feature revealed in the larger exposure in 1987 raises some serious difficulties for such an interpretation. While an open ditch may require revetting to prevent erosion, reasons for lining the base of such a feature are not readily apparent. The lining of drainage ditches in prehistory with brushwood to improve water movement is known at, for example, Fengate, Cambridgeshire (Pryor 1984). The stones at Redcliff are indeed water-worn, but the local supply of beach shingle would be abraded in any event, and given that the feature merges with a wider surface downslope, an alternative interpretation can be offered. Perhaps the feature is better understood as a cutting through the natural subsoil to lessen the gradient of slope at this point. Heading towards the shoreline, which in the first century AD could have been some tens of metres to the south, this may be a roadway constructed to offer a shallow gradient for the movement of goods up from and down to the waterline. However, there remain many questions: why is it so narrow (could this relate to the movement of livestock?) and why is there not more evidence for repairs? Until further excavations expose the area to each side of the feature, we can only speculate.

To the east of this feature, and associated with its alteration and revettment, the ground level appears to have been raised. Gleying of the material that comprises the made-up area suggests that groundwater may have been a problem. 'Floor debris' laying on the more or less level top of this area demonstrated that it had been used as an extensive occupation surface. A slightly disturbed hearth was contemporary with this horizon. These floor debris deposits were found to contain a range of mid first century imported fine wares, comprising Tiberio-Claudian (c. AD 14-54) decorated Samian, Gallo-Belgic platter forms, a White Ware butt beaker and Terra Rubra beakers. To the northwest this surface partly overlays a narrow trench cut perhaps for a fence or wall. To the east of the occupation surface, at the extreme eastern edge of the excavated area, a deep gully contemporary with the surface yielded an important pottery group including decorated Samian, Terra Nigra and sherds of a south Spanish olive oil Amphora. Later activity on site shows that the now largely infilled cutting had still a land management function, for a shallow ditch appears to have been cut through its upper filling. Next to it a shallow, square-cut pit was dug, but its purpose remains enigmatic.

Finds from the site included several Corieltauvian coins, pointing to cross-river contact with that tribe at this period (May pers. comm.), as well as brooches of first century AD type, a copper alloy toilet spoon with wire-twist stem, fragments of blue glass, and several iron nails and other fittings. A small iron knife with a bone handle and copper alloy pommel was also recovered. A fragment of leather from the base of one feature indicates that impeded drainage on site may provide conditions favourable for the preservation of organic remains in certain contexts.

The composition of the pottery assemblage confirms the dating of the site to the middle decades of the first century AD. An extensive range of Roman imported wares is represented. These constitute the earliest identified Roman imports north of the Humber. Though the range of types now known from the site has been extended through the recent excavations, the close correlation with the early imported wares recorded at Old Winteringham, as previously identified by V. Rigby (Stead 1976), remains evident. The absence of like assemblages of this date in the immediate hinterlands of these two sites suggests the likelihood of the arrival of these exotic wares via the Humber rather than by an overland route from the south of Britain.

The Terra Sigillata component comprises a small proportion of the fine wares. Nevertheless, it provides a firm dating pointer since it includes sherds of 'Arretine' as well as 'early' forms such as the Dragendorff type 15/17 platter and the type 24/25 cup. The imports also include a range of types which will have been manufactured in Gallia-Belgica, specifically bead-rimmed wall-sided mortaria, White Ware flagons and butt beaker forms, together with comparatively large quantities of Terra Nigra and Terra Rubra platters and cups. These are likely to be of Tiberio-Claudian date. The presence of Amphora sherds from Dressel form types 2-4 and 28, plus Camulodunum (Hawkes and Hull 1947) Type 139 (in a Campanian fabric), implies that at around the time of the Roman conquest of the south, Mediterranean wine was being consumed at Redcliff. It is of particular interest, with regard to both the dating of the site and its interpretation, that no horizon of deposits containing exclusively pottery of a late Iron Age tradition has been encountered (nor indeed has an aceramic horizon). The proportion of extra-regional imported wares in the assemblage relative to the 'locally' produced coarse wares is remarkably high.

Conclusions

The features and finds from the Redcliff excavations to date point to cliff-top settlement contemporary with the Roman occupation of southern Britain around AD 43-70, though the start date for this *floruit* may pre-date AD 43 by one or perhaps two decades. At this time the Humber's position at the eastern extremity of the imperial frontier in Britannia provided the means by which political and economic contact between north and south could be defined, exploited and controlled. Redcliff would have been ideally placed to traffic prestige goods from the imperial periphery into the native north in exchange for goods and consumables to supply and equip a Roman army based to the south of the estuary at Lincoln, or possibly established even closer to the opposite bank (Creighton this volume).

The economic relationship between Rome, her empire and its fringes was based on a dynamic traffic of goods, services and obligations flowing inwards and outwards, operating through different mechanisms - for example, taxation, treaty obligations, free trade and controlled traffic - at different places and times according to the prevailing political and economic circumstances (Cunliffe 1988). Between the Roman south and the as yet unconquered north, where the main power-base, the Brigantes tribe, were ruled by the client-queen Cartimandua, there seems likely to have existed with the Parisi an expedient political and economic relationship based on mutual benefit. Through Redcliff the local Parisian élite may have provided produce and other resources in exchange for exotic manufactured goods, the distribution and traffic of which may have been strictly controlled in order to enhance and maintain their status (see also Creighton this volume). Such 'prestige goods economies', as they have been termed, were a feature of the frontier zones of the Roman Empire just as they were to be with the British Empire 1800 years later. Redcliff offers a great opportunity for observing this relationship, the impact of the Roman invasion and the native response to it.

Acknowledgements

Work at Redcliff forms part of a project by Hull City Museums in conjunction with members of the University of Durham Department of Archaeology. The work is funded by the Society of Antiquaries of London, the Royal Archaeological Institute and the British Academy with assistance from English Heritage. The generous sponsorship and support of the landowners, Capper Pass Ltd and RTZ, is gratefully acknowledged.

References

Bisat, W.S. (1932). Glacial and post-glacial sections on the Humber shore at North Ferriby. *Transactions of the Hull Geological Society* 7, 83-95.

Corder, P. and Davies Pryce, T. (1938). Belgic and other early pottery found at North Ferriby, Yorkshire. *Antiquaries Journal* 18, 262-77.

Corder, P., Wright, C.W. and Wright, E.V. (1939). The pre-Roman settlement of the Parisi at North Ferriby. *The Naturalist* 1, 237-43.

Crowther, D.R. (1987a). Sediments and archaeology of the Humber foreshore. In: *East Yorkshire Field Guide* (ed. S. Ellis) pp. 99-105. Quaternary Research Association, Cambridge.

Crowther, D.R. (1987b). Redcliff. *Current Archaeology* 104, 284-5.

Crowther, D.R. and Didsbury, P. (1988). Redcliff and the Humber. In: *Recent Research in Roman Yorkshire*, British Archaeological Reports (British Series)193 (ed. J. Price and P.R. Wilson) pp. 3-20. British Archaeological Reports, Oxford.

Cunliffe, B. (1974). *Iron Age Communities in Britain*. Routledge and Kegan Paul, London.

Cunliffe, B. (1988). *Greeks, Romans and Barbarians: spheres of interaction*. Batsford, London.

Gaunt, G.D. and Tooley, M.J. (1974). Evidence for Flandrian sea-level changes in the Humber estuary and adjacent areas. *Bulletin of the Geological Survey of Great Britain* 48, 25-41.

Hawkes, C.F.C. and Hull, M.R. (1947). *Camulodunum: first reports* on the excavations at Colchester 1930-9, Reports of the Research Committee of the Society of Antiquaries of London No. 14. London.

May, J. (1976). *Prehistoric Lincolnshire.* History of Lincolnshire Committee, Lincoln.

Pryor, F.M.M. (1984). *Excavations at Fengate, Peterborough, England: the fourth report,* Northamptonshire Archaeological Society Monograph No.2. Northampton.

Stead, I.M. (1976). *Excavations at Winterton Roman Villa and other sites in North Lincolnshire 1958-67,* Department of the Environment Archaeological Report No. 9. HMSO, London.

14

The Humber frontier in the first century AD

J. Creighton

Introduction

In AD 43 the Claudian forces crossed the Channel, bringing closer into Rome's sphere of interest a series of political units which were developing in Iron Age Britain, such as the Trinovantes, the Catuvellauni, the Iceni and the Corieltauvi. In many ways the internal workings of these tribes can never be known to us. Even their very names are by no means immune to academic scrutiny and revision (Tomlin 1983). Nevertheless, historical sources do point to a complex political scene requiring flexibility in its manipulation by the Roman conquerors. The actual form this contact took varied from clientship (the Iceni) to straightforward annexation (the Trinovantes and Catuvellauni). Unfortunately, in the case of the Corieltauvi the historical sources fail to reveal quite how this territory fell into Roman hands. However, what can be told from the archaeological evidence is that by *c.* AD 47 the Roman army had extended its occupation to cover the entire length and breadth of Corieltauvian territory. By AD 50 the Ninth Legion had moved forward to be based at Lincoln. A military presence was also established at Old Winteringham on the banks of the Humber, indicated by specific types of metalwork, building and road construction (Stead 1976), and on the Lincolnshire Wolds a fort was built at Kirmington, at a date as yet unknown, but probably between *c.* AD 47 and *c.* AD 70 (Fig. 14.1).

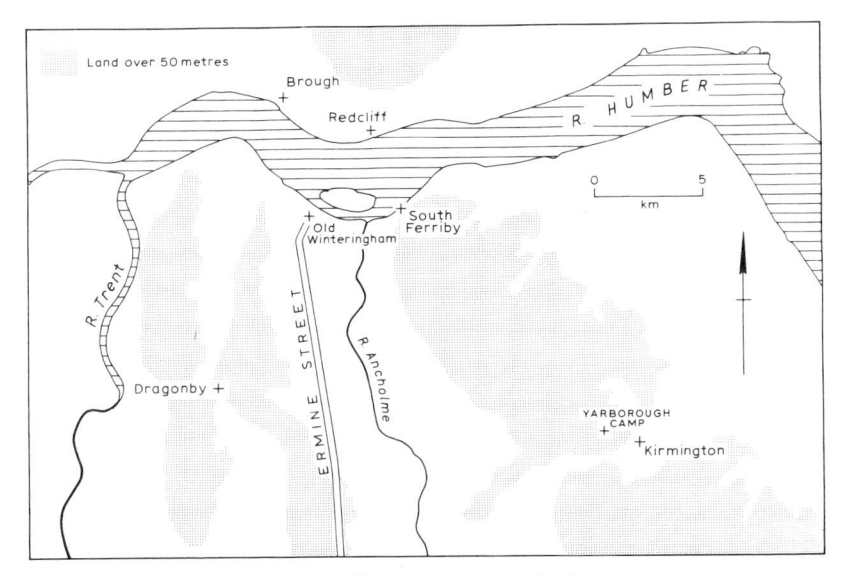

Fig. 14.1. The main Iron Age and Roman settlements in the area.

The Humber, even before the Roman invasion, had represented the boundary between two distinct Iron Age societies. To the south, Corieltauvian society was developing large nucleated settlements at sites like Dragonby, Kirmington, Sleaford and Ancaster (May 1976a), whereas to the north, in the area identified with the Parisi, no settlements of this complexity can be identified. On the other hand, before the invasion this area showed itself to be a cohesive cultural entity by the existence of a very distinctive burial rite, the square-barrow tradition, the best known element of which was the earlier Yorkshire Wold chariot burials (Stead 1965, 1979). The Humber boundary was also where the Romans decided to halt their advance north. Twenty years or so were to pass before the armies moved across the estuary, building forts at Brough, Hayton and Stamford Bridge as they made their way north towards York. This advance took place *c*. AD 70, perhaps under the governorship of Vettius Bolanus or Q. Petilius Cerealis, but again the historical record is unclear.

This chapter considers the effect of the Humber frontier on the communities of this area during the late Iron Age and the ensuing Roman 'frontier' and 'post-frontier' periods by examining particular categories of sites and finds. The quality of the data may be highly variable, particularly with regard to unstratified surface finds that have been accumulated without rigorous and compatable methodologies. Nevertheless, significant patterns and trends do emerge, which are best seen as relating directly to events and processes in the first century AD, rather than to inherent biases or weaknesses in the data.

The sites

Figure 14.1 illustrates the main sites in the discussion. Dragonby and Old Winteringham are located on the Lincoln Edge, with Kirmington and South Ferriby taking up corresponding positions on the Lincolnshire Wolds, while on the north bank only two Iron Age/early Roman settlements of any size are known, Brough and Redcliff (North Ferriby).

In order to begin to investigate social change, it needs to be seen how these settlements reacted to the political changes that were taking place at the time. Did sites contract or expand in response to changing circumstances? This question is most easily answered for the north bank sites. Redcliff and Brough seem almost chronologically exclusive. Brough had a late start, with the earliest coin known being a *dupondius* of Vespasian (AD 69-79) (Wacher 1969), whereas Redcliff begins at a much earlier date, with Republican and Neronian coins occurring (Crowther and Didsbury 1988). The imported pottery tells the same story. Figure 14.2 shows the forms of Terra Nigra and Terra Rubra found on the sites. Redcliff mainly comprises material showing a Claudian and Neronian emphasis, whereas Brough is only represented by Form 16, a late type which is commonly found in early Flavian contexts on military sites in the north. It is at this early Flavian date (AD 69-81) that the archaeological material from Redcliff markedly tails off, suggesting that Redcliff was replaced as the north bank harbour at the date of the advance north, and the establishment of a fort at Brough.

In contrast, neither Dragonby, South Ferriby, Kirmington nor Old Winteringham can be said to have been occupied during quite such discrete periods. The simple examination of the presence or absence of various forms of pottery is not of help here, since all four sites have

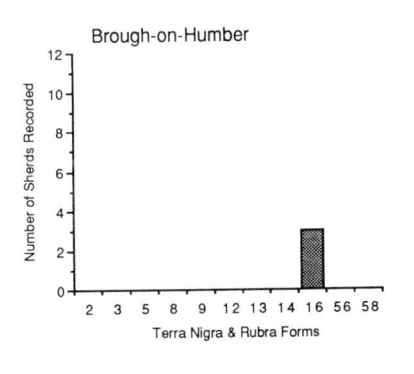

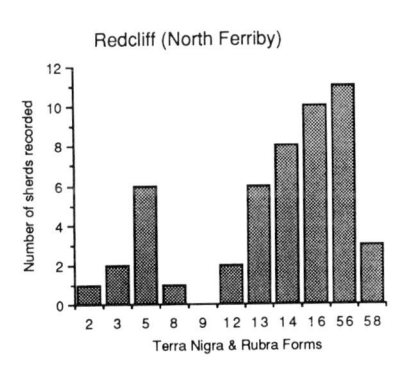

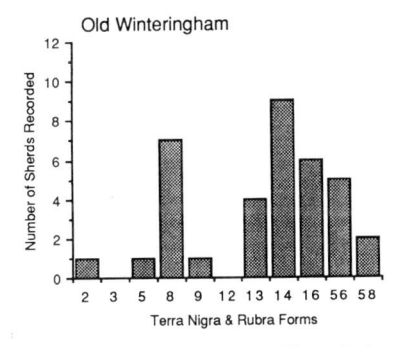

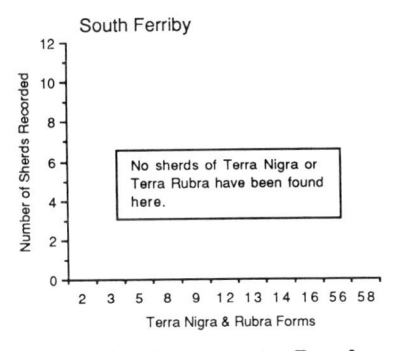

Fig. 14.2. Terra Nigra and Terra Rubra from sites on the Humber bank. Data from Wacher (1969), Stead (1976) and Crowther and Didsbury (1988); typology from Hawkes and Hull (1947).

turned up material of Iron Age, frontier and post-frontier date. Also, not all the sites have been excavated; both Kirmington and South Ferriby lack the large ceramic assemblages which have been acquired through excavation at Dragonby and Old Winteringham (May 1970, Stead 1976). However, fieldwalking and metal-detecting coverage has accumulated a body of data which allows comparisons between sites, especially on the basis of Iron Age coins and bow brooches.

The Iron Age coins

The Corieltauvi had developed their own coin series well before the Roman invasion. Their silver series started off uninscribed, derived from the Gallo-Belgic C and British I series. However, some time in the first century AD, names start to appear on the coinage, for example AVN COST, VEP CORF and DVMN TIGIR (Allen 1963). These have often been taken to illustrate the names of rulers or, when more than one name appears on the coin, joint magistrates. Despite their native Iron Age origins, certain hoards show that many of the coins continued in circulation beyond AD 47 into the Roman period in some areas. The Lightcliff hoard (near Halifax) contained many Corieltauvian coins hoarded together with Roman *denarii* which dated to the invasion, and the Honley hoard (near Huddersfield), from nearby, contained five inscribed coins and 18 *denarii* of which the latest were of the emperor Vespasian (AD 69-79) (Whitwell 1982). This means that Iron Age coins on their own need not imply a pre-conquest site. However, a site with a higher proportion of uninscribed (earlier) to inscribed (later) coins may have been occupied more intensively at an earlier date than a site with a lower proportion. On this basis, Figure 14.3 indicates that the youngest site is Old Winteringham, showing an even higher proportion of inscribed coinage than the Claudian/Neronian site at Redcliff. South Ferriby, Kirmington and Dragonby appear to have relatively older assemblages.

The brooches

There are large assemblages of bow brooches from the sites, ranging from a collection of 89 from Dragonby to 155 from Old Winteringham. These numbers provide a data base which it is possible to examine methodically in an attempt to build a chronological view of the varying brooch use and loss on a site. This has been done by creating a 'brooch profile' for each site, using a method similar to one often used on Roman coinage (cf. Casey 1980). The technique is derived from Brown (1986).

Each assemblage has been divided up into a series of brooch types, each of which has been assigned to a certain date range (Fig. 14.4a). However, the chronology of Roman brooches is by no means firmly established, and these date ranges, derived from Mackreth (1973) and Brown (1986), are not definitive. It should be noted that in the brooch typology used here, the 'La Tene 3' category includes a number of Nauheim derivatives and early Colchester types.

The Humber frontier in the first century AD

Site Finds (as a percentage)

(35) South Ferriby	
(80) Kirmington	
(33) Dragonby	
(39) Redcliff	
(36) Old Winteringham	

% Inscribed   % uninscribed

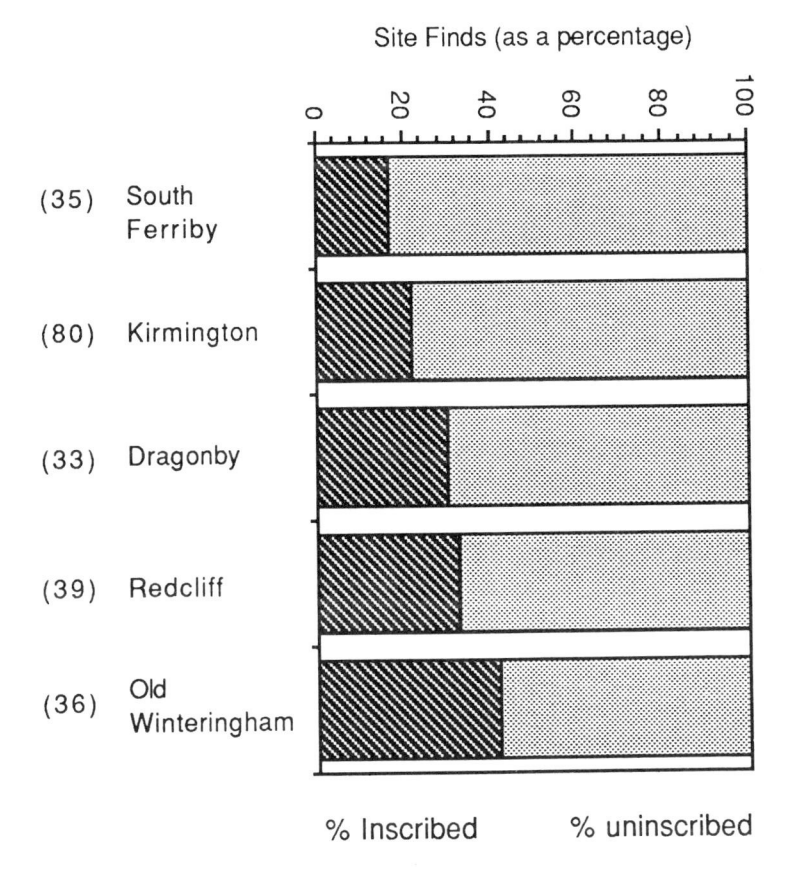

Fig. 14.3. Corieltauvian coinage. Figures in brackets indicate number of coins at each site. Data from May (1984).

A 'factor value' is established for each type of brooch per site using the following equation:

$$\text{Factor value} = \left(\frac{f}{t}\right)\left(\frac{1000}{N}\right)$$

where f = number of brooches of a specific brooch type
       t = time span of a specific brooch type
       N = total number of brooches from the site.

The latter half of this equation standardises the data from different

188   *Humber Perspectives*

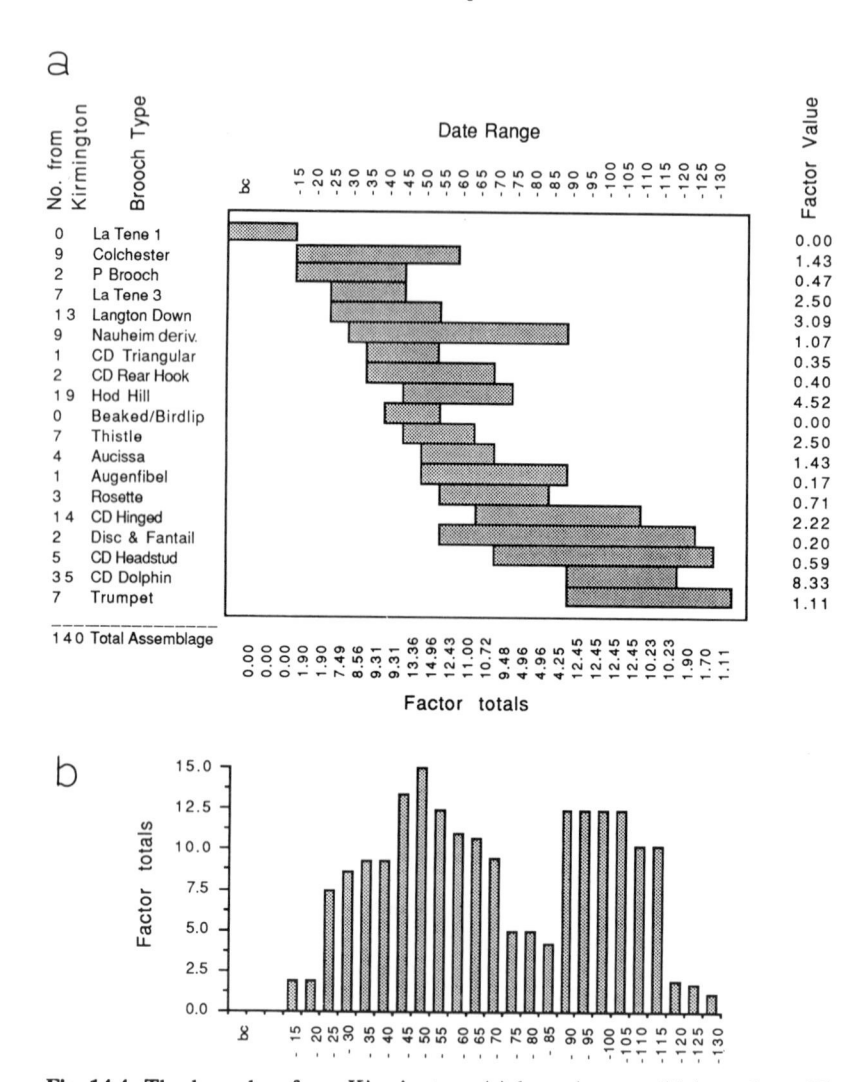

a

No. from Kirmington	Brooch Type	Factor Value
0	La Tene 1	0.00
9	Colchester	1.43
2	P Brooch	0.47
7	La Tene 3	2.50
13	Langton Down	3.09
9	Nauheim deriv.	1.07
1	CD Triangular	0.35
2	CD Rear Hook	0.40
19	Hod Hill	4.52
0	Beaked/Birdlip	0.00
7	Thistle	2.50
4	Aucissa	1.43
1	Augenfibel	0.17
3	Rosette	0.71
14	CD Hinged	2.22
2	Disc & Fantail	0.20
5	CD Headstud	0.59
35	CD Dolphin	8.33
7	Trumpet	1.11
140	Total Assemblage	

Factor totals: 0.00, 0.00, 0.00, 1.90, 7.49, 8.56, 9.31, 13.36, 14.96, 12.43, 11.00, 10.72, 9.48, 4.96, 4.25, 12.45, 12.45, 12.45, 10.23, 1.90, 1.70, 1.11

b

Fig. 14.4. The brooches from Kirmington: (a) brooch type, (b) brooch profile. Brooches from Scunthorpe Museum and the private collection of Alan Harrison.

sites, at which the total number of brooches may differ, and therefore enables direct comparisons to be made between different site lists. For each time slice, all the factor values of current brooch types are then added up, resulting in factor totals which can be plotted against the time slices to give a 'brooch curve'. These values in effect represent the number of brooches being lost on a site, varying through time. The curve for Kirmington is shown in Figure 14.4b. The other three sites produced similar curves, indicating that the basic shape of the curve is more a factor of brooch production and supply to the area than a function of the history of the individual sites. However, the curve shapes do show some differences, and an average curve was therefore constructed from the four sites, weighting each equally in order to examine how each site deviates from it. The results are shown in Figure 14.5, the vertical scale being the deviation from the average line, quantified in terms of the standard deviation of the data. There is a mathematical problem with this method; strictly speaking one should not use a standard deviation around a mean created from standardised data (for example percentages), since this does not take into account the variability in the error margins of the individual values which went to create the mean. Nevertheless, the results show a consistency which suggests that it is a useful exercise.

From the turn of the century until c. AD 60 the predominantly positive residuals at Dragonby indicate a higher rate of loss than that indicated by the four-site-average. This is in keeping with it being a major Iron Age centre. However, from c. AD 60 the residuals are all negative, indicating relatively less brooch activity. The gradual decline from high to low activity takes place from c. AD 50-90 and perhaps indicates Dragonby's relative decline in importance after it was by-passed by Ermine Street, the new direct route to Old Winteringham, probably constructed c. AD 50.

Kirmington shows almost the reverse picture to Dragonby. From about AD 50 it enters into a period of increased activity, with growth tailing off c. AD 90. The final three negative residuals are less easy to interpret, as they are based on only a small sample of late bow brooches (the Headstud and Trumpet brooch-types) continuing in use after the main fashion for bow brooches had died out. Otherwise this growth accords with a nucleated Iron Age settlement which, through growth and increasing prosperity, developed into a thriving Romano-British small town.

Old Winteringham shows minimal activity before AD 45, after which it is the scene of a sudden rise in brooch use and loss. This phenomenon lasts from AD 45-70, the period when the archaeological evidence suggests a military presence at the site, and a time at which

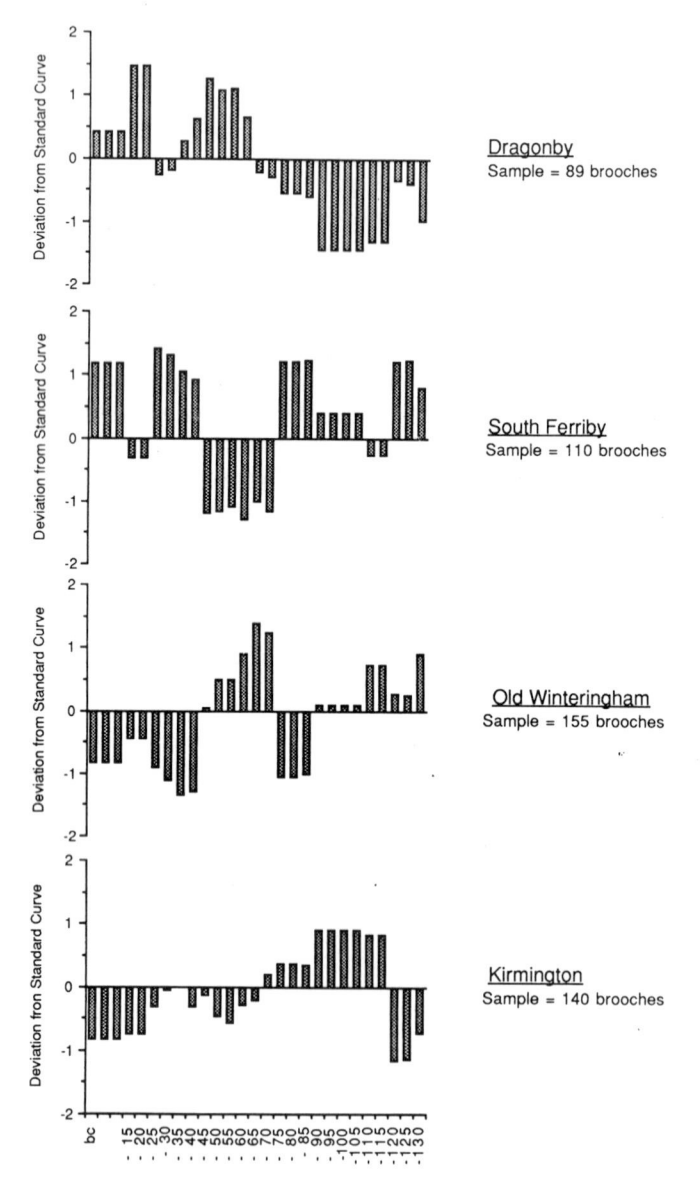

Fig. 14.5. Deviation of brooch profiles from the average profile.

the Humber still acted as a frontier. The northward move of the army to Brough and beyond in c. AD 70 is shown by a marked but short-lived decline. By AD 90 the curve is again positive, corresponding to the establishment of the settlement as a minor town at the end of Ermine Street.

Up until the Roman invasion the residuals at South Ferriby are largely positive. This is in keeping with the site's interpretation as a major Iron Age centre, as also suggested by the presence of a couple of large early Iron Age coin hoards (Allen 1963). The frontier period (c. AD 45-70) appears to have treated the site badly, with a marked decrease in activity, contrasting with Old Winteringham's increase. From then on the site re-established itself.

A model of settlement change

The above observations can now be drawn together with the other archaeological evidence to create a dynamic model of settlement change in the area in the first century AD.

Phase 1: the late Iron Age (pre c. AD 47)
Dragonby can claim to have been a major Iron Age centre on the basis of the spread of material over 20 acres, the dating of the material, the excavations conducted there (May 1970) and the brooch analysis. Kirmington, alas, has not been excavated. However, at 50 acres, it has a larger spread of material than Dragonby. The Iron Age coins show an early bias, and the brooch analysis shows a site in a continual state of growth. Also in the vicinity of the site is the banked enclosure of Yarborough Camp (Fig. 14.1), and the site of the find of the Ulceby hoard of gold torcs and horse trappings (May 1976b). Unfortunately, much of the site at South Ferriby has now been lost to the Humber, but when it was washed away at the turn of the century a lot of metalwork was recovered. This included a couple of large Iron Age hoards dating to before the appearance of the inscribed issues. Even without the hoards, the ratio of inscribed to uninscribed coins found from the site lies heavily in favour of it being an early establishment. The brooches indicate strong activity before the Roman conquest.

Old Winteringham has the latest coin assemblage and also has minimal brooch activity in its pre-conquest phase. When Stead excavated the site in 1964-5 he stated 'The coins and pottery suggest that the settlement was founded about the middle of the first century AD, and it seems likely that the Romans occupied a virgin site' (Stead 1976 p. 18). Excavations were also carried out in 1981-2 by Humberside Archaeological Unit, producing mainly third and fourth century AD material. In a brief statement of what was found it was said that '... numerous surface finds recorded over many years suggest that the settlement extended over some 70 acres and was preceded by an Iron Age settlement of some size' (Whitwell 1983 p. 103). However, since neither excavation demonstrated major Iron Age occupation, and since the surface collection of brooches and coins has a demonstrably late bias, the argument for a major Iron Age site at Old Winteringham is found wanting.

If Dragonby, Kirmington and South Ferriby were the three major Iron Age sites in the area, it is interesting to note that they are almost equidistant from each other (Fig. 14.1), each exploiting its own hinterland without encroaching on its neighbour. Between these sites there must have been many smaller farmsteads. One example was found beneath Winterton Villa (Goodburn 1980), and one suspects that many other villas in the area also had Iron Age origins. Little material culture from the Parisi can be noted on the south side of the Humber, and only a few sites on the north bank have turned up any Dragonby style wheel-made pottery (Halkon this volume). Since Redcliff appears to start sometime in the Claudian period, no major pre-frontier settlements are known on the north bank, suggesting that exchange between the Corieltauvi and Parisi was at a minimum.

Phase 2: the frontier period (c. AD 47-70)
At this time Old Winteringham was established as a new settlement on a virgin or near-virgin site. The archaeological evidence suggests some kind of military presence, although no actual fort has ever been identified. The early section of the Roman coin-list is amply represented, with 22 pre-Claudian coins as well as many Claudian bronze copies (A. Harrison pers. comm.). Military metalwork is present, including some auxiliary scale armour, and the types of building construction revealed in the 1964-5 excavations were considered by Stead (1976) to be consistent with military occupation. Fine pottery was imported to the site, including Terra Nigra and Terra

Rubra from the Low Countries (and also possibly from southeast Britain) as well as some South Gaulish Samian. The brooch analysis is consistent with this picture, showing an intense burst of activity during this phase.

This new imposition must have had a dramatic effect on the pre-existing situation. The new road to Old Winteringham, Ermine Street, by-passed the old major centre of Dragonby, and the latter's brooch data indicate that a decline set in. At South Ferriby the brooch activity also declines dramatically relative to the earlier period. Both sites therefore appear to have suffered from the creation of Old Winteringham. Such a decline due to a new nearby military site may be seen elsewhere in the country, for example the decline in Bagendon's importance due to the nearby new foundation at Cirencester. In contrast, the Kirmington brooch evidence shows continued growth, perhaps due to the creation here of a Roman fort. This was only recently discovered by aerial photography, and as yet it has not been archaeologically dated. Thus there was a situation where new Roman military sites were disrupting the existing settlement hierarchy.

At the same time changes were starting on the north bank with the establishment of Redcliff. If there was little trade across the river before, why should a trading site on the north bank have become necessary? Part of the answer must surely lie in the increased richness of the material culture on the south bank relative to the north. In this context the position of the Parisian élite on the north bank can be postulated by reference to some models of social change used for a later period in history (Hodges and Whitehouse 1983 p. 92):

> The most effective means of enhancing chiefly status is to establish a trade partnership with another leader who can offer prestigious commodities in exchange for goods raised by taxation. Trade partnerships of this kind are of signal importance for developing economies for they offer a possibility of swiftly accelerating the political position of the leader ... As the volume of trade increases between the trade partners, Kings or Chiefs inevitably are forced to confine the commerce to specific trading places. If they do not, the commodities may be siphoned off to subjects who can afford such things, and the initial

purpose of the exchange system will be defeated. Thus in many complex pre-market societies there are administered trading settlements that may appear to be colonies because they are mostly inhabited by alien merchants, and yet in terms of jurisdiction they are urban communities belonging to the native élite. Historians know such sites as emporia ...

Seen in such terms, Redcliff would have been a kind of regulated trading centre on the north bank, engaged in a trading partnership with the Roman Empire to the south (see also Crowther *et al.* this volume). The assemblage of Terra Nigra and Terra Rubra forms from this site matches extremely well with that of Old Winteringham (Fig. 14.2), suggesting that the source of supply to them both was the same, or conversely that the Redcliff material was all imported across the Humber from Old Winteringham itself. The date limits of Redcliff seem to fit in very closely with the parameters of this phase, which suggests that the site's whole *raison d'être* was based on the Humber operating as a frontier. Had the site been primarily an agricultural rather than trading settlement, it could be expected to have continued after this phase as a farmstead, villa or agricultural village. The current excavations at Redcliff are beginning to shed further light on the site's economic role (Crowther *et al.* this volume).

The temporary decline in brooch activity at South Ferriby could possibly be related to this controlled exchange between Old Winteringham and Redcliff. No Terra Nigra or Terra Rubra has been recorded from South Ferriby, although this may be more a factor of recovery than any kind of real absence. A ceramic assemblage is therefore badly needed in order to see how this non-military site fared on the frontier during this period; was it receiving prestige goods similar to those at Old Winteringham and Redcliff, or was it being politically left out in the cold?

Phase 3: the frontier moves forward (c. AD 70-80)
When the Roman army crossed the Humber in *c.* AD 70, Redcliff lost its *raison d'être* and was superceded by a new creation at Brough. A 4.5 acre auxiliary fort was built here, and remained in full occupation until *c.* AD 80 (Wacher 1969). It is not known when the military occupation at Old Winteringham ended, but AD 70 seems as good a

time as any, since to have two military bases only a mile or so apart on each side of the river may have been rather excessive, although by no means impossible. The brooch data imply a decrease in activity between AD 70 and 85, which might indicate this two-decade-old creation suffering in its turn at the hands of Brough.

Life seems to have resumed at South Ferriby; its naturally advantageous position at the end of a trackway along the Wolds, with access along the rivers to a large number of new markets, must have helped it. It may also have provided Kirmington with its easiest access to the sea. Judging from the brooch evidence, Kirmington itself continued to grow, while Dragonby continued to decline. The latter site's role as a market centre seems to have been largely usurped by Old Winteringham. Its by-passing during the construction of Ermine Street, and Old Winteringham's closer proximity to the river system, may have been the leading factors.

Phase 4: the Roman Civitates (c. AD 80 onwards)
Old Winteringham and Kirmington eventually developed into Romano-British small towns. Presumably, by AD 80 there would have been little need of a fort at Kirmington, and both sites would have continued as civilian settlements. South Ferriby has a coin list which would imply a similar development, but since the site has now been lost to the Humber the size of the settlement can only be speculated upon. Dragonby, however, does not appear to have turned into a small town, although the published details would certainly warrant describing it as an important agricultural village, possibly with iron production continuing to be an important factor in its existence. The auxiliary fort at Brough was abandoned around AD 80, and a civilian settlement seems to have slowly developed there. Along the Humber other settlements grew up, possibly taking advantage of the new trading and supply routes forming within the province. For example, at the mouth of the River Ancholme a site turning up late first and second century AD material is known at South Ferriby Brickyard (Loughlin and Miller 1979), and wasters found from the site indicate pottery production. Further upstream another settlement appeared, this time on the north bank at Faxfleet (Sitch this volume). Trade and exchange along the Humber would appear to have been on the increase. In the countryside Iron Age farmsteads developed into villas, for example Winterton (Stead 1976,

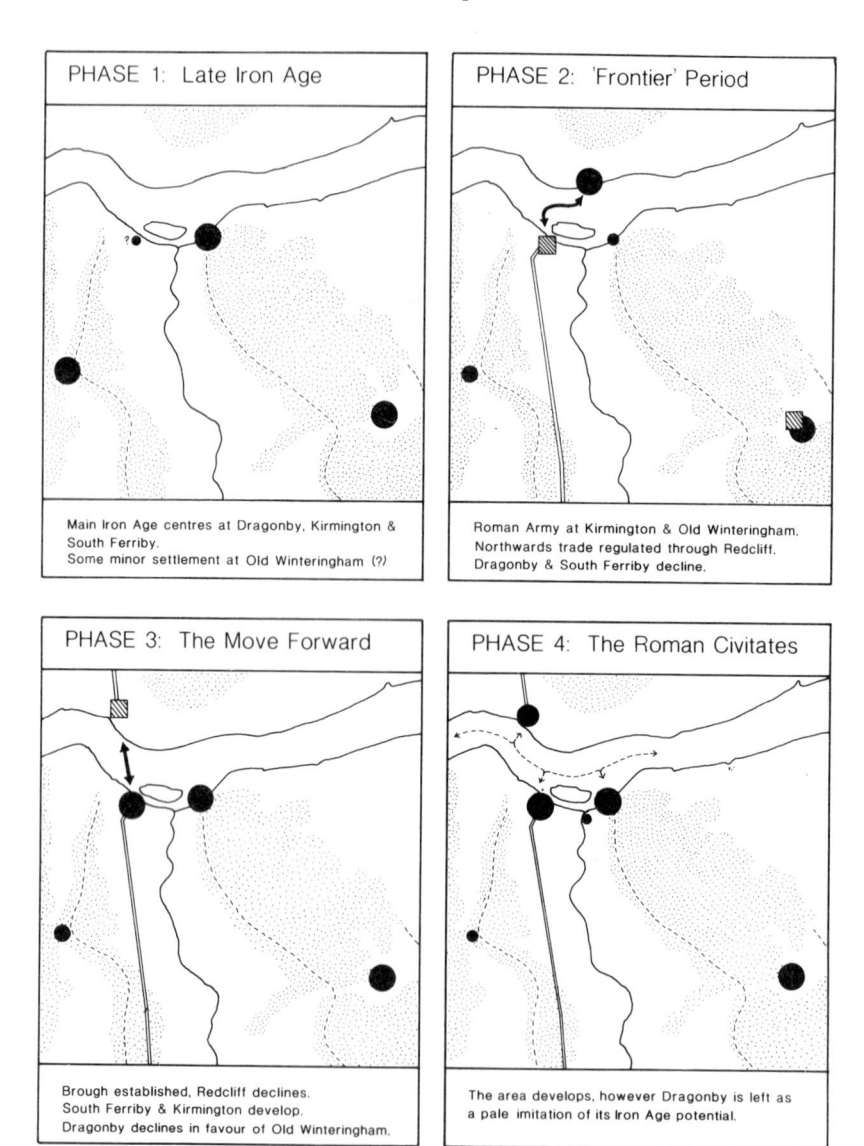

Fig. 14.6. A model of settlement change in the first century AD.

Goodburn 1980), so that by the third and fourth century the area was materially very rich and densely occupied.

The model, summarised in Figure 14.6, attempts to draw together many kinds of archaeological data. As the excavation reports of Dragonby, Redcliff and Old Winteringham appear, this model may have to be revised or discarded. Until then, however, it is offered as a framework within which to view the changing landscape of the upper Humber during the years of the Roman conquest.

Acknowledgements

I would like to thank David Crowther and Kevin Leahy, of Hull and Scunthorpe Museums respectively, for allowing me to examine their collections of material, as well as Alan Harrison who allowed me access to his own private collection. I must also thank Jeffrey May for letting me see some of the Dragonby material before its publication. Much of the research for this paper was conducted during a Sites & Monuments Record enhancement project for Humberside Archaeology Unit, sponsored by the Manpower Services Commission.

References

Allen, D.F. (1963). *The Coins of the Coritani*, Syllogue of the Coins of the British Isles 3. British Museum, London.

Brown, R.A. (1986). The Iron Age and Romano-British settlement at Woodcock Hall. *Britannia* **17**, 1-58.

Casey, P.J. (1980). *Roman Coinage in Britain*. Shire Publications, Aylesbury.

Crowther, D. and Didsbury, P. (1988). Redcliff and the Humber. In: *Recent Research in Roman Yorkshire*, British Archaeological Reports (British Series) 193 (ed. J. Price and P.R. Wilson) pp. 3-20. British Archaeological Reports, Oxford.

Goodburn, R. (1980). Winterton. *Lincolnshire History and Archaeology* **15**, 80.

Hawkes, C.F.C. and Hull, M.R. (1947). *Camulodunum*. The Society of Antiquaries, London.

Hodges, R. and Whitehouse, D. (1983). *Mohamed, Charlemagne and the Origins of Europe*. Duckworth, London.

Loughlin, N. and Miller, K.R. (1979). *A Survey of Archaeological Sites in Humberside*. Humberside Libraries and Amenities, Hull.

Mackreth, D. (1973). *Roman Brooches*. Salisbury and South Wiltshire Museum, Salisbury.

May, J. (1970). Dragonby: an interim report on excavations on an Iron Age and Romano-British site near Scunthorpe, Lincolnshire, 1964-9. *Antiquaries Journal* **50**, 222-45.

May, J. (1976a). The growth of settlement in the Later Iron Age in Lincolnshire. In: *Oppida: the beginnings of urbanisation in Barbarian Europe*, British Archaeological Reports (Supplementary Series) 11 (ed. B. Cunliffe and T. Rowley) pp. 163-79. British Archaeological Reports, Oxford.

May, J. (1976b). *Prehistoric Lincolnshire*, History of Lincolnshire 1. History of Lincolnshire Committee, Lincoln.

May, J. (1984). The major settlements of the Later Iron Age in Lincolnshire. In: *A Prospect of Lincolnshire* (ed. N. Field and A. White) pp. 18-22. N. Field and A. White, County Offices, Lincoln.

Stead, I.M. (1965). *The La Tene Cultures of Eastern Yorkshire*. Yorkshire Philosophical Society, York.

Stead, I.M. (1976). *Excavations at Winterton Roman Villa and other sites in North Lincolnshire*, Department of the Environment Archaeological Reports No. 9. HMSO, London.

Stead, I.M. (1979). *The Arras Culture*. Yorkshire Philosophical Society, York.

Tomlin, R.S.O. (1983). Non Coritani sed Corieltauvi. *Antiquaries Journal* **63**, 353.

Wacher, J.S. (1969). *Excavations at Brough-on-Humber, 1958-61*, Research Report 25. Society of Antiquaries, London.

Whitwell, J.B. (1970). *Roman Lincolnshire*, History of Lincolnshire 2. History of Lincolnshire Committee, Lincoln.

Whitwell, J.B. (1982). *The Coritani: some aspects of the Iron Age tribe and the Roman Civitas*, British Archaeological Reports (British Series) 99. British Archaeological Reports, Oxford.

Whitwell, J.B. (1983). Old Winteringham. *Lincolnshire History and Archaeology* **18**, 103.

15

Exploitation of the alluvium of the lower Hull valley in the Roman period

P. Didsbury

Introduction

The historically and archaeologically attested landscapes of the lower Hull valley are the result of human interaction with, and modification of, a physical infrastructure of extremely recent origin. The River Hull may have originated as a pro-glacial stream, running south along the western margin of the retreating Dimlington Stadial ice sheet (Sheppard 1956, Catt this volume), and, in common with other drainage channels in the Humber basin in the early post-glacial (Flandrian or Holocene) period (Gaunt and Tooley 1974), appears to have undergone a phase of pronounced fluvial incision, cutting through great depths of glacial deposits in response to the low sea level then occurring in the estuary. Indeed, in parts of the Hull valley the till has been completely eroded, so that post-glacial deposits rest directly upon the Upper Cretaceous chalk (de Boer *et al.* 1958). As higher temperatures began to melt the ice sheet, sea level in the Humber estuary rose quite rapidly, from a postulated -18 m OD at *c*. 8000 years ago to -9 m OD at *c*. 7000 years ago, and ultimately there commenced processes of alluviation within the deeply incised channels which have continued to the present day. In addition, rising ground-water encouraged the formation of peat deposits in various parts of the valley, those in the south being subsequently overlain by alluvium of estuarine origin. The soil map of the area (Soil Survey of England and Wales 1983) shows ground-water gleys of the Wallasea 1 association developed in alluvium and extending approximately as far north as Beverley, where they begin to give way to more organic-rich ground-water gleys on the mixed alluvium and fen peat of Downholland 3, which dominates most of the rest of the valley, thereby permitting a convenient division of it into upper and lower parts.

Human activity in the area may thus be seen as responses to a physical base comprising two main elements - first, the heavy, clayey till margins of the valley, interspersed with better drained areas of coarser textured glaciofluvial deposits, such as those on which the villages of Cottingham and Leconfield are sited, and second, the valley floor itself, where a partially eroded morainic topography is submerged beneath alluvium once supporting either saltmarsh or freshwater fen, and through which protrude higher 'islands' of till, as at Sutton, Tickton and Wawne. Clearly, any consideration of human activities in the valley must take close account of the geomorphological changes to which it has been subject throughout the Flandrian, changes which affect not only the interpretation of archaeological material, but also its very availability. Thus, a 'peat and bog oak' layer occurring between -9.15 and -11.58 m OD at the Market Place, Hull (Gaunt and Tooley 1974) represents an early Flandrian mixed-forest environment which may well have been exploited by later Mesolithic groups before the onset of estuarine conditions *c.* 7000 years ago. There is in fact no period from the early Flandrian to the eighteenth century AD (Harris 1959) in which the valley, whatever its morphological state, would not have represented a rich variety of floral and faunal resources (reeds, peat, grazing, wildfowl, fish) to nearby populations. However, our expectations regarding the exploitation of its lower areas often depend very much on what can be learnt of settlement on its higher and drier clay and gravel components where the archaeological evidence is more accessible, and not deeply buried beneath later overburden.

In her studies of the historical topography of the East Yorkshire wetlands, Sheppard (1956, 1958) envisaged little human activity in the valley before the Anglo-Saxon period, when the till was supposed to have witnessed the first large-scale clearance of its natural forest cover; the area of estuarine alluvium south of Beverley was considered to have occupied an arm of the Humber until early medieval times (Fig. 15.1), and the freshwater fens in the central part of the valley were thought to have been unattractive to early populations. The valley had lain outside the collecting areas of such nineteenth century fieldworkers as J.R. Mortimer and Canon Greenwell, and the lack of archaeological data available to June Sheppard was reinforced by then current archaeological opinion as to the late exploitation of the heavy lowland clays of eastern England. In the last 30 years, however, this picture has been radically altered by increased archaeological fieldwork; the lowland tills of northeast England were probably as intensively settled as lighter upland soils by the first century AD (Hazelgrove 1984), and prehistoric and Romano-British exploitation of wetland environments is now evidenced from several parts of England and Wales (Thompson 1980). The history of forest clearance is now also more fully understood (Flenley this volume). It is the intention of this chapter to illustrate briefly some of the ways in which archaeological discoveries and research over the past three decades have altered our perceptions of the exploitation of the alluvium in the lower Hull valley in the Roman period.

Archaeological work

The present writer has suggested elsewhere, in the course of a general survey of the archaeology of the lower Hull valley at this period (Didsbury 1988), that a large part of the alluvium upon which Hull and its suburbs now stand was available for exploitation by the beginning of the first millennium AD. That this might be the case first became apparent during the author's collation of recorded finds of Roman material in the city in an attempt to understand the setting of a second to fourth century AD site at Greylees Avenue on the west bank of the River Hull, excavated by Hull Museums in 1984 (Crowther and Didsbury 1985). Museum and literature search quickly raised the number of finds from the seven recorded by Loughlin and Miller (1979) to over fifty, consisting for the most part of small collections of potsherds or single coins.

The discovery of Roman pottery during the course of excavations in Hull's Old Town had already led to speculation about the possibility

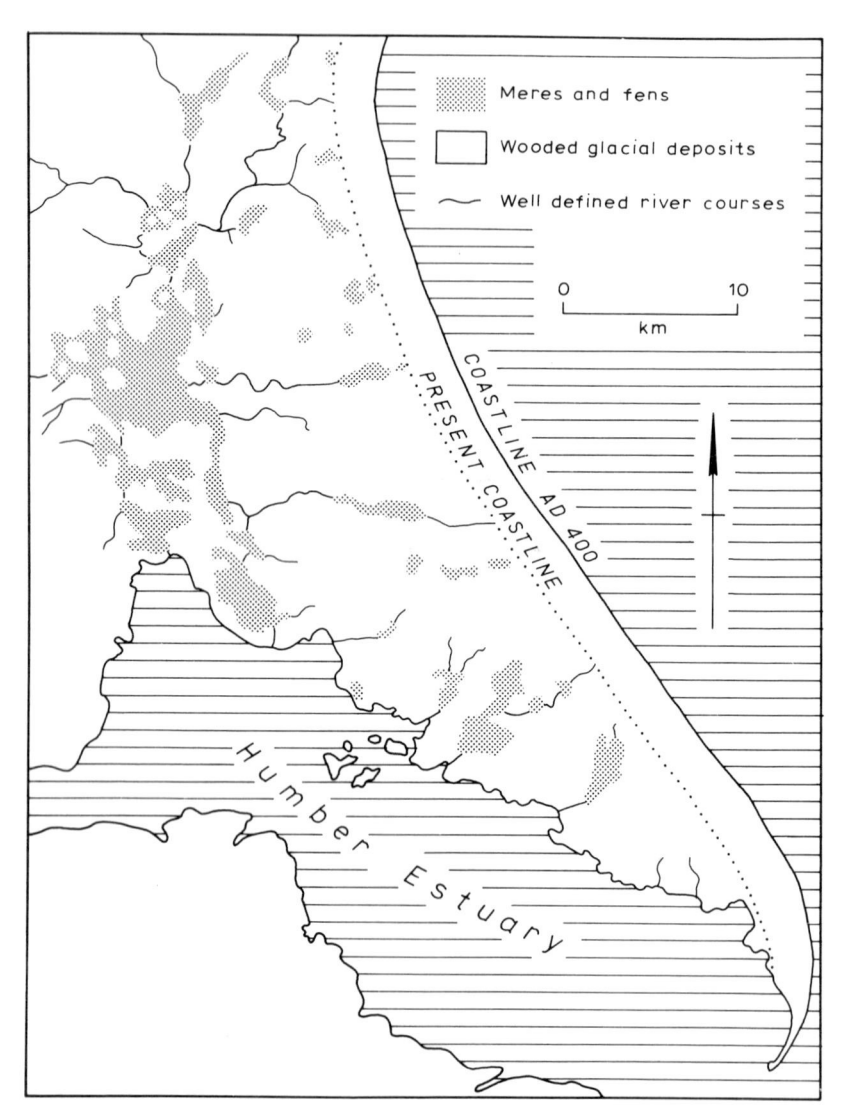

Fig. 15.1. Holderness in AD 400 (after Sheppard 1956).

of a Roman land surface sealed by later alluvium in parts of the city (Bartlett 1971), but it is clear from Museum archives that Roman *coins* found in the city had generally been explained away as modern or 'souvenir' losses, and no systematic attempt had been made to record them. Souvenir deposits can be a real problem, as Casey (1985) has demonstrated, and the Second World War serviceman returning from foreign parts and casually disbursing coins with which to confuse the numismatic record is probably not an entirely spectral figure. However, invoking him in respect of an entirely unremarkable coin from the Trier mint, excavated from some depth in the garden of a house which the finder had occupied for over 30 years, is a clear indication that negative expectation was acting to influence the response to archaeological data (*Hull Museums Correspondence* - unpublished correspondence between J. Bartlett and T. Heroneau, October 1959). There proved in fact to be almost no indication of anything extraordinary in the Hull coin list compiled by the present author; only one coin, a loosely provenanced third century billon *tetradrachm* from Alexandria (Lonsdale 1966), was eventually excluded from consideration, and, after close examination of a variety of factors which might have occasioned deposition, it seemed reasonable to conclude that the majority of these coin finds represented original site losses.

A map lodged at Hull Museums showing the location of boreholes within the city and the depth of till deposits beneath the alluvium had suggested to Peter Armstrong in the 1970s (pers. comm.) the possibility of a link between areas of higher relief and Romano-British findspots, but the small amount of material then known allowed no definite conclusions to be drawn. The new body of evidence, however, when plotted on to a map of the alluvium-buried till surface prepared by Valentin (1957), also from borehole data, suggested that a statistical correlation between finds of Roman material and the height of the till was indeed observable. To summarise this evidence briefly (Didsbury 1988), analysis suggested that alluvial areas over till lying higher than -3.8 m OD were probably no longer permanently under water in the Roman period, and constituted a surface capable of being settled or otherwise managed almost a millennium earlier than suggested by Sheppard.

The pattern of fluctuation of Mean Sea Level in the Humber estuary appears very similar to that around the coasts of northwest

England (Gaunt and Tooley 1974), which can be reconstructed in some detail (Tooley 1980). Where levels can be compared directly with those in northwest England they appear to be some 4 m lower, the latest period for which this systematic difference can be demonstrated being in the Iron Age - the 'Lytham VIII' transgression cycle of Tooley (1980). If it were maintained subsequently, then Mean Sea Level at the beginning of the Roman period could have been as low as -3 m OD in parts of the Humber estuary. Wacher (1969) postulated a Mean Sea Level of -1.6 m OD at Brough in the later third century AD. Although it is impossible to be more precise than this, both figures may serve to illustrate the range of sea levels in question. In view of the fact that two-thirds of the estuarine alluvium have an underlying till surface between 0 and -3.8 m OD (Fig. 15.2), it is clearly not far-fetched to suggest that by the Roman period, after several thousand years of alluvial deposition, parts of it could have afforded an 'inhabitable' surface.

It is well to remember that Sheppard's judgement as to the date at which the alluvium had first afforded an inhabitable land surface was itself also an essentially archaeological one, relying not on geomorphological data, which were lacking, but on the fact that historical documentary evidence for the beginning of settlement around the end of the first millennium AD was at that time contradicted by no known body of pre-medieval archaeological material. There now exists, however, a substantial and gradually expanding data base which can be coherently interpreted in the light of the present state of knowledge of the valley's morphology, and which future work may do more to elucidate. It may be noted here that a considerable number of boreholes has been sunk in Hull since Valentin's investigations, and these would allow a refinement of his mapping of the till surface, thereby providing an invaluable aid to the future interpretation of Romano-British material from the city.

Until very recently the only proven settlement sites of the period in the extreme south of the Hull valley were situated on the till islands of Sutton and Wawne; round buildings and enclosures probably belonging to the first century AD (although whether they pre- or post-date the Roman conquest is uncertain) had been excavated by John Bartlett and the East Riding Archaeological Society at Saltshouse Road in 1962 (Hull Museums 1966, Challis and Harding 1975), and a 12 m length of ditch containing third century Roman pottery had been

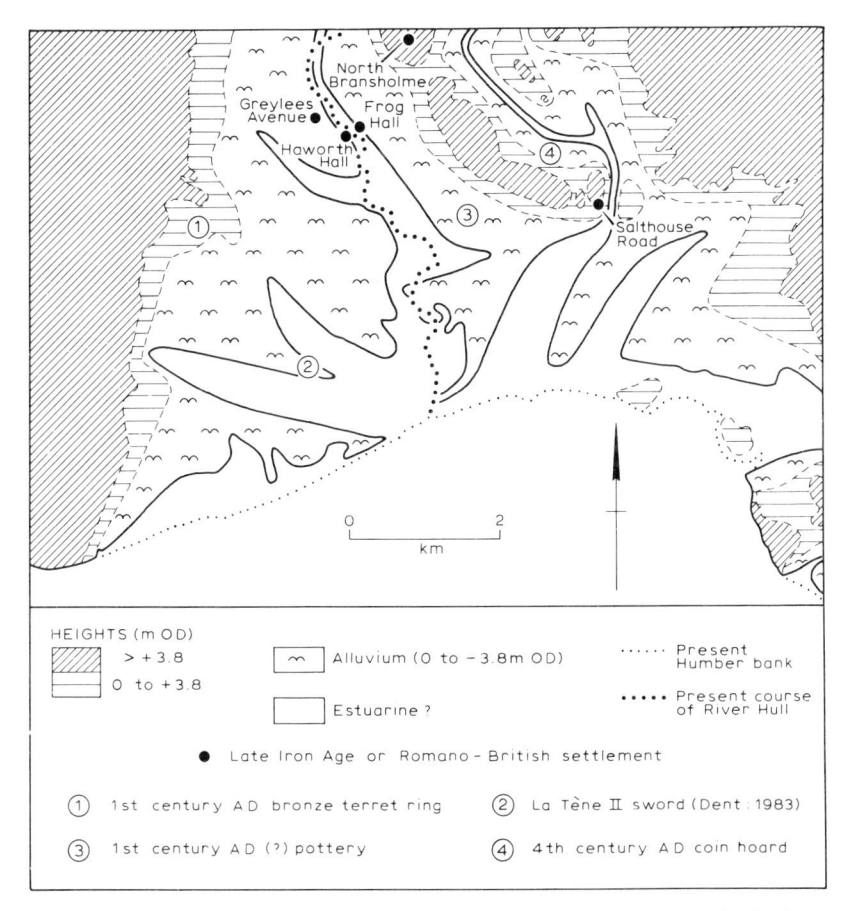

Fig. 15.2. Late Iron Age and Romano-British settlements and findspots in the lower Hull valley.

recorded by Peter Armstrong at North Bransholme in 1975 (Fig. 15.2). Although Romano-British pottery had also come to light at several places along the banks of the River Hull in the 1960s, notably at Haworth Hall and Frog Hall (Fig. 15.2), these finds appeared anomalous in terms of the geomorphological state of the lower valley as then perceived, and were largely ignored, although Eagles (1979) suggested that at Haworth Hall a slight eminence near the water's edge may have been used as a seasonal fishing or wildfowling establishment. Although such interpretations seemed an inadequate response to both the quantity and quality of pottery involved, it was not until excavations by Hull Museums in 1984 at Greylees Avenue (Fig. 15.2) that actual settlement close to the present course of the river in the Roman period could be demonstrated (Crowther and Didsbury 1985).

The nature of the exploitation

Unstratified material at Greylees Avenue suggested activity there from perhaps the late first century AD, and the excavated portion of an apparently extensive ditch system was receiving dumped pottery by as early as $c.$ AD 180, continuing as a visible earthfast feature appropriate for the disposal of various classes of domestic rubbish until the later fourth century. Apart from constituting the earliest evidence for drainage/land-management in this marginal landscape, the ditches and their contents offered a tantalising glimpse of settlement on the alluvium and the possible economic strategy being practised there. The large quantity of bone material, though not yet fully analysed, would be consistent with primary butchery on a site at least partly involved in animal husbandry, and the nature of dumped building materials may indicate the presence of a Romanised establishment in the vicinity.

Whatever the precise course of the River Hull during the Roman period, it seems that sites such as Haworth Hall and Greylees Avenue must have been essentially riparian, and that by the late second century there was almost linear occupation along stretches of the lower Hull, similar to that along Roman roads in the region. Such sites would have been well placed to command river transport facilities as well as the rich ecological resources of broad tracts of saltmarsh well suited to the summer pasturing of livestock. Indeed, some degree of exposure to both the regional and international trade characterising the Humber at this period (Sitch this volume) is suggested in the ceramic record at Greylees Avenue, the former by large quantities of (shell-tempered) Dalesware from Lincolnshire in an early third century context, and the latter by, among other possible imports, a greyware bowl with a horizontally inturned rim which has as its closest parallel a mid second century form from Speicher in

Germany (V. Rigby pers. comm.).

Perhaps the most interesting aspect of the alluvium in the first four centuries AD is the possibility that it was being exploited in the interests of animal husbandry in much the same way, and from similar settlement foci, as in the twelfth and thirteenth centuries when, as Blashill noted as long ago as 1892, the meadows and pastures (ings and carrs) upon which the city of Hull now stands had been of economic importance not only to settlement on the till island of Sutton, but also to areas of already 'ancient enclosures and tillage' along the east bank of the River Hull. As Figure 15.2 suggests, this pattern of settlement and economy may have recapitulated what had been the case during the earlier period, a parallelism which Boon (1980) has also noted in the Gwent Levels of southeast Wales. The first century AD settlement at Saltshouse Road, where large amounts of animal bone indicate an at least partly pastoral economy, is excellently sited to have exploited the differing resources of the till and the alluvium. A further environmental attraction of the area may be suspected from the name of the pastures to the east of the site in the late twelfth and thirteenth century, for references in the Chronicle of Meaux Abbey (Rolls Series 1866-8) to 'in salinis de Suttona' suggests that 'les Saltz' may have referred specifically to the presence of pits for the evaporation of salt (Med. Lat. *salinum*), rather than simply to areas of saltmarsh grazing (Smith 1937).

Whether such economic activity characterised the area in the early first millennium AD, as in the second, must remain speculative, but that parts of the carrlands surrounding the Sutton clays were similarly accessible in both periods has recently received confirmation with the discovery in 1987 by Tony Bibby, of seventeen bronze coins between the North and East Carrs (Fig. 15.2). The coins all date from the period AD 330-5, and those with legible mint marks come from western mints (B. Sitch pers. comm.). There are indications that the coins were originally in *rouleaux*, and they undoubtedly represent the remains of a hoard which, unlike the other hoards in the vicinity, had been buried not in the till, but in alluvium with an underlying till surface higher than -3.8 m OD. The find suggests not only the probability of undiscovered settlement of this period on the adjacent till itself, but also that these lower areas in the fourth century were still in a state which made it both possible and appropriate to conceal coin there in the reasonable expectation of its later recovery.

Unfortunately, although we can now demonstrate settlement along the banks of the Hull and on the islands of till throughout the Roman period, there is still insufficient evidence to judge how settlement and economic activity may have developed during those four centuries. The few finds of late Iron Age date from the alluvium (Fig. 15.2 findspots 1-3) suggest, on the face of it, that exploitation of this deposit was a post-conquest development. It should be borne in mind, however, that Roman artefactual material, especially coinage, is far more likely to be recognised, and thus be reported, than, say, an abraded sherd of hand-made Iron Age pottery. It remains likely, nevertheless, that the economic management of the alluvium received its greatest stimulus from the imposition of the Roman economy. While this may imply no more than the need to produce a surplus in order to pay taxes, it should be remembered that military involvement in the development of similar estuarine tracts for stockraising has been demonstrated in the Wentlooge and Caldicot Levels in Gwent (Boon 1980, Allen and Fulford 1986), and it is possible that the existence of large tracts of rich potential grazing within the hinterland of *Petuaria* (Brough), some 11 km to the west, would not have gone unnoticed by the authorities there. There is, as yet, no evidence to show whether a road heading eastnortheast from *Petuaria,* and visible on aerial photographs as far as Swanland (Ramm 1973, Loughlin and Miller 1979), continued any further, but if it did it could well have reached the higher alluvial area somewhere in the north of present-day Hull, serving such sites as Greylees Avenue and linking *Petuaria* with an economically valuable resource base.

References

Allen, J.R.L. and Fulford, M.G. (1986). The Wentlooge Level: a Romano-British saltmarsh reclamation in South-east Wales. *Britannia* **17**, 91-117.

Bartlett, J. (1971). The Medieval walls of Hull. *Kingston upon Hull Museums Bulletin 3 & 4*, 1-28.

Blashill, T. (1892). *Sutton in Holderness and the Monks of Meaux.* British Archaeological Association, London.

Boon, G.E. (1980). Caerleon and the Gwent Levels in early historic times. In: *Archaeology and Coastal Change* (ed. F.H.

Thompson) pp. 24-36. Society of Antiquaries, London.
Casey, J. (1985). Roman coinage of the fourth century in Scotland. In: *Between and Beyond the Walls: essays on the prehistory and history of North Britain in honour of George Jobey* (ed. R. Miket and C. Burgess) pp. 295-304. J. Donald, Edinburgh.
Challis, A. and Harding, D.W. (1975). *Later Prehistory from the Trent to the Tyne,* British Archaeological Reports (British Series) 20. British Archaeological Reports, Oxford.
Crowther, D.R. and Didsbury, P. (1985). Excavation of a Romano-British ditch at Greylees Avenue, Hull. In: *CBA Forum 1984-5* pp. 11-16. Council for British Archaeology Group 4, Hull.
de Boer, G., Neal, J.W. and Penny, L.F. (1958). A guide to the geology of the area between Market Weighton and the Humber. *Proceedings of the Yorkshire Geological Society* **31**, 157-209.
Dent, J.S. (1983). The impact of Roman rule on native society in the territory of the Parisi. *Britannia* **14**, 34-44.
Didsbury, P. (1988). Evidence for Romano-British settlement in Hull and the Lower Hull Valley. In: *Recent Research in Roman Yorkshire,* British Archaeological Reports (British Series) 193 (ed. J. Price and P.R. Wilson) pp. 21-35. British Archaeological Reports, Oxford.
Eagles, B.N. (1979). *The Anglo-Saxon Settlement of Humberside,* British Archaeological Reports (British Series) 68. British Archaeological Reports, Oxford.
Gaunt, G.D. and Tooley, M.J. (1974). Evidence for Flandrian sea-level changes in the Humber estuary and adjacent areas. *Bulletin of the Geological Survey of Great Britain* **48**, 25-41.
Harris, A. (1959). *The Open Fields of East Yorkshire.* East Yorkshire Local History Society, York.
Haselgrove, C. (1984). The Late Pre-Roman Iron Age between the Humber and the Tyne. In: *Settlement and Society in the Roman North* (ed. P.R. Wilson, R.F.J. Jones and D.M. Evans) pp. 9-27. Bradford University and Yorkshire Archaeological Society.
Hull Museums (1966). *Recent Archaeological Discoveries from East Yorkshire,* Hull Museums Publications 216. Hull Museums, Hull.

Lonsdale, A. (1966). Recent finds. *Transactions of the Yorkshire Numismatic Society* **2**, 63-5.

Loughlin, N. and Miller, K.R. (1979). *A Survey of Archaeological Sites in Humberside.* Humberside Libraries and Amenities, Hull.

Ramm, H. (1978). *The Parisi.* Duckworth, London.

Rolls Series (1866-8). *Chronica monasterii de Melsa.*

Sheppard, J.A. (1956). The Draining of the Marshlands of East Yorkshire. Ph.D. thesis, University of Hull.

Sheppard, J.A. (1958). *The Draining of the Hull Valley.* East Yorkshire Local History Society, York.

Smith, A.H. (1937). *The Place Names of the East Riding of Yorkshire and York.* English Place Name Society, Cambridge.

Soil Survey of England and Wales (1983). *Soils of England and Wales, Sheet 1, Northern England.* Ordnance Survey, Southampton.

Tooley, M.J. (1980). Theories of coastal change in Northwest England. In: *Archaeology and Coastal Change* (ed. F.H. Thompson) pp.74-86. Society of Antiquaries, London.

Valentin, H. (1957). Glazialmorphologische Untersuchungen in Ostengland. *Abhandlungen der Geographische Institut der Freien Universitat, Berlin* **4**, 1-86.

Wacher, J.S. (1969). *Excavations at Brough-on-Humber, 1958-61,* Research Report 25. Society of Antiquaries, London.

Part III
URBAN ORIGINS AND DEVELOPMENT

16
The archaeology of the Grimsby-Cleethorpes area
P.J. Wise

Introduction

The adjacent towns of Grimsby and Cleethorpes lie at the mouth of the Humber estuary on the Lincolnshire Marsh, a narrow strip of coastal plain which stretches to the Lincolnshire Wolds some 10 km to the southwest. The majority of the plain comprises Skipsea Till (Catt this volume), which reaches the sea at Cleethorpes as a low eroded cliff. Along the coast to the north and south of Cleethorpes are estuarine alluvial deposits of clays and silts. This location must always have been attractive for trade and settlement for immigrants crossing the North Sea or travelling up the east coast of England. Fish was readily available in the estuary, salt could be produced on the beach, while the hinterland could support a variety of agriculture. It is somewhat surprising, therefore, that the area has received little attention from professional archaeologists; it has been left very much to local amateurs to collect and salvage the area's archaeology. This chapter aims to synthesize their efforts.

Prehistory

The first settlers in the area are likely to have been Neolithic farmers about 4000 BC, who would have found the coastal plain covered by

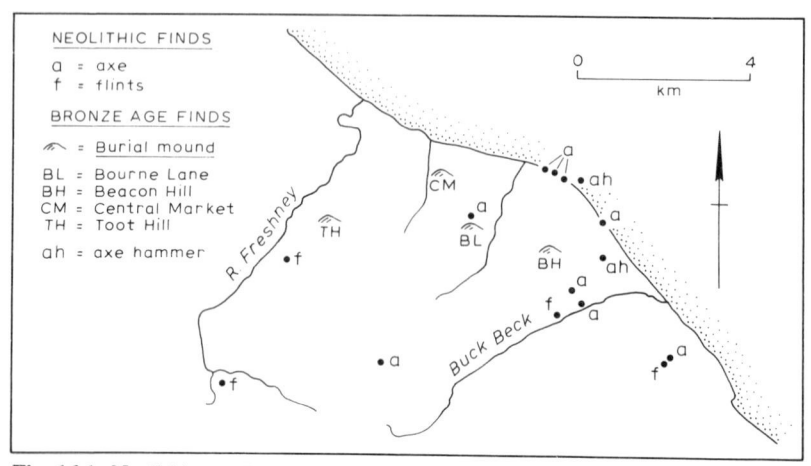

Fig. 16.1. Neolithic and Bronze Age finds from Grimsby and Cleethorpes.

broad-leaved woodland of oak, birch and alder (Flenley this volume). The stumps of these trees are very occasionally revealed at exceptionally low tides on Cleethorpes beach. The prevailing climate during this period was warmer and drier than that of the present and hence there could have been quite large islands of dry ground within the coastal marshes. The main evidence for human occupation is the ground stone and flint axes found right across the coastal plain (Fig. 16.1). An interesting cluster of eight is recorded from Grimsby-Cleethorpes, of which four are made of epidotised tuff from the Great Langdale axe factory in Cumbria, and two of flint, perhaps from Grimes Graves in Norfolk. Although these axes indicate that forest clearance was taking place, there is little evidence for settlement. One possible site is close to the River Freshney in Laceby parish, where two flint scrapers, a perforated bone pin and a few pottery sherds were found, while nearer the coast at Little Coates a similar riverside location produced microliths, flakes, cores, a plano-convex knife and a leaf-shaped arrowhead (Loughlin and Miller 1979). Occupation was also likely in the Humberston area, where flint implements have been found (Loughlin and Miller 1979). The evidence for burial practice is limited to a wooden cyst or 'rude dugout' with the possible remains of a cremation, discovered in Grimsby (Cooke 1898).

During the Bronze Age (2000-600 BC) the Grimsby-Cleethorpes area continued to be densely settled, although the archaeological evidence is almost exclusively from burial mounds (Fig. 16.1). Three round barrows are recorded, at Toothill (Little Coates), Beacon Hill (Cleethorpes) and Bourne Lane (Grimsby). Toothill was described in 1903 as being 'a huge mound with an irregular ground plan ... an elliptical contour (and) composed chiefly of sand and sandy clays' (Johnson 1912 p. 72). During its levelling for sand in the following year, a complete human lower jaw and an urn were recovered. Beacon Hill lies on a low morainic ridge and was excavated in 1935. In the centre was found a large collared urn which contained four smaller vessels as well as cremated remains and charcoal. Nearby there was a single small collared urn and a further secondary burial in the top of the barrow which may have been disturbed when the mound became a beacon in AD 1377 (Sheppard 1935). It is believed that there may be an undisturbed primary burial beneath the barrow and other secondary burials inserted into the body of the mound. The round barrow at Bourne Lane was destroyed by building work in 1948, when a collared biconical urn containing cremated bone and a bronze pin were recovered. An excavation beneath the barrow revealed a grave containing cremated bone and charcoal, but no pottery (Hannigan 1948).

It is quite possible that there were once other Bronze Age burial mounds in the Grimsby-Cleethorpes area. In 1825 the Reverend George Oliver opened two barrows in Little Coates, one of which contained 'charred wood and other marks of burning' and the other a 'broken urn and some bones' (Oliver 1825). It is interesting to note that in 1961 the small hill known as Holme Hill in Grimsby was flattened and a human skeleton uncovered (*Grimsby Evening Telegraph 1961*). However, two mounds at Old Clee, when excavated in 1959, were found to be the remains of a medieval kiln or saltern and a possible mill mound, neither with any evidence for burials (Hurst 1960).

As with the Neolithic evidence, there have been several finds of stone tools, the most significant being the recent discovery of an axe-hammer from the 'sunken forest' on Cleethorpes beach (Leahy 1986). The axe is made of quartz dolerite from the Whin Sill in Northumberland, and had been fitted with a poplar wood haft which gave a radiocarbon date of *c.* 1400 b.c. At least two other axe-

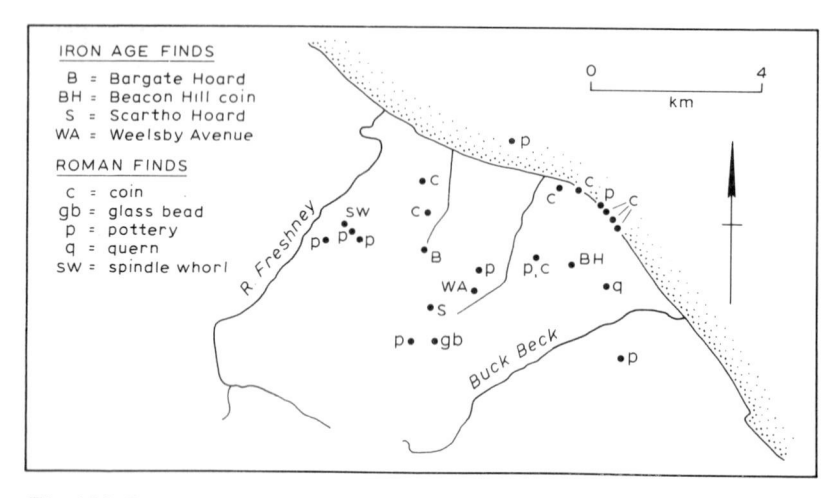

Fig. 16.2. Iron Age and Roman finds from Grimsby and Cleethorpes.

hammers have been found in the area.

By the Iron Age (600 BC-AD 43) the climate had become similar to that of the present time and colder, wetter conditions encouraged the formation of peaty fen. On a till spur projecting into the surrounding marshes in what is now Weelsby Avenue, Grimsby, a small Iron Age settlement was established during the first century BC (Figs 16.2 and 16.3). Excavations since 1976 by John Sills and Gavin Kinsley have shown that there were two distinct phases of occupation. During the initial, solely agricultural phase, the settlement consisted of an enclosure about 40 m square, formed by a single bank and ditch, the latter shallow and flat-bottomed with expanded terminals at the south-facing entrance. Within this earthwork were two roundhouses of differing diameters (9.5 and 5.5 m) and a four-poster granary. Evidence for cereal cultivation is provided by a fragment of rotary quern, and the large quantities of animal bone indicate the rearing of sheep, cattle and horses. The pottery from this phase is handmade and comprises a distinctive slack profile jar which comes in a variety of sizes. This pottery makes up over 90% of the total recovered from the site and is very similar to that produced in the Arras culture of the Yorkshire Wolds (see especially Danes Graves and Burton Fleming in Challis and Harding 1975 fig. 31, Stead 1979 fig. 33).

A number of changes define the second phase of the settlement,

Fig. 16.3. The Weelsby Avenue Iron Age Settlement being constructed on the site of the original in 1987.

the most significant being the introduction of bronze-working. Three dumps of metallurgical debris have been found in the fill of the enclosure ditch. This debris includes moulds, crucibles and slag, and from a preliminary analysis it appears that terret rings and bridle bits were being cast. The crucibles are of the typical three-cornered Iron Age type. There is also some evidence of iron-working, including a possible iron bloom. Elsewhere in the ditch a further dump of clay firebricks may have come from the kiln used to fire the clay moulds. Two other changes were the introduction of imported wheel-thrown pottery, and physical changes in the site's appearance, including the re-cutting of the enclosure ditch to form a major earthwork. Lastly, the inhabitants appear to have displayed human skulls at the entrance to the settlement, a practice also recorded at Bredon Hill, near Evesham, and Stanwick in Yorkshire (J. Sills pers. comm.).

Two hoards of Iron Age gold coins and two single finds are known from the area (Fig. 16.2). The first hoard was found in 1851 by a labourer excavating footings for a windmill in Scartho, and consists of two Gallo-Belgic and four British-type coins (Allen 1947). The second hoard was unearthed in 1954 in Bargate, Grimsby, and consists of four Gallo-Belgic type coins (Dolley 1955), with a fifth coin found separately in 1985. A single Corieltauvian coin dated *c.* AD 40 was found near Beacon Hill in 1937 (Allen 1963), while in the 1970s a stater was recovered from a load of topsoil thought to have come from Weelsby Road, Grimsby, not far from the Iron Age settlement (J. Sills pers. comm.). The six Gallo-Belgic coins were imported into the Grimsby region from either northern France or more likely southeastern Britain, which, following the establishment of Roman Gaul in the mid first century BC, enjoyed extensive trading contacts with the continent (Allen 1963, May 1976). The four British-type coins, plus a single find from West Ravendale parish on the Lincolnshire Wolds, date to *c.* 40-20 BC and are more common in the South Midlands and North Thames regions.

The concentration of Gaulish and south British coin types around Grimsby is also seen at Sleaford, a mint and major settlement site. The evidence would thus suggest the existence of a trading settlement at Grimsby, either at Weelsby Avenue itself or, as May (1984) has recently suggested, at an undiscovered site closer to the coast. The cultural affinities of such a settlement might well have been as close with the inhabitants of the north bank of the Humber as with those of the south. Boats capable of crossing the Humber had been in existence since the North Ferriby boats of the early Bronze Age (McGrail this volume), and by the late Iron Age the journey was probably made on a regular basis.

The Roman period

The evidence for the Roman period (AD 48-410) is difficult to assess because it is limited to chance finds of coins and pottery, and there have been no scientific excavations of possible settlement sites (Fig. 16.2). Most of the material found is probably evidence for farming activity, but there is the possibility that the finds from Cleethorpes beach may be linked to the salt industry, known especially from sites around Ingoldmells to the south. Whitwell (1982) has recently suggested the existence of a major Roman settlement in the Grimsby area which may even have served as a naval base in the late Roman period. He points to the similarity of the Freshney haven with other sites on the south bank, such as Barrow Haven, Goxhill Haven and

East Halton skitter, where Roman pottery has been found. A naval base at Grimsby would have been ideally placed to protect the entrance to the Humber estuary. Eight Roman coins have been found in the area, with the majority coming from Cleethorpes beach; the distribution comprises three first century AD, two second century and three fourth century coins.

A settlement site is believed to be located on a raised spur at Old Clee, where a quantity of grey ware sherds and a coin of Constantine I (AD 306-37) have been found. A second site is suspected near the Weelsby Avenue Iron Age Settlement, where a range of Romano-British pottery dating from the second to fourth centuries was found behind the Peaks Lane Fire Station. At Weelsby Avenue itself, a Roman field drain was found running along the north-facing line of the Iron Age enclosure ditch, although pottery evidence indicates that the Iron Age Settlement was abandoned some 50 years before the arrival of the Romans (J. Sills pers. comm.). The discovery of Romano-British pottery including Samian, Castor and shell-gritted wares between 1947 and 1950 points to the existence of a third settlement on a small knoll at Little Coates golf course (Loughlin and Miller 1979). Scattered finds of Roman material are also recorded from elsewhere in Little Coates (pottery and spindle whorl), and at Scartho (pottery and glass bead), Humberston (pottery) and Cleethorpes (quern). As well as five coins, Cleethorpes beach has produced a coarseware rim sherd and a mortarium sherd, to which can be added the pottery lamp dredged up from Grimsby Docks in 1930 (Loughlin and Miller 1979).

The Anglo-Saxon period

The archaeology of the area during the Anglo-Saxon period (AD 410-1066) is marked by an extreme paucity of evidence, which is possibly explained by a marine transgression across the coastal plain at the close of the Romano-British period. Settlement would thus have been restricted to the higher ground on the edge of the Lincolnshire Wolds, where two Pagan Saxon inhumation cemeteries of the fifth to seventh centuries are recorded at Welbeck Hill (Irby-on-Humber) and Laceby (Loughlin and Miller 1979). At Holton-le-Clay excavations near St Peter's Church revealed traces of a Middle Saxon occupation site on a raised mound of glacial till and sand. Associated with a layer of chalk fragments were animal bones, oyster shells and three sherds of an Ipswich Ware-type jar. From elsewhere on the site were recovered fragments of a maximum of twelve handmade vessels of the late seventh/eighth centuries (Sills 1982).

There is no other evidence for Anglo-Saxon settlement, despite the Saxon architecture of parts of Old Clee and Scartho churches and the Saxon place names of Brigsley, Great and Little Coates, Healing and Waltham. Scandinavian settlement of the area had certainly begun by AD 866, when, according to the twelfth century writer Geoffrey Gaimar, the Danes crossed the Humber at Grimsby on their way to attack York (Gillett 1970). Although Scandinavian place names are present at Bradley, Barnoldby, Laceby, Scartho and Weelsby, the only archaeological evidence for settlement in Grimsby before AD 1100 is a fragment of decorated bone comb from Brighowgate and two sherds of late Saxon Torksey ware (Hannigan 1957, G. Watkins pers. comm.).

The medieval period

The first archaeological evidence for Grimsby's medieval past was recorded in 1913, when 'historic stones' and 'a number of bones' were discovered at a site in the Old Market Place (*Grimsby News* 10 January 1913). The stones were believed to have come from St Mary's Church, a twelfth century building which was amalgamated with the present parish church of St James in 1586 and by 1600 had been demolished (Fig. 17.1 this volume). In the 1950s and 60s there were scattered finds of medieval pottery, such as the jug found in George Street in 1957 and a handle sherd from the Dock Offices in 1961 (*Grimsby Evening Telegraph* 6 July 1961, Loughlin and Miller 1979). More numerous were the finds from Brighowgate in 1957, which included a bone comb side plate, pottery of thirteenth to fourteenth century date, tiles, nails, animal bones and oyster shells (Hannigan 1957). In 1970 a building site between Victoria Street and Sanctuary Lane produced finds of Humberwares (*c.* 1300-1550), Cistercian Wares (*c.* 1500-1600) and Raeren Stoneware of fifteenth and sixteenth century date from the Rhineland. There was also a plain medieval floor tile and fragments of roof furniture (Trevitt *et al.*

1971). Two carved stone heads are known from Grimsby, one of thirteenth or fourteenth century date found near the site of the Austin Friary in 1969 and the other, probably earlier in date, from Wellowgate discovered in 1983 (*Grimsby Evening Telegraph* 19 August 1983). Most recently, in 1987, the writer recovered three sherds of Cologne-Frechen salt-glazed stoneware of sixteenth or seventeenth century date and a possible twelfth century jug shoulder sherd from a development site at 52 Victoria Street, Grimsby.

Excavations to find medieval Grimsby began in 1986 when members of the Humberside Archaeology Unit dug two trial trenches near the junction of the Riverhead and the West Haven at Baxtergate Car Park to locate the medieval waterfront. A sequence of waterfronts was discovered, including that associated with the eighteenth century widening and deepening of the Haven and an earlier structure of fourteenth century date some 15 m west of the present-day water's edge. Although disturbed, this medieval waterfront was of timber construction and may be compared with examples recorded from Hull, Norwich, King's Lynn and London (Fig. 16.4). Among the finds from the excavation were a decorated floor tile which may have come from the Austin Friary, various bronze clothes fittings, two fragments of animal bone with butchery evidence and several leather shoe fragments (B. Whitwell pers. comm.).

During the medieval period the Grimsby area is recorded as having a total of eight religious houses, that is two abbeys, two friaries, a nunnery, two hospitals and a hermitage. Such a concentration of religious houses can be compared elsewhere in Lincolnshire with Lincoln (19), Stamford (18), Boston (8) and Grantham (5), and indicates the importance of those in holy orders to the life of the town (Knowles and Hadcock 1953). None of the Grimsby houses was wealthy and several were frequently in debt. Only three of the houses have ever produced archaeological finds, the remainder being known solely from scattered and incomplete historical references (Victoria County History 1906, Knowles and Hadcock 1953, Gillett 1970).

The first religious house to be excavated was the priory of St Leonard, which was a nunnery established under the protection of Wellow Abbey before 1184 (Fig. 17.1 this volume). The site of the priory is now located near the College of Technology, and in 1962 a small area was examined which produced three burials, some pottery

Fig. 16.4. The medieval waterfront at Grimsby excavated in 1986.

sherds and an arch moulding with dog-tooth decoration (Caborn 1962). During the 1960s excavations were also conducted on the site of Humberston Abbey, a Benedictine house founded in *c.* 1160, where the remains of the abbey church, the warming room and other claustral buildings were found (Kirkby and Tailby 1974). As well as two coffined burials from the abbey church, an important assemblage of late medieval pottery was recovered from the reredorter drain. This has been discussed by Hayfield (1984), who noted the presence of jugs, urinals and cisterns in Humberwares and Toynton-Bolingbroke fabrics.

The location of the Austin Friary in Grimsby is shown on a map of 1600, the oldest surviving survey of the town. The friary lay in an area bounded by the West Haven, Flottergate and Sanctuary Lane (Fig. 17.1 this volume), land which has undergone major redevelopment since 1969 as the Riverhead Shopping Centre. In that year several discoveries of human bones were made in this area and these probably came from the Friary burial ground (*Grimsby Evening Telegraph* 3 July 1969, 7 October 1969). Also in 1969 a large quantity of pottery and a whetstone were recovered from a telephone cable trench at the corner of Flottergate and Sanctuary Lane. Unfortunately, the pottery from this site became mixed with a group of pottery from a site in Princes Avenue before full identification had been made. However, for convenience the assemblage will be referred to as the Austin Friary group. There are approximately 200 sherds, some of which have been published by Hayfield (1985).

The earliest pottery in the Austin Friary group are two sherds of late Saxon Torksey Ware (*c.* 825-1075) referred to above. From the twelfth and early thirteenth centuries comes a small amount of pottery including fine sandy wares from a probable central Lincolnshire source (Hayfield 1985), Scarborough Whitewares, including an aquamanile fragment, and a sherd of developed Stamford Ware. The period *c.* 1100-1400 is represented by sherds of coarse sandy wares produced at several sites on both sides of the Humber and shell-tempered wares from a kiln site near Lincoln. The majority are, however, orangewares of the later suspension glazed type dating to *c.* 1200-1350. Orangewares are known from both sides of the Humber, and Hayfield (1985), on the basis of a sub-group clustered around Grimsby, has suggested a kiln site somewhere in the vicinity. However, the Austin Friary orangewares have exact parallels with pottery found in Hull and Beverley, and it seems more likely that one central production site at Beverley supplied the distribution area (G. Watkins pers. comm.). Certainly there were trade links with Beverley, for in 1395 Grimsby's new town hall was built using bricks and roof tiles produced in Beverley (Gillett 1970). In 1970 finds made during construction work in Victoria Street included roof tile fragments of Beverley type (Trevitt et al. 1971). Also present in the Austin Friary group was a large quantity of Humberwares produced between c. 1300 and 1550 and coming in this case from kilns at either Thornton Curtis (Hayfield 1985) or Thornholme Priory (G. Watkins pers. comm.).

During 1987 exploratory excavations were conducted on the site of the Austin Friary at Baxtergate Car Park by the Humberside Archaeology Unit (B. Whitwell pers. comm.). Further sherds of Stamford Ware, shell-tempered ware, orangewares and Humberwares were recovered, as well as pottery from Beverley/Scarborough, Lincoln and Saintonge in southwest France. The excavation uncovered alternate clay floor surfaces and ash levels which, together with two possible stone bases for timber uprights, suggest a timber and wattle-and-daub building. Similar structures are known from Blackfriargate in Hull and Dyer Lane in Beverley, of twelfth and thirteenth century date. This building at the friary site may either be evidence for occupation before its foundation in 1293, or temporary accommodation while the masonry buildings of the friary were under construction, as at Guildford (Clarke 1984).

Conclusions

The archaeology of the Grimsby-Cleethorpes area is as rich and varied as the natural resources upon which local communities have relied for thousands of years. Much may have been destroyed, yet much remains for modern investigation and analysis; recent work at Weelsby Avenue and elsewhere shows what can be achieved.

Ten years ago Miller identified urban development as 'the single most significant threat to the archaeology of Grimsby' (Loughlin and Miller 1979 p. 228). Today new development is continuing within the area of the medieval borough, and the threat shows no sign of disappearing in the foreseeable future. Considerable opportunities for rescue archaeology will therefore exist, and it is to be hoped that sufficient resources will be available to record Grimsby's past before the evidence has gone forever.

Acknowledgements

I would like to express my thanks to Ben Whitwell and John Sills who read and commented upon draft versions of this paper. I have also received considerable help from Dave Tomlinson, Alison Williams, Linda Pinkham, Gareth Watkins, Kevin Leahy and Tony Page.

References

Allen, D.F. (1947). Ancient British coins from Lincolnshire. *Numismatic Chronicle 6th series* **7**, 65-8.

Allen, D.F. (1963). *The Coins of the Coritani,* Syllogue of the Coins of the British Isles 3. British Museum, London.

Caborn, E. (1962). A Report on the Excavations made on a Site near Nun's Corner, Grimsby in February 1962. Unpublished manuscript.

Challis, A.J. and Harding, D.W. (1975). *Later Prehistory from the Trent to the Tyne,* British Archaeological Reports (British Series) 20. British Archaeological Reports, Oxford.

Clarke, H. (1984). *The Archaeology of Medieval England.* Colonnade, London.

Cooke, J.H. (1898). Neolithic life in Lincolnshire. *The Naturalist,* 221-4.

Dolley, M. (1955). Grimsby treasure trove 1954. *Numismatic Chronicle 6th Series* **15**, 242-3.

Gillett, E. (1970). *A History of Grimsby.* Oxford University Press, London.

Hannigan, R.N. (1948). Bronze Age Site in Grimsby. Unpublished manuscript.

Hannigan, R.N. (1957). Archaeological notes. *Lincolnshire Architectural and Archaeological Society Reports and Papers, 103.*

Hayfield, C. (1984). A Late-Medieval pottery group from Humberston Abbey, South Humberside. *Lincolnshire History and Archaeology* **19**, 107-10.

Hayfield, C. (1985). *Humberside Medieval Pottery*, British Archaeological Reports (British Series) 140. British Archaeological Reports, Oxford.

Hurst, J.G. (1960). Medieval Britain in 1959. *Medieval Archaeology* **4**, 139-65.

Johnson, W. (1912). *Byways in British Archaeology*.

Kirkby, A.E. and Tailby, A.R. (1974). *The Abbey of St. Mary and St. Peter, Humberston, Lincolnshire*. Waltham Toll Bar School, Private publication.

Knowles, D. and Hadcock, R.N. (1953). *Medieval Religious Houses in England and Wales*. Longman, London.

Leahy, K. (1986). A dated stone axe-hammer from Cleethorpes, South Humberside. *Proceedings of the Prehistoric Society* **52**, 143-52.

Loughlin, N. and Miller, K.R. (1979). *A Survey of Archaeological Sites in Humberside*. Humberside Libraries and Amenities, Hull.

May, J. (1976). *Prehistoric Lincolnshire*, History of Lincolnshire 1. History of Lincolnshire Committee, Lincoln.

May, J. (1984). The major settlements of the Later Iron Age in Lincolnshire. In: *A Prospect of Lincolnshire* (ed. N. Field and A. White) pp. 18-22. N. Field and A. White, County Offices, Lincoln.

Oliver, G. (1825). *The Monumental Antiquities of Great Grimsby*. Isaac Wilson, Hull.

Sheppard, T. (1935). Bronze Age burials - Beacon Hill, Cleethorpes. *Lincolnshire Notes and Queries* **23**, 129-32.

Sills, J.A. (1982). St. Peter's Church, Holton-le-Clay, Lincolnshire. *Lincolnshire History and Archaeology* **17**, 29-41.

Stead, I.M. (1979). *The Arras Culture*. Yorkshire Philosophical Society, York.

Trevitt, E.H., Russell, E. and Russell, R. (1971). Archaeological notes. *Lincolnshire History and Archaeology* **6**, 12.

Victoria County History (1906). *Lincolnshire, Vol. 2*. Victoria Histories of the Counties of England, London.

Whitwell, J.B. (1982). *The Coritani*, British Archaeological Reports (British Series) 99. British Archaeological Reports, Oxford.

17

The historical development of Grimsby and Cleethorpes

R.W. Ambler

Introduction

The position of the adjacent settlements of Grimsby and Cleethorpes at the mouth of the Humber meant that the sea was a common influence on the lives of both communities. However, their development took different courses; although the inhabitants of those secondary settlements (or 'thorpes') of the ancient parish of Clee which were situated on the coast were involved in seafaring, especially fishing, it was Grimsby which developed as a port. In the second half of the nineteenth century Cleethorpes became a seaside resort and residential area linked to Grimsby as the growth of the port's population caused it to spread out of its ancient boundaries and into the parish of Clee. This chapter examines the development of both settlements from medieval times to the present day, focusing in particular on their economic functions.

The medieval period

Grimsby's haven provided a natural landing place for ships and the medieval town grew up at a point where a relatively high clay ridge,

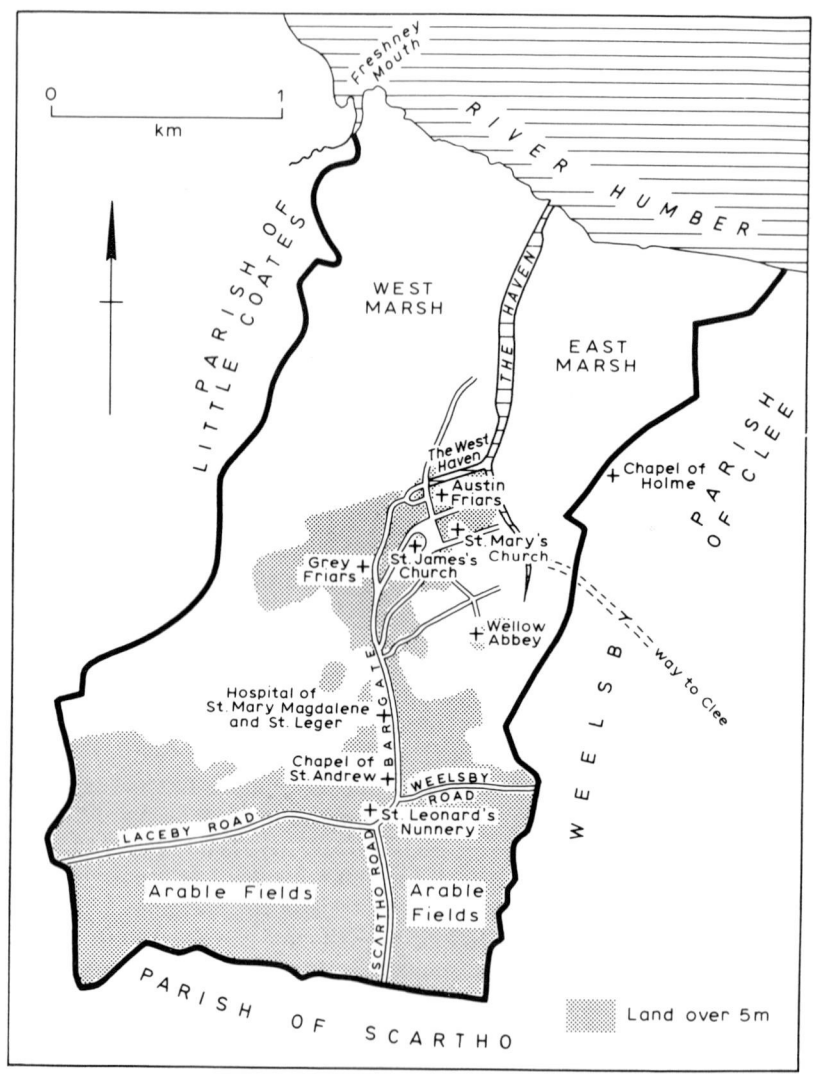

Fig. 17.1. Medieval Grimsby, showing the position of the town in relation to the 5 m contour. Sources: Gillett (1970), Public Record Office MP B/14, Plan of Grimsby *c.* 1600, unpublished maps based on Grimsby Bailiffs' extent books prepared by Mr E. Caborn.

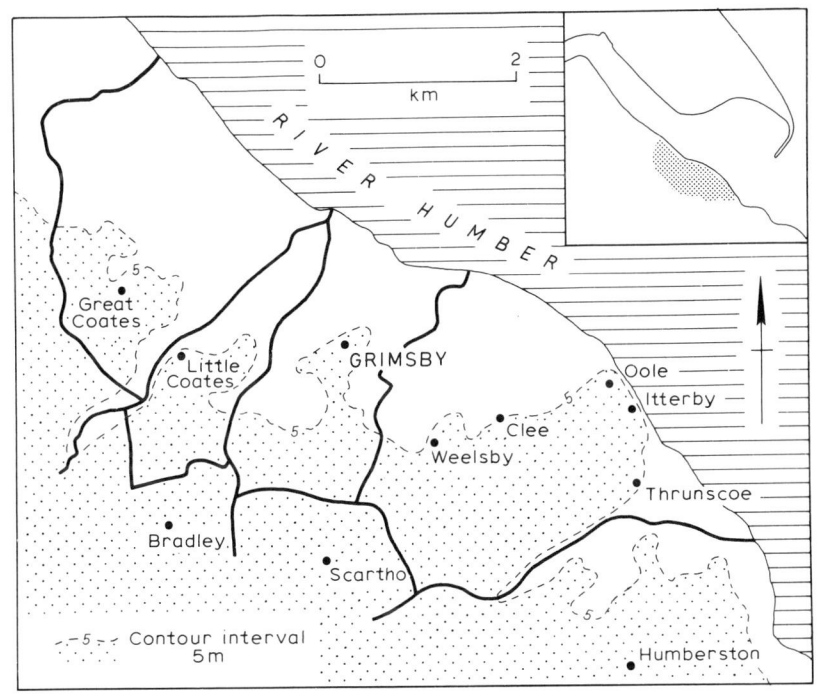

Fig. 17.2. The ancient boundaries of Cleethorpes, Grimsby, Great Coates and Little Coates.

marked by the 5 m contour, reached down to the waterside (Fig. 17.1). The shape of Grimsby's boundaries and its relatively small area of under 2000 acres, compared with over 3500 acres in Clee, suggest that the town, to which there are literary references as early as AD 866, may have been a later development between Clee to the east and Great and Little Coates to the west (Fig. 17.2). The natural advantages which Grimsby enjoyed did not mean that its haven was the only landing place in the area; goods were also brought ashore at various creeks and outfalls in neighbouring parishes, and the haven at the mouth of the Freshney stream on the boundary of Great and Little Coates continued to be important until the late fifteenth century (Gillett 1970). Grimsby was, however, the place to which these goods were taken to be traded, and in the 1270s the men of Walter de la Linde, lord of Laceby, and of Gilbert of Little Coates were said to be impeding their passage to and from the Freshney (Anon. 1812,

Gillett 1970).

Grimsby had already begun to be clearly distinguished as an urban settlement by late in the reign of Henry II (1154-89), when the town was first described as a borough and its inhabitants as burgesses (Stenton 1920, Hill 1965, Rigby 1982). By 1194 its customs and liberties were sufficiently well developed to be used for the new borough of Pontefract. These privileges and the right to hold an annual fair of 15 days were confirmed by two charters obtained from King John in 1201 (Gillett 1970, Rigby 1982). While Grimsby developed as a town the people of the neighbouring parish of Clee inhabited the scattered settlements of Itterby, Thrunscoe and Weelsby, with the village now known as Old Clee at their centre. Clee and these 'thorpes' of Clee were included in Domesday Book in 1086, while Hole (later known as Houll or Oole) is first mentioned in the early twelfth century (Figs 17.2 and 17.3).

The extent of the meadowland in Clee in Domesday Book is an indication of the rich natural resources which the area possessed and was a feature it had in common with Grimsby at this period (Foster and Longley 1924). In so far as the earlier organisation of the arable land of Clee and its thorpes can be inferred from a 1601 terrier of the parish's glebe land and a map of 1749, Old Clee, Thrunscoe and Weelsby each had separate open field systems while Oole and Itterby shared what became a three field system (Fig. 17.4). Weelsby's open fields had been enclosed by their owner, the nearby abbey of Wellow, by the early sixteenth century (Ambler et al. 1987). The 1601 terrier shows that all the arable open field land belonging to the vicar of Clee lay within the fields belonging to Old Clee, an indication that they represented the old core of the parish's farming system from which the church was first endowed, while the field systems of the thorpes developed later (Taylor and Taylor 1980, Lincolnshire Archives Office Glebe Terriers vol. 5 fols 221-2).

However, the people of Clee did not look only to these fields for their livings, and just as merchandise was being brought to Grimsby from neighbouring creeks and landing places, fish from Clee was also part of the trade of the borough (Anon. 1812). The fact that a tithe in fish was due to the monastery of Wellow from the chapel which had been established at Itterby for the convenience of the inhabitants of the coastal settlements is a further indication of its importance in the local economy (Owen 1975, South Humberside Area Record Office

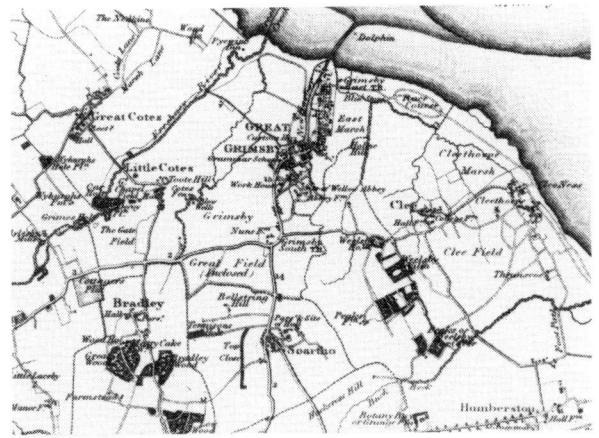

Fig. 17.3. Grimsby, Cleethorpes and district in the 1820s. The medieval core of Grimsby can be seen with the rectilinear new northern extension of the town into the East Marsh along the east side of New Harbor (*sic*). The village of Clee is shown as a distinct settlement, while two of the coastal thorpes of Clee are marked as Cleethorpe. Although they are not named on this map, Oole is to the north and Itterby to the south, while the largely deserted site of Thrunscoe is shown further to the south. The site of Weelsby is thought to be in the area marked as Weelsby House. From A. Bryant (1828) *Map of the County of Lincoln, 1825-27*.

Grimsby Court Book I 394v).

The thirteenth century *Lay of Havelock the Dane* describes how the legendary origins of Grimsby were associated with the sale of fish, and so encapsulates an important aspect of the town's economic life which reaches back beyond written records (Skeat 1868). Ordinances made in 1258 specified herring and mullet as well as other fish among the items of which the sale was to be regulated, and an indication of the international dimensions of this trade were the special provisions made for the fishermen of France and Flanders (Anon. 1906, Rigby 1982). Something of the pattern of distribution of Grimsby fish in the late thirteenth century can be seen in the disputes which involved the detention of 300 fresh herring at Laceby, and interference with Grimsby trade, including herring, on the River Trent at Stockwith (Anon. 1812). The fish trade continued to play a part in Grimsby's economy throughout the Middle Ages. In September 1385 as many as twenty boats with herring were said to have been forestalled at Grimsby so that the people could not get their food (Kimball 1962). Fishmongers were prominent among the

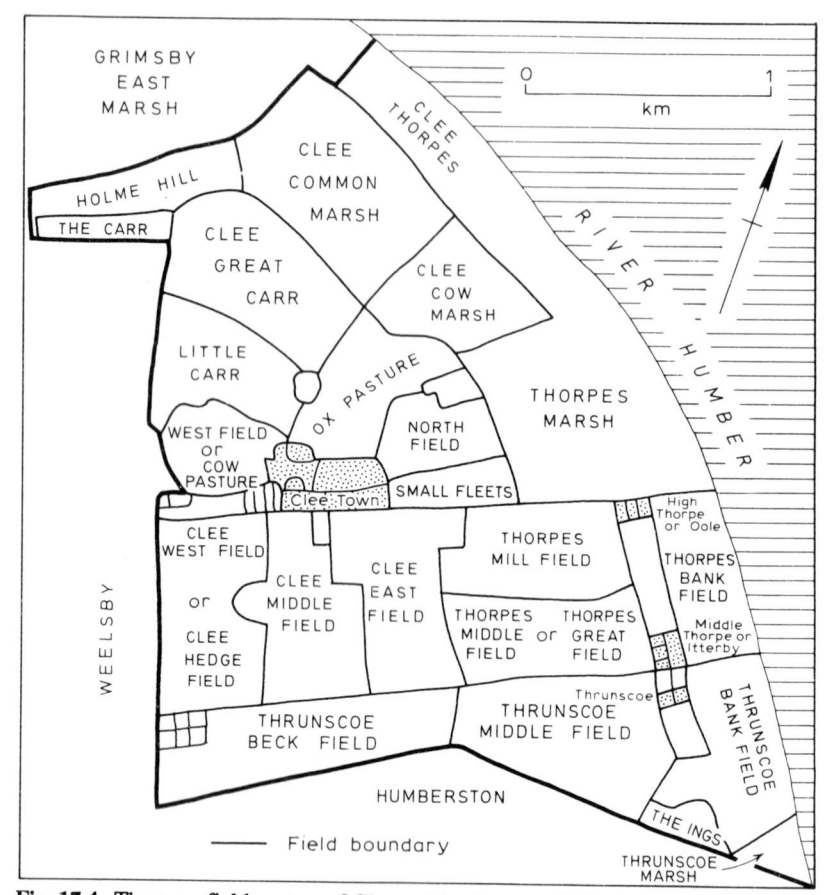

Fig. 17.4. The open field system of Clee and its thorpes, 1749. Source: Baker (1953) based on a copy of a lost original formerly at Sidney Sussex College, Cambridge.

London merchants who traded in the town. They did not, however, deal only in fish; for example, John Lovekyn, a 'stockfishmonger', was licensed to carry corn to London from Barton-upon-Humber and Grimsby in 1356 (Rigby 1982).

There were fishermen who were based on Grimsby such as the William who was sued before the royal justices in 1202 by another William, son of Gunni, but much of the fish which was landed in the port seems not to have been caught by local men, and as early as the 1190s fishermen from Filey were in Grimsby (Stenton 1926, Gillett

1970). From the mid thirteenth century Scarborough, Bridlington and Filey fishermen, as well as others from places nearer the port such as Cleethorpes, Tetney, Saltfleet and Stallingborough, appear in the Grimsby borough court records (Pawley 1984). Grimsby's concern to protect its trade was shown in 1321-2, when the town's burgesses successfully petitioned Parliament against markets which they said were being held by the inhabitants of Clee, Itterby, Oole, Thrunscoe and Humberston, and attracting merchants who had once gone to Grimsby; three years later it was found, as a result of a further complaint, that only fish and no other goods were being unloaded at Oole (Anon. undated, Rigby 1982, Pawley 1984, Platts 1985). Nonetheless, the complaints made by Grimsby did not prevent the Earl of Richmond and Lancaster from obtaining the right to hold a weekly market at Thrunscoe on Thursdays, together with a yearly fair at Michaelmas (Figs 21.1 and 21.2 this volume). The timing of the fair may have been connected with the east coast herring and mackerel fishery as it moved south in the late summer and early autumn (Anon. 1916a, Pawley 1984, Platts 1985).

If trade in fish remained a constant element in the economy of Grimsby until the sixteenth century, its other commercial activity changed during the course of the Middle Ages. Some of the town's earliest recorded commercial links were with Norway, which exported such items as hawks, falcons, furs and wool in the eleventh and twelfth centuries, and Scandinavian links remained important into the thirteenth century. In 1230 the cargoes on Norwegian boats included pine, boards and oil, while in return grain was sent to Norway out of Grimsby. A reference to a Flemish ship sold at Grimsby in the twelfth century is a rare indication of trade to places other than Scandinavia at this period, and German merchants first appeared in Grimsby in 1242. However, apart from this, little is known of trade at this period, although there were Spanish merchants in the town in 1228 and French ships put into the port in 1230. The wool trade was of little importance to the port; although the monastery of Wellow and the nuns of St Leonard sold wool to an Italian merchant in the early fifteenth century, it was as shipowners rather than as merchants that Grimsby men were probably involved in Lincolnshire's wool trade in the Middle Ages (Hill 1965, Gillett 1970, Rigby 1982, 1984, Pawley 1984).

Grimsby's traditional links with Scandinavia began to decline significantly in the fourteenth and fifteenth centuries under increasing pressure from the Hanseatic merchants abroad and from the development of the ports of Boston and Hull at home, although the second half of the fourteenth century seems to have been something of an Indian summer for the town, when the number of complaints about its fortunes diminished. Trade links with the Low Countries became of greater importance, with the growth of an export trade in such foodstuffs as ale, wheat, beans, peas and oats, and a more limited trade occurred with France, especially Calais (Rigby 1982).

As the port's international role diminished, its coastal trade became of greater relative importance in the town's economy, together with the commercial activity which was generated by fishing and local marketing and manufacturing. Grimsby's position gave it trading connections via the Ouse and Trent into Yorkshire and the Midlands, as well as the coastwise links as far as Scotland in the north and London in the south. Peat for fuel had been brought down the Humber from the twelfth century onwards after being dug in the Doncaster, Goole and Howden area, while grain was shipped from Grimsby to Newcastle, with coal as the main return cargo, from the fourteenth century. In 1389 John Hesilden was selling wheat and peas to traders in Hartlepool while men from Northumberland were among the people trading in wheat and malt out of Grimsby. In 1392 Adam de Hayton was found not guilty in the borough court of causing the loss through negligence of Thomas de Fountenay's ship *la Marie* with £10 worth of coal. The main cargoes sent coastwise to the south were basic foodstuffs such as wheat, oats, beans and malt, especially for the London market (Gillett 1970, Rigby 1982). This coastal trade continued to be important into the sixteenth and seventeenth centuries. Grimsby ships made a number of trips to Newcastle during the summer months, bringing back coal, while craft from other ports periodically put into Grimsby. The pattern of trade with the North East which developed during this later period was occasionally varied when a cargo of general merchandise and grain was taken out of the port (Public Record Office E190/303/1, 3 and 4, E190/307/17, Port Books of Kingston upon Hull 1565-7, 1580-1).

The sixteenth to eighteenth centuries: a period of decline

Grimsby ships were involved in the great summer Icelandic cod fishery of the fifteenth and sixteenth centuries, but the masters of the vessels were frequently from Clee and Cleethorpes, and Grimsby's contribution was to provide capital rather than men for the voyage (Gillett 1970, Pawley 1984). A survey of fishing and ferry boats in Lincolnshire in 1565 showed, however, that there were only seven craft at Cleethorpes of between a half and three tons which were owned by nine people, and there was none at Grimsby (Pawley 1984, Public Record Office SP 12/38/23 i). By the seventeenth century the number of boats at Cleethorpes had declined even further, and in 1628 when a muster of vessels, seafarers and fishermen was taken it was said that although there were five fishermen in Cleethorpes none of them was a boat owner. From the end of the sixteenth century until the development of the oyster trade in the eighteenth century, what fishing there was in Cleethorpes appears to have been largely carried out from the shore using nets and traps (Pawley 1984, Ambler et al. 1987, Public Record Office SP 16/138/60).

There is evidence of some trade in timber from Norway in the seventeenth century but this declined, and in the eighteenth century what was left of Grimsby's international trade came via Hull, with an occasional ship discharging its cargo into smaller boats to transfer ashore. In the ten years from 1775 to 1784 this happened on average between three and four times a year, while by 1785 to 1794 it had dropped to less than once a year (Jackson 1971, Public Record Office E190/318/3, 318/5, 323/18, 328/5, 329/10, 333/15, 333/20, 333/21, Port Books of Kingston upon Hull 1637-8, 1679-80, 1684-5, 1696-7). The town's merchant community dwindled as its inhabitants turned their backs on the sea and began to become more dependant for their livelihoods on the town's fields and pastures, as well as its role as a local marketing centre. Edward Popple and Christopher Clayton, who died in 1665 and 1679 respectively, both left quantities of timber among their stock in trade, and a great deal of Popple's came from Norway, but their place among the leading inhabitants of the town was taken by farmers, corn merchants and attorneys, giving Grimsby the type of social structure which could be found in many inland market towns (Jackson 1971, Lincolnshire Archives Office Inv 165/138 and 180/3).

The general decline in the fortunes of the town was reflected in its population figures (Table 17.1) which, even allowing for underestimation in the first quarter of the eighteenth century, seem to have moved steadily downwards from around 1400 in 1377 to about 850 in 1524, until by the eighteenth century Grimsby was little larger than its rural neighbour of Clee (Rigby 1982). The Revd Abraham de la Pryme visited Grimsby in 1697 when he found it to be 'but a little poor town, not a quarter so great as heretofore'. It had been 'very great and rich formerly, by its having a larg [sic] spacious haven which brought great trafic [sic] to the town.' He gave the reason for the destruction of the haven as 'the Humber's wearing away the huge cliff at Cleythorp, and bringing it and casting it all into Grimsby haven or river' and reported that work was in progress to dig out the haven and 'bring vessels to the townside again' (Jackson 1870 pp. 153-5). The problems connected with the haven were not new. As early as 1255 Grimsby had been granted a toll to help to support work on the port, and when John Bek was commissioned with the sheriff of Lincoln in November 1280 to enquire into a proposed diversion of the Freshney it was in an effort to unblock the 'sand and earth' which had accumulated in the haven. This was the result of extremely high tides which occurred from the second half of the thirteenth century bringing an accumulation of sand and silt on to the coast (Anon. 1901, Robinson 1981, Rigby 1982, Pawley 1984). Nothing appears to have been done, however, and complaints about the condition of the haven continued to be made into the fourteenth century, although what was described as a new port had been built by 1341 (Anon. 1916b, Rigby 1982). This West Haven, which still remains substantially intact, was excavated from the common pasture called the 'Somertymyng' (Fig. 17.1) (Gillett 1970). In 1660 a committee was appointed to restore the haven, but it was not until 1697 that work was begun to divert the Freshney into the West Haven and so scour it and the old haven of sediment (Anon. 1895, Gillett 1970).

The nineteenth and twentieth centuries

In 1787 plans were made to revive Grimsby's fortunes by carrying out further excavations on the haven and creating a dock. After a series of financial and engineering vicissitudes stretching over a number of

Table 17.1. The population of Clee and Grimsby, 1563-1981.

	1563 Households (estimated population)	1605 Communicants (estimated population)	1642 Adult males (estimated population)	1676 Communicants (estimated population)	1705-23 Average number of families (estimated population)	1801 Number of inhabitants	1851	1901	1951	1981
Clee	22									
Utterby	18									
Houll	14	200	72	-201	78	387	1034	12 578+	29 557	35 637
Thrunscoe	16	(300)	(216)	(301)	(331)					
Weelsby	6									
	(361)									
Grimsby	145	500	No return	168*	94	1524	8860	63 138	94 557	92 596
	(834)	(750)		(714)	(399)					

Sources: Census Reports 1801-1981, Cole (1912), Foster (1926), Hodgett (1975), Whiteman (1986).

* This return is almost certainly for families.

\+ The population of Cleethorpes after the 1889 Grimsby Extension Act.

years, John Rennie, the eminent civil engineer, was first consulted and then appointed engineer for the project. The new dock, at that time the largest in Britain, was opened on 30 December 1800, although the work was still incomplete. However, the rural hinterland on which the dock depended for its prosperity was not large enough, and after a period of modest growth the trade of the port stagnated. There was also an initial rise in the population of the town which was greater than anywhere else in north Lincolnshire in the first decade of the nineteenth century, but after 1811 and until 1841 Grimsby's growth was little different from that of other towns of the area (Jackson 1971).

The Ashton under Lyne and Manchester Railway Company began to seek an outlet to the east, and in 1844 decided to build a line to Grimsby. Plans to construct a new dock were also drawn up and in 1845 the Haven Company voted to amalgamate with the railway. In 1846 work was begun on the great coffer dam which was to extend three-quarters of a mile out into the Humber, enclosing the area in which the 20 acre Royal Dock was to be built. The dock was completed by March 1852 and brought into use two months later (Jackson 1971, Dow 1985). The port's first fish dock of about 6 acres was completed in 1857 and fishermen came to the port, encouraged by the Deep Sea Fishing Company, which had the backing of the Great Central, Great Northern and Midland Railway Companies (Tye and White 1970, Dow 1985). These were the first stages in a process of dock development in Grimsby which was not to come to an end until the completion of the Number 3 Fish Dock in 1934 (Figs 17.5 and 17.6) (Edwards 1951). The Union Dock, which linked the Old Dock and the Royal Dock, was opened in 1879. A year later a new 26 acre dock leading out of the Old Dock was also completed, and both were named Alexandra in honour of the Princess of Wales (Dow 1985). In 1866 the first fish dock was doubled in size and a second dock, completed in 1878 and known as Number 2 Fish Dock, was built out of it. This 11 acre dock was enlarged again to 16 acres between 1897 and 1900 (Tye and White 1970, Dow 1985).

The railways provided Grimsby with the hinterland that it had lacked in the early nineteenth century, linking the port with the south Yorkshire coalfield as well as the industrial areas of Lancashire and the Midlands. The net tonnage of cargo handled in 1854 was 163 000, and had reached 3 777 000 by 1911. However, the shift of traffic to

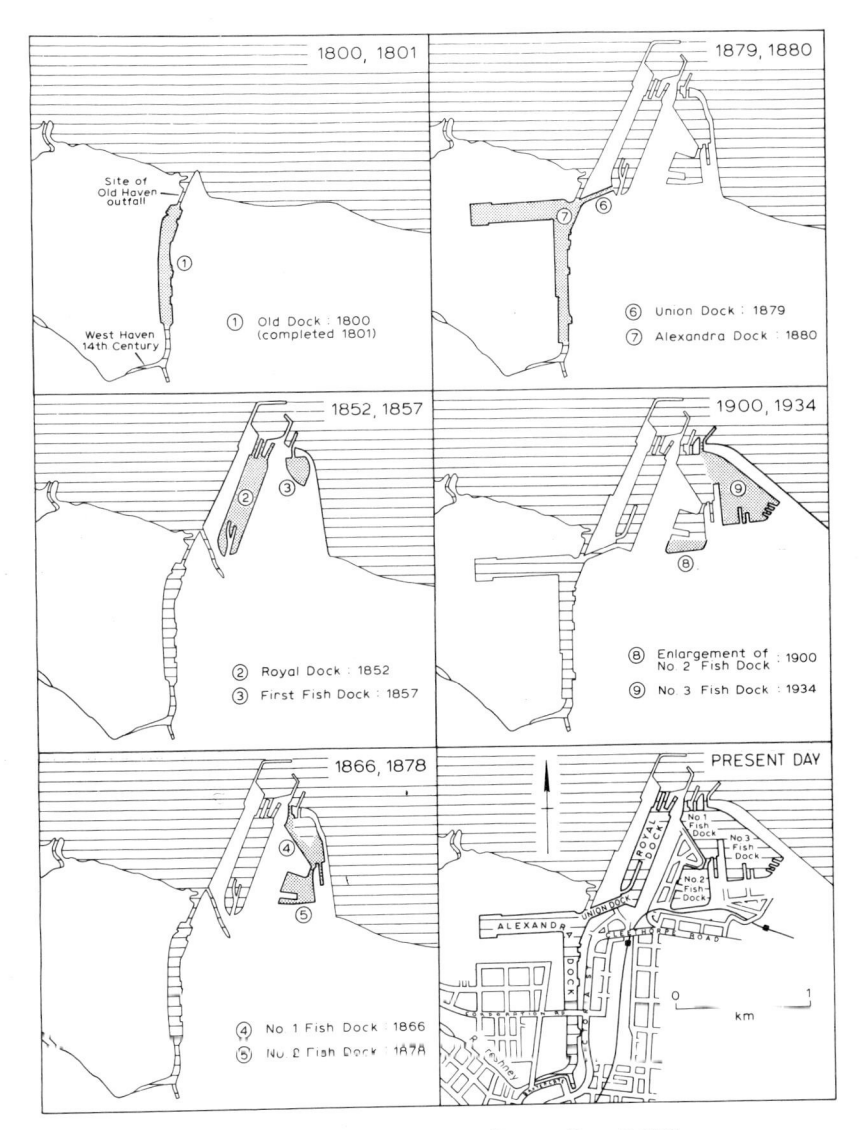

Historical development of Grimsby and Cleethorpes

Fig. 17.5. The development of Grimsby docks. Source: Dow (1985).

Fig. 17.6. Aerial view of Grimsby docks, 1988. The course of the original haven leading into the Humber is to the left of the Royal Dock with its distinctive water tower, part of the hydraulic system provided to operate locks and quayside facilities. The Fish Docks are to the right, and Alexandra Dock runs across the centre of the photograph, crossed by a new motorway extension. The medieval West Haven can be seen in the extreme bottom right of the picture.

Immingham, together with a fall in exports as a result of reduced shipments of textile goods and machinery, iron and steel in the period between the wars, meant a subsequent reduction in the volume of Grimsby's trade, which had fallen to 619 700 tons by 1938. After the Second World War this grew again to a peak of 1 489 800 in 1956, declining to 638 100 in 1962 (Edwards 1951, Hiner 1965, Tye and White 1970). Since the 1960s the port has diversified its cargo handling and storage facilities; from 1975 the bulk of its import traffic has been in cars and Danish foodstuffs, while exports have been varied, but chiefly in manufactured goods (Jones and North 1987).

The expansion of the fish docks in the nineteenth century was matched by a rapid growth in the amount of fish landed at Grimsby. In 1855 188 tons of fish were landed from British vessels, and this had increased to about 30 000 tons by 1871 when there were 302 vessels fishing from the port. The beginning of steam fishing in 1881 increased fish landings still further and, although sailing smacks had fished off Iceland, the greater range of the new boats together with diminishing fish stocks in the North Sea led to more distant voyages being undertaken. By 1911 fish landings at Grimsby were 190 000 tons, excluding foreign landings, and although the total weight of landings dropped in the inter-war period, the industry did not cease to expand since the value of prime and fresh fish remained high. In 1921 there were 622 fishing vessels in the port. The level of landings from British vessels recovered to reach 198 000 tons by 1951, but from the 1950s there was a moderate decline in the weight of fish landed. However, this also happened in other British fish ports, and Grimsby's share of the total amount of fish landed in the country remained unchanged at about 20% (Alward 1932, Edwards 1951, Hiner 1965, Gillett 1970). Declining catch rates in the early 1970s together with steep rises in fuel costs had already raised doubts about the future viability of the distant-water industry, when the introduction of fishing limits by the European Economic Community, a 50 mile limit by Iceland, 200 mile Exclusive Economic Zones by Norway, Canada and Greenland, and Britain's entry into the European Economic Community closed many traditional fishing grounds. Grimsby's landings of fish from British vessels fell from 166 000 tons in 1970 to 24 200 in 1983, and the port slipped from second to fourth in the country in the value of its landings, although foreign vessels helped to maintain its role as a major landing port (Symes 1987a).

As the town's population and the demand for housing grew in the second half of the nineteenth century (Table 17.1), Grimsby began to spread from its ancient centre first to fill in the building lots which had been laid out and partially developed on the east side of the Old Haven, then over the former grazing lands of the East Marsh (Fig. 17.3). By 1872 all this land had been disposed of for building, while development of part of the parish of Clee adjoining Grimsby's northeastern boundary, which became known as New Clee, increased the population of this area from 325 in 1861 to 2058 in 1871. The Great Grimsby Improvement Act of 1869 enabled the town's corporation to bridge the Old Dock and develop the West Marsh as building land after Corporation Bridge was opened in August 1872. From the 1870s Edward Heneage, the landlord of the

Weelsby estate to the south of the East Marsh, opened it up for leasehold development to create a residential area of good quality housing.

It was not only in those areas of the parish of Clee adjacent to Grimsby that housing began to develop to meet the needs of a growing population. The extension of the railway from Grimsby to Cleethorpes in 1863 meant that it was possible to reside there and go by train daily to work in Grimsby (Ambler 1981). However, Cleethorpes' attraction was not only that it had spare building land. Indeed, development was initially inhibited because the ground landlord of a considerable area of Clee, Sidney Sussex College Cambridge, charged relatively high rents for its leases. It was the fact that Cleethorpes was a seaside resort which helped to make it a desirable place to live, although the attitude of residents to day-trippers was sometimes ambivalent (Aspinall 1976, Ambler 1981).

Cleethorpes' beginnings as a resort dated back to the late eighteenth century and its modest development was enhanced by the coming of steam packet services to the Humber, which brought visitors from an increasingly wide area in the 1820s, 30s and 40s, some of whom were to stay for relatively long periods. The arrival of the railway at Grimsby further increased the number of visitors and brought the first day-trippers. These became more important when the railway was extended to Cleethorpes itself, so that the residents and longer term visitors became differentiated from 'the shoals of operatives from the Yorkshire and Lancashire districts' who crowded to the seaside (Fowler 1880, Ambler 1981). At first the resort had few amenities. A pier was opened in 1873, and in 1886 the Manchester, Sheffield and Lincolnshire Railway Company, who had taken over the seafront, laid out a promenade and pleasure gardens (Ambler 1981) (Fig. 17.7). In the 1920s an area on the seafront to the south of the town which had been used as golf links was developed as a bathing pool and boating lake, and in 1935 the urban district council bought back the pier, promenade and gardens from what had become the London and North Eastern Railway Company. The sea front to the north of the resort was gradually developed as an area of seaside amusements and stalls from the end of the nineteenth century (Baker 1953).

Cleethorpes has continued to be both a seaside resort and a residential neighbour to Grimsby. No detailed estimates of the

Fig. 17.7. Aerial view of the sea front at Cleethorpes, 1974. The pier is in the centre with the North Promenade and railway station above. Below the pier are the promenade and pleasure gardens, with residential development behind the sea front. The thorpe of Oole was situated in the area to the middle left.

number of visitors it currently attracts are available, but it is certain that they do not reach the 230 000 ordinary and 72 000 excursion passengers who it was claimed visited it in 1881 (Ambler 1981, Symes 1987b). Its short summer season means that for most of the year its importance is as a place of residence for its inhabitants.

Residential development has closed the gap between Grimsby and Cleethorpes and also covered the farmland within the former parish of Clee, obliterating its ancient boundaries and the separate settlements of its thorpes. The 1889 Grimsby Extension Act moved the boundary of Grimsby to incorporate New Clee, the old village of Clee and the Weelsby suburb developed by Edward Heneage, bringing a substantial

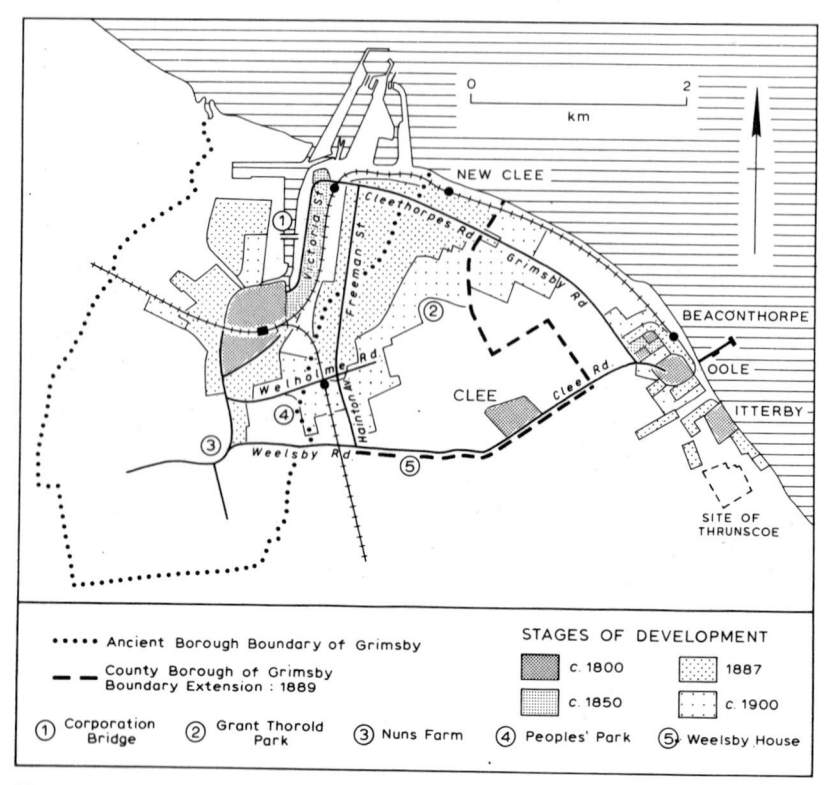

Fig. 17.8. The growth of Grimsby and Cleethorpes in the nineteenth century. Sources: Ordnance Survey maps, Wright (1982).

increase in the town's population, which had reached 63 138 by 1901 (Fig. 17.8, Table 17.1). Further extensions followed in 1922 and 1927, when Cleethorpes also made gains, including parts of the neighbouring parish of Humberston where suburban development was beginning to take place. This was part of a wider movement of population generated by the growth of Grimsby, but which also sustained the growth and development of Cleethorpes despite the loss of land and people to the borough. As part of the 1927 boundary adjustments Grimsby's boundaries were also extended to absorb its former village neighbours of Little Coates, parts of Bradley and Weelsby, together with most of Scartho. Further additions in the 1950s brought Great Coates into Grimsby (Fig. 17.9), but none of these extensions was sufficient to compensate for the movement of

Fig. 17.9. The growth of Grimsby and Cleethorpes in the twentieth century. Source: Ordnance Survey Maps.

population away from the older town centre, so that Grimsby's population dropped from 94 557 in 1951 to 92 596 in 1981 (Table 17.1) (Baker 1953, Gillett 1970).

Grimsby had grown up on a relatively small area of land and although, like its neighbour Clee, part of its economy was based on agriculture, its fortunes were closely linked to the sea and its port was the basis for the town's development in the nineteenth century. This link began to be weakened after the Second World War, when attempts were made to diversify Grimsby's economy and the borough began to purchase land outside its boundaries for industrial use (Hiner 1965). Clee, with its larger area of land, had been less dependent on maritime activity, but its population had included seafarers and fishermen as well as farmers, while the development of Cleethorpes as a resort had reinforced these ties. The urban development of the nineteenth and twentieth centuries obliterated the ancient boundaries between the two towns, as well as eventually causing them to spread out into their former rural neighbours; although a strong sense of identity remains within the individual communities, they have developed together to become the largest conurbation in south Humberside.

Acknowledgements

I am indebted to Mrs A.J. Kay and Mr A. Dowling for permission to use unpublished long essays and dissertations prepared as part of their degrees in Regional and Local History at the University of Hull, to Mr A. Marriott for advice on geographical literature on the towns, to Dr S. Pawley for references to sixteenth and seventeenth century surveys of ships and boats at the Public Record Office, to Dr G. Platts for clarifying references to markets at Clee, Itterby, Oole, Thrunscoe and Humberston, to Dr S.H. Rigby for elucidating events which led up to the construction of the West Haven, to Mr E.H. Trevitt for material on the development of Cleethorpes as a seaside resort, to Mrs B. Watkinson for references to the *Calendar of Charter Rolls* and also, with the late Mr L. Watkinson, for references to Grimsby probate inventories and for advice on the topography of the towns, to Mr D. Wattam of Grimsby Reference Library for his assistance with local material, especially maps of the towns, and to Mr M. Wright of National Westminster Bank South Humberside Business Centre for help in locating Figure 17.6.

References

Alward, G.L. (1932). *The Sea Fisheries of Great Britain and Ireland.* Albert Gait, Grimsby.
Ambler, R.W. (1981). Cleethorpes: the development of an East Coast resort. In: *Ports and Resorts in the Regions* (ed. E.M. Sigsworth) pp. 179-90. Humberside College of Higher

Education, Hull.
Ambler, R.W., Watkinson, B. and Watkinson, L. (eds) (1987). *Farmers and Fishermen: the probate inventories of the ancient parish of Clee, south Humberside, 1536-1742*, Studies in Regional and Local History No. 4. School of Adult and Continuing Education, University of Hull.
Anon. (1812). *Rotuli Hundredorum Temp Henry III and Edward I*. London.
Anon. (1895). *Historical Manuscripts Commission 14th Report, Appendix part VIII: the manuscripts of Lincoln, Bury St. Edmunds and Great Grimsby Corporations; and of the Dean and Chapters of Worcester and Lichfield, &c., C7881*. HMSO, London.
Anon. (1901). *Calendar of Patent Rolls, Edward I 1272-1281*. HMSO, London.
Anon. (1906). *Calendar of Charter Rolls, Vol. 2 Henry III-Edward I 1257-1300*. HMSO, London.
Anon. (1916a). *Calendar of Charter Rolls, Vol. 5 15 Edward III-5 Henry V 1341-1417*. HMSO, London.
Anon. (1916b). *Calendar of Inquisitions Miscellaneous, Vol. 2. Edward II - 1-22 Edward III 1307-1349*. HMSO, London.
Anon. (undated). *Rotuli Parliamentorum; ut et Petitiones, et Placita in Parliamento tempore Edwardi R. I*, Vol. 1. Record Commission, London.
Aspinall, P.J. (1976). Speculative builders and the development of Cleethorpes, 1850-1900. *Lincolnshire History and Archaeology* **11**, 43-52.
Baker, F. (1953). *The Story of Cleethorpes and the Contribution of Methodism during Two Hundred Years*. Trinity Methodist Church, Cleethorpes.
Cole, R.E.G. (ed.) (1912). *Speculum Dioeceseos Lincolniensis*, Lincoln Record Society Vol. 4, Lincoln.
Dow, G. (1985). *Great Central*, Vols 1 and 2. Ian Allan, London.
Edwards, K.C. (1951). Grimsby and Immingham: a port study. *Tijdschrift voor economische en sociale geografie* **42**, 382-6.
Foster, C.W. (ed.) (1926). *The State of the Church in the Reigns of Elizabeth and James I ...*, Lincoln Record Society Vol. 23, Lincoln.
Foster, C.W. and Longley, T. (eds) (1924). *The Lincolnshire*

Domesday and the Lindsey Survey, Lincoln Record Society Vol. 19, Lincoln.

Fowler, J. (1880). *Richard Waldo Sibthorpe: a biography.* W. Skeffington & Son, London.

Gillett, E. (1970). *A History of Grimsby.* Oxford University Press for the University of Hull, Oxford.

Hill, F. (1965). *Medieval Lincoln.* Cambridge University Press, Cambridge.

Hiner, O.S. (1965). Economic developments in the Grimsby-Immingham area since 1945. *Tijdschrift voor economische en sociale geografie* **56**, 21-32.

Hodgett, G.A.J. (1975). *Tudor Lincolnshire.* History of Lincolnshire Committee, Lincoln.

Jackson, C. (ed.) (1870). *The Diary of Abraham de la Pryme, the Yorkshire Antiquary.* Surtees Society, Durham.

Jackson, G. (1971). *Grimsby and the Haven Company.* Grimsby Public Libraries, Grimsby.

Jones, P.N. and North, J. (1987). Ports and wharves. In: *Humberside in the Eighties* (ed. D.G. Symes) pp. 97-111. Department of Geography, University of Hull.

Kimball, E.G. (ed.) (1962). *Records of Some Sessions of the Peace in Lincolnshire 1381-1396 Vol. II The Parts of Lindsey.* Lincoln Record Society, Lincoln.

Owen, D.M. (1975). Medieval chapels in Lincolnshire. *Lincolnshire History and Archaeology* **10**, 15-22.

Pawley, S. (1984). Lincolnshire Coastal Villages and the Sea, *c.* 1300-*c.* 1600: economy and society. Ph.D. thesis, University of Leicester.

Platts, G. (1985). *Land and People in Medieval Lincolnshire.* History of Lincolnshire Committee for the Society for Lincolnshire History and Archaeology, Lincoln.

Rigby, S.H. (1982). Boston and Grimsby in the Middle Ages. Ph.D. thesis, University of London.

Rigby, S.H. (1984). Urban decline in the later middle ages: the reliability of the non-statistical evidence. In: *Urban History Yearbook, 1984* (ed. D. Reeder) pp. 45-60. Leicester University Press, Leicester.

Robinson, D.N. (1981). *The Book of the Lincolnshire Seaside.* Barracuda Books, Buckingham.

Skeat, W.W. (1868). *The Lay of Havelok the Dane.* Early English Text Society, London.

Stenton, D.M. (ed.) (1926). *The Earliest Lincolnshire Assize Rolls A.D. 1202-1209,* Lincoln Record Society Vol. 22, Lincoln.

Stenton, F.M. (1920). *Documents Illustrative of the Social and Economic History of the Danelaw from Various Collections,* Records of the Social and Economic History of England and Wales Vol. 5. Oxford University Press for the British Academy, London.

Symes, D.G. (1987a). The fishing industry. In: *Humberside in the Eighties* (ed. D.G. Symes) pp. 23-32. Department of Geography, University of Hull.

Symes, D.G. (1987b). Tourism. In: *Humberside in the Eighties* (ed. D.G. Symes) pp. 123-31. Department of Geography, University of Hull.

Taylor, H.M. and Taylor, J. (1980). *Anglo-Saxon Architecture,* Vol. 1. Cambridge University Press, Cambridge.

Tye, A. and White, P. (1970). *An Industrial History of Grimsby and Cleethorpes.* Lincolnshire Industrial Archaeology Group, Lincoln.

Whiteman, A. (ed.) (1986). *The Compton Census of 1676: a critical edition,* Records of Social and Economic History, New Series Vol. 10. Oxford University Press for the British Academy, London.

Wright, N.R. (1982). *Lincolnshire Towns and Industry, 1700-1914.* History of Lincolnshire Committee for the Society for Lincolnshire History and Archaeology, Lincoln.

18

The geographical shaping of Hull from pre-industrial to modern times

M.T. Wild

Hull's historical status

The large majority of major English towns and cities fall into two common types according to their historical experience: 'early starters', such as York, Norwich and Exeter, which were highly important centres in pre-industrial times but, from the late eighteenth century to quite recently, saw considerable decline in their relative standing, and 'late starters', typified by Manchester, Birmingham and Bradford, which for centuries were not very significant, but during the Industrial Revolution emerged as major concentrations of population and economic activity. Hull shares with a few other English cities (notably Bristol, Coventry, Nottingham and Newcastle) the distinction of being exceptional, for here each historical episode - medieval period, mercantile era, Industrial Revolution and modern age - contributed substantially to the shaping of the urban form. Indeed, Hull's historical evolution exhibits much of the strong *continuity* widely experienced amongst the towns and cities of continental Europe (Mumford 1961).

For more than four centuries Hull's position in the ranking-order of English urban centres changed by only ten places. The 1524/25 Lay Subsidies indicate that it was England's nineteenth largest urban community. Nearly 150 years later the Hearth Tax returns of the

1660s and 70s showed that it had moved up slightly to sixteenth position, at a time when Manchester, Birmingham, Sheffield and Leeds had yet to feature in any list of the country's foremost twenty-five cities (Patten 1978). Hull's continued commercial expansion during the eighteenth century and its strong involvement in the economic growth of the Industrial Revolution stimulated some further improvement in its ranking. Measured in population terms it achieved eleventh position in 1801 and 1851. Hull's highest-ever ranking, ninth, was attained in 1951, but since then it has slipped to twelfth.

The pre-industrial town

From the end of the Middle Ages to the onset of the Industrial Revolution the population growth of Hull was slow and irregular. The Poll Tax returns show that 693 families were living in Hull in 1377. Assuming the average size of a family to be between four and five, this represents a population within the range of 2772-3465. Three centuries later their numbers had risen to between 6200 and 6900 (Forster, G. 1969). By 1770, just before the opening of 'The Dock' (later known as Queen's Dock) effectively marked the commencement of Hull's 'Industrial Age', the population had risen to 15 392 (Williams 1969). Even so, a few more years passed before the town first began to experience any noteworthy extensions to a physical form and structure that had been laid out in the final decade of the thirteenth century and had been fortified by walls and gateways during the years 1321-4. There had been some changes, however. Since the Civil War Hull had developed primarily as a leading commercial port rather than continuing as a strategic naval base with a secondary trading function. Inside the town itself many new buildings, especially merchant houses, had replaced old medieval properties, and there had been much infilling of vacant plots and spaces. Not only had the population increased to about five times its former level, but it had also become more socially differentiated. The Hearth Tax returns of Hull, as analysed by G. Forster (1969), show this trend occurring as early as the late seventeenth century. In 1673 as many as 19% of Hull households were considered to be too poor to pay the tax, but at the other end of the social spectrum 14.5% of taxable households lived in very substantial dwellings with more than five hearths. Comfortable residences of the wealthy concentrated along the 'higher' section of High Street in the northern part of the town, while greater numbers of humble cottages were hidden away along the alleyways and narrow lanes nearer the Humber and the River Hull confluence.

Hull is well provided with historical maps and plans. Early versions were drawn before cartography became a precise profession, but one of them, Hollar's map of *c*. 1640, does contain much useful information. Figure 18.1, based on this plan, shows the town almost wholly confined inside one of the strongest systems of urban defences in the country. Outside the medieval walls only the hamlets of Drypool and Trippet, and some buildings in front of Beverley Gate, disturbed the flat scene of enclosed fields and reclaimed wetland. Inside the town the two distinctive components of the medieval street framework - the 'fishbone' structure focusing on the winding axis of High Street, and the later 'grid-iron' layout of Edward I's planned extension west of Lowgate and Market Place - remained virtually intact. Dwellings, warehouses, workshops, churches and civic institutions were all accommodated within an intra-mural area of just 90 acres. However, the density of buildings varied greatly. It was very high in the streetblocks lying between the River Hull and High Street, and also in some situated between High Street and Market Place (Fig. 18.1). This intense concentration close to the Old Harbour reflected the commanding significance of the port function.

The congestion eased considerably west of Market Place and Lowgate; there was even some open space, mostly gardens, tofts and orchards. Indeed, adjoining the town wall along Scale Lane, Dagger Lane and Blanket Row, a few undeveloped streetblocks still remained. The existence of this open space meant that urban growth could continue as an internal process, wholly contained within the medieval defensive *enceinte*. Eventually, however, the entire intramural space became filled with buildings, as Defoe (1948 ed. p. 244) observed in his visit to Hull in 1726: 'The town is exceedingly close built, and should a fire ever be its fate, it might suffer deeply on that account; 'tis extraordinary populous, even to an inconvenience, having really no room to extend itself by buildings.' Even so, another half-century elapsed and Hull's population increased by a further 6000 before any significant urban growth occurred beyond

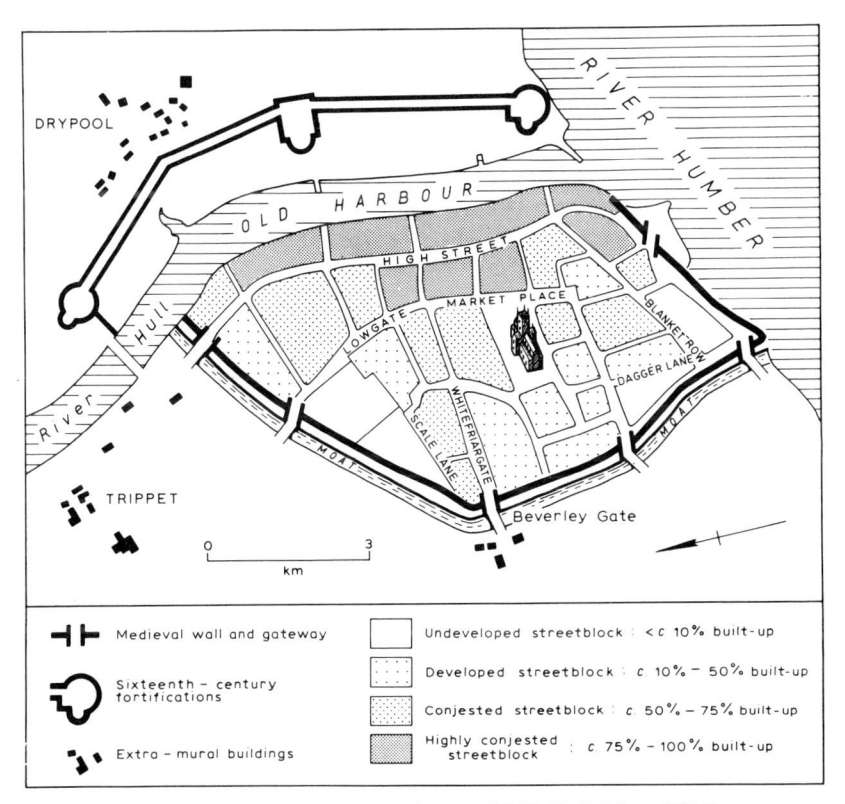

Fig. 18.1. The shape of Hull in c. 1640. Source: W. Hollar's Map of Hull.

the confines of the Old Town.

Urban growth during the Industrial Revolution

The Industrial Revolution came to Hull during the final quarter of the eighteenth century, bringing three inter related developments, each of which had a profound effect on the geographical evolution of the town. First, there was a huge surge in the quantity of trade, with the total tonnage of foreign-going shipping entering and leaving the port increasing from 63 795 tons in 1772 to 165 743 in 1800 (Williams 1969); there were also large increases in coastal and river trade. Second, an era of vigorous industrial expansion was initiated, led by shipbuilding, oil seed extracting and sugar refining, and third, the population growth rate accelerated sharply.

The rapid growth of shipping, and the obvious inability of the constricted Old Harbour to cope, prompted the construction of the port's first dock. Completed in 1778, The Dock necessitated the demolition of the northern section of the town wall and also the removal of Beverley Gate (demolition of other sections and gates followed during the 1780s and 90s). This was a prelude for the first extension of Hull since the reign of Edward I. Industrial expansion, now mainly in the form of factories, warehouses and construction yards, spread northwards, concentrating along the banks of the River Hull where materials and products were easily transported. In the meantime residential development responded to the quickening demographic trend. The Hull Dock Company estate, which lay immediately to the north of the new dock, was sold in 1781 and quickly became Hull's first residential suburb (Fig. 18.2). For several decades a community of wealthy traders, shipowners and professional people lived here and in adjoining streets. A few years later much poorer quality housing, for dock labourers, seafarers and factory workers, appeared to the west of the Old Town in South Myton (Fig. 18.2). This was the origin of the Hessle Road area, Hull's largest sector of working-class housing.

By 1817 Hull's physical area covered 258 acres, which was nearly three times the size of the Old Town, excluding its small post-1801 extension on to land reclaimed from the Humber foreshore (this area, between Humber Street and Nelson Street, was developed in the early 1800s following the 1801 Ferry Boat Dock Act and covered no more than 4 acres). However, the physical growth of Hull during the late eighteenth and early nineteenth centuries did not greatly outpace the population trend (Fig. 18.3); this period was one of 'intensive' urban extension, characterised in Hull and other industrialising cities by high housing densities, compact manufacturing quarters and little open land.

Goodwill and Lawson's 1856 *Plan of Kingston upon Hull* indicates that the main directions of urban growth had continued to be northwards and westwards, although for the first time there had also been some significant expansion eastwards at Witham and Drypool (Fig. 18.2). The industrial belt alongside the River Hull now stretched beyond Wincolmlee and included several factory-workers'

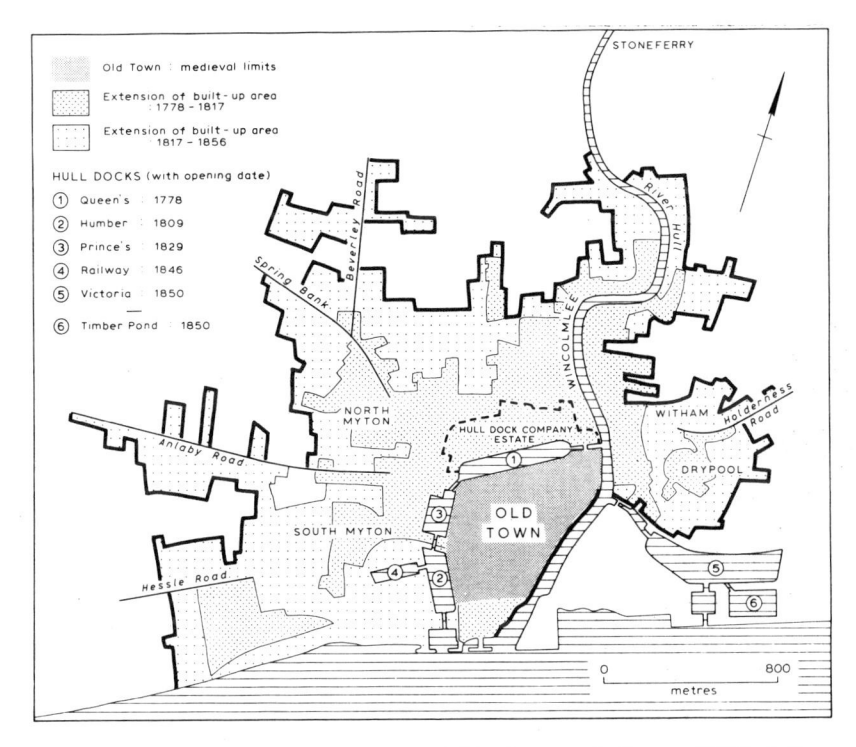

Fig. 18.2. Physical growth of Hull, 1778-1856. Sources: J. Craggs (1817) *A New Plan of the Town of Kingston upon Hull and its Environs*, Goodwill and Lawson (1856) *A Plan of Kingston upon Hull*.

communities. Progressive westwards growth of the city had extended the Hessle Road 'sector' beyond a mile from the Old Town. At its eastern end there existed an area noted for its appalling housing conditions and poverty. This, the slum quarter of South Myton, consisted almost entirely of closely-packed, back-to-back, courtyard housing with only tunnel entrances (Forster, C. 1969).

The oldest courts in Hull were in the Old Town (Fig. 18.4a) where most had been built in the eighteenth century, when the infilling process was at its height, and had been fitted into the intricate framework of medieval curtilages, or 'burgage plots' (Conzen 1960). Forster (1972) argues that the courts in South Myton, and elsewhere in North Myton, Drypool and within the industrial belt of the River Hull, were 'regularised' adaptations of these earlier structures.

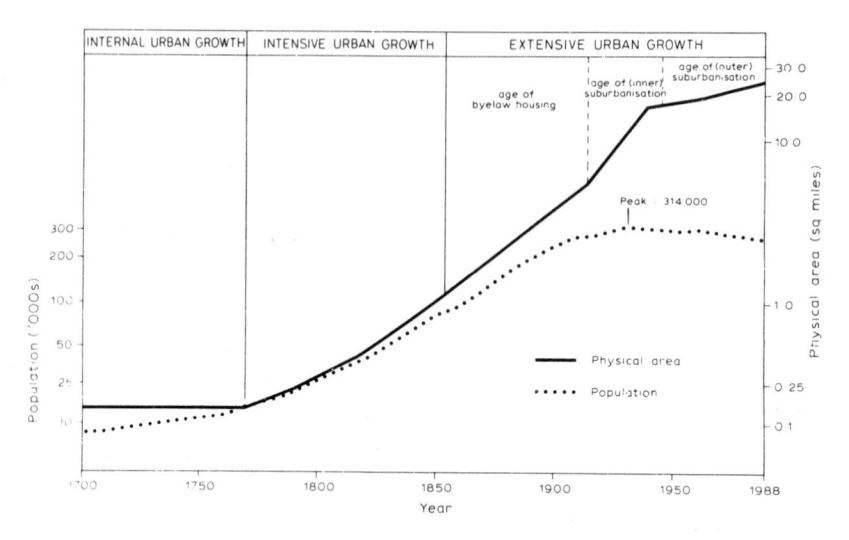

Fig. 18.3. Urban growth and population growth in Hull, 1700-1988.

Although their dimensions differed - the courts outside the Old Town were much more orderly arranged (Fig. 18.4b) - both versions had the same poor quality housing, lack of sanitation and degree of overcrowding.

Very different were the spacious residences which accommodated Hull's growing middle-class population. These were mostly villa-type houses forming linear suburbs alongside the principal thoroughfares leading out from the city. By the middle of the nineteenth century Spring Bank, Beverley Road and Anlaby Road (Fig. 18.2) had become the most fashionable places to live. Here, on the city's northwestern and western outskirts, there was cleaner air and easy access to the city centre and Paragon Railway Station (opened in 1848).

Urban growth, 1854-1914

The date 1854 is highly significant in the geographical evolution of Hull, for this was the year when the city, through the Local Board of Health, introduced the first byelaws imposing 'minimum

The geographical shaping of Hull 257

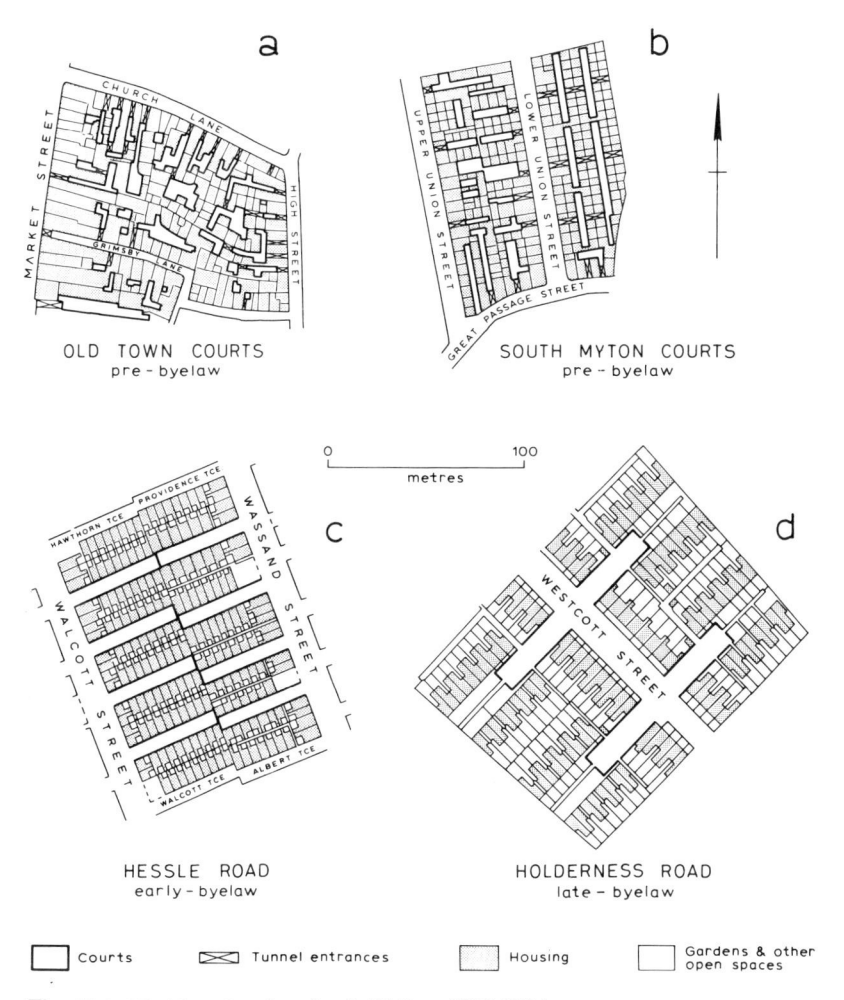

Fig. 18.4. Working-class housing in Hull, c. 1770–1914.

standards' on all new housing construction. They covered such urgent needs as adequate sanitation, street lighting and building materials, but particularly important were the stipulations concerning new courtyard housing. These did not forbid all forms of residential courts, but they did demand substantial improvements in their design. Tunnel entrances and back-to-back housing were prohibited, and the dimensions of all new courts were standardised to a minimum width of 20 feet and a maximum length of 120 feet (Forster 1972) (Fig. 18.4c). Subsequently a second set of byelaws, introduced in 1893, widened and shortened these limits to 24 and 100 feet, and also demanded larger houses and space for small front and rear gardens (Fig. 18.4d). Forster's survey, conducted in 1965 when slum-clearances were still largely confined to the pre-1854 areas of the city, counted as many as 38 450 houses in Hull built to the minimum standards defined by the nineteenth century byelaws (Forster, C. 1969). Of this total, 20 810 (or 54%) were in permitted open-entrance courts; the rest were constructed as plain terrace-rows.

Byelaw housing was not only better built and healthier than the pre-1854 slums, but it also produced lower housing densities (Fig. 18.4). This tendency, along with the creation of urban parklands (Pearson Park in 1860, West Park in 1885, East Park in 1887 and Pickering Park in 1911), the increasing scale of new industrial plants and the use of more land for railways and public buildings, stimulated a change from 'intensive' to 'extensive' urban growth (Fig. 18.3). Between 1851 and 1911 the number of people living in Hull multiplied by 211%. This was a more rapid increase than occurred in most English cities during this period, but now it was greatly exceeded by the 409% expansion of the physical area, from 1.1 square miles in 1854 to 5.6 in 1914.

By 1914 Hull had become a major industrial and port city with a population approaching 300 000. The byelaw housing was distributed within the post-1854 parts of three large working-class residential districts - the Hessle Road area in the west, the streets leading off Spring Bank, Beverley Road and Newland Avenue in the northwest, and, representing the first large-scale urban growth in East Hull, the quickly spreading suburbs (including James Reckitt's 'garden village', begun in 1907) which focused principally on Holderness Road (Fig. 18.5). Dwellings for the middle classes continued to occupy positions facing the more prestigious arterial roads and their main connecting 'avenues'. However, the opening of Pearson Park in 1860 formed a nucleus for an extensive, fashionable suburb which, by 1914, had spread northwestwards to include The Avenues.

Until 1850 the port of Hull had been the Old Harbour and the constricted group of 'town' docks - Queen's Dock, Prince's Dock, Humber Dock and Railway Dock - situated around the northern and

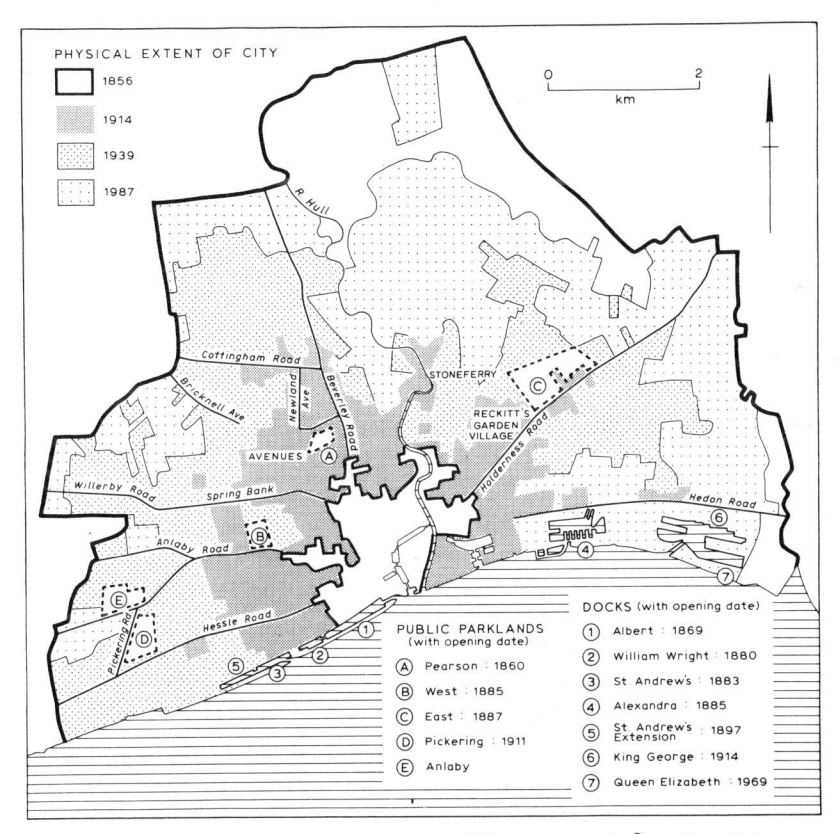

Fig. 18.5. Physical growth of Hull, 1856-1987. Sources: Goodwill and Lawson (1856) *A Plan of Kingston upon Hull*, M. Harland (1914) *Plan of the City of Kingston upon Hull*, A. Brown and Son (1939) *New Plan of Hull*, Personal field-survey (1987).

western limits of the Old Town. Commencing with the opening of Victoria Dock in 1850, the second half of the century saw major extensions to the dock system. Along the Humber bank west of the River Hull confluence, Albert Dock was completed in 1869, followed by William Wright Dock (1880), St Andrew's Dock (1883) and St Andrew's extension (1897) (Fig. 18.5). To the east, Victoria Dock, with its Timber Pond and Earle's shipbuilding yard, was the only development until the construction of Alexandra Dock (1885). Covering 53 acres, this was Hull's largest dock before the opening of

King George Dock in 1914.

Port expansion, in conjunction with Hull's growing regional importance and its widening railway links, encouraged substantial industrial growth, led by oil seed crushing, paint making, engineering, leather working, corn milling, cotton spinning and fish processing (Brown 1969). Apart from engineering, which has always been more widely distributed within the city, and fish processing, which was first located near Albert Dock and later moved to the vicinity of St Andrew's Dock, manufacturing continued to concentrate on sites close to the River Hull. By 1914 the industrial axis had thickened and spread as far upstream as Stoneferry.

At the same time, the city centre was assuming something of its present shape, location and character. Before and during the Industrial Revolution it had remained historically fixed within the Old Town around Market Street, Lowgate, Silver Street, Whitefriargate and Myton Gate (Fig. 18.6). However, by the middle of the nineteenth century the Old Town was suffering from its isolation (created by the 'town docks') and its disorderly congestion of buildings, and many businesses were forced to close or move out to better positions (Wild and Shaw 1974). By 1881 most of Hull's principal central shopping streets were outside the Old Town; the main focus was represented by Savile Street, Paragon Street, Carr Lane, Carlisle Street, West Street and the southeastern section of Prospect Street (Fig. 18.6). By 1914 the expansion of the shopping core, often at the expense of old residential properties, had progressed a stage further to include George Street, Brook Street, the whole length of Prospect Street and the newly constructed King Edward Street and Jameson Street. In the Old Town only Market Street and Whitefriargate were still included.

As the nineteenth century evolved, an increasing quantity and proportion of the city's retail and services outlets were established in suburban locations, mostly 'invading' residences fronting the main roads. The largest of these arterial concentrations of shops and other business premises still survive today along Hessle Road, Anlaby Road, Spring Bank, Beverley Road, Newland Avenue and Holderness Road.

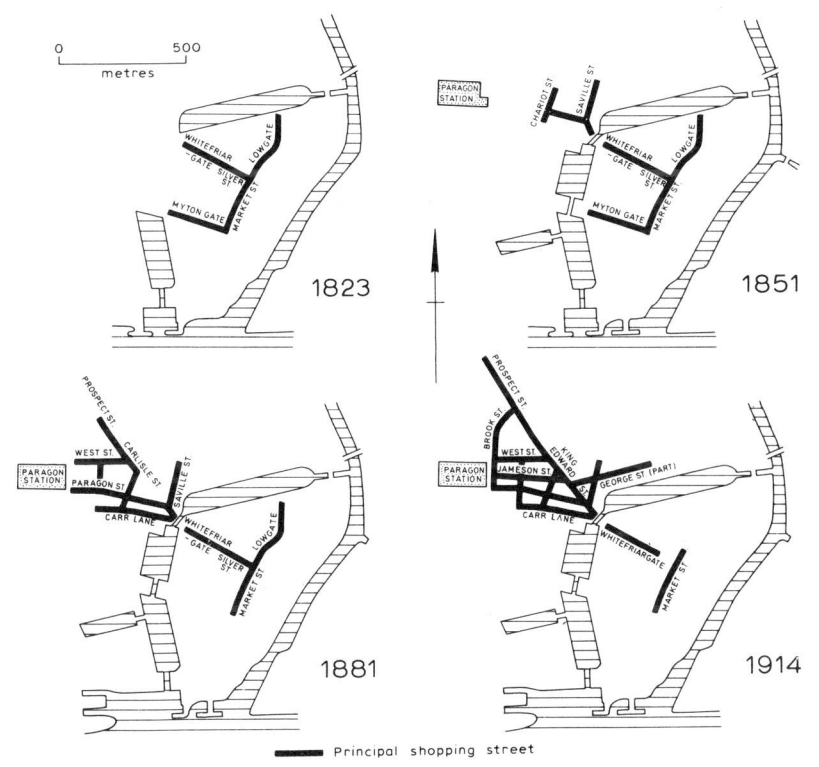

Fig. 18.6. Geographical spread of Hull's central shopping streets, 1823-1914. The analysis is based on the Trades Directories of Baines (1823), White (1851) and Kelly (1881, 1914).

Residential extension and internal change since 1918

Since 1918 Hull's geographical development has been far too extensive and complex to be discussed within the confines of this chapter in anything other than a selective manner. From this point onwards, therefore, attention is focused on the *residential dimension* of urban change. Above all other issues, this had the most important bearing on the shaping of the city and also had the widest human significance. Other aspects of post-1918 change have been more specific and more localised, the most notable being the modernisation of the city centre, including its reconstruction after the Second World War, the changing character and location of industrial development and the decline and new uses of the dock system.

Municipal and private suburbia
The First World War marked a major turning point in the history of urban housing in Britain. Until then the large majority of dwellings, more than 90% in England and Wales (Burnett 1978), had been constructed for private-rental tenure. The change came from two markedly different directions, first from the 1918 Tudor Walters Report and the 1919 Housing and Town Planning Act (or 'Addison' Act) which ushered in the first extensive programmes of municipal housing provision in almost all sizeable British towns and cities (a few cities, most notably Liverpool, did bring in quite large-scale programmes of municipal-council housing provision before 1918/19), and second from the sudden shift in middle-class preference in housing tenure, from rentals and leases to owner-occupance. The former direction was instrumental in creating 'municipal suburbia' while the latter led to 'private suburbia'.

Hull shared strongly in the growing civic enthusiasm for providing municipal housing. Before the 'Addison' Act the Corporation had constructed only 181 dwellings, mostly tenements built to rehouse people displaced from a small slum-clearance area in South Myton (Fleming 1986). However, between 1919 and 1939 just over 10 000 Corporation homes were completed. Of these, as many as 96% were built as municipal suburbia on six new estates situated around the periphery of the city (Fig. 18.7). In order of size they were the East Hull estate (3019 dwellings), North Hull estate (2336), Orchard Park (1741), Gipsyville (1380), Greatfield (823) and Derringham Bank (572). The design of each adhered strictly to the Tudor Walters guidelines - semi-detached or short four-unit rows, formal cottage-type houses, front and rear gardens, geometrically planned wide streets, green verges with space for tree-planting and a maximum density of just twelve dwellings per acre (Edwards 1981).

Between 1945 and 1964 a further 13 072 council dwellings were completed, including 2500 emergency prefabs built just after the war for people who had lost their homes through bombing (Fleming 1986). Four inter-war estates, East Hull, North Hull, Greatfield and Derringham Bank, were enlarged, but most new council homes were built in the three additional estates of Bilton Grange (2839 dwellings), Longhill (2088) and Boothferry (1694). It should be noted that

The geographical shaping of Hull

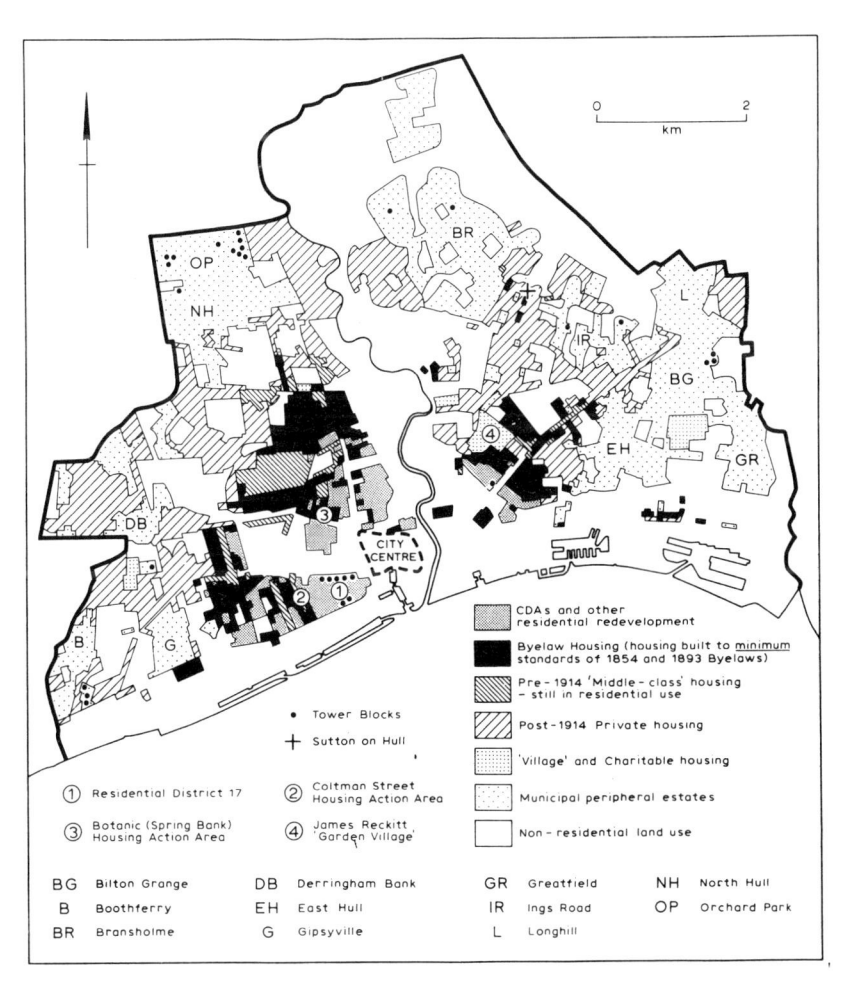

Fig. 18.7. Residential areas in Hull, 1988. Based on personal field-survey (1988).

Greatfield, Bilton Grange and Longhill lie in the eastern part of the city where land was cheaper and in easier supply. The development of these estates, and the later Ings Road estate, gave Hull a degree of physical symmetry that had never existed in the past. It also gave east Hull's housing profile a predominantly municipal character.

The heaviest wave of municipal, or council, housing construction, however, came during the late 1960s and the 1970s. Since 1964 the number of council-built homes has nearly doubled from 23 500 to 45 500, and today they account for 47% of all housing in the city (Gill 1987) - this percentage does not include the 9151 (August 1987) council houses sold under the terms of the 1979 'Right to Buy' Act. Nearly one-fifth of this huge increase was built in the inner residential districts in conjunction with residential redevelopment after extensive slum-clearance, but the housing programme was still dominated by completions in peripheral estates. There were three major projects here in the post-1964 period - Orchard Park in North Hull, which was extended by 3500 dwellings, the new Ings Road estate (3000) and the 'satellite' community of Bransholme (Fig. 18.7). The latter, with its 9240 council homes and more than 20 000 residents, is Hull's largest and most controversial housing scheme. Most of the people housed here had been moved from the eastern part of the Hessle Road area, where slum-clearances were being vigorously pursued during the late 1960s and early 70s. Criticism centered partly on its rather bleak and remote location on the extended northern edge of the city, and partly on the poor visual and living quality of its tower blocks and maisonettes (most of the high-rise developments have been classified as unfit for habitation and have recently been demolished). Such a marked departure from the long-established density and design traditions of Tudor Walters also occurred in certain other municipal developments, notably in the groups of tower blocks in the Orchard Park extension and earlier in Residential District 17 within the city's first extensive residential redevelopment zone.

During the inter-war period the spread of private suburbia occurred as long ribbons of houses and bungalows following most suburban main roads and bus routes; typical examples are Pickering Road, Willerby Road, Bricknell Avenue and Cottingham Road (Figs 18.5 and 18.7). This unplanned urban sprawl has been criticised for its unco-ordinated development, wastage of land and harmful environmental effects (Buchanan 1958). The quality of private housing varied considerably, reflecting differences in social status and incomes of its predominantly middle-class occupants (Edwards 1981). Detached and semi-detached houses of various sizes and designs were universal but, more so in Hull than in other cities, terrace-rows were also widespread. What these dwelling types had in common, however, was an architecture and external appearance deliberately designed to differentiate them from their municipal counterparts. Bay windows quickly became standard features even in the cheapest private houses, and by the 1930s gabled fronts and arched porches also became characteristic.

The pattern of private suburbia began to change towards the end of the inter-war period. The 1935 Restriction of Ribbon Development Act imposed limits on the further spread of ribbon suburbs and, in so doing, encouraged the appearance of small private-housing estates usually filling tracts of undeveloped land between main roads. Also, increasing car-ownership and declining availability of new residential sites within Hull itself encouraged building firms to turn to nearby villages and small towns in 'outer' suburbia beyond the city boundary. A ring of dormitory settlements soon emerged, mostly in the west and northwest where there were pleasant environmental conditions and good road and rail communications.

During the post-war period the building of owner-occupance housing in Hull was overshadowed by the massive quantity of council-house construction, and was also substantially exceeded by the private development taking place as 'rural suburbanisation' in Hull's quite extensive commuter belt (Wild this volume). As indicated by the population trend - a very modest 6% increase during 1911-31, and a 17% decline since 1931 - people with the choice were moving out from the city in increasing numbers.

Municipal and private suburbia, together with increasing use of land for industry, new roads, recreational space, schools and hospitals, brought a near-trebling of Hull's physical area during the age of 'inner' suburbanisation, from 1919 to 1939. Within the city's administrative boundary such a remarkable pace of growth was never achieved again (Fig. 18.3). This was not through any slowing down of urban extension during the post-war period, but because of its shift in emphasis from the city itself into outer suburbia. Since 1945 Hull's physical area has grown by 44%, with the largest contribution coming from the Bransholme development. The city now covers 23.6 square miles, which is more than twenty times the size of mid nineteenth century Hull and about 160 times that of the Old Town.

Slum clearances and residential redevelopment
In a piecemeal and small-scale way, the origins of slum clearances in

Hull, as in other cities, can be traced back into the nineteenth century. Outwards growth of the city centre, expansion of industrial premises and construction of important public buildings involved localised destruction of slum properties. The first municipal clearances came in the 1890s when 602 dwellings, mostly in South Myton and Drypool, were demolished under the terms of the 1890 Housing of the Working Classes Act (Fleming 1986). Subsequently the pace increased, and by the 1930s it was running at an average rate approaching 500 dwellings per annum. This, however, was still far short of what was required; even the destruction of about 5000 houses through bombing during the Second World War, 3000 of which were slums (Fleming 1986), was little more than the 'tip of the iceberg'.

The eventual breakthrough came with the 1947-57 series of planning legislation, which gave local authorities sufficient finance and legal machinery (for compulsory purchases) to undertake programmes not only of extensive slum-clearances but also of residential rebuilding within defined Comprehensive Development Areas (CDAs). Hull took this opportunity of greatly accelerating the removal and redevelopment of its slum quarters, and between 1955 and 1984 as many as 25 500 unfit dwellings were cleared (Kingston upon Hull City Planning Office 1986). The whole area of pre-byelaw housing, lying between the edge of the city centre and Hull's 1854 physical limit, was redeveloped. Altogether 6400 new council homes have been built within the various CDAs into which this zone was divided during the late 1950s and the 1960s. Hull's earliest and most publicised CDA scheme, Residential District 17, which was approved in 1959 to deal with the notorious slum quarter of South Myton, replaced 2500 court dwellings and back-to-backs with 1400 tower-block flats and maisonettes. The very large difference between numbers of cleared slums and numbers of replacement homes built *in situ* in clearance areas as a whole meant that about half of the affected households had to move to the peripheral estates. Accordingly slum-clearance and redevelopment have activated considerable depopulation of the inner city.

Over the last decade there has been a major change in emphasis away from replacement and towards improvement of outdated housing. For this grants have been made available to property owners, resulting in the scattered but quite widespread occurrence of residential renovation within the remaining areas of byelaw housing

(Fig. 18.7). The City, often in partnership with housing associations, has extended its activity in inner-city housing improvement, with the designation of two special Housing Action Areas (Coltman Street, off Hessle Road, and 'Botanic', immediately north of Spring Bank) for concentration of effort and resources. Housing Associations have also been involved in the construction of new houses in various parts of the city, including recent residential regeneration in the Old Town. The shift in policy from redevelopment to improvement has had the effect of preserving, rather than continuing the obliteration of, historical residential structures.

Acknowledgements

The author wishes to thank Patricia King, map curator of Hull University Map Library, for her assistance, and the Kingston upon Hull Director of Housing for provision of figures relating to Corporation/council-housing completions.

References

Baines, E. (1823). *History, Directory and Gazetteer of the County of York*, Vol. 2. E. Baines, Leeds.

Brown, L. (1969). Modern Hull. In: *The Victoria County History of the County of York, East Riding, Volume 1, The City of Kingston upon Hull* (ed. K.J. Allison) pp. 215-77. Oxford University Press, London.

Buchanan, C.D. (1958). *Mixed Blessing: the motor in Britain*. Leonard Hill, London.

Burnett, J. (1978). *A Social History of Housing 1815-1970*. David & Charles, Newton Abbot.

Conzen, M.R.G. (1960). Alnwick: a study in Town Plan analysis. *Institute of British Geographers Transactions* **27**, Special Edition.

Defoe, D. (1948). *A Tour through England and Wales*, Vol. 2. Everyman Edition, London.

Edwards, A.M. (1981). *The Design of Suburbia: a critical study in environmental history*. Pembridge Press, London.

Fleming, D. (1986). *Homes for the People: the story of council housing in Hull,* Malet Lambert Local History Reprint Vol. 67, Hull.

Forster, C.A. (1969). The Historical Development and Present-Day Significance of Byelaw-Housing Morphology, with particular reference to Hull, York and Middlesbrough. Ph.D. thesis, University of Hull.

Forster, C.A. (1972). *Court Housing in Kingston upon Hull,* University of Hull Occasional Papers in Geography No. 19, Hull.

Forster, G.C.F. (1969). Hull in the 16th and 17th centuries. In: *The Victoria County History of the County of York, East Riding, Volume 1, The City of Kingston upon Hull* (ed. K.J. Allison) pp. 90-173. Oxford University Press, London.

Gill, D. (ed.) (1987). *Humberside Facts and Figures 1987.* Humberside County Council, Hull.

Kelly, J. (1881). *Directory of Hull, Beverley and the East Riding.* Kelly's Directories Ltd, London.

Kelly, J. (1914). *Kelly's Directory of Hull and Neighbourhood.* Kelly's Directories Ltd, London.

Kingston upon Hull City Planning Office (1986). Housing Refurbishment Policy. Unpublished paper.

Mumford, L. (1961). *The City in History.* Secker & Warburg, London.

Patten, J. (1978). *English Towns 1500-1700,* Studies in Historical Geography. Wm Dawson and Sons, Folkestone.

White, F. (1851). *General Directory and Topography of Yorkshire.* Sheffield.

Wild, M.T. and Shaw, G. (1974). Locational behaviour of urban retailing during the nineteenth century: the example of Kingston upon Hull. *Institute of British Geographers Transactions* **61**, 101-18.

Williams, J.E. (1969). Hull, 1700-1835. In: *The Victoria County History of the County of York, East Riding, Volume 1, The City of Kingston upon Hull* (ed. K.J. Allison) pp. 174-214. Oxford University Press, London.

19

The archaeology of Beverley

D.H. Evans

Introduction

Water played a major role in the early life of Beverley for a number of reasons. The town owed a great deal of its success to its siting adjacent to the River Hull. This gave rise to its early development as a port, as it offered an outlet not only for the products of its own industries (notably cloths, bricks and tiles), but also for those of the surrounding hinterland. The poor drainage of much of the marshland to the east (the 'Carrs') also ensured that the location of the town at the western end of a string of islands (e.g. Tickton, Routh and White Cross) controlled one of the few dry crossing-points of this part of the Hull valley. In addition the various water courses which then flowed into Beverley Beck largely dictated the elongated shape of the medieval town and its winding streets. This is no longer so immediately apparent as most of them have disappeared as a result of the culverting of streams and lowering of the water-table by the sinking of numerous wells within the town, although some streams such as the Walker Beck survived late enough to be recorded on the early Ordnance Survey maps. Furthermore, water played a vital role in many of the town's industries. Crafts such as dyeing, fulling, tanning, potting and brick or tile making are all highly water-intensive, and simply could not have existed without a reliable, constant source. It is therefore hardly surprising that streams such as the Walker Beck are named after the trade (fulling) which exploited them. Lastly, even the name of the town is descriptive of the fundamental part which water played in this area - the lake or stream of the beavers. A twelfth century account of the miracles of St John mentions a lake surrounding the town and flowing out into the churchyard; although this description probably contains an element of poetic exaggeration, it is a useful reminder that the limits of early settlement were greatly conditioned by factors of drainage, and that we may need to think in terms of 'islands' of settlement being separated by areas of marsh, pools and streams at the time of the Norman Conquest.

Pre-Conquest Beverley

Recent environmental work in various parts of the town suggests that much of the pre-urban landscape was dominated by a mixture of oak woodland and wetland elements - pools, marshes and wet grassland (Hall and Kenward 1980, Sanders and Armstrong 1983, Armstrong *et al.* forthcoming, Evans and Tomlinson forthcoming). As such, it is likely to have been exploited by prehistoric hunters in much the same way as the lowlands to the east (Gilbertson this volume). Neolithic activity, accompanied by some clearance, is suggested by redeposited finds of polished axeheads at Hengate and Lurk Lane (Fig. 19.1). Iron Age settlement is attested by the square ditched barrows on the Westwood to the west of the town. Shallow ditches, perhaps representing plot boundaries of a cultivation system, were located at Lurk Lane, and could be of any date from later prehistoric to early Anglo-Saxon. Similar ditches were also noted at Constitution Hall, Flemingate.

The nature of Roman settlement in Beverley is at present uncertain, but there is a steadily growing quantity of Roman finds from sites throughout the town. This material ranges in date from the late first or early second century to the later fourth century and includes Flavian/Trajanic (AD 69-116) and later samian, greywares, Nene Valley colour-coated wares, coins, three glass bangle fragments, glass tesserae and large quantities of brick and tile. Although much of this is redeposited, it is mostly found in medieval construction dumps of soil which are unlikely to have come from any

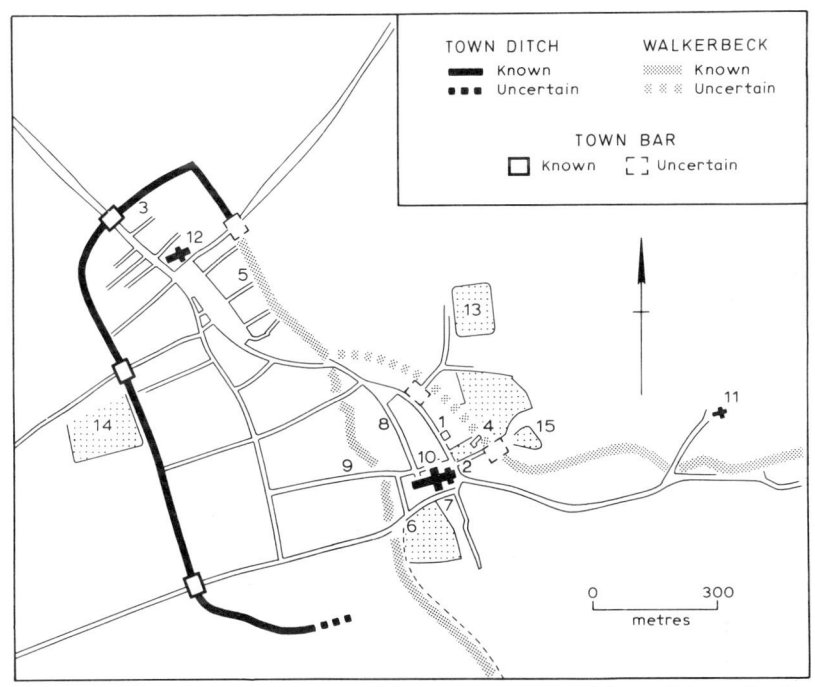

Fig. 19.1. The medieval town of Beverley, showing the positions of the main sites mentioned in the text. 1 Eastgate, 2 Constitution Hall, 3 Wylies Road, 4 Dominican Friary, 5 Dyer Lane, 6 Hall Garth, 7 Lurk Lane, 8 Highgate, 9 Minster Moorgate, 10 The Minster, 11 St Nicholas' Church, 12 St Mary's Church, 13 Preceptory of Knights Hospitallers, 14 Franciscan Priory, 15 St Nicholas' Hospital.

great distance. As yet, the only Roman site which has been found within the town is on the south side of Wylies Road. Here a small V-shaped ditch was found at the edge of an excavation across the medieval defences. It contained a number of fairly complete pots of late second or early third century date (*contra* Frere 1986), suggesting settlement on the better-drained gravels to the south.

The choice of Beverley by Bishop John for the siting of his monastery of Inderauuda at the beginning of the eighth century was of crucial importance to the later development of the town. The identification of Inderauuda ('in the wood of the men of Deira') with Beverley was for a long time unproven; however, textual analysis of an early eleventh century list of saints' resting-places shows that the section which links St John with Beverley ('Beferlic') had been compiled by the middle of the ninth century (Rollason 1978), and as there is no hint of an earlier translation of his remains from anywhere else, the identification of these two place names as relating to a single site seems secure. The last vestiges of doubt were removed by the discovery at Lurk Lane of a substantial stretch of the precinct ditch of this Anglian monastery and some of its outlying industrial buildings. Although its church has not yet been located by excavation (it probably lies somewhere beneath the present Minster), fragments of window glass and lead window came from these levels show that this church was a stone building with glazed windows (cf. the contemporary buildings at Jarrow and Monkwearmouth). Dating of the site is provided by Middle Saxon pottery and other finds, and is corroborated by a series of radiocarbon dates (a.d. 680-885 from the secondary silting in the precinct ditch, and a.d. 780-980 from the Phase 4A occupation levels). The occupation of this first monastery traditionally ended in a Danish raid of *c.* AD 866. The evidence from Lurk Lane suggests that the equivalent Phase (4A) ended with the concealment of a purse-hoard of twenty-three coins in *c.* AD 851, the year that the great Viking army first over-wintered in England. Whilst it might be tempting to suggest that the monastery was abandoned some fifteen years earlier than its traditional sacking, the failure to recover this hoard might merely reflect the problems involved with relocating such a small cache. Nevertheless, it does illustrate the prevailing climate of fear and uncertainty in mid ninth century Northumbria (for further details of the excavation see Armstrong *et al.* forthcoming).

The monastery seems to have been abandoned for half a century or more, and then re-established as a college of secular canons in the early tenth century. Tradition has it that it was re-founded under King Athelstan in AD 937. The archaeological evidence is far less precise, but the primary levels of the second monastery include a coin from the Viking kingdom of York, which could have been lost as late as AD 930, and there are certainly other objects and pottery which indicate tenth century occupation. Perhaps this was indeed re-founded by Athelstan; alternatively, perhaps he endowed an institution which was already in the throes of rebirth. Either way the site has produced one of the most important collections of Anglo-Scandinavian finds in Northumbria, outside of York itself. The structural evidence shows that once again this part of the precinct contained a number of industrial buildings during the tenth and eleventh centuries. However, whereas the ninth century buildings had been associated with iron-smithing, these later structures were associated with lead and glass-working, and were clearly providing the fixtures and fittings (glazed windows and sheets of roofing lead) for new stone buildings which were being erected elsewhere in the precinct. Substantial building activity is documented through much of the early and mid eleventh century under successive Saxon Archbishops, but routine maintenance of existing buildings would clearly have been needed throughout this period.

At the northern end of the town the church of St Mary is also reputedly an Athelstan foundation. Although the earliest extant masonry is of twelfth century date, the church clearly pre-dates the medieval street system which is on a markedly different alignment, almost at a diagonal to it. The emergence of a parish church at such an early date suggests that some sort of domestic settlement was firmly established here, distinct from the religious community to the south. Whether this was a nucleated settlement or a collection of dispersed steadings is a moot point; certainly there is insufficient evidence to argue for proto-urban nuclei. However, it seems that such settlement was probably sited on the same outcrop of gravel which was favoured by its Roman predecessor. Contemporary activity in the area between St Mary's and the monastery to the south is evidenced by the find of a scramasax (a single-edged long knife) from Butcher Row (Sanders and Armstrong 1983) and by land reclamation from a pond on Eastgate (Evans and Tomlinson forthcoming).

Post-Conquest Beverley

Within a century of the Norman Conquest Beverley had emerged as a town with borough status (granted by the 1120s). By 1377 it was the eleventh largest town in England and one of the three major towns in Yorkshire, the other two being York and Hull. Four major factors for this rise can be proposed. The first was its association with the cult of St John, who continued to be one of England's major saints during the Middle Ages; his banner was even carried at Agincourt, alongside that of St George. This association was fundamental in securing for the men of Beverley most of their favourable trading privileges. It also probably brought a steady income into the town from pilgrims. Traditionally, it saved the town from being looted by the Normans during the 'Harrying of the North'. A second, related factor was the patronage of the Archbishops of York, who became the sole lords of the manor. These two factors ensured that Beverley continued to have an importance in the religious world which far outreached its nominal status within the Archdiocese. Hence it continued to boast a major church despite the fact that its Minster status had long since been redundant. Thanks to these connections, Beverley in the mid twelfth century enjoyed more fairs than York itself. Only rarely did this association with the Archbishop work to the disadvantage of the town, for example when the entire town was excommunicated in 1200 because of its association with Archbishop Geoffrey (Stubbs 1871). A third factor was the siting of the town adjacent to the River Hull. Prior to the emergence of Hull as a port during the thirteenth century, Beverley was the major port for the Hull valley and the Wolds, and enjoyed a thriving coastal and continental trade. This is amply illustrated by finds from excavations throughout the town. Its major continental links were with the ports of the Low Countries and northern France, but connections with the Baltic, southwest France, Iberia and the Mediterranean are also evident. Its coastal trade is illustrated by links with other Yorkshire ports (e.g. Scarborough), but finds such as the seal of an Aberdeen merchant, or a number of London lead brooches, demonstrate the extent of its trade. A final factor in the success of the town was the rise of its cloth industry and the popularity of the colours used by its dyers. Its products became fashionable both along the eastern seaboard and in Europe, and became the town's main export. Other industries such as tanning and brick and tile making played an important role in the town's economy, but did not supplant the cloth industry until c. 1400, by which time the town was in decline. Its fortunes slumped during the fifteenth century (Kermode 1987), and took a further downfall with the demise of its college of secular canons at the Dissolution (Neave this volume).

The historical background to the town during the Middle Ages is thus well understood. Archaeology has been able to contribute to this picture in three specific areas. The first is on the life of the religious communities, notably within the college of secular canons attached to the church of St John, and in the Dominican Friary. The second concerns the town's main industries (dyeing, fulling, tanning, potting and brick and tile making). Finally, it can also shed light on specific aspects of the development of particular streets and on the town defences. By contrast, very little is known of the domestic housing of the period for any level of society in the borough, from the Archbishop downwards. A study of surviving buildings adds little to the picture, for none survives from before the fifteenth century, and even those from the sixteenth century are likely to be unrepresentative, and heavily refurbished at a later date.

Excavations at Lurk Lane revealed a wholesale reorganisation of the Minster complex at about the time of the Norman Conquest, and that this was accompanied by major landscaping of most of the area to the south. Although this work may have been initiated by the last of the Saxon Archbishops, it is more likely to have been the work of the Normans. A succession of aisled buildings was uncovered, spanning the period from the later eleventh to the later sixteenth centuries. Briefly summarised, those of the eleventh and twelfth centuries were earth-fast post buildings, those of the thirteenth and fourteenth centuries were padstone-based buildings, and the latest buildings were of interrupted sill construction. The initial identification of this complex was that it was part of the Bedern (the residence of the Vicars Choral), but in fact it was probably one of the prebendal houses, or perhaps represents guest accommodation.

One of the major features of the medieval levels at Lurk Lane (Fig. 19.2) was the recognition of the 1188 fire horizon. The chronicler Roger of Howden records that a disastrous fire broke out in the town on 20 September 1188, resulting in the destruction of most of the town and substantial damage to the church of St John (Stubbs 1869). At Lurk Lane the Phase 6C hall was destroyed by fire, sealing beneath the debris a number of new coins struck in 1180 or very shortly thereafter, and several complete pottery vessel profiles. This offers a useful time capsule, as very little appears to have been disturbed from these levels. The general chronology of the site is confirmed by a succession of underlying and overlying deposits, dated by associated coins, dendrochronology and archaeomagnetically dated hearths (Armstrong *et al.* forthcoming). It thus provides a useful fixed point in the chronology of Beverley. A by-product of this fire is the enormous quantity of Romanesque masonry from the Minster and its associated buildings, which was

Fig. 19.2. The foundations of medieval buildings at Lurk Lane seen from the north. In the foreground is a succession of aisled buildings up to the sixteenth century, with a thirteenth century stone annex of the Minster complex in the background.

subsequently reused throughout Beverley either as building stone (e.g. in the Minster itself) or as rubble; fragments have been found reused as padstones (at Lurk Lane and Eastgate), as packing in pits, rubble in paths and as infilling of deep ponds and pits. The main value of this material is that it gives a major insight into the form of the Saxo-Norman Minster and its associated buildings, which have otherwise disappeared from view. Hence we can now identify a major building programme which was proceeding in the Minster complex in the middle years of the twelfth century, but which was otherwise undocumented. Some of this work seems to have involved the same group of masons who were at work at Fountains and Jervaulx Abbeys in the 1170s.

At the Dominican Friary an important series of excavations has done much to establish the layout of the precinct and its principal buildings, and to correct earlier misconceptions (Armstrong and Tomlinson 1987). More recently, the eastern ends of the church and chapter house have been uncovered, and a second and outer late medieval cloister has been excavated.

The limits of the early medieval town were tightly defined by topographic factors, notably by areas of wetland, woods and commons. Expansion to the south was effectively prohibited by the location of the Archbishop's palace at Hall Garth, and by his hunting park beyond (Barley 1983). The area immediately to the north of the Minster traversed several areas of wetland. As a result, there was comparatively little early domestic settlement around the Minster, the commercial centre of the town being concentrated to the north around the Saturday Market area and adjacent streets. The intervening marshy areas seem, despite their apparent 'central location', to have enjoyed a peripheral status. As such, they formed a natural focus for industries which needed a ready supply of water. Excavations on the east side of Eastgate revealed just such a pattern of tenement use, with anti-social industries such as smithing, dyeing and fulling being carried out within a few hundred metres of the Minster until the middle years of the fourteenth century.

The dominant industry on the Eastgate site was dyeing, as evidenced by a great succession of industrial hearths with interlinked complexes of timber vats and drains, some of which were still lined with traces of madder and wool-fats (Fig. 19.3). Further evidence of this industry is supplied by numerous finds of dyeing plants such as woad, weld and bog myrtle, and by impressive collections of associated artefacts such as stone mullers (used to break up the plant stems), mortars and spindle whorls (Evans and Tomlinson forthcoming). Documentary evidence suggests that by the later thirteenth century Eastgate properties were being rented by numerous small tradesmen such as masons and carpenters, and that this still formed a type of industrial suburb. The following century was to see a shift towards residential or domestic settlement. Another area in which the dyeing and fulling industry was located lay further to the north on the edge of the Walker Beck. Excavations at Dyer Lane uncovered similar evidence to that found at Eastgate, although not on such a dramatic scale. Once again, timber vats and drains were associated with objects such as stone mullers and spindle whorls.

Leather-working was another of Beverley's major industries, although tanning pits have been located only on Flemingate (Sanders and Armstrong 1983). These dated to the eleventh or twelfth centuries, but later tanneries clearly existed somewhere on the edges of the medieval town as cobbling and shoemaking are

Fig. 19.3. Timber vats and drains of mid twelfth century date which formed part of the dyeing complex at Eastgate.

attested at numerous sites. Large quantities of shoe parts and leather waste are found on the Eastgate site from the early twelfth century onwards (Evans and Tomlinson forthcoming). Substantial amounts of leather objects and waste fragments were also recovered from a complex of pits dating from the tenth to the thirteenth centuries in Wilbert Lane and Butcher Row (Sanders and Armstrong 1983).

The last of Beverley's major industries concerned the production of pots, bricks and tiles. These were often, but not invariably, made by the same craftsmen, and hence can be considered here as a single industry. This was located in a loosely-defined industrial suburb on the southeast side of the medieval town in the Beckside and Grovehill areas. Some nine production sites within this suburb are now known either from fieldwork or from documentary records, and these span the period from the later twelfth to the mid seventeenth century. No pottery kilns have yet been located, but two major dumps of pottery wasters were found at the Albion Court site in 1985, and at an earlier site by the River Hull in 1947-8. Tileries are much better known from the documentary records, and a recent excavation at Annie Reed Road revealed six tile kilns and several associated timber sheds (Youngs *et al.* 1987). Subsequent geophysical work on this site has revealed a further five kilns. All the excavated kilns were producing flat roof tiles during the mid and later thirteenth century. The pattern of land use in this area seems to have consisted of renting plots for a set number of years, followed by the abandonment of the site once a clay source had been exhausted, or if other factors, such as causing an environmental nuisance, prompted the owner not to renew a lease.

Sections across the town defences have been obtained in only two areas. At the northern end of the town, at Wylies Road, a 3 m deep ditch was cut into the well-drained gravel subsoil; its base was revetted by some sort of hurdling. The full width of the town defences could not be established at this point (Hughes 1985). At the southern end of the town the boundary ditch ('defences' is too grand a word) was a mere 0.7 m deep and 2.1 m wide at Long Lane (Sanders and Armstrong 1983). However, the smaller scale of this earthwork may simply reflect the problems of digging deep ditches in clay. Nevertheless, the disparity between these works suggests that at Beverley the role of the town ditches was primarily one of demarcation of the limit of the town's authority, rather than one of defence.

Attempts at improvement of drainage have been observed at a number of locations within the town at dates varying between the late twelfth and later fourteenth centuries. Many of the medieval street surfaces have been raised by the deposition of massive dumps of chalk and building stone on top of rafts of brushwood and occasionally of timber. These were first observed by Stephenson (1895) during the construction of many of the nineteenth century sewers, but they have been more recently seen at Oswaldgate and Butcher Row (Sanders and Armstrong 1983) in late twelfth/early thirteenth century levels. Similar attempts at improving the drainage of individual burgage plots have been observed at Long Lane and Chantry Lane (Sanders and Armstrong 1983) and at Highgate (Watkins and Williams 1983).

The future of Beverley's past

The last decade has seen a great deal of work devoted to the exploration of much of the central area of the medieval town, and the choice of sites has inevitably been dictated by the developers. Although it has contributed much useful information about aspects of the medieval town, the range of that information has been limited, and there are still substantial areas about which we know very little. A plot of the excavated sites shows that work has been concentrated on the southern and eastern sides of the town (Fig. 19.1), with the end result that we know more about peripheral industries than we do about residential housing or shops. The situation has been further hindered by the lack of available frontages for excavation; nowhere has a complete tenement been excavated.

Now that the centre of the town is largely protected as a conservation area, development is inevitably shifting towards the peripheral areas of the medieval town, and particularly to its outlying suburbs. The known sites which are at risk are mainly those of religious houses, such as the friaries, leper houses, hospitals and the preceptory of the Knights Hospitallers (Miller *et al.* 1982). Of equal interest are areas of early or potentially early settlement (e.g. St Mary's Manor site), and the industrial suburbs such as Grovehill, with its documented ceramic industries. Archaeological priorities are therefore changing as the focus and pace of development change.

However, because of the very nature of the sites which are now being threatened, it is becoming more difficult to persuade planners to impose archaeological conditions on sites which are less dramatic, or to persuade funding bodies to part with ever-dwindling sources of finance. Consequently, for the immediate future the outlook for archaeology in Beverley is bleak.

References

Armstrong, P. and Tomlinson, D.G. (1987). *Excavations at the Dominican Priory, Beverley, 1960-1983*, Humberside Heritage Publication 13. Humberside Leisure Services, Hull.

Armstrong, P., Tomlinson, D.G. and Evans, D.H. (forthcoming). *Excavations at Lurk Lane, Beverley, 1979-1982*. University of Sheffield.

Barley, M.W. (1983). Review of 'Beverley: an archaeological and architectural study'. *Archaeological Journal* 63, 456-7.

Evans, D.H. and Tomlinson, D.G. (forthcoming). *Excavations at 33-35 Eastgate, 1983-86*. University of Sheffield.

Frere, S.S. (ed.) (1986). Roman Britain in 1985: 1. Sites explored. *Britannia* 17, 385-6.

Hall, A.R. and Kenward, H.K. (1980). The interpretation of biological remains from Highgate, Beverley. *Journal of Archaeological Science* 7, 33-51.

Hughes, J. (1985). *An Excavation on the Town Defences of Beverley*. Humberside Archaeological Unit, Beverley.

Kermode, J.I. (1987). Merchants, overseas trade, and urban decline: York, Beverley, and Hull, c. 1380-1500. *Northern History* 23, 51-73.

Miller, K., Robinson, J., English, B. and Hall, I. (1982). *Beverley: an archaeological and architectural study*, Royal Commission on Historic Monuments Supplementary Series No. 4. HMSO, London.

Rollason, D.W. (1978). Lists of saints' resting-places in Anglo-Saxon England. *Anglo-Saxon England* 7, 61-93.

Sanders, G.B. and Armstrong, P. (1983). A watching brief on the Beverley high level drainage scheme. *East Riding Archaeologist* 7, 52-70.

Stephenson, W. (1895). Beverley in Olden Times. *Archaeological Journal* **52**, 271-9.

Stubbs, W. (ed.) (1869/71). *Chronica Magistri Rogeri de Hovedene*, Rolls Ser. 51 Vol. 2. London.

Watkins, J.G. and Williams, R.A.H. (1983). An excavation in Highgate, Beverley, 1977. *East Riding Archaeologist* **7**, 71-84.

Youngs, S., Clark, J. and Barry, T. (1987). Medieval Britain and Ireland in 1986. *Medieval Archaeology* **31**, 110-91.

20

Post-medieval Beverley

D. Neave

Sixteenth century decline

Around 1540 John Leland, 'king's antiquary', visited Beverley and he noted that it was a very large town 'welle buildid of wood', but that the once important cloth manufacture was 'much decayid' (Woodward 1985 p. 8). By that date the town's medieval prosperity (Evans this volume) was clearly on the wane, for an Act of 1535 had named Beverley, along with other towns, as having many houses in the principal streets in great ruin and decay (MacMahon 1973). Although it is impossible to verify this general statement, the deterioration of the town's economy was clearly exacerbated by the Reformation. The dissolution of the town's two friaries and the wealthy preceptory of the Knights Hospitallers in the late 1530s was followed in 1548 by the termination of the collegiate status of Beverley Minster. The property and wealth of the Minster were confiscated and its staff of at least seventy seven was reduced to four. The final loss of rights of sanctuary in 1540 also had an impact on the town's status and population; between 1478 and 1539 469 people fleeing from some crime or debt had sought refuge in the town (MacMahon 1973).

The decline seemingly continued throughout the sixteenth century, for in 1599 it was claimed that the town 'heretofore verie ritch and populous is nowe become very poore and greatly depopulated in so muche as there are in the same fower hundred tenements and dwellinge-houses utterly decayed and uninhabited' (Poulson 1829 p. 338). The transference of trade to Hull and dissolution of the Minster are given as the main causes. Notwithstanding its apparent decline, Beverley remained a leading marketing and trading centre in the region, and its continued importance was confirmed by the grant of a charter of incorporation in 1573 (Poulson 1829).

Seventeenth and eighteenth century development

During the first half of the seventeenth century the town suffered from two severe outbreaks of the plague (in 1604 and 1610) and from the repercussions of the Civil Wars. Beverley, as an open town without defences, was adversely affected through its proximity to the twice-besieged Parliamentary stronghold of Hull. Bloody skirmishes were fought in and around Beverley in 1643, and both Royalist and Parliamentarian forces plundered the town (MacMahon 1973). However, these events, and the financial and other depredations suffered by leading local families for their involvement with the Royalists, had little long-term impact on the town, and by the late seventeenth century Beverley was emerging from its post-medieval decline. For example, in 1695 Edmund Gibson noted that Beverley was 'of late much improv'd in its buildings' and two years later Celia Fiennes found it 'a very fine town for its size ... the buildings are new and pretty lofty' (Woodward 1985 pp. 41 and 48). Marketing and the processing of agricultural produce were still the basis of the town's economy, but it was also developing as the administrative capital of the East Riding and as a social centre.

At the beginning of the eighteenth century there were two weekly markets. That held on Wednesdays was discontinued soon after 1731, but the Saturday market is still flourishing today (MacMahon 1958). The latter's importance in the eighteenth century is evidenced by the splendid surviving market cross erected in 1711-14, and by the building of butchers' shambles in 1753 and fish shambles in 1777 (MacMahon 1958). Butchers constituted the largest group in the market, occupying some forty-five stalls (Humberside Record Office DDBC/16/103, 128). Of the numerous fairs, the most important was the Cross fair at Ascensiontide which

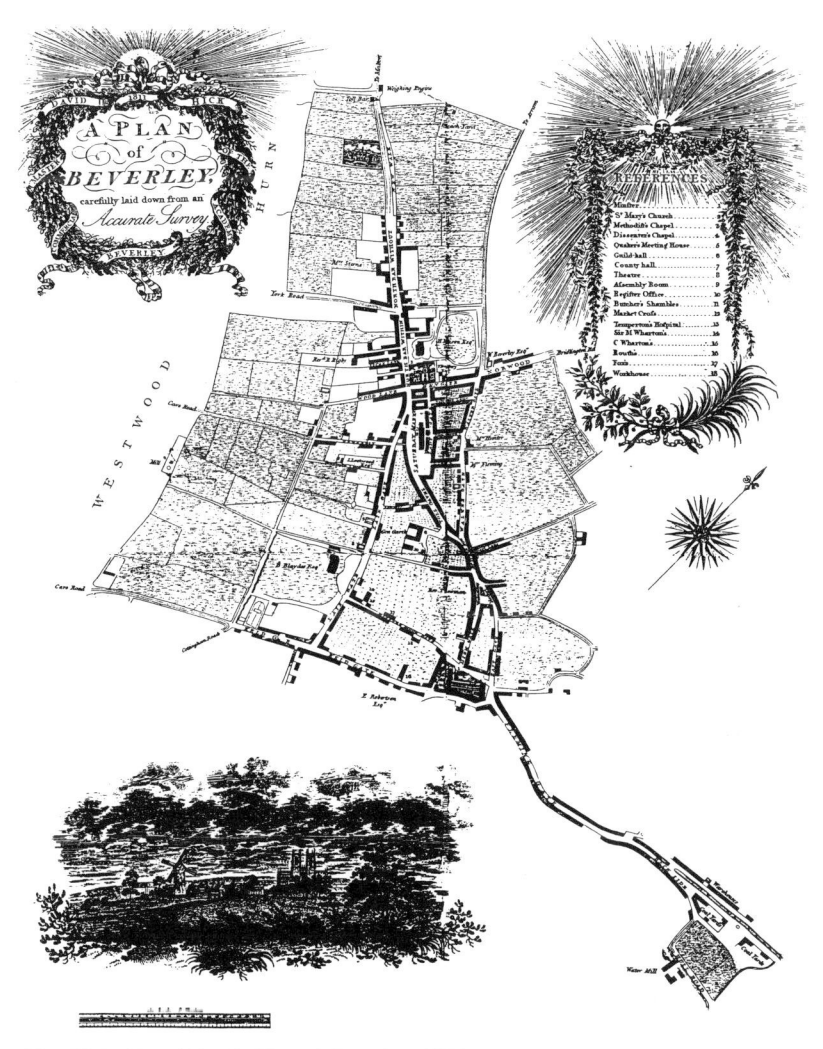

Fig. 20.1. David Hick's *Plan of Beverley*, 1811.

was widely known for the 'mercery' and 'haberdashery ware' sold there by London merchants. The merchants had their shops in Highgate (Fig. 20.1), which was otherwise called Londoners' street. However, increasingly few London merchants attended the fair in the later seventeenth century, and by the mid eighteenth century their empty shops were being replaced by houses (MacMahon 1958, Humberside Record Office DDBC/16/175).

The Londoners' goods were carried via the River Hull and Beverley Beck, which were of commercial importance to the town well into this century. The corporation spent considerable sums on improving the beck following the Beck Acts of 1727 and 1745, culminating in the construction of a lock at the junction with the River Hull in 1802-3 (MacMahon 1971). Land communications were also greatly improved in the eighteenth century. The road linking Hull and Beverley was turnpiked in 1744, and by 1769 all the main roads leading to Beverley had similarly come under turnpike trusts (MacMahon 1964).

Agricultural improvements in the East Riding from the 1760s led to a great increase in the corn trade, and in 1825 the front of the butchers' shambles was converted to a corn exchange (MacMahon 1958). Cattle and corn provided the main raw materials for the principal trades and industries of the town which, in the late seventeenth century, were said to be the production of malt, oat-meal and tanned leather (Woodward 1985). Only freemen were allowed to exercise a trade in the town, but the strict control of the guilds declined from the sixteenth century. By 1724 only the brotherhoods of the mercers, carpenters, tailors, bakers, bricklayers, oatshillers, butchers, shoemakers and the combined fraternity of tanners and skinners remained of the thirty-eight guilds recorded in the fourteenth century (Poulson 1829). Tanning was the most prominent industry in the eighteenth century, and shoemakers, of whom there were sixty-seven in 1774, the most numerous craftsmen (Beverley Reference Library *Copy of Poll 1774*). During this century maltsting and oat-meal making declined, but the associated trades of brewing and corn milling expanded. In the same period, nursery gardening emerged and by 1829 the firm of George and William Tindall, with a staff of fifty, was the major employer in the town; less well known were the mint plantations which flourished off Hull Road and Grovehill Road during the Napoleonic Wars (Oliver 1829).

Although a large proportion of the population was engaged in trades and crafts, Beverley was not considered a 'town of trade' by visitors in the Georgian period. For example, the actor-manager Tate Wilkinson stated that the town was 'chiefly supported by the genteel private families that reside there in continuance' (Wilkinson 1790). The genteel families, whose fine houses and large gardens still determine the character of Beverley, were attracted to the town because of its position as a social centre. By 1700 Beverley was providing entertainments and specialist services for the periodic gatherings of local gentry at the quarter sessions which had become permanently based in the town (Forster 1973). Beverley's role as the capital of the East Riding was emphasised in 1708 when it was chosen as the location for the newly established registry of deeds for the East Riding and Hull (MacMahon 1958). By the mid eighteenth century the town had also become the centre for all the county militia and lieutenancy meetings (Norfolk 1965).

Georgian Beverley's social life revolved around horse races, assemblies, concerts and theatrical performances. A race course was laid out on the Westwood in the late seventeenth century. The course was moved to a new site on the Hurn by 1765 and a grandstand was built there two years later (Poulson 1829, MacMahon 1958). Fine new assembly rooms, the scene of social gatherings, balls and interminable card parties, were opened in Norwood in 1763 (Humberside Record Office DDBC 21/99) (Fig. 20.2). Regular visits by theatrical companies based in York and then Richmond began around 1730, and the first purpose-built playhouse was opened in Walkergate in the 1750s (Tillott 1961, Hall and Hall 1973). Beverley also had its 'spa'; from the late seventeenth century a well on Swine Moor had been resorted to for bathing and drinking. A new wellhouse was built in 1747 and the spa continued to be used until the second decade of the nineteenth century (Humberside Record Office DDBC/16/160, Beverley Corporation Records BC/IV/1/1). Finally, the essential promenading place was provided in the 1780s with the laying out of the tree-lined New Walk (MacMahon 1958).

The numerous inns of the town (there were 48 licensed alehouses in 1725), which fared best during parliamentary elections, were the centres of social life for the bulk of the population. The chief inns were the Tiger and Blue Bell, the latter renamed the Beverley Arms after rebuilding in 1796 (Hull University Library DDMM/29/40 and DDX/60/3). The town and county were largely administered from these two inns, although the town council officially met in a fine Guildhall that was rebuilt in 1762 (MacMahon 1958, *York Courant* 28 November 1752). A Sessions House, the meeting place of the East

Fig. 20.2. Norwood c. 1900. In the centre are the Assembly Rooms (1761-3), now demolished, and on the right Norwood House (c. 1765).

Riding justices, was built at the end of New Walk in 1807-14, and from here the East Riding was ruled.

By the early nineteenth century the modest half-timber and thatch buildings which still predominated in the 1660s had been almost totally replaced by more substantial brick and tile houses and shops. Among the surviving large houses of this period are Newbegin House (c. 1690), Norwood House (c. 1765) (Fig. 20.2) and Lairgate Hall (c. 1760-70) (Hall and Hall 1973). Later, the middle-and upper-class development was chiefly in the form of semi-detached or terraced houses. Much of the expanding population was, however, housed in cramped yards off the older streets. It was not until the later eighteenth century that development really began outside the town's medieval boundaries, for Beverley's population in the early nineteenth century was little different from what it had been in the late Middle Ages. In 1552 a population of some 5000 was claimed, but this probably included a larger area than the built-up town (MacMahon 1973). Nevertheless, an estimate of 2800 inhabitants 120 years later, based on the Hearth Tax returns, suggests

Table 20.1. Population of Beverley, 1801-1981.

1801	5401	1891	12 539
1811	6035	1901	13 183
1821	6728	1911	13 654
1831	7432	1921	13 469
1841	7574	1931	14 012
1851	8915	1951	15 504
1861	9654	1961	16 031
1871	10 218	1971	17 132
1881	11 425	1981	19 687

Sources   Page (1913 p. 499); HMSO *Census: County Reports, East Riding 1921-71, Humberside 1981.*

considerable decline (Humberside Record Office Microfilm of Hearth Tax Returns 1672). Diocesan visitation returns and parish registers indicate a rise to about 3300 by 1760 and then a much more rapid rise to the 1801 census figure of 5401 (Borthwick Institute York Bp.V.1764/Ret.1 nos. 56-7, Humberside Record Office PE 1/4,6-7 and PE 129/6-10).

Nineteenth and twentieth century expansion

The steady population rise throughout the nineteenth century (Table 20.1) reflects the increasing industrialisation of the town. This was particularly marked in the first three decades of the century with the expansion of tanning and the founding of a firm of agricultural machinery makers that became known throughout the world. William Hodgson established a tannery in Flemingate in 1812, which was steadily enlarged until it was employing some 400 men by the end of the century (Bulmer 1892, MacMahon 1973), and in 1825 William Crosskill opened an iron foundry in Mill Lane (Fig. 20.3); this developed rapidly, making a wide range of iron articles and patented agricultural machinery, including the celebrated clod-crusher. The

Fig. 20.3. Crosskill's Iron Works, 1861.

expansion of the firm was greatly assisted by the opening of the Hull-Bridlington railway line through Beverley in 1846 and the outbreak of the Crimean War in 1854. Large contracts were obtained for the supply of carts, shells and other military equipment, and at one stage some 800 men were employed at the foundry. However, the post-war slump and a serious fire in 1860 led to severe financial problems and, although the business was taken over in 1864, it finally closed in 1878 (MacMahon 1973).

The other major nineteenth century Beverley industry was shipbuilding at Grovehill. A minor industry throughout the eighteenth century, it expanded during the Napoleonic Wars when ships of several tons were built. Then followed a period of decline until the industry revived in the late nineteenth century, building steam trawlers for the Hull fishing industry; in 1892 the largest shipyard, Cochrane, Cooper & Schofield, with 400 workmen, vied with Hodgson's tannery as the chief employer in the town. In the years 1884-1900 Cochrane's launched 245 ships. They were followed at the yard by Cook, Welton & Gemmell from 1901-63. In 1918 Armstrong's Patents was established in Eastgate, making shock absorbers for the growing motor industry.

The shipyard, Hodgson's and Armstrong's remained Beverley's major employers until they either closed or left the town in the late 1970s. Although today there are various flourishing industries, including light engineering and caravan manufacture, the main employment comes through Beverley's position as a thriving shopping centre and as the administrative centre of both the county of Humberside and the East Yorkshire Borough of Beverley. It is also a highly desirable residential town and has recently experienced a rapid increase in population (Table 20.1) associated with large-scale housing development to the north, east and south, although the still-surviving common pastures of Westwood and the Hurn have restricted development westwards.

References

Bulmer, T. (1892). *History, Topography and Directory of East Yorkshire.* Preston.
Forster, G.C.F. (1973). *The East Riding Justices of the Peace in the Seventeenth Century.* East Yorkshire Local History Society, York.
Hall, I. and Hall, E. (1973). *Historic Beverley.* W. Sessions, York.
MacMahon, K.A. (1958). *Beverley Corporation Minute Books 1707-1835,* Yorkshire Archaeological Record Series vol. 122. Yorkshire Archaeological Society, Leeds.
MacMahon, K.A. (1964). *Roads and Turnpike Trusts in Eastern Yorkshire.* East Yorkshire Local History Society, York.
MacMahon, K.A. (1971). 'Beverley and its beck: borough finance and a town navigation 1700-1835. *Transport History* **4**, 121-43.
MacMahon, K.A. (1973). *Beverley.* Dalesman Books, Clapham.
Norfolk, R.W.S. (1965). *Militia, Yeomanry and Volunteer Forces of the East Riding.* East Yorkshire Local History Society, York.
Oliver, G. (1829). *History of Beverley.* M. Turner, Beverley.
Page, W.B. (1913). *Victoria County History, Yorkshire, vol. 3.* Constable, London.
Poulson, G. (1829). *Beverlac,* 2 vols. G. Scaum, London.
Tillott, P. (ed.) (1961). *Victoria County History: City of York.* Oxford University Press, London.
Wilkinson, T. (1790). *Memoirs of His Own Life.* Wilson Spence and

Mawman, York.

Woodward, D. (ed.) (1985). *Descriptions of East Yorkshire: Leland to Defoe.* East Yorkshire Local History Society, Beverley.

21

The small towns of south Humberside

R.W. Ambler

Introduction

Some of the largest settlements in south Humberside in 1603, when figures on which to base an estimate of relative size become available, already had a long history as marketing centres, but markets and fairs did not flourish in all the places which had been granted the right to hold them, nor was the size of a place always linked to market town status. Changes in patterns of trade and commerce could cause well-established centres to decline and small settlements to grow, so that fluctuations in the fortunes of the small towns of south Humberside after 1603 represent the later stages of a longer process of less easily quantifiable town development. This chapter examines briefly this development from the Middle Ages to the present day, concentrating in particular on the growth of towns as market centres and the role of water transport via the Humber and its tributaries.

The Middle Ages

Barton-upon-Humber and two adjoining settlements in the soke of Kirton in Lindsey - Burton upon Stather and Thealby - were the only markets in the area mentioned in Domesday Book in 1086. The Humber ferry at Barton must have been a factor in the town's growth and development, while the toll on trade which Gilbert de Gand's men were said to have taken at Barton is a further indication of a level of commercial activity which supported a population density three times the norm for rural areas in 1086 (Foster and Longley 1924, Darby 1971, Bryant 1981). The market at Barton and that belonging to Kirton both seem to have had a continued existence until the early part of the thirteenth century, when they were moved from their usual day of Sunday to Monday and Tuesday respectively (Anon. 1889, Stenton 1926). By this period Brigg, which owed its importance to its location at a crossing point of the River Ancholme where there was a bridge by 1218, had also begun to develop as a market centre (Barley 1936). Wine was being traded there in the 1180s and a market was already established by the early thirteenth century (Anon. 1911, Stenton 1938). Brigg's position was enhanced by its location on the main route from Lincoln north to the Humber ferry at Barton, which also passed through Kirton in Lindsey (Hill 1965).

Water-borne traffic was a further important element in the development of trade and commerce in south Humberside in the Middle Ages. Burton upon Stather's position on the River Trent made it a major outlet for the trade of the area. Its two great fifteen day fairs in late October/early November and late May/early June, the longest in south Humberside, attracted traders who dealt on a large scale (Anon. 1908, Lincolnshire Archives Committee Archivists' Report 9 p. 31). Brigg's market and fairs also benefited from trade on the Ancholme, therefore it was a matter of considerable concern when the river was obstructed in 1294 and 1295 (Anon. 1895, Barley 1936).

The number of settlements granted the right by charter to hold markets and fairs in the period 1234 to 1383, and especially in the thirteenth century, is an indication of the growing amount of commercial activity in the period (Figs 21.1 and 21.2) (Miller and Hatcher 1978, Platts 1985). The charters which the lords of such places as Appleby and Bonby obtained in 1267 and 1318 respectively may represent an over-optimistic assessment of their commercial potential, but at other places such as Goxhill and Laceby these grants of markets and fairs were associated with substantial communities, even if they were still large villages rather than towns (Glasscock 1975). Goxhill was among the larger settlements of the area until the early eighteenth century, by which time it had no market and continued to be principally a farming community.

The small towns of south Humberside 295

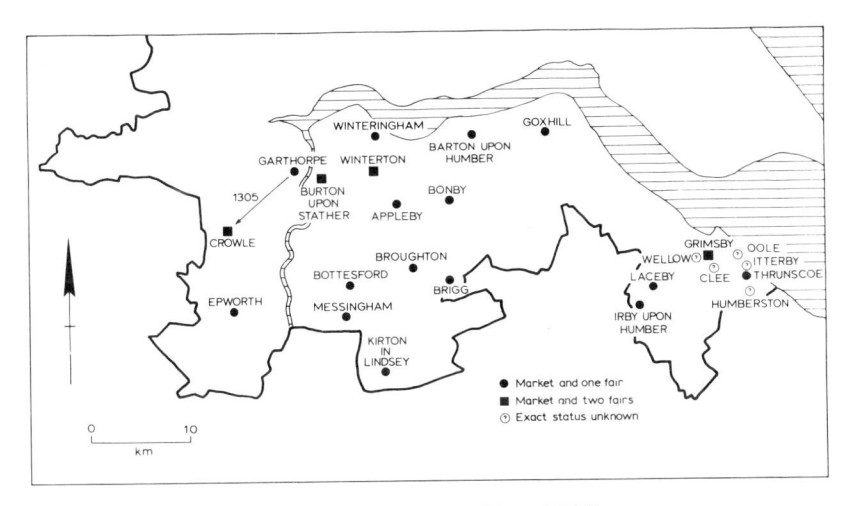

Fig. 21.1. Medieval markets and fairs. Source: Platts (1985).

Barton-upon-Humber probably passed the peak of its prosperity by the early thirteenth century as Hull grew to become a rival for the trade of the Humber (Allison 1969, Platts 1985). It did, however, continue to flourish as a port and appears frequently in the lists of places providing vessels impressed for royal service in the fourteenth century. In the same period Barton merchants were involved in overseas trade in wool and wine (Ball 1856, Brown 1908, Gillett and MacMahon 1980, Pawley 1984). Other creeks and havens such as Burton upon Stather, East Halton, Immingham and Owston Ferry were also involved in the wool trade and had vessels impressed, but did not develop into recognisably urban communities (Owen 1929, Beresford and Finberg 1973, Pawley 1984, Platts 1985).

The sixteenth and seventeenth centuries

The coastal and river trade which had been important to marketing centres such as Barton, Brigg and Burton upon Stather in the Middle Ages continued to play a part in the local economy, but there was a decline in the number of settlements on the south bank of the Humber which had vessels engaged in trade, and also in the number of craft which used them, due at least in part to the silting of havens (see also

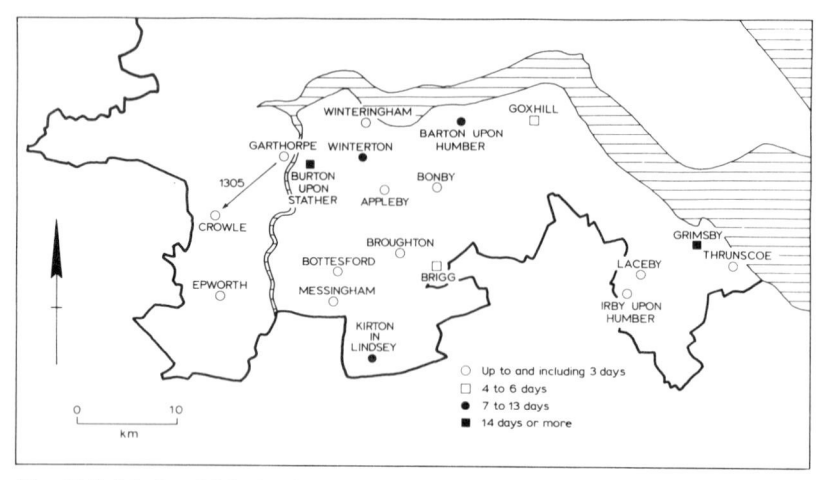

Fig. 21.2. Medieval fairs by duration. Source: Platts (1985).

Ambler this volume). A survey made in 1565 of the fifteen places with harbours, creeks and landing places between Cleethorpes and Burton upon Stather showed that, excluding Grimsby, only Barrow, Barton, Burton upon Stather and Winteringham had any settlement associated with them (Pawley 1984, Public Record Office S.P. 12/38/23).

The most important market centres in south Humberside in the seventeenth century were Barton, Burton upon Stather, Brigg and Kirton in Lindsey (Fig. 21.3). However, this did not necessarily mean that they were the largest places in the area; the villages of the Isle of Axholme (Haxey, Belton, Epworth and Crowle) continued to occupy this position into the nineteenth century because of the rich natural resources of the area (Thirsk 1957) (Table 21.1). Barton's Humber ferry was said in 1673 to 'add good advantage to the Town, which is large and straggling', but its market was described as 'indifferent'; Kirton, 'a very good' town, had a 'considerable' market for provisions, but the decline of Burton upon Stather from its position as an important centre of trade in the Middle Ages was already marked (Blome 1673 pp. 142-3). It was not among the larger places of south Humberside from the early seventeenth century (Table 21.1), and the market there was, according to the Revd Abraham de la Pryme, a local clergyman writing in 1695, 'inconsiderable' and held

The small towns of south Humberside

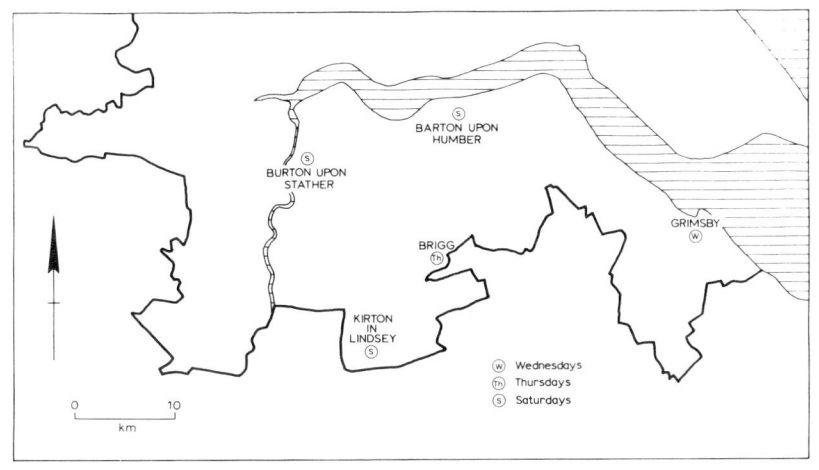

Fig. 21.3. Markets in the seventeenth century showing day on which held. Source: Blome (1673).

in the 'worst market place' he had ever seen (Jackson 1870 pp. 59, 137). He also noted the continuing prosperity of Brigg, 'a pretty large town' with 'a good trade', as well as the decay of the former markets at Broughton, Winterton and Winteringham (Jackson 1870 pp. 128, 132). Henry Best, from Elmswell in east Yorkshire, noted how the south bank markets fitted into a wider network of trade in the mid seventeenth century. When conditions were favourable, Lincolnshire men came over to the Hull markets on Wednesdays and Saturdays, buying oatmeal from Beverley traders which they then carried to 'sell againe in brigg-markette and other marketts thereabouts' (Woodward 1984 p. 106).

The importance of Barton and Brigg as retail and service centres from the late sixteenth to the eighteenth centuries can be seen from the presence in the towns of a range of tradesmen and craftsmen, including merchants, victuallers, butchers, drapers, glovers, bakers, tailors, chandlers, shoemakers and surgeons (Lincolnshire Archives Office, Parish card index of ecclesiastical records sub Barton-upon-Humber and Brigg). The needs of the people who resorted to them for trade and business were also reflected in the number of alehouses in the towns in 1633, when Brigg had 23 and Barton 21 (Lincolnshire Archives Office, Lindsey Quarter Sessions, Alehouse Recognisances 1632-8).

Table 21.1. The ten largest settlements in south Humberside in rank order, 1603-1981, excluding Grimsby, Cleethorpes and Scunthorpe.

1603	1642	1676	1705-23	1801	1851	1901	1951	1981
Crowle	Haxey	Haxey	Haxey	Barton-upon-Humber	Barton-upon-Humber	Barton-upon-Humber	Barton-upon-Humber	Immingham
Belton	Belton	Belton	Epworth	Haxey	Brigg	Brigg	Brigg	Bottesford
Haxey	Barton-upon-Humber	Owston Ferry[2]	Belton	Epworth	Crowle	Barrow upon Humber	Waltham	Barton-upon-Humber
Barton-upon-Humber	Epworth	Crowle	Barton-upon-Humber	Crowle	Barrow upon Humber	Crowle	Crowle	Humberston
Epworth	Barrow upon Humber	Barton-upon-Humber	Crowle	Brigg	Haxey	Haxey	Immingham	Brigg
Stallingborough	Goxhill	Epworth	Owston Ferry	Kirton in Lindsey	Kirton in Lindsey	Epworth	Winterton	Winterton
Goxhill	Crowle	Goxhill	Brigg[1]	Barrow upon Humber	Epworth	Kirton in Lindsey	Barrow upon Humber	Waltham
Kirton in Lindsey	Brigg[1]	Brigg[1]	Kirton in Lindsey	Owston Ferry	Owston Ferry	Belton	Broughton	Broughton
Owston Ferry	Kirton in Lindsey	Barrow upon Humber	Goxhill	Winterton	Winterton	Winterton	Kirton in Lindsey	Haxey
Brigg[1]	Owston Ferry	Althorpe[3]	Barrow upon Humber	Broughton	Scawby	Broughton	Haxey	Crowle

[1] Returned with Wrawby parish. [2] May include West Butterwick. [3] May include Amcotts.

Sources: Census Reports 1801-1981, Cole (1912), Foster (1926), Webster (1984), Whiteman (1986).

The eighteenth and nineteenth centuries

By the middle of the eighteenth century there were ten settlements in south Humberside, excluding Grimsby, which had annual fairs (Fig. 21.4). Of these, Crowle and Kirton had two a year. Their trade was predominantly in agricultural produce, and those at Belton, Crowle and Epworth reflected the local economy of the Isle of Axholme by dealing in hemp and flax; Haxey, Kirton, Messingham and Winterton were also concerned with 'merchandizing goods' (Owen 1756). All except Belton, Haxey, Messingham, Winteringham and Winterton had weekly markets in 1792. Some of these may have revived as a result of increasing agricultural prosperity. Epworth market was said to have been well attended, with considerable business being transacted there until the end of the Napoleonic Wars, but when prices began to drop, farmers were obliged to go to Doncaster and other places to find buyers for their produce (Stonehouse 1839). Whatever the relationship between the development of markets and agricultural prosperity, there was a strong association between the size of towns and their function as marketing centres in the late eighteenth and into the nineteenth century, so that, with the exception of Barrow upon Humber, Broughton, Goxhill and Owston Ferry, all the area's largest places had markets or fairs during this period (Table 21.1). It was claimed in 1690 that Owston had 'anciently' had a weekly market which had been revived during the Commonwealth, but its chief importance in the early nineteenth century was as a port on the River Trent from which the agricultural produce of the Isle of Axholme was despatched.

The introduction of steam packet boats on the Humber and Trent in the early nineteenth century meant that the inhabitants of villages near the rivers could go to the larger markets at Hull, Gainsborough and Newark, while hawkers came by boat into the area (Stonehouse 1839, Beckwith 1966). This concentration of marketing at the expense of the older centres of south Humberside continued in the nineteenth century and can be analysed by studying the destination of carriers in the mid nineteenth century (Fig. 21.5). Even allowing for the fact that carriers coming from out of the area are not shown, Brigg was the most important market town in the area, with Barton and Grimsby also having significant roles. Links with Hull were also strong, but Winteringham and Winterton had ceased to have any

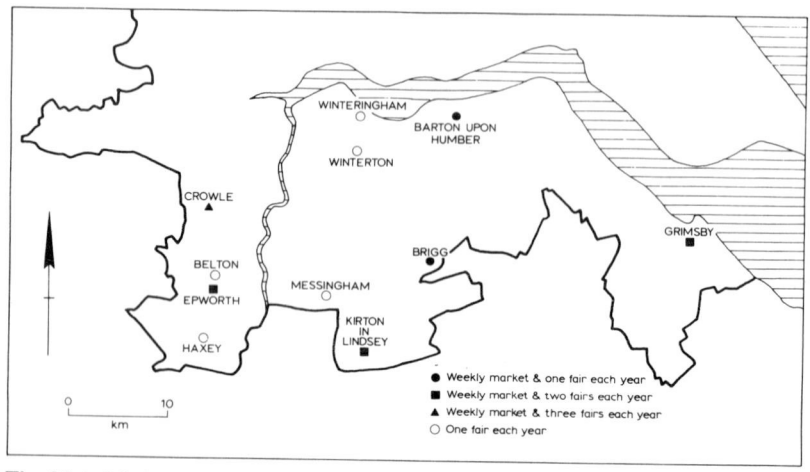

Fig. 21.4. Markets and fairs in the eighteenth century. Source: Owen (1756, 1792).

importance in this respect.

In his account of the towns of Lincolnshire, including Brigg, in the 1720s, Defoe (1948 ed.) had noted their strong links with the agricultural economy of the area, and it was on this basis that the development of south Humberside's market towns was built. When Cary Elwes succeeded to his Brigg estate in 1752 he responded to the town's rising prosperity by leasing land for building. His encouragement of brick and tiled buildings, using the products of his developing brickyards, began to change the appearance of a town which had hitherto been built largely of mud and stud with roofs of thatch (Jackson 1965, Henthorn 1987). The fortunes of the tradesmen, craftsmen and professional people who occupied these new premises were closely tied up with those of the agriculturalists who lived in the area. Until the uplands of the Lincoln Edge and Lincolnshire Wolds were enclosed in the late eighteenth and early nineteenth centuries, the warrens on them provided rabbit skins for a considerable fur trade based on the town. Corn milling, seed and bone crushing, oil cake manufacture, the production of agricultural machinery and later the manufacture of artificial fertiliser became established in Brigg and characterised its industrial activity in the nineteenth century, while Henry Spring's lemon curd factory was begun in the 1880s in response to new consumer demands (Wright

The small towns of south Humberside 301

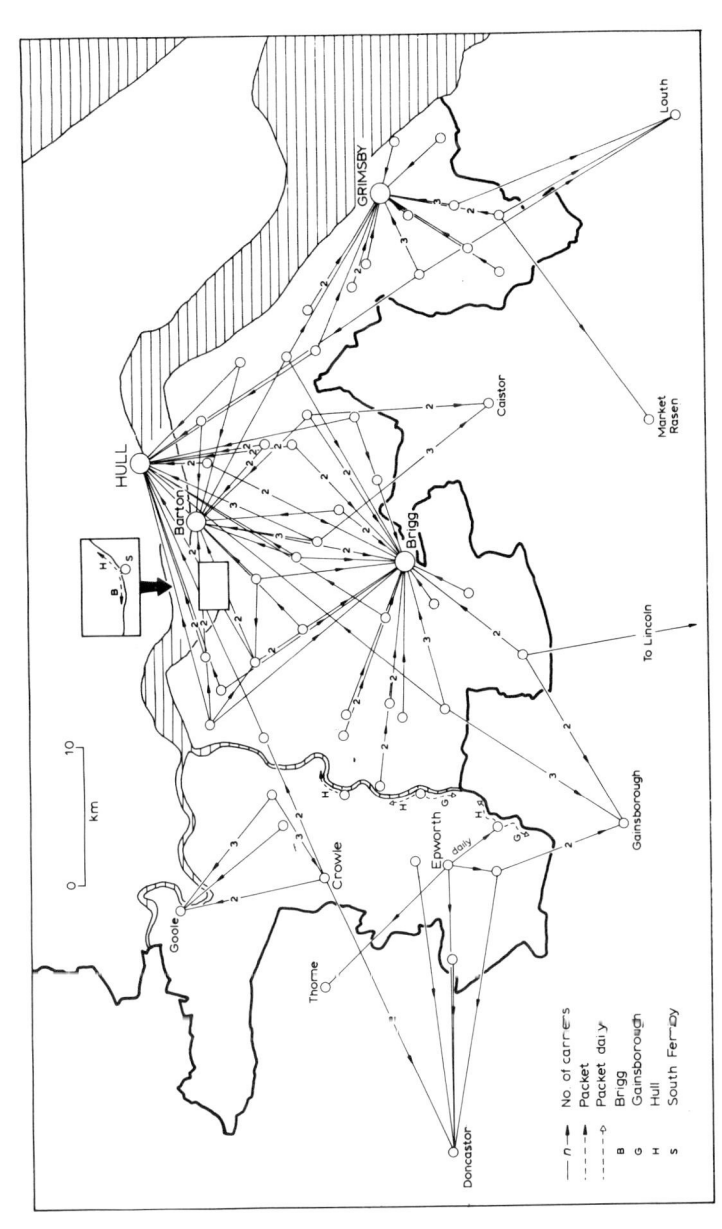

Fig. 21.5. Carriers in the mid nineteenth century. Source: White (1856).

1982, Henthorn 1987).

Like Brigg, brick and tile making developed at Barton in the eighteenth century, and from 1767 the Hall family were manufacturing rope in the town (Anon. 1975). While both industries expanded considerably in the nineteenth century, work in agriculture continued to provide the greatest single opportunity for employment in Barton. As well as rope making, the manufacture of sailcloth also reflected the town's position on the Humber. Harrison's bell foundry, which was located in the town for just over 50 years in the late eighteenth and early nineteenth centuries, would also have benefited from transportation along the Humber. Other trades and occupations at Barton included chalk quarrying, with the associated manufacture of whiting, together with tanning and leather preparation, and the town also had a large candle factory until the 1920s (Anon. 1978, Wright 1982). Hoppers, the local cycle manufacturers, diversified their activities into car manufacture for a period in the early twentieth century, building car bodies on a chassis produced by a Wolverhampton company (Wright 1982). This industrial base contributed to the growth and development of Barton and Brigg, making them the largest towns in south Humberside from the nineteenth and into the twentieth century (Table 21.1). It helped to set them apart from the other communities of the area, which, whatever their status had been in the past, had become large villages.

The twentieth century

It was not until the twentieth century that the spread of industry along the south bank of the Humber began to erode the older pattern of urban development. The establishment of a new port at Immingham in 1912, and the broadening of its trade from an early dependence on coal, iron and steel to a new phase of development in the 1960s in response to the growth in oil storage and chemical industries on the Humber bank near the port, meant that the population of what was a small village of 241 people in 1901 had grown to 11 506 by 1981 (Leafe 1967). This made it the area's largest community apart from Grimsby, Cleethorpes and Scunthorpe. The latter spread into the parish of Bottesford, while the growth of Grimsby and Cleethorpes greatly increased the population of the villages of Humberston and

Waltham. By 1981 Bottesford and Humberston had become the second and fourth largest settlements in south Humberside (Table 21.1).

The old towns of Barton-upon-Humber and Brigg, together with the larger Isle of Axholme villages of Haxey and Crowle, still retained a place as some of the larger communities of south Humberside (Table 21.1), giving an element of continuity to the historical development of the area into the second half of the twentieth century. It was, however, in the new industries such as fertilisers, pigments and man-made fibres, together with the growth of oil refining capacity, that the greatest capital development was taking place, and these industries no longer had a specifically urban base (Jones 1987).

Acknowledgements

I am grateful to Dr J. Bellamy for assistance with references to rope manufacture at Barton-upon-Humber, to Dr D.R.J. Neave for references to markets in the seventeenth century and to Barton-upon-Humber probate inventories, and to Dr S. Pawley for references relating to shipping at the Public Record Office.

References

Allison, K.J. (ed.) (1969). *The Victoria History of the County of York, East Riding, Vol. 1, The City of Kingston upon Hull*. Oxford University Press for the Institute of Historical Research, Oxford.

Anon. (1889). *First Report of the Royal Commission on Market Rights and Tolls*, Vol. 1. HMSO, London.

Anon. (1895). *Calendar of Patent Rolls, (Edward I, 1292-1301)*. HMSO, London.

Anon. (1908). *Calendar of Charter Rolls, Edward I-Edward III Vol. 3 (1300-1326)*. HMSO, London.

Anon. (1911). *The Great Roll of the Pipe for the Twenty-Ninth Year of the Reign of King Henry the Second A.D. 1182-1183*, The Pipe Roll Society Vol. 32, London.

Anon. (1975). *The Story of the Hall-mark*. Cloister Press, Heaton Mersey.

Anon. (1978). *Barton on Humber in the 1850's, Part Two, The Town and the People*. Barton Branch Workers' Educational Association, Barton-upon-Humber.

Ball, H.W. (1856). *The Social History and Antiquities of Barton-upon-Humber*. M. Ball, Barton-upon-Humber.

Barley, M.W. (1936). Lincolnshire rivers in the Middle Ages. *Lincolnshire Architectural and Archaeological Societies Reports and Papers* New Series **1**, 1-22.

Beckwith, I.S. (1966). Transport in the Lower Trent Valley in the eighteenth and nineteenth centuries. *East Midland Geographer* **4**, 99-106.

Beresford, M.W. and Finberg, H.P.R. (1973). *English Medieval Boroughs: a handlist*. David and Charles, Newton Abbot.

Blome, R. (1673). *Britannia: or a geographical description of the kingdoms of England, Scotland and Ireland, with the isles and territories thereto belonging*. T. Roycroft for R. Blome, London.

Brown, R. (1908). *Notes on the Earlier History of Barton-on-Humber, Vol. 2, A.D. 1154-1377*. Elliot Stock, London.

Bryant, G.F. (1981). *The Early History of Barton on Humber: prehistory to the Norman Conquest*. Barton Civic Society and Barton Branch Workers' Educational Association, Barton-upon-Humber.

Cole, R.E.G. (ed.) (1912). *Speculum Dioeceseos Lincolniensis ...*, Lincoln Record Society Vol. 4, Lincoln.

Darby, H.C. (1971). *The Domesday Geography of Eastern England*. Cambridge University Press, Cambridge.

Defoe, D. (1948). *A Tour through England and Wales*. Everyman edition, London.

Foster, C.W. (ed.) (1926). *The State of the Church in the Reigns of Elizabeth and James I ...*, Lincoln Record Society Vol. 23, Lincoln.

Foster, C.W. and Longley, T. (eds) (1924). *The Lincolnshire Domesday and the Lindsey Survey*, Lincoln Record Society Vol. 19, Lincoln.

Glasscock, R.E. (ed.) (1975). *The Lay Subsidy of 1334*, Records of Social and Economic History, New Series Vol. 2. Oxford

University Press for the British Academy, London.
Gillett, E. and MacMahon, K.A. (1980). *A History of Hull*. Oxford University Press for the University of Hull, Oxford
Henthorn, F. (1987). *A History of 19th Century Brigg*. F. Henthorn, Stamford.
Hill, F. (reprint 1965). *Medieval Lincoln*. Cambridge University Press, Cambridge.
Jackson, C. (ed.) (1870). *The Diary of Abraham de la Pryme, the Yorkshire Antiquary*. Surtees Society, Durham.
Jackson, G. (1965). Cary Elwes - Lord of Brigg. *The Lincolnshire Historian* 2, 1-13.
Jones, P.N. (1987). The structure and distribution of manufacturing industry. In: *Humberside in the Eighties* (ed. D.G. Symes) pp. 49-65. Department of Geography, University of Hull.
Leafe, R.V. (1967). The port of Immingham. *East Midland Geographer* 4, 127-42.
Miller, E. and Hatcher, J. (1978). *Medieval England: rural society and economic change 1086-1384*. Longman, London.
Owen, L.V.D. (1929). Lincolnshire and the wool trade in the Middle Ages - a note. *Associated Architectural Societies Reports and Papers* 39, 259-63.
Owen, W. (1756). *An Account Published by the King's Authority of all the Fairs in England and Wales ...* W. Owen, London.
Owen, W. (1792). *Owen's New Book of Fairs*. W. Owen, London.
Pawley, S. (1984). Lincolnshire Coastal Villages and the Sea, c. 1300-c. 1600: economy and society. Ph.D. thesis, University of Leicester.
Platts, G. (1985). *Land and People in Medieval Lincolnshire*. History of Lincolnshire Committee for the Society for Lincolnshire History and Archaeology, Lincoln.
Stenton, D.M. (ed.) (1926). *The Earliest Lincolnshire Assize Rolls A.D. 1202-1209,* Lincoln Record Society Vol. 22, Lincoln.
Stenton, D.M. (ed.) (1938). *The Great Roll of the Pipe for the Fifth Year of the Reign of King John, Michaelmas 1203,* The Pipe Roll Society, New Series Vol. 16, London.
Stonehouse, W.B. (1839). *The History and Topography of the Isle of Axholme, being that part of Lincolnshire which is west of the Trent.* Longman, Rees, Orme and Co., Simpkin Marshall and Co., W. Pickering, London.

Thirsk, J. (1957). *English Peasant Farming: the agrarian history of Lincolnshire from Tudor to recent times.* Routledge and Kegan Paul, London.

Webster, W.F. (ed.) (1984). *Protestation Returns 1641-2, Lincolnshire.* Nottingham.

White, W. (1856). *History, Gazetteer, and Directory of Lincolnshire ...* W. White, Sheffield.

Whiteman, A. (ed.) (1986). *The Compton Census of 1676: a critical edition,* Records of Social and Economic History, New Series Vol. 10. Oxford University Press for the British Academy, London.

Woodward, D. (ed.) (1984). *The Farming and Memorandum Books of Henry Best of Elmswell, 1642,* Records of Social and Economic History, New Series Vol. 8. Oxford University Press for the British Academy, London.

Wright, N.R. (1982). *Lincolnshire Towns and Industry, 1700-1914.* History of Lincolnshire Committee for the Society for Lincolnshire History and Archaeology, Lincoln.

22

Market towns of the Humber north bank, 1700-1850

M.K. Noble

Introduction

The settlement structure of the north bank of the Humber is largely homogeneous in character, comprising farms, villages and market towns, with only the large urban centres of Hull and York disturbing this pattern. The foundations of the regional urban system had been established by the start of the fifteenth century after the granting of markets and fairs to almost forty communities (Fig. 22.1). This initial phase of urban genesis was followed by a process of rationalisation in the number of towns. Of the original thirty-nine market centres, only ten retained their market status at the start of the sixteenth century, while two new towns had appeared by this date and two additional centres were established in the following century (Adams 1680, Owen 1770, McCutchcon 1940, Everitt 1976). The fifteenth and sixteenth centuries were a time of fluctuating fortunes for many market centres. Some towns disappeared, while others, such as Patrington and Hornsea, temporarily lost their market status only to re-emerge in the regional marketing system at a later date.

The reasons why so many towns disappeared are not altogether clear, but are likely to include population decline caused by localised epidemics or famines, initial overprovision of market centres and improved transport and communications. By the start

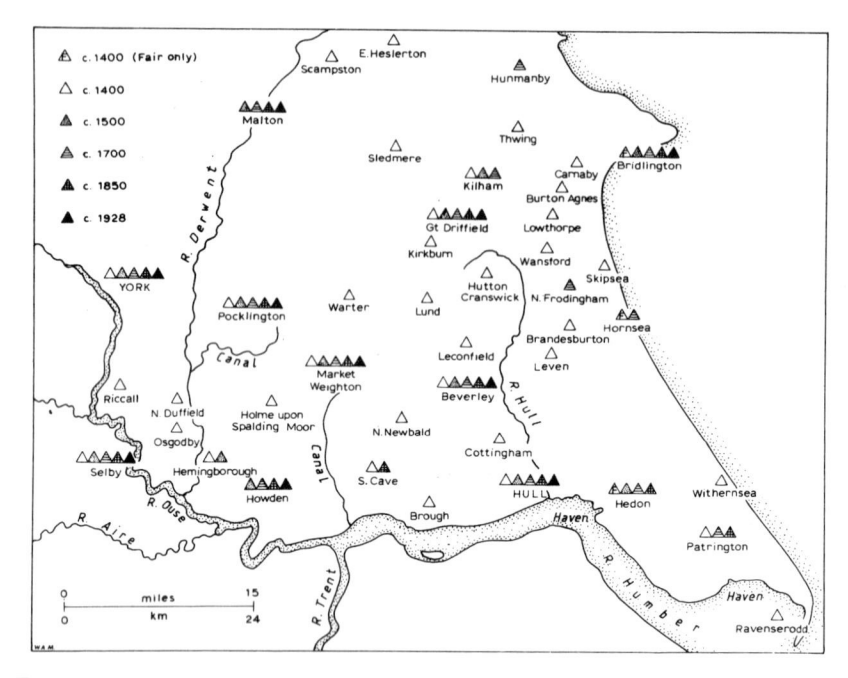

Fig. 22.1. Market centres of the Humber north bank c. 1400-1928.

of the eighteenth century only seventeen market centres, fifteen of which can be classified as market towns or country towns, remained on the north bank of the Humber (Fig. 22.1). In the ensuing centuries of improved communications there was clearly insufficient space for all of these towns to retain their status and continue to service the region; by the middle of the nineteenth century the number of market centres had been reduced to thirteen and by the first decades of the twentieth century they numbered only ten (Ministry of Agriculture and Fisheries 1928).

Selective urban growth among market towns was an important aspect of the regional urban system in the period after c. 1700. This chapter seeks to examine the changes that occurred in their population and function, and also the factors, in particular those related to transportation links, which ensured the survival and growth of some centres but the demise of others. Since space is limited, such an examination can only be brief, but further details are available in Noble (1983).

Demographic and functional changes

Over the period *c*. 1700 to 1850 a process of demographic urbanisation occurred in the north bank region as the urban population increased from 35% to 49% (calculations of urban population include all settlements which held a weekly market at the start of the study period, *c*. 1700). However, the proportion of the region's urban population resident in market towns rose only slightly from 15% to 17%, and their share of the total urban population on the Humber north bank fell, from 44% to 34%, indicating an increasing concentration of population in the regional centres of Hull and York, and a rationalisation among small towns (population estimates have been obtained from Hearth Tax Returns for 1674, Ollard and Walker 1928-32 and census returns for 1801 and 1851). Over this period the demographic fortunes of market towns and their growth experiences varied both temporally and spatially. At the start of the eighteenth century only one of the towns contained more than 2000 inhabitants, and many had populations of less than 1000 (Table 22.1). During the next 150 years, as populations increased, there occurred diversification in the population size levels of market centres, and by the middle of the nineteenth century a clear urban size hierarchy had emerged. Beverley remained at the top of the hierarchy, but numerous changes of relative position occurred between the remaining towns (Table 22.1). Some towns began to decline and lose their relative standing, while others made a bid for regional or sub-regional dominance (Fig. 22.2). It is interesting to observe that the leading towns to emerge in demographic terms each had a degree of 'port' status, enjoying either a river, canal or coastal location, suggesting that the presence or absence of a navigational link was a significant determinant of selective urban growth (see later).

As in the case of population growth, the functional development of towns between 1700 and 1850 was not a uniform process. Some market centres acquired new functions, for example banks, veterinary surgeons and specialised merchants and retailers such as stationers and booksellers, confectioners and fruiterers, and so increased their status within the region, but others were neither able to duplicate existing functions and services nor extend their range. Those towns which came to dominate servicing within the region each had well developed transportation links. Beverley, Malton, Selby and Great

Table 22.1. Population change in market towns of the Humber north bank, c. 1700-1851.

c. 1700 Town	Pop.	c. 1750 Town	Pop.
Beverley	2790	Beverley	4000
Bridlington	1580	Bridlington	2370
Malton	1465	Malton	2170
Selby	1235	Selby	1350
Howden	930	Pocklington	1050
Pocklington	755	Howden	800
Hunmanby	750	Market Weighton	740
Great Driffield	660	Great Driffield	700
Market Weighton	635	South Cave	650
Patrington	535	Hunmanby	540
Hedon	525	Patrington	450
South Cave	505	Hedon	450
Kilham	500	Kilham	450
Hornsea	435	North Frodingham	300
North Frodingham	380	Hornsea	220

1801		1851	
Beverley	5401	Beverley	8915
Malton	3662	Malton	6156
Bridlington	3130	Bridlington	5839
Selby	2861	Selby	5320
Howden	1552	Great Driffield	3963
Pocklington	1502	Pocklington	2543
Great Driffield	1411	Howden	2491
Market Weighton	1183	Market Weighton	2001
Patrington	894	Patrington	1827
Hunmanby	757	Hunmanby	1291
South Cave	707	Kilham	1247
Hedon	592	Hedon	1027
Kilham	588	Hornsea	945
Hornsea	533	South Cave	937
North Frodingham	365	North Frodingham	846

Driffield each had access to good water communications which facilitated the concentration of functions. Some of the towns occupying an intermediate position in servicing, for example Market Weighton and Pocklington, also had such links, but generally these were less well developed. Many of the region's market towns, however, possessed few distinctive attributes that might have enabled them to increase their regional standing but did, through their weekly

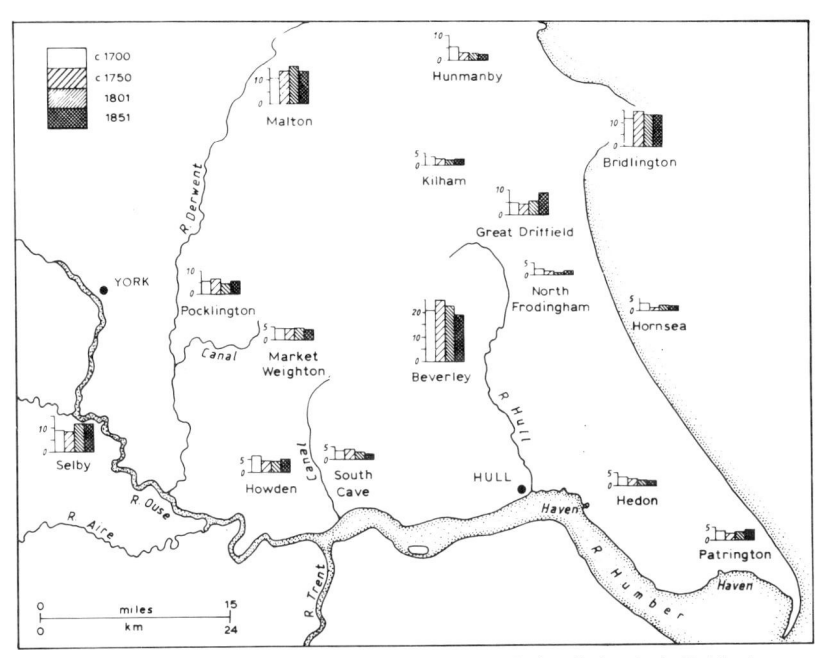

Fig. 22.2. Percentage of regional market town population living in individual centres c. 1700-1850.

markets and less frequent fairs, have functions that made them significant service centres within the regional settlement system. Indeed, some fairs, for example Howden's October horse fair, attracted buyers from as far afield as Russia, Prussia, Germany, France and Spain, while Market Weighton's September fair was said to be 'probably the greatest sheep fair in the kingdom with 70 000 to 80 000 animals annually exposed for sale' (Bigland 1812, Strickland 1812, *Hull Advertiser* 1 October 1841, 6 October 1843, 4 October 1844).

During the course of the eighteenth and nineteenth centuries most markets and fairs held in small towns came to specialise in trading particular products, with those places that failed to specialise having a less assured future and less healthy growth rate. The main products traded were either corn or livestock, and Figure 22.3 shows spatial patterns of specialisation within the region. The large quantities of produce handled by local markets, which could amount to thousands of quarters of wheat or hundreds of livestock on any given market

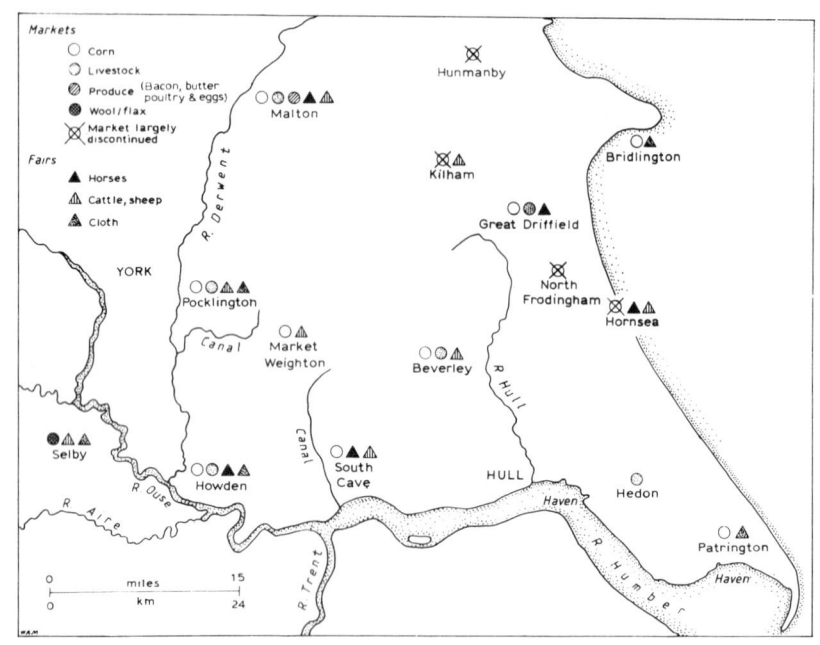

Fig. 22.3. Market specialisation *c.* 1800.

day, are incisive evidence of the wealth that could be brought to small towns via their markets and of the important role they played in the regional economy (Marshall 1788).

Developments in trading were reflected in the developing social standing of market towns. From the middle of the eighteenth century several towns, for example Beverley and Great Driffield, acquired leisure and social facilities such as theatres, horse races, assembly and reading rooms, eating houses, clubs and societies to cater for the growing upper and middle classes of urban society. Other towns, however, proved unable to expand their existing levels of social provision significantly; in places like Patrington such facilities were largely absent before the second half of the nineteenth century, and most social activity focused on local inns, as indeed did town administration and trade (Everitt 1973).

Analysis of demographic and functional changes occurring among market towns of the Humber north bank suggests that transport functions were a crucially important factor in determining growth. One of the simplest measures of the differential importance of the towns as transportation focal points is obtained by analysing the spatial extent and frequency of carrier services arriving at, and leaving, the towns in any given week. These data, obtained from Barfoot and Wilkes (1790-8), Baines (1823) and Slater (1849), demonstrate that there were marked variations in the nodal importance of the various centres (Fig. 22.4). Those situated on major thoroughfares or with direct access to navigational links experienced the healthiest growth rates, while those lacking these attributes either saw little alteration to, or an erosion of, their regional standing. Four types of growth experience can be recognised, namely dynamic growth, expansion, stability and decline (Noble 1983, 1987) (Fig. 22.5).

The Humber and its tributaries as a factor in market town development

In the period after 1700 the volume of agricultural produce to be marketed substantially increased under the impetus of widespread enclosure and improvements in farming methods. Market trade was undoubtedly strongest in those towns that had viable transportation links, particularly with the network of waterways that bounded the region. In 1762 William Porter, one of the chief instigators of the Driffield Canal of 1767, wrote 'if a canal could be made from here to Hull, Driffield would soon emerge as one of the best market towns in the East Riding'. He had good foresight, for between c. 1750 and 1850 Great Driffield became the most important corn market in the region and by 1798 was said to be 'frequented by more agriculturalists than any other market town in the East Riding'. By the middle of the nineteenth century 100 000 quarters of grain were exported annually via the town's canal (Humberside County Record Office DDX 128/27 and DDX 17/15).

The possession of navigational links was, for a number of reasons, arguably the most significant factor in determining the relative standing of market towns. First, they enabled certain towns to function as ports and thereby provided them with an outlet for marketable produce; second, they introduced raw materials in greater quantities than could reasonably be carried by

314 *Humber Perspectives*

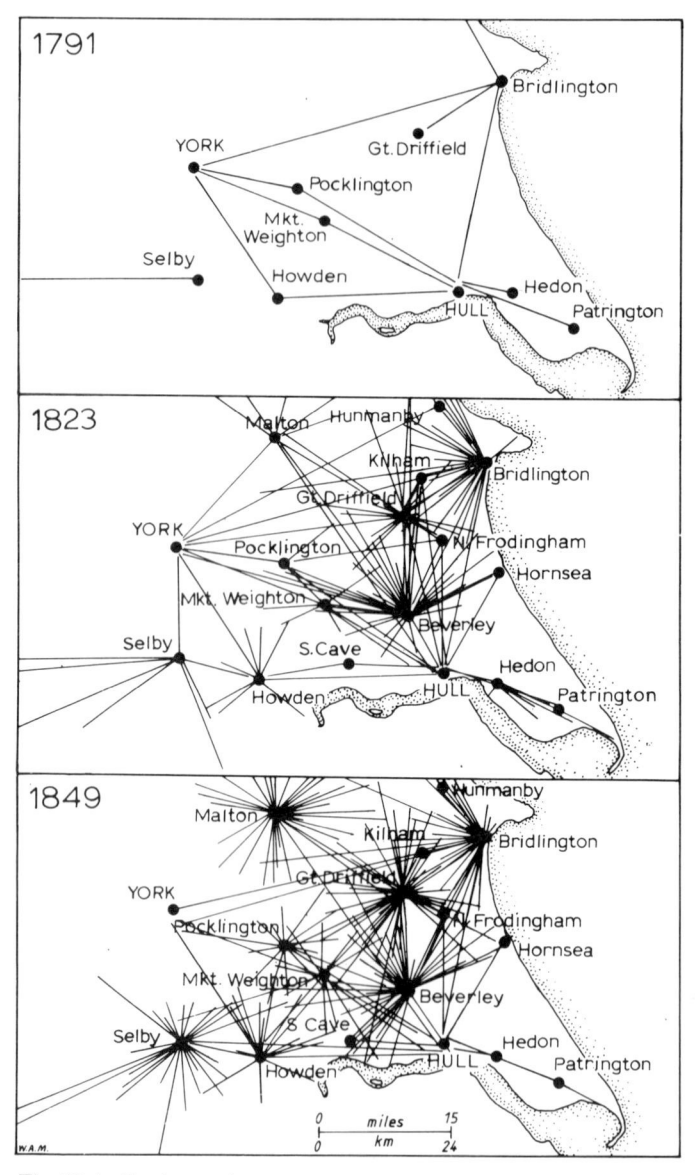

Fig. 22.4. Carrier services to market towns, 1791-1849.

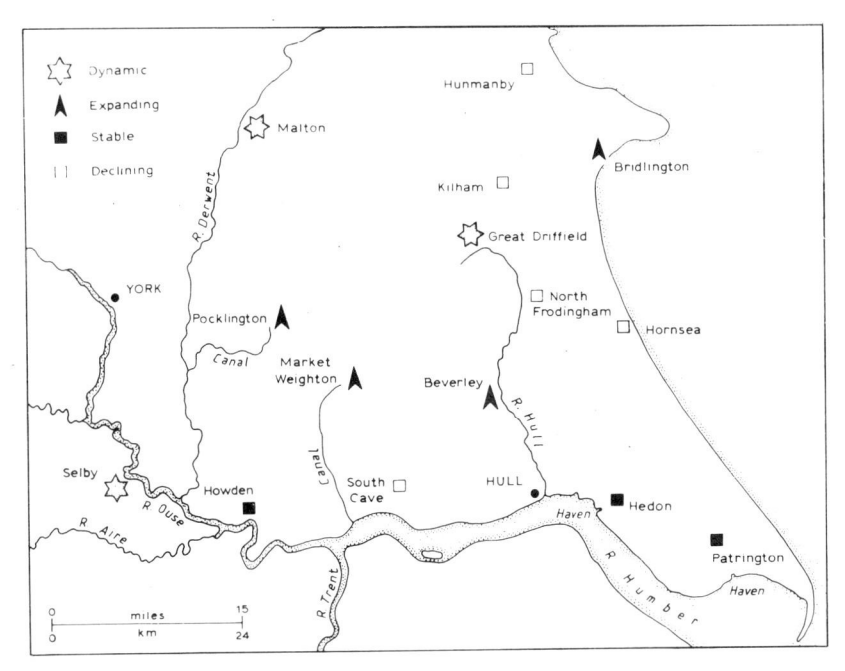

Fig. 22.5. Growth experiences of market towns c. 1700-1850.

road, thus enabling industrial expansion; third, they encouraged trade and widened urban trading horizons, and finally, they could ensure continued economic viability at a time when demographic and economic growth was increasingly focused on larger urban centres such as Hull and York. Navigational accessibility, together with a greatly improved road network, gave certain market towns enhanced nodality, making them centralised trading centres (Fig. 22.6).

Over the course of the eighteenth and nineteenth centuries those market towns associated with navigational schemes - Malton via the Derwent Navigation (1702), Beverley Beck (cleansed and deepened 1727), Patrington Haven (improved 1761), Driffield Navigation (1767), Market Weighton Drainage and Navigation (1772), Hedon Haven (deepened and improved 1774), Selby Canal (1778) and Pocklington Canal (1814) - were able to participate in intra- and inter-regional water-borne trade. Although the details of these various schemes are well documented (Duckham 1972, Hadfield 1972), few detailed records concerning the number of ships and the

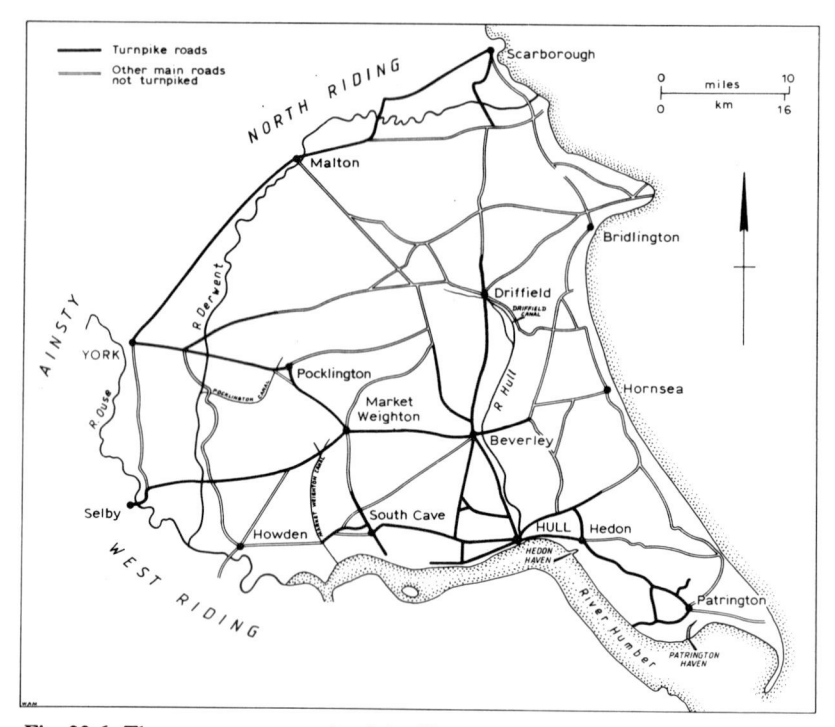

Fig. 22.6. The transport network of the Humber north bank c. 1830 (from Noble 1985).

type and tonnage of goods imported and exported to towns via their navigations have survived, and it is often the comments of contemporaries that provide the most insight into trading patterns. Following the opening of the Derwent Navigation, Malton was accounted to have become a place of 'considerable internal commerce' due to its 'facility for the transmission of corn, butter, hams and other articles of provision to Hull, Leeds and various places' (Tuke 1800 p. 310, Slater 1849 p. 315). The improvement of Beverley Beck afforded 'great facilities to trade by opening up a communication with the Humber and coals are brought in large quantities to the staiths for the interior supply of the East Riding', while the trade of the town of Market Weighton was said to be 'considerably improved by means of a navigable canal to the Humber' (Baines 1823 pp. 158 and 365). The 'brisk market town' of Selby, situated in close proximity to the Ouse and having a navigable canal to Leeds, had the advantage of being an unloading point for goods from the West Riding and a principal thoroughfare. By the first quarter of the nineteenth century more than 800 vessels docked at the town annually from places such as Wakefield, Leeds, Huddersfield, Manchester and London, giving Selby a 'flourishing trade' and 'an expeditious intercourse of commerce between the great manufacturing districts and Hull' (Baines 1823 p. 273, Slater 1849 p. 408).

An important factor in determining the success of navigation schemes in the development of town trade was the character and level of financial support, particularly that which a town drew from other areas, since this ensured that an area more extensive than the immediate hinterland became linked to the town, resulting in higher trade flows (Ward 1974, Noble 1981). The Driffield canal, for example, received high levels of external support, and by the early nineteenth century twenty-seven vessels traded regularly between Driffield and the West Riding via the Humber (Duckham 1972, Humberside County Record Office DDIV 1). A second factor of significance was the physical location and characteristics of the scheme. On navigations where the canal basin or river wharfage point was located at some distance from the town, as was the case for both the Market Weighton and Pocklington canals, or where physical problems such as silting and dredging served to limit the volume of trade that might be handled, potential benefits to the town were generally held in check (Noble 1981). For example, at the small haven of Hedon, shipping was affected by problems of maintenance and silting to such an extent that boats entering the haven scarcely had time to load or unload before the tide turned and left them stranded; it received only ten vessels per month at the close of the eighteenth century. Patrington Haven, some 15 miles downriver, also suffered from problems of silting, but managed to attract greater volumes of trade; on average twenty boats per month each carrying 70 tons entered the haven. In spite of these problems, however, both towns traded successfully with the West Riding and London (Head 1836, Humberside County Record Office DDPK 6/3).

Most navigational trade was related either to agricultural products or to industries associated with the agricultural economy. The grain trade dominated exports and by tonnage exports of grain and other agricultural products accounted for approximately 30% of all trade.

Exports of wheat and barley were of particular significance, especially from towns with specialised grain markets such as Great Driffield, Market Weighton and Malton, the latter exporting more than 56 000 quarters of grain in 1796 (Bigland 1812, Hadfield 1972 vol. 1, Humberside County Record Office DDMW 7/463 and DDIV 1,2). Principal imports were coal, lime, bone dust, gravel, sand, manure, timber and occasionally products used in local industries. For example, during the 1830s large quantities of bark were imported via Pocklington canal for use in the town's then flourishing tanning industry (Humberside County Record Office DDBD 56/2 and Public Record Office RAIL 1112/46).

Although many towns which failed to acquire direct navigational links saw their trade restricted, several of them did use the region's waterways for the transhipment of goods. For example, considerable quantities of corn were purchased each market day in the small market settlement of South Cave and 'shipped on the Humber for many of the towns in the West Riding, the back cargoes consisting of firestone, lime, flags and coal, together with commodities for domestic use and consumption' (Slater 1849 p. 52). In Howden, where attempts to gain support for constructing a canal from the River Ouse to the town in the 1790s had failed, goods and passengers regularly used the neighbouring township of Howden Dike to make the journey via the Ouse and Humber to Selby and Hull (Barfoot and Wilkes 1790-8 vol. 3, Hadfield 1972 vol. 2).

Conclusions

Accessibility to water-borne communications was a factor of major significance in enabling towns to develop localised advantages and to widen and strengthen their marketing and trading networks, and cannot be underestimated in explaining selectivity of growth in the regional urban system. It would be wrong, however, to assume that transportational links with the Humber and other waterways was the only element determining patterns and processes of differential growth among the region's market towns. Although it was of central importance, other factors, among them migration, economic structure, geographical location and competition, also played a role (Muller 1977, Noble 1987). What is perhaps of significance, however, is the way in which transportation links underlie so many of these other explanatory variables.

References

Adams, J. (1680). *Index Villaris: or an alphabetical list of all cities, market towns, parishes, villages and private seats in England and Wales.* London.

Baines, E. (1823). *History, Directory and Gazetteer of the County of York,* 2 vols. Leeds. Reprinted as *Baines' Yorkshire* (1969), David and Charles, Newton Abbot.

Barfoot, P. and Wilkes, J. (1790-8). *The Universal British Directory of Trade, Commerce and Manufacture,* 6 vols. Champante and Whitrow, London.

Bigland, J. (1812). *The Beauties of England and Wales: volume 16 Yorkshire.* London.

Duckham, B.F. (1972). *The Inland Waterways of East Yorkshire 1700-1900.* East Yorkshire Local History Society, York.

Everitt, A.M. (1973). The English urban inn, 1560-1760. In: *Perspectives in English Urban History* (ed. A.M. Everitt) pp. 91-137. MacMillan, London.

Everitt, A.M. (1976). The market town. In: *The Early Modern Town* (ed. P. Clark) pp. 168-204. Longman, London.

Hadfield, E.C.R. (1972). *The Canals of Yorkshire and North East England,* 2 vols. David and Charles, Newton Abbot.

Head, G. (1836). *A Home Tour through the Manufacturing Districts of England in the Summer of 1835.* Murray, London.

Marshall, W. (1788). *The Rural Economy of Yorkshire.* London.

McCutcheon, K.L. (1940). *Yorkshire Fairs and Markets.* Thoresby Society Publications, Leeds.

Ministry of Agriculture and Fisheries (1928). *Markets and Fairs in England and Wales: Part 3 northern markets.* HMSO, London.

Muller, E.K. (1977). Regional urbanisation and the selective growth of towns in North American regions. *Journal of Historical Geography* 3, 21-39.

Noble, M.K. (1981). Inland navigations and country towns: the case of eastern Yorkshire c. 1750-1850. In: *Ports and Resorts in* the Regions (ed. E.M. Sigsworth) pp. 79-100. Humberside College of Higher Education, Hull.

Noble, M.K. (1983). Growth and Development of Country Towns: the case of eastern Yorkshire c. 1700-1850. Ph.D. thesis, University of Hull.

Noble, M.K. (1985). Urban settlement. In: *A Guide to Local Studies in East Yorkshire* (ed. B. Dyson) pp. 102-25. Hutton Press, Cherry Burton.

Noble, M.K. (1987). Growth and development in a regional urban system: the country towns of eastern Yorkshire, 1700-1850. In: *Urban History Yearbook 1987* (ed. D. Reeder) pp. 1-21. Leicester University Press, Leicester.

Ollard, S.L. and Walker, P.C. (ed.) (1928-32). *Archbishop Herring's Visitation Returns, York Diocese, 1743,* Yorkshire Archaeological Society Record Series, vols 71, 72, 75, 77, 79. Yorkshire Archaeological Society, Leeds.

Owen, W. (1770). *Book of Fairs.* A Godbid and J. Playford, London.

Slater, I. (1849). *Commercial Directory of Yorkshire and Lincolnshire.* Leeds.

Strickland, H.E. (1812). *A General View of the Agriculture of the East Riding.* London.

Tuke, J. (1800). *General View of the Agriculture of the North Riding of Yorkshire.* London.

Ward, J.R. (1974). *The Finance of Canal Building in Eighteenth Century England.* Oxford University Press, Oxford.

23

The rise and decline of Goole as a Humber port

J.D. Porteous

Introduction

Goole was created by the Aire & Calder Canal Company (A&C) as the prime outlet for the canal-borne trade of the West Riding of Yorkshire (Hanson 1949). Originally relying upon the River Aire, the company built a canal to Selby in 1788 (Unwin 1964). By the early nineteenth century, however, the Selby Canal had proved inadequate for the traffic (Duckham 1965), and the engineer John Rennie was called in to suggest an alternative. Rennie found the Ouse below Selby and the lower Aire to be quite as inadequate for navigation as the Selby Canal. He therefore proposed a new canal which would leave the Aire at Knottingley and debouch into the River Ouse at Goole (Leather 1819). This canal was opened with due ceremony on 20 July 1826 with toasts wishing 'Success to the Port of Goole.' This chapter proposes to examine, since these early beginnings, the rise and subsequent decline of Goole as a Humber port.

The new port

Goole was founded in the district of Marshland in the extreme eastern section of the West Riding of Yorkshire. In this southern portion of the Vale of York the tidal rivers Ouse, Wharfe, Derwent, Aire, Don and Trent meet to form the Humber estuary. The Humberhead region is thus a landscape of extreme flatness, somewhat reminiscent of Holland in its sweeping distances and innumerable rivers and dykes (Dugdale 1772). Before the 1820s Goole was notable only as the outfall of the Dutch River, created in the early seventeenth century by Dutch engineers engaged in large-scale drainage operations. Goole township itself contained only 450 persons in 1821, five years before the completion of the A&C canal. At this time the Humberhead market towns of Howden (2080 population in 1821), Thorne (2713) and Selby (4097), the latter two with major shipping interests, were all growing in size, especially Selby at the lowest Ouse bridge-point.

This obscurity was to change drastically when the Knottingley-Goole Canal entered the township parallel to the Dutch River (Porteous 1969a). A number of buildings stood in the way of the canal, and almost the whole of this community, with smithy, inns and mill, was razed in the name of progress. On its site was built the town of Goole, with an extensive dockland which rapidly rose into regional prominence. In the early nineteenth century the A&C had immense commercial and social importance in industrial Britain; indeed, it was facetiously referred to as the fourth estate of the realm. It is not surprising, therefore, that the founding of Goole was reported not only by the Yorkshire press but also in London newspapers. The *Hull Advertiser* best illustrates the impact of Goole on the locality; in the years immediately following 1826 scarcely a month passed without some reference to the new port. From 1834 few major directories failed to mention Goole, and by 1853 the town was an established entity, even on the 6-inch sheets of the Ordnance Survey.

Goole, the last of a series of canal ports built between 1760 and 1830, was planned on an altogether more extensive scale than previous terminals. Grandiose port development schemes were created by the engineers Rennie and Leather (Fig. 23.1). The final plan (Fig. 23.2) involved both ship and barge docks, connected by inner locks via an intermediate basin to separate river locks. Shipping congestion in the Ouse was to be avoided by allowing vessels to wait in the harbour basin. Although the water level in the docks was maintained by canal water, the whole system could be used as a vast lock, vessels riding in with the tide.

Built as planned, the system was remarkable for its unified conception; the harbour basin, 250 x 200 ft with a draught of 18 ft,

The rise and decline of Goole

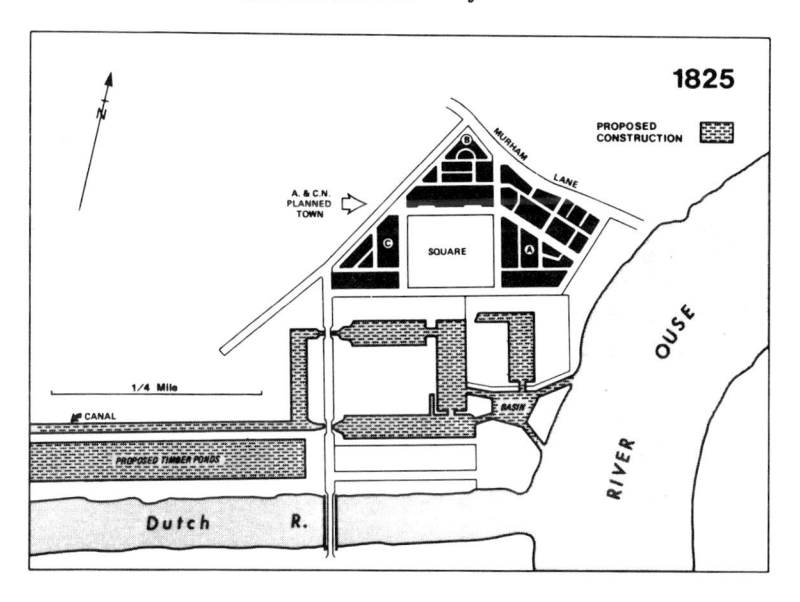

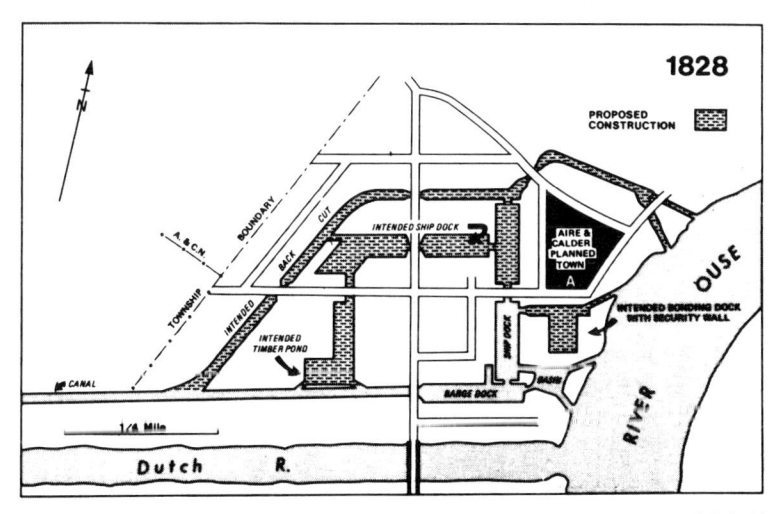

Fig. 23.1. Grandiose port and town development plans for Goole, 1825-8 (from Porteous 1977).

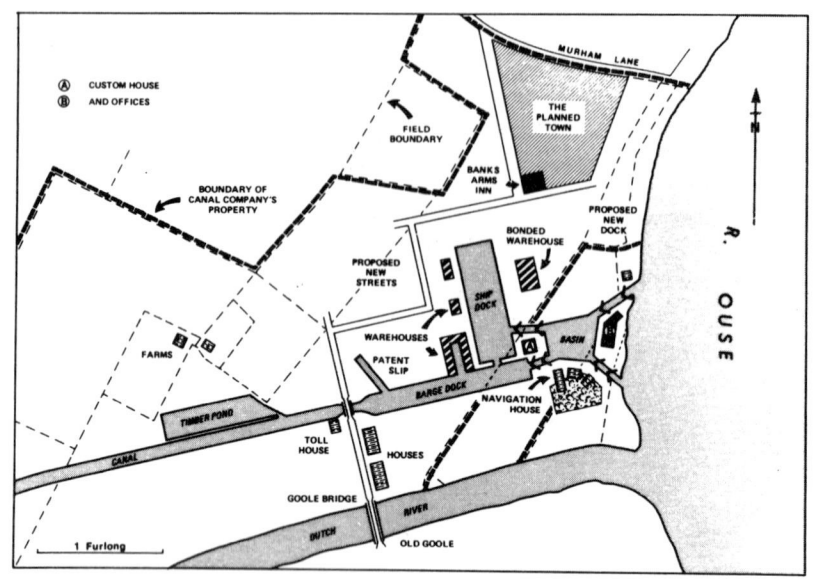

Fig. 23.2. The port and town of Goole as built, c. 1831 (from Porteous 1977).

and the barge dock, 900 x 150 ft with a draught of 10 ft, were fully interconnected. While the ship dock was planned to take up to 60 river vessels, its partner was calculated to accommodate about 200 small coasting and inland craft. Warehouses, offices, customs house and ship repair facilities quickly arose.

The new A&C canal soon proved its worth; the line was responsible for 40% of all A&C income by 1851. Grain and wool were upstream staples, while coal vied with textiles in the downstream trade. The company actively promoted Goole at the expense of its erstwhile establishment at Selby, and Goole was also fortuitously established during a period of stagnation at Hull, whose indecision over dock construction provided an opportunity for growth for several upriver ports. Hull's opposition to the new port rose to a fever pitch in 1828 when Goole was commissioned as a port for foreign trade, with port limits extending upstream from the Trent outfall to include all the Ouse tributaries.

Despite the obstacles placed in its way by Hull and Selby (East 1931), Goole in the 1830s had seemingly triumphed. Sailings between Goole and continental ports were frequent, and vessels traded as far afield as Archangel and North America. Regular processions of carriers' flyboats on the canal were matched by a daily service of speedier steam packets between Goole and West Riding coach points. At this time Goole became a tourist attraction, with extensive entries in several guide books; some visitors even broke into verse (Phillips 1834, Parsons 1835, Holland 1837).

The new town

In the 1820s and 30s Goole was a true frontier settlement, and quickly became known for inconvenience, lack of supplies, the high price of provisions and the usual lawlessness associated with nineteenth century navvies. The obvious solution to these problems was to build a town to serve the docks (Porteous 1969b). In a splendid example of recycling, spoil excavated from the new dock basins was used for brick-making, and many of the 20 000 bricks used for facing the early buildings came from this source. The new town therefore arose bodily from the ground on which it stood, a growth capped entirely with imported slate.

Although a very elaborate planned town was first envisaged, only one-third of it was authorised by the A&C (Fig. 23.1). The first task was to lay out the major streets and, because of the liability to flooding, these were built up several feet above the general land surface; material for this operation again emerged from current dock operations. A private census taken in 1826 showed that of the population of 1223 (nearly three times the 1821 figure), most were accommodated in workmen's huts with a high level of overcrowding, and a crash building programme was therefore inaugurated to solve this problem.

The result was the creation of 'New Goole', a triangular settlement which by the 1840s contained over 250 buildings. From the start, each street was planned to perform some specific function, and building-unit shape and size varied accordingly. Aire Street became the major commercial street, with stores, inns and saloons, while Ouse Street was built unusually wide to accommodate an open market and East Parade's imposing structures were intended for the professional classes. Behind these facades the poor were clustered in small terraced cottages. The southeast corner of the town, with the

Banks Arms (built by Sir Edward Banks, the chief contractor), the Public Rooms, the Commercial Buildings and the chapel, was the hub of the town, as befitted the nearest point to the docks. The architecture of early Goole displayed considerable and impressive uniformity as a result of the A&C's rigorous control. Formal terraced uniformity and an outward display of quiet opulence were the keynotes.

An awkward position

Created at the high noon of the Canal Age, Goole soon found itself in a difficult position both temporally and geographically, and the great hopes which attended the port's inauguration were not wholly fulfilled. Its foreign trade was stifled by Hull competition, and its trading problems after the first flush of the 1830s also arose from the development of rail carriage as an alternative mode of transportation (MacTurk 1880, Porteous 1977). Having failed to crush the new port by attempting to impose its dock dues on Goole ships, Hull played a major part in the promotion of a Hull-Leeds railway, designed to supersede completely the movement of goods by canal and river via Goole. This railway, opened in 1840, caused a decline in Goole's shipment of both coal and textiles.

The new town rallied, however, by expanding its industrial base (shipyards, chemicals and agricultural processing) and by acquiring a rail connection of its own. As early as 1829, railways were proposed to connect Goole with West Riding towns, and the A&C directorate soon realised that to oppose railways blindly in favour of its canal would be to invite ruin. Consequently, several competing railways endeavouring to obtain tidewater outlets near Goole were invited into the town (Porteous 1969c). The successful railway, the Wakefield, Pontefract & Goole Railway (Hopkinson 1964), later part of the Lancashire and Yorkshire Railway (L&YR), was completed in 1848, along with the Railway Dock, newly built to accommodate its traffic (Fig. 23.3). The North Eastern Railway (NER) also reached the port in 1869.

Initially kept out of Hull by the manoeuvres of the NER, the L&YR developed Goole as its major east coast outlet, particularly for the export of West Riding coal. This activity was furthered by the

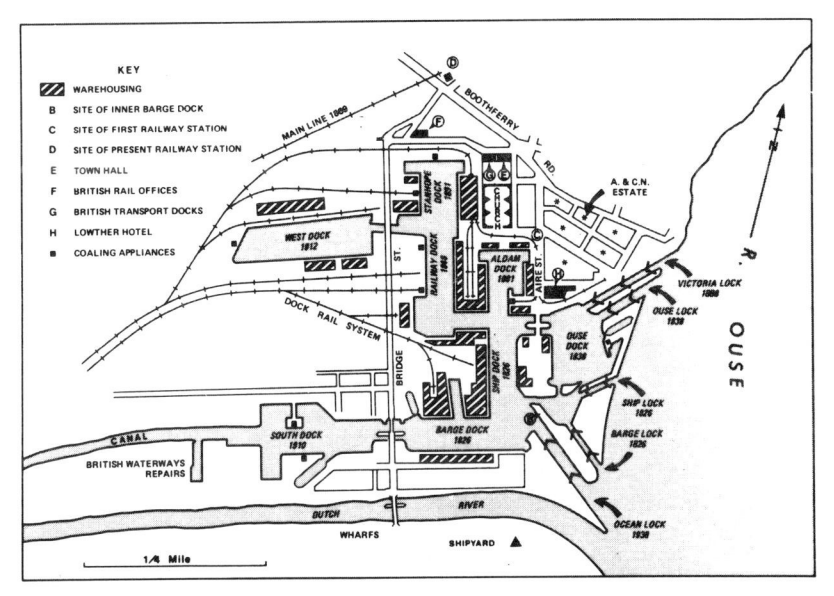

Fig. 23.3. Dock development at Goole, 1826-1938 (from Porteous 1977).

founding of the Goole Steam Shipping Company in 1864, backed by both the A&C and L&YR. The most important single improvement, however, was the invention by the A&C manager, W.H. Bartholemew, of the compartment boat train system. In operation until recently, this system involved the organisation of up to nineteen rectangular steel barges (known as 'Tom Puddings') into an amphibious goods train. At Goole, hydraulic lifts, lifting each compartment from the water, tipped its contents into the hold of a waiting collier. This cheap and efficient means of bulk mineral transport enabled the A&C to hold its own as a coal carrier, against intense railway competition, until the First World War.

Sustained by coal movement on both rail and a revolutionised canal system, Goole revived in the late nineteenth century, with a renewed improvement in the dock system from the 1870s (Fig. 23.3). The construction of Aldam Dock (1881), Victoria River Lock (1888), Stanhope Dock (1891), Victoria Pier extension (1908) and South and West Docks (1910-12) more than doubled Goole's dock space, static for a generation, in thirty years. In conjunction, the Lower Ouse Improvement Scheme of 1884 permitted vessels of 2000 tons to reach

Goole for the first time.

By the turn of the century trade was booming. In the period 1865-1904 the number of foreign vessels entering the port rose from 400, of 70 000 tons, to 1360, of 555 000 tons. In a similar period the tonnage both entered and cleared coastwise rose fivefold, while the tonnage of registered steam craft over 50 tons burden increased fiftyfold. A similar expansion occurred in the registration of canal boats at Goole, which rose from 400 in 1878 to 814 in 1899. In 1913, its peak year, the port of Goole handled 3 895 514 tons of traffic and 1 448 555 NRT of shipping. Consequently, Goole became a major growth centre, its population rising dramatically from 4618 in 1851 to 20 916 in 1911.

This was not to last, however. During the First World War the enemy occupation of its foreign trading partners, and the transfer of many of its vessels to government use, dealt the port a savage blow. Between the wars the import trade never wholly recovered, although coal exports remained high. Some improvement was expected with the opening of Ocean Lock in 1938, but the necessary large-scale improvement of the River Ouse was frustrated by the Second World War. The sheer cost of improving the Humber itself has since discouraged substantial attempts at river amelioration, so that Goole shipping remains subject to the difficulties involved in navigating tortuous channels (Duckham 1967). Little recent dock expansion has therefore occurred, and the dockland of 1913, with 39 acres of water in eight commercial docks, has remained almost unchanged into the modern period. Furthermore, although the town has physically expanded via redevelopment of the old A&C centre and the development of peripheral housing estates, its population has remained stagnant, at about 20 000, from 1911 to the present.

Goole's future

Created at an awkward time (a canal port at the beginning of the Railway Age) and in an awkward position (high up a river sometimes difficult to navigate and readily by-passed by more efficient transportation modes), Goole has had to struggle hard since 1913 to maintain even its late nineteenth century size and economic strength. Always at the mercy of circumstances beyond its control, the town has been successively crippled by two wars, coal strikes, the loss of foreign markets and failure to develop a major alternative to its stagnating shipping function (Porteous 1977).

Its awkward geographical position has been crucial, for the town was readily by-passed by railways in the nineteenth century and even more so by roads in the twentieth. The opening of Boothferry Bridge in 1929 and of the M62 motorway half a century later did little to aid Goole as traffic thundered by between the industrial Pennine towns and the coastal ports. Locked into a palaeotechnic economy, Goole's position during the twentieth century has been one of unenviable stagnation. Still largely dependent upon its port, Goole's shipping functions have received further blows since the 1970s with the development of small wharves at a number of riverside locations on the Ouse and Trent (Jones and North 1987). These have received impetus, and Goole has correspondingly declined, with the absorption of the town, once an independent borough, into the largely rural borough of Boothferry after 1974.

Rural councillors now form a majority on Boothferry Council, and analysis of their statements since 1974 suggests that they strongly agree with government support for the development of alternatives to the established ports. Despite the appeals of Goole-based councillors, as well as dock workers, unions and official agencies, small ports such as Howdendyke, a few miles upriver from Goole, have enormously increased their cargo-handling capacity in recent years (Porteous 1988). Users of such facilities argue that small river wharves have a much quicker turn-round than established ports, and that they handle only certain low-value cargoes, such as bulk powders and ingots, leaving automobile imports, for example, for established ports such as Goole. As this situation has arisen only in the last decade or so, no balanced assessment of the effects of the development of small wharves on Goole can yet be given. It may be significant, however, that Boothferry councillors were united in trying to prevent the further development of small wharves on the Trent in 1986-7, arguing that such developments outside Boothferry's boundaries would adversely affect Goole.

Conclusion

It would not be out of place to liken Goole's predicament to that of an overspecialised species confronted with drastic ecological change. Evolutionary success demands flexibility, a characteristic naturally lacking in a town built by a single commercial company for a specific purpose. Goole was conceived at a time when a pattern of settlement dispersion based on road and river traffic was giving way to urban concentration based on canals and railways. The late twentieth century is a time of renewed settlement dispersion in an era of dominant road traffic. Goole's gallant attempt at adaptation to these new economic realities, in the shape of industrial estates and new lines of exports and imports, has succeeded in maintaining the town at its 1911 population peak, but significant future growth does not seem likely. Today Goole rewards the patient and curious visitor with a working example of a port created in an era when canals were considered the ultimate in transport innovation.

References

Duckham, B.F. (1965). Selby and the Aire & Calder Navigation. *Journal of Transport History* 7, 84-8.

Duckham, B.F. (1967). *The Yorkshire Ouse*. David & Charles, Newton Abbot.

Dugdale, W. (1772). *The History of Imbanking and Drayning*. Bowyer & Nichols, London.

East, W.G. (1931). The port of Kingston-upon-Hull during the Industrial Revolution. *Economica* 11, 190-212.

Hanson, J.L. (1949). Transport Development in West Yorkshire from the Industrial Revolution to the Present Day. Ph.D. thesis, University of London.

Holland, J. (1837). *The Tour of the Don*. Sheffield Mercury, Sheffield.

Hopkinson, G.G. (1964). Railway projection and construction in south Yorkshire and south Derbyshire 1830-50. *Transactions, Hunter Archaeological Society* 9, 8-26.

Jones, P.N. and North, J. (1987). Ports and wharves. In: *Humberside in the Eighties* (ed. D.G. Symes), pp. 97-111. Department of

Geography, University of Hull.
Leather, G. (1819). *A Plan of the Proposed Canal from Knottingley to Goole*. Garside Local History Collection, Public Library, Goole.
MacTurk, G.G. (1880). *A History of the Hull Railways*. Hull Packet Office, Hull.
Parsons, E. (1835). *The Tourist's Companion*. Whittaker, London.
Phillips, J. (1834). *A Trip to Goole on board the Sythe: a poem*. Peck & Smith, Hull.
Porteous, J.D. (1969a). *The Company Town of Goole: an essay in urban genesis*, University of Hull Occasional Papers in Geography No. 12. University of Hull. Reprinted Hull University Press 1988.
Porteous, J.D. (1969b). Goole: a pre-Victorian company town. *Journal of Industrial Archaeology* 6, 105-13.
Porteous, J.D. (1969c). A new canal port in the Railway Age: railway projection to Goole 1830-1914. *Transport History* 2, 25-47.
Porteous, J.D. (1977). *Canal Ports: the urban achievement of the Canal Age*. Academic Press, London.
Porteous, J.D. (1988). *Planned to Death*. Manchester University Press, Manchester.
Unwin, R.W. (1964). The Aire & Calder Navigation: I - the beginnings. *Bradford Antiquary* New Series **42**, 47-63.

24

The development of Scunthorpe

D.C.D. Pocock

Introduction

Scunthorpe did not evolve over long centuries - it was developed in a few decades. It did not grow out of a relationship to the surrounding countryside, but sprang up through attributes of site, being built adjacent to, and in parts actually on, the ironstone deposits of the Lower Lias (Catt this volume), which were to prove the town's 'brown gold'. Given this mineral base as its *raison d'être*, Scunthorpe has always been to a degree an 'industrial island' (Armstrong 1981) within a predominantly rural region. Any contextual setting, therefore, is to be sought in terms of relative advantage of the area within the evolution of the country's iron and steel industry. Although Scunthorpe does not appear within this context until the second half of the nineteenth century, the industrial island is currently producing nearly one-fifth of the UK total steel output. This chapter recounts the history of the rapid rise of this activity and the consequent emergence of an iron and steel town.

The iron and steel industry

The key figure in initiating the industry was Rowland Winn, later the first Lord St Oswald. He it was who discovered the ore and had it analysed, persuaded ironstone companies to take up leases to extract the stone and iron-masters to erect smelting plants and, not least, championed the crucial rail connection with Yorkshire and the rest of industrial England. In the beginning Winn was stimulated by the conviction that the strata on his estate resembled those of the Cleveland area of northeast Yorkshire, and in 1859 (two decades before the arrival of the Geological Survey) he discovered beds of 'undoubted ironstone'. Analysis confirmed his conviction, and in 1860 the first extraction of the mineral began on the Winn estate, on which leases were delimited in linear strips for a fair allocation of exposed and concealed beds on the East Common and beyond the Lincoln Edge escarpment respectively (Pocock 1964).

For the first five years the ore was moved out of the district for smelting at Elsecar, near Barnsley. Initially, transport was by horse-drawn carts to the Trent and thence by the Keadby and Sheffield Canal to Elsecar. In 1861 two sections of narrow-gauge railway were built to a new wharf at Gunness, connected in the middle section over the Trent Cliff escarpment by a self-acting incline or 'gin', whereby descending ore-loaded trucks automatically pulled up the empty ones. During 1860-61 a certain amount of calcining was done at Gunness in a further effort to reduce costs of transporting the low-grade mineral, but in January 1864 Keadby bridge was opened, carrying the railway across the Trent. Winn had been striving for this link since his first discovery of ironstone, having purchased or exchanged land to achieve a wayleave, provided much of the capital and skilfully engineered the necessary Act of Parliament. The line linked the South Yorkshire Company's terminus at Keadby with the Manchester, Sheffield and Lincolnshire line at Barnetby, ten miles to the east (Daff 1968, Henthorn 1981). This made possible the import of coal and coke, and hence the establishment of an orefield smelting industry, which offered a greater permanence and higher return than did an activity engaged solely in the excavation of a non-renewable resource.

Iron-smelting began immediately (Kendall 1938, Pocock 1963a, Daff 1973). The capital for the first two works (Trent and Frodingham, both set up in 1864) came from businessmen established in south Yorkshire; geographical proximity and the financial encouragement offered by Winn were perhaps the decisive factors. The owners of the Trent works, W.H. and G. Dawes, already possessed a blast-furnace plant and rolling mills at Elsecar, and had been supplied for five years with Frodingham ironstone under the very first mineral lease concluded by Winn. In the case of the Frodingham works, Joseph Cliff, a firebrick-maker at Wortley, near Leeds, overcame the lack of previous knowledge of iron-smelting by procuring assistance from Stockton-on-Tees both to erect and manage his Frodingham Iron Company. A year later the North Lincolnshire Iron Company was established, largely through the efforts of Daniel Adamson, a boiler-maker from Hyde, near Manchester. Most of the remainder of the capital also came from Lancashire. Unlike the first two companies, the North Lincolnshire did not extract its own ironstone; the agreement, as with subsequent ventures, was for the smelting plant to be supplied from Winn's own mining company. Ten years later, when another three works were established, much of the capital was from more distant areas; both the Lindsey and Redbourn Hill plants were associated with Birmingham investors, while the Appleby works attracted Scottish capital.

The first six plants were all placed within little more than one mile of each other, alongside or related to the railway (Fig. 24.1). Lysaght's works, erected in 1912 at Normanby Park on land belonging to the Sheffield family, was the only one not located on the actual ore seams. Its siting, however, followed the earlier plants in turning its back on a waterside location. Disadvantages of a Trentside location would have been loss of valuable agricultural land and possible difficulties of drainage and building foundations on the deep alluvium, although the obvious advantages would have been a short, simple journey for the ore to meet canal-borne coke at a waterside site, with ready means for exporting the product. Interestingly, in 1859 Winn did briefly seek to purchase land beside the Trent. The statement in *Kelly's Directory* for 1861 that ironworks were about to be erected at Gunness may have been encouraged by Winn's brief interest, with perhaps further evidence seen in the calcining at Gunness by the Dawes. The latter were also planning their Trent Ironworks at this time, but not at Trentside. The brief moment in history passed, therefore, and the chief port of the district came to be Immingham, on the Humber south bank, 19 miles to the east. The district thus became dependent on rail transport which, it could be argued, slowed its growth compared with Middlesbrough, where early advantage of a tidewater location was taken. An orefield location,

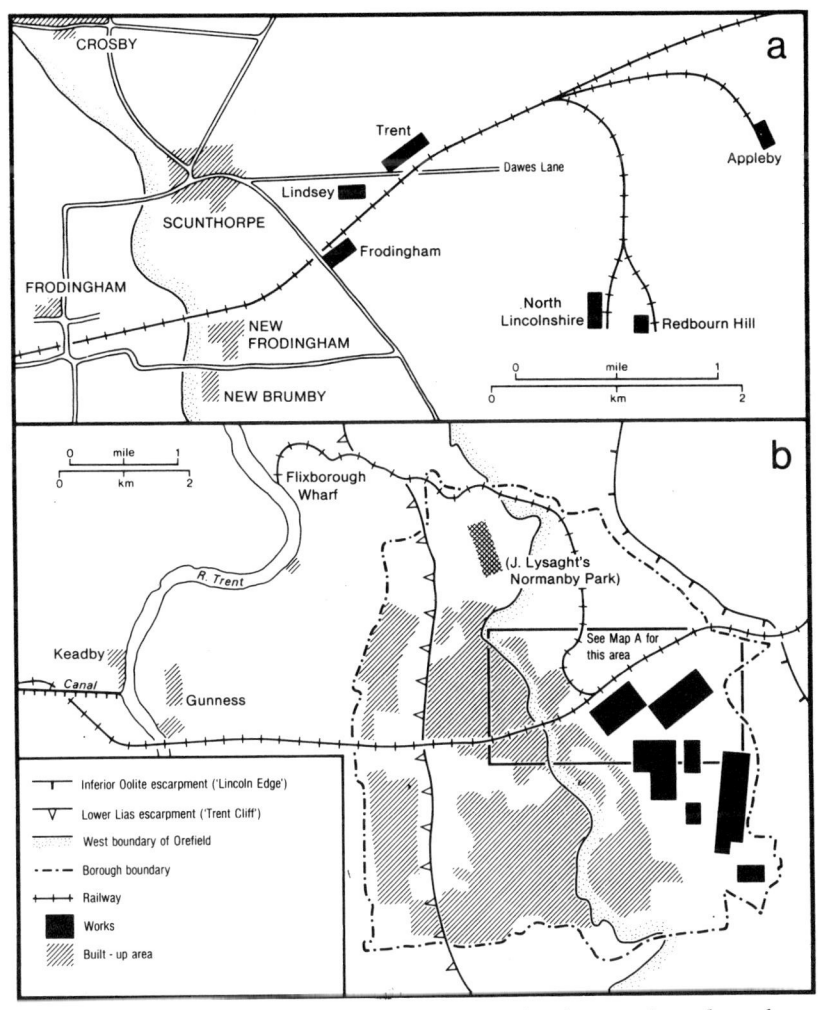

Fig. 24.1. (a) Early ironworks and (b) present-day iron and steel works at Scunthorpe.

however, could be justified in terms of the leanness of the deposit, initially a 30% iron content on the exposed or lightly-covered beds, but already averaging nearer 20% by 1918. Orefield smelting therefore made sense, although, with a lack of a nearby market, it was still possible to argue, as Burn (1940 p. 181) did in his national survey of the industry, that 'what they gained on the ore, they might lose on the trains'. The latter has been given a further twist from time to time, since rail facilities within the district have proved inadequate for the industry's demands.

The early twentieth century saw the absorption of the plants by outside concerns, mainly re-rollers wishing to gain control of their own sources of material, and the subsequent addition or expansion of steel-making capacity. In 1917 the Frodingham plant, which in fact had made the district's first steel in 1890, was taken over by the United Steel Company, with its parent works in Sheffield (Walshaw and Behrendt 1950, Ayres 1965). The Frodingham unit had earlier absorbed the Appleby plant (1912); to this was subsequently added the North Lincolnshire (1931) and Trent works (1936). The Redbourn plant was taken over in 1905, eventually becoming part of Richard Thomas and Company in 1917, when steel capacity was added (Davies 1951). Lysaght's, which began as an integrated iron and steel unit in 1912, became part of the Guest, Keen and Nettlefold group in 1919 (John Lysaght Ltd 1957).

Scunthorpe thus entered the inter-war period with three major companies, each with an integrated iron and steel unit. The addition of coke plants and, importantly, ore-preparation plants contributed to Scunthorpe becoming the lowest cost producer in the country. This was reflected in its contribution to national steel output increasing from 3% to 10%. It also led in the 1920s to Stewarts and Lloyds acquiring the North Lincolnshire site with plans for another large steelworks, although the project was frustrated by being unable to obtain sufficient ore reserves. Again, in the 1930s Richard Thomas wished to transfer its tinplate industry to low-cost Scunthorpe, but was persuaded by the Government on social grounds to build in South Wales.

After 1945 the district further increased its position within the British iron and steel industry, both during the general years of expansion in the 1950s and 60s and during the period of rationalisation and retraction since the mid 1970s (Hopkinson 1981, Pocock 1981). This reflected the continued exploitation of its locational advantages by the three separate companies prior to the 1967 nationalisation, followed by the choice of Scunthorpe by the British Steel Corporation as one of its five major steel-producing centres. Until the 1970s a vital component was the continuing advance in ore preparation, which now included the universal application of sintering. The content of the blast-furnace charge, however, changed dramatically under the challenge of foreign ores; Northampton Sands ironstone, which, for reasons of complementarity and a higher iron content, had grown to rival the local ore in importance, ceased altogether, and even the local Frodingham ironstone has now been reduced to the role of a flux, the tonnage consumed becoming a mere 2% of its peak two decades ago. The foreign ore, two-and-a-half times richer in iron than the local beds, is brought by rail from a special deep-water terminal at Immingham, thereby giving an ironic twist to Burn's earlier aphorism.

All the latest modernisation, which has included the replacement of open-hearth by oxygen steelmaking, is concentrated in the area around and to the south of the original six units, the former Lysaght's site being abandoned in 1981. The total capacity (but not output, given the world imbalance of potential supply and actual demand) is now in excess of five million tons from a workforce only half that at the time of nationalisation. The 7300 who remain, however, still form by far the largest component of employment in a town which owes not only its distinctiveness, but its very existence, to the industry.

The iron and steel town

The exploitation of the Frodingham ironstone deposit gave rise to the steel town of Scunthorpe. Its history falls into two obvious episodes, divided by the amalgamation in 1919 of the five separate parishes which today constitute the borough. At the time of amalgamation the population was 25 000, having risen from a mere 1400 at the opening of the first ironworks; today it is a borough of some 67 000.

The five original villages, spaced at intervals, north to south, along the gentle dip slope of the Lower Lias, showed markedly different responses to the advent of industry (Table 24.1). Scunthorpe itself experienced early and continuous expansion, but Crosby to the north and Frodingham and Brumby to the south remained 'closed' townships or parishes until the present century. The increase which did occur in the latter two was on two 'planted' sites, New Frodingham and New Brumby, some distance from the ancient villages. The fifth and most southerly village, Ashby, experienced slow but continuous increase. The explanation for the differential

Table 24.1. Population of the five parishes in the Scunthorpe area, 1861-1918.

Year	1861	1871	1881	1891	1901	1911	1918
Crosby	235	288	304	299	364	3339	5575
Scunthorpe	368	701	2126	3481	6750	10 171	12 312
Frodingham	113	577	1306	1384	1369	1734	1750
Brumby	204	178	560	756	904	1197	2004
Ashby	503	669	1462	1634	1843	3237	3735
Total	1423	2413	5758	7573	11 232	20 580	25 376

Sources: Census volumes, 1861-1911; 1918 from County of Lincoln - Parts of Lindsey, *Inquiry ... into Proposals for the Amalgamation and Extension of Areas of Local Government in the Ironstone District of North Lincolnshire, 1-3 October 1918.* Lincolnshire County Council, Lincoln.

growth rates, and the associated disposition of settlement, lies in patterns of land ownership, an underlying mosaic which was dovetailed into the coarser network of the elongated strips of the townships (Pocock 1970).

Over two-thirds of the total area in enclosure awards or tithe apportionment earlier in the nineteenth century was in the hands of four families - Sheffield, Winn, Beauchamp and Skipworth. Winn and Beauchamp were responsible for the two early plantations mentioned above which were located adjacent to each other, although divided by the township boundary, and nearly a mile from the smelting works. The houses in Winn's compact block of six streets were allocated to workers in the six ironworks on his land, as well as to his own quarrymen; Earl Beauchamp's two streets were for the workers in his quarries. Apart from these early forays, the two landowners did not directly participate in any further housing, but concentrated on their business commitments. The Sheffield family similarly concentrated on their mineral land, not releasing any land for residential purposes until the turn of the century, by which time the village of Scunthorpe had spread to both its northern and southern boundaries and thence, with the ironworks to the east, in a confined development westwards. Its rapid growth was made possible as a result of the varied pattern of land ownership in proximity to the village. With Ashby, it had the largest number of owners and number of separate parcels not belonging to the lord of

Table 24.2. Number of shops in the five parishes in the Scunthorpe area, 1861-1918.

Year	1861	1885	1905	1918
Crosby	2	1	7	67
Scunthorpe	5	50	173	275
Frodingham	2	9	4	6
Brumby	2	7	13	17
Ashby	9	16	37	51
Total	20	83	234	416

Source: *Post Office Directory of Lincolnshire.* Kelly, London.

the manor within the village. Speculative development in Ashby, however, was hindered by its more distant location. In both settlements, however, housing extension was accompanied by commercial development, so that early growth laid the foundation of the present borough's two major shopping centres, linear-fashion along the two High Streets. The distribution of shops, in fact, provides a good summary statistic of commercial growth (Table 24.2). Other indicators confirm the pre-eminence of Scunthorpe; in 1918, for instance, it possessed the district's co-operative society and retail market, the only three cinemas and eight of the area's nine banks. Scunthorpe's hegemony in civic matters, however, was less willingly acknowledged or easily achieved (Pocock 1963b).

As the progressive and expanding urban centre, Scunthorpe had made its first application to the County Council for amalgamation of the ironstone district in 1903. It argued the case for economic advantage and for the complementary nature of itself and Brumby and Frodingham Urban District. The latter two, which had combined to achieve urban status in 1894, and thus kept pace with their much larger neighbour, administratively at least, interpreted the same facts as indicating Scunthorpe's lack of prudence and a dissimilarity between authorities. With Sheffield, Oswald (formerly Winn) and Beauchamp considering the application premature, it is perhaps little wonder that the County Council rejected it, even though three of its five representatives found in favour. There followed a decade-and-a-half of acrimony before the inevitable amalgamation was suddenly agreed, and instituted in 1919. Landowners and ironmasters were then unanimously in favour and brought pressure to bear on the authorities. The catalyst was the request by the Ministry of Munitions to the local companies for a large increase in steel production, the consequence of which was the need for a rapid provision of 3-4000 houses. Interestingly, the only contention came at the end of the inquiry and concerned the name of the unified district. It had been assumed, and indeed was part of Scunthorpe's compromise, that Frodingham would be the choice, the argument being that it was the older settlement, and as such had been the ecclesiastical parish for the three adjacent parishes (including Scunthorpe); its name had also been given to the ironstone deposit (and district) and to the largest works. The persistence of the vicar of Scunthorpe and his Citizens' League, however, forced a compromise, and all three names were retained in the official title. This persisted until 1936 when, on achieving borough status, Brumby and Frodingham were dropped, quietly and without incident.

The removal of Trentside's low-lying ings and carrs in the redrawing of boundaries at amalgamation gave Scunthorpe its present, compact area (there has recently been a small easterly extension to incorporate the latest steelworks' extension). Given this compact area, several general restrictive forces on subsequent urban growth may be recognised (Fig. 24.2). The eastern third of the area, for instance, was actual or potential quarryland and the iron and steel zone. Any overlap of residential growth with the ferruginous beds either occurred before the extent of the ore was known or was the later, deliberate sterilising of the thinnest, westernmost layers. Westwards from the ironstone beds the gentle, dry dip slope of the Lower Lias offered no physical barrier until the low but uninterrupted escarpment of the Trent Cliff was reached. This may be deemed, at least during the early phases, as a potential barrier to growth. Expansion southwards was restricted from the outset by the course of the railway, with only two crossings in the central and eastern part of the borough. In the eastern half the built-up area was further disrupted in the inter-war years by the creation of extensive marshalling yards parallel to the main line, and another barrier, although less serious, was the construction of the A18 trunk road through the middle of the area as a town by-pass in 1933.

The disposition of parish boundaries, being at right angles to the

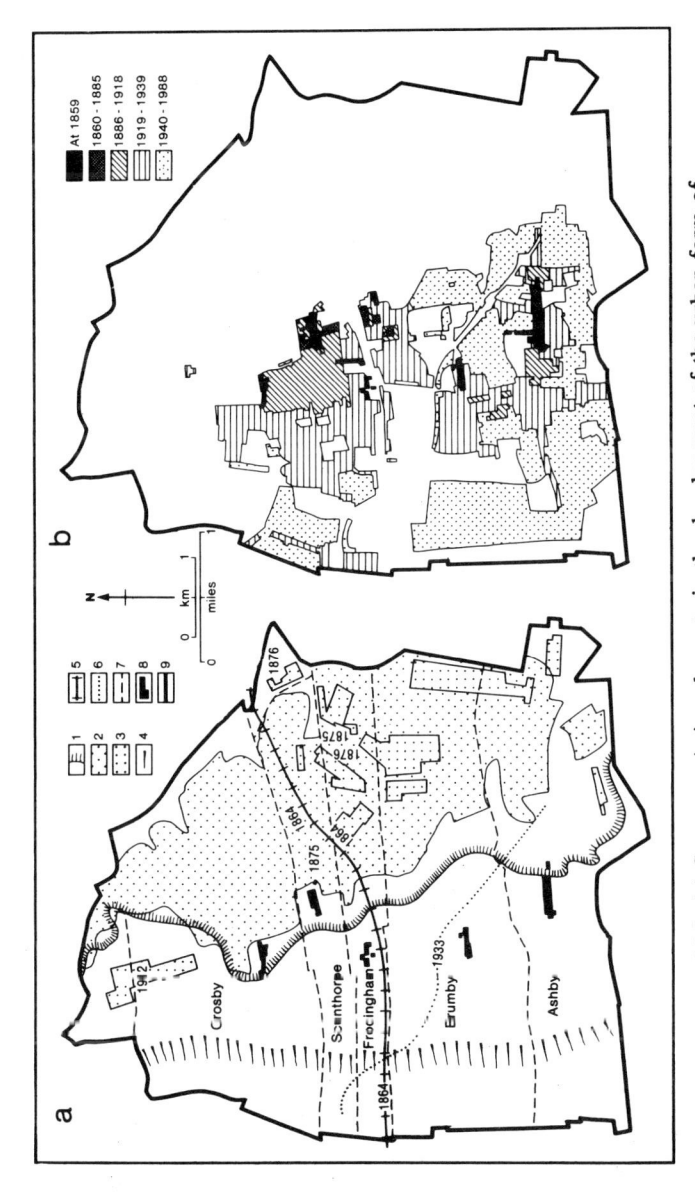

Fig. 24.2. (a) Some restrictive elements in the development of the urban form of Scunthorpe. 1 Western boundary of Frodingham ironstone, 2 Quarried area, 3 Iron and steel works (with opening dates), 4 Lower Lias escarpment ('Trent Cliff'), 5 Railway, 6 A18 trunk road, 7 Former township/parish boundary, 8 Villages in 1859, 9 Borough/District boundary. (b) Growth in residential built-up area from 1859.

north-south extent of the ore deposit, had contributed to an uneven ironstone exploitation and urban response from the beginning. The underlying mosaic of land ownership was given new significance with the large-scale acquisition in 1918 of parts of the Oswald and Beauchamp estates by the ironmasters ahead of the expected expansion. Four separate companies collaborated to form the Frodingham Estate Company and purchased 445 acres, plus a brickworks at Thorne, for the purpose of erecting a garden city. In anticipation of its own expected expansion, Richard Thomas and Company formed the Redbourn Village Society and acquired another 330 acres. The remaining company, John Lysaght's, had purchased 27 acres adjacent to its works for its own model village. In the event the various plans were largely unrealised, and the visible legacy has been one of detail rather than general form. Fewer than 400 houses were erected by the five companies between 1918 and 1925, over half of them by the Redbourn Village Society to the west of New Brumby, in a compact area forming the only recognisable quarter. Even this represented but one-fifth of the projected layout. The remainder were scattered in small or even individual lots.

The contribution of town planning to urban form has become increasingly evident since the 1947 Act, although its foundations were laid in the inter-war period (Bowyer 1959). The newly-formed Urban District passed a resolution to prepare a town-planning scheme in 1920, and an outline plan covering the town and an equivalent area outside its boundaries was prepared by Abercrombie and Johnson within a few months (Scunthorpe and Frodingham UDC *Minutes of Town Planning Committee 1920-30*, 21 February 1924 pp. 10-24). Although the partnership between council and consultants was relatively short-lived, several of the latter's broad recommendations can be recognised in the present town. These include the joining of the separate northern and southern parts of the town by extensive building in Frodingham and Brumby, the erection of a civic centre in the central area and a careful development along the western scarp face. All three achievements were only finally realised in the last two decades. Earlier, and more detailed, is the tangible contribution of Sir Patrick Abercrombie in the heavy, but classical, design of some housing in the eastern part of the corporation's Crosby estate.

With something like nine-tenths of Scunthorpe's physical development having taken place since the amalgamation of the five villages in 1919, it is perhaps little wonder that those presently in authority are able to project their town as an 'industrial garden city', an image which has been supported in the active restoration of derelict industrial land (North and Spooner 1987). At the same time, however, it remains ineluctably a steel town, with the motto, 'The heavens reflect our labours', hardly less appropriate than when first chosen. Further, despite its recent link to the country's motorway system, Scunthorpe remains an 'industrial island'. But, then, on almost any criterion, social or political, as well as economic, Scunthorpe represents a unique development within its regional setting.

References

Armstrong, M.E. (ed.) (1981). *An Industrial Island: a history of Scunthorpe*. Scunthorpe Borough Museum and Art Gallery, Scunthorpe.

Ayres, H.S. (1965). A hundred years of ironmaking at Appleby-Frodingham. *Journal of the Iron and Steel Institute* **203**, 1081-93.

Bowyer, F.J. (1959). *The Development of Scunthorpe*. Scunthorpe Corporation, Scunthorpe.

Burn, D.L. (1940). *The Economic History of Steelmaking, 1867-1939*. Cambridge University Press, Cambridge.

Daff, T. (1968). A local line made good. *Railway Magazine* **114**, 132-6.

Daff, T. (1973). The establishment of ironmaking at Scunthorpe. *Bulletin of Economic Research* **25**, 104-21.

Davies, S.G. (1951). The growth of Redbourn, 1871-1951. *Richard Thomas & Baldwin Quarterly* **11**, 3-7.

Henthorn, F. (1981). The coming of the railway. In: *An Industrial Island: a history of Scunthorpe* (ed. M.E. Armstrong) pp. 39-45. Scunthorpe Borough Museum and Art Gallery, Scunthorpe.

Hopkinson, C.F. (1981). The development of iron and steel technology in Scunthorpe 1919-1974. In: *An Industrial Island: a history of Scunthorpe* (ed. M.E. Armstrong) pp. 120-7. Scunthorpe Borough Museum and Art Gallery,

Scunthorpe.
John Lysaght Ltd (1957). *The Lysaght Century, 1857-1957*. John Lysaght, Scunthorpe.
Kendall, O.D. (1938). Iron and steel industry at Scunthorpe. *Economic Geography* **14**, 271-81.
North, J. and Spooner, D.J. (1987). Land for industry. In: *Humberside in the Eighties* (ed. D.G. Symes) pp. 67-78. Department of Geography, University of Hull.
Pocock, D.C.D. (1963a). Iron and steel at Scunthorpe. *East Midland Geographer* **3**, 124-38.
Pocock, D.C.D. (1963b). Scunthorpe and Frodingham: early struggles in civic history. *Appleby-Frodingham News* **16**, 33-40.
Pocock, D.C.D. (1964). Stages in the development of the Frodingham ironstone field. *Institute of British Geographers Transactions and Papers* **35**, 105-18.
Pocock, D.C.D. (1970). Land ownership and urban form in Scunthorpe. *East Midland Geographer* **5**, 52-61.
Pocock, D.C.D. (1981). Change and expansion in iron and steel from 1919. In: *An Industrial Island: a history of Scunthorpe* (ed. M.E. Armstrong) pp. 111-20. Scunthorpe Borough Museum and Art Gallery, Scunthorpe.
Walshaw, G.R. and Behrendt, C.A.J. (1950). *The History of Appleby-Frodingham*. Appleby-Frodingham Steel Company, Scunthorpe.

Part IV
THE EMERGING REGION

25

Iron Age and Romano-British settlement in the southern Vale of York and beyond: some problems in perspective

M. Millett

Introduction

Since 1983 various members of the Department of Archaeology at Durham University have been involved in researching the Iron Age and Romano-British settlement in the southern Vale of York, and some of the results of this work have been presented in earlier chapters of this volume (Halkon, Sitch, Creighton, Didsbury). This chapter presents some of the background to these research projects, and comments on some of the broader issues with which they are concerned.

In comparison with some areas of southern England, the Iron Age and Romano-British periods in Lincolnshire and Yorkshire are remarkably poorly known, with the exception of some very limited categories of evidence. Some of these, like water transport (McGrail this volume), the Iron Age burial rite (Stead 1979) and the major Roman towns (Wacher 1975), do provide an invaluable contribution on a national scale, but other aspects have a less impressive record. Recent work by Dent (1982, 1983) and Haselgrove (1984) has gone some way towards codifying the more mundane yet important settlement evidence from the Yorkshire region, and these studies inevitably form the foundations for current research. Nonetheless, settlement archaeology does not have a high profile, despite the considerable potential that has been shown by Halkon's survey (1987, this volume), the excavations within our project and those underway at North Cave (Dent 1987) and Lingcroft Farm (Frere 1987). Disappointingly, the highest profile work remains the hunt for 'rich' burials of the Arras type (Selkirk 1987) rather than the pursuit of knowledge about society and the economy within the overall settlement system of the ordinary people.

In our own work we have been trying to examine the settlement pattern against the environmental and economic background. In undertaking this, doubts have emerged in my mind about whether the categories within which East Yorkshire is currently viewed are appropriate, defined as they are by the prevailing southern-based view of the British Iron Age. This may be less true on the south bank of the Humber, where the patterns emerging within the territory of the Corieltauvi seem more closely related to the southern Iron Age, with the presence of lowland nucleated centres, coinages and imported pottery (May 1976) comparing closely with the centralised systems so effectively explored by Cunliffe (1978) which seem so well adapted to the social processes which constitute Romanisation (Millett in press). This model, however, is not so consistent with the available evidence from East Yorkshire, and since the southern model seems, albeit unconsciously, to have framed many approaches to the evidence in the recent past, the significance of the peculiarities of the Yorkshire pattern are in danger of being overlooked.

Settlement patterns

To sketch the evidence briefly, we have a predominantly dispersed pattern of Iron Age settlement on the Yorkshire Wolds, with most of the evidence represented by burials within square-barrow cemeteries (Stead 1979) (Fig. 25.1). These betray wealth which is at least as spectacular as anything from the southern Iron Age, but which is distinguished by its decentralised character and its occurrence in funerary contexts. To the west of the Wolds, in the Vale of York, the limited environmental evidence shows that woodland clearance came comparatively late in the middle Iron Age (Millett and

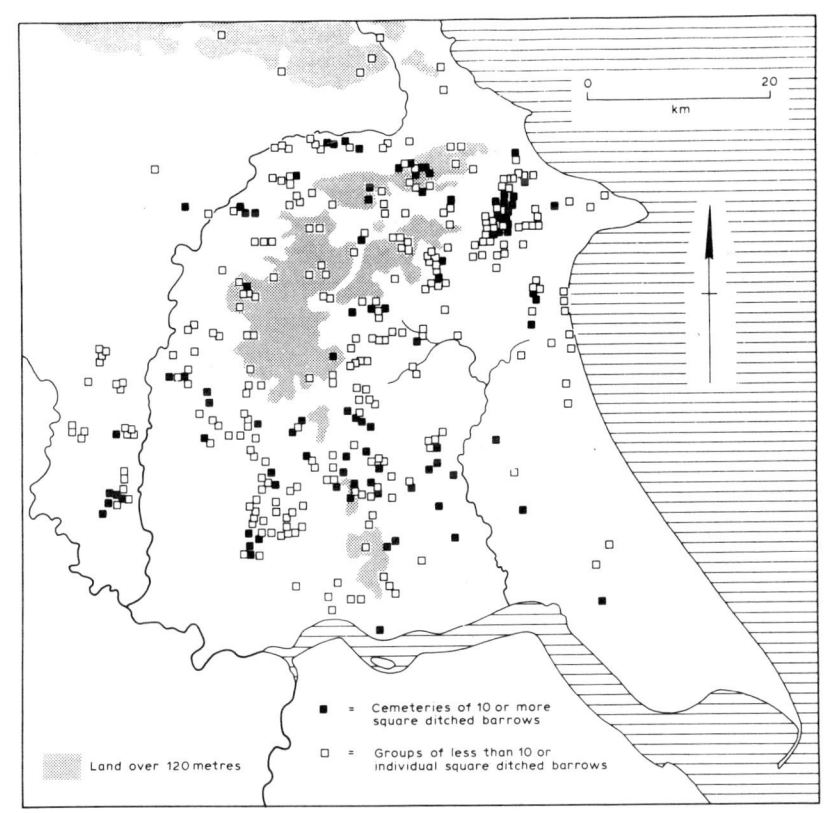

Fig. 25.1. Distribution of Iron Age square barrows north of the Humber.

McGrail 1987). This area lies on the edge of the main barrow distribution, but was densely settled from the late Iron Age onwards. The wet and wooded lowlands, combined with the Humber, suggest a model of relatively isolated development of the Parisi. This isolation remained significant into the late Roman period, as shown by Evans' (1985) seminal study of East Yorkshire pottery; the fourth century pottery assemblages remained a remarkably coherent and self-contained entity.

This cultural homogeneity should not, however, be confused with isolationism, since Hodder (1982) has demonstrated most clearly that there are a number of contemporary instances in which a clearly-defined cultural identity is strongly maintained by material cultural symbols, but where trade or exchange also regularly takes place across the boundaries. This type of exchange across the well-defined and long-lived Humber boundary may well provide a context for the apparently heavy use of the Humber system for water transport (McGrail this volume), the transfer of kiln technology from the south to the north bank (Swan 1984), the transport of Dragonby-type pottery into Yorkshire (Halkon this volume) and the possible movement of iron ore from south to north to supply the substantial iron manufacturing industry which seems to have existed around the River Foulness (Millett and Halkon 1988, Halkon this volume). In this sense the Humber may be seen as both boundary and access to the clearly-defined cultural group of the Parisi. The same seems true of the Vale of York, to a lesser extent, but this area remained a substantial western boundary until into the Roman period. The settlements on the western edge of the Vale of York are thus peripheral to the settlement system, although nonetheless significant for that.

Settlement within the territory of the Parisi seems to have lacked the dominant focal nucleated settlements which characterise the southern British Iron Age. Although we have the significant early hillfort of Grimthorpe on the western Yorkshire Wolds (Stead 1968), Staple Howe on their northern edge (Brewster 1963) and the major but ill-understood coastal site of Danes' Dyke on Flamborough Head in the east (Ramm 1984), these sites lie on the peripheries, and the core of the settlement area seems to have been characterised by a far less centralised pattern comprising farmsteads, hamlets and their attendant burials. Even when Romanisation brought changes to this pattern, the urban centres which emerged (Redcliff/Brough-on-Humber, Malton, Shiptonthorpe and York) remained peripheral to the main landmass, and the spectacular sites, including the mosaics of the Petuaria school, were rural, with the urban centres (with the exception of York) remaining uninspiring (Fig. 25.2). Indeed, the preceding Roman military phase, with its attendant forts and road construction, seems also to have by-passed the core of the territory, focusing its concerns on the Brigantes to the west and north (Breeze and Dobson 1985) (Fig. 25.3).

This pattern does not seem to be a coincidence, as I have argued elsewhere that the essence of the Roman system was that it worked through the native system, and Romanisation was therefore limited by

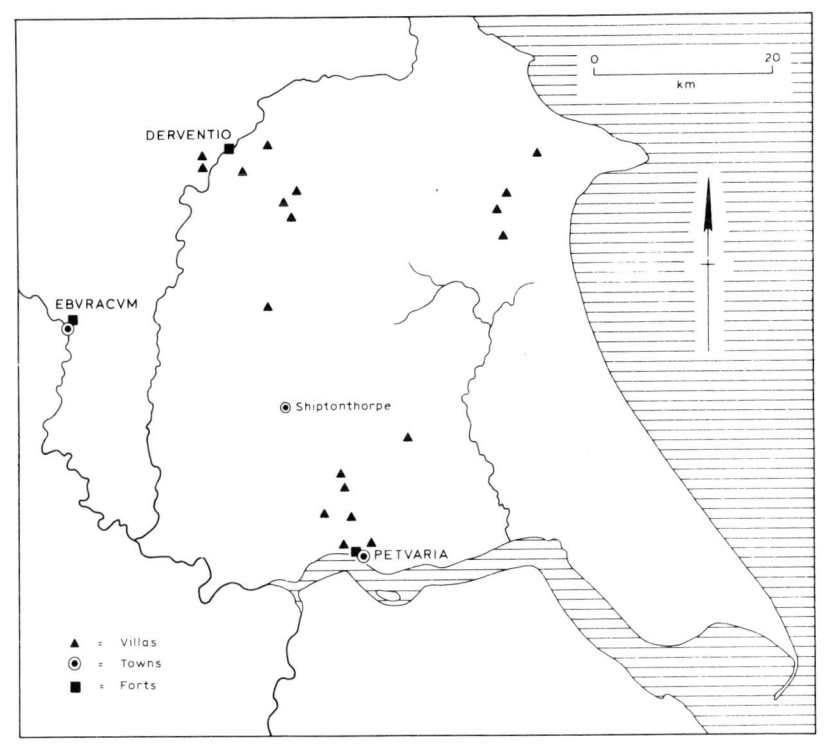

Fig. 25.2. Roman settlement after the first century AD.

the extent of native social evolution (Millett in press). Furthermore, the nature of Roman control was that it worked through the native élites. Rome could, and did, conquer, coerse and control native societies from the top downwards; Romanisation thus worked best in centralised societies. That we have no evidence for any sustained anti-Roman activity in East Yorkshire suggests that the Parisi came over to Rome and were incorporated through coersion or co-operation. The military dispositions in the *Civitas Parisiorum* remained focused on the enemy beyond the territory, and it is my belief that the legionary base at York was deliberately placed at a neutral boundary location, facing, threatening and observing the Brigantes. The routes to that target territory were the *raison d'être* of the military installations, all of which lie along them (Breeze and

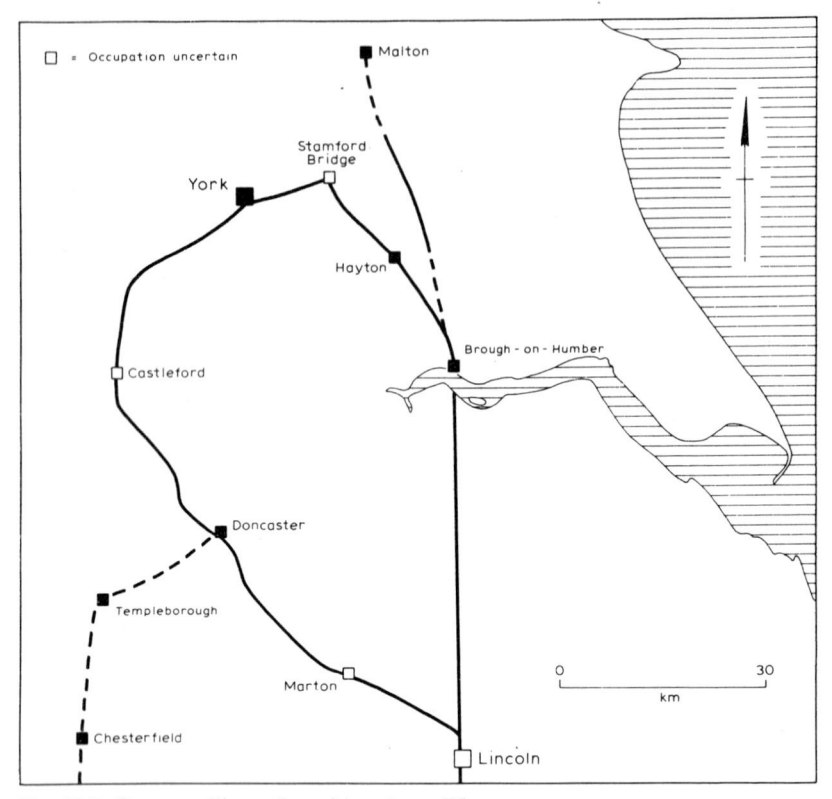

Fig. 25.3. Roman military dispositions in AD 75.

Dobson 1985). It thus seems to me that the Roman military were essentially irrelevant to the social and economic development of the territory except in indirect ways, and even in these their effect is as likely to have been negative and destructive as a positive stimulus to growth (Millett in press).

The difficulties over the identification and characterisation of the *chef lieu* of the *civitas* are thus a result of the continuity of the predominantly dispersed system of native power, which we do not yet understand because it has not been made a focus of study. The town of *Petuaria* is both remarkably peripheral in location, and presumably largely irrelevant to native social needs. It may be that the model proposed for the development of London as a centre of incoming traders based on a neutral social and physical boundary (Millett in press) is equally appropriate for sites around the Humber (cf. Creighton this volume). The lack of success of these sites in comparison with London may be the result of the less favourable geographical location, or the central place concept being inappropriate to the nature of the native system of the Parisi.

Continuity of power seems the most appropriate model for this region, and I see no reason why such a continuity cannot be postulated for the change from Roman to Anglian, although the present evidence is able neither to support nor refute this hypothesis. It seems significant that rural settlement sites similar to Elmswell, Garton (Congreve 1937, 1938), which are the most likely to generate new information in relation to this question, have not been the subject of recent research and excavation.

Future research

If one is willing to accept a model of social organisation based on a rich but unfocused, acephalus (headless) rural settlement system, as evidenced by the Iron Age burials and Romano-British villas, then some investigation of the working of the social and economic system is required. This is a particularly interesting problem as far as Roman Britain is concerned because it does appear to be a rare example of the successful Romanisation of an essentially decentralised native society. It is our failure to realise that models based on central places are inappropriate to the Iron Age in East Yorkshire that has led us into research which has not resolved these problems (cf. Haselgrove 1986). The Holme-on-Spalding-Moor survey has begun to provide some of the data, but much more work is needed before any definite answers can be formulated. Meanwhile, I can perhaps contribute to future research by codifying a few of the relevant questions.

As regards the Iron Age, we need to attempt first to examine the rural settlements and cemeteries afresh in order to establish the extent to which the society, although decentralised, was part of a dispersed heirarchy. It should be a priority to attempt to characterise the nature of the economies of the rural sites. Any settlement excavation without adequate environmental sampling is thus wholly unjustifiable. The nucleated sites also need to be examined, particularly in relation to their economic functions and territorial roles, if any. Special attention needs to be paid to the establishment of artefact distribution patterns within the territory of the Parisi, and the nature and distribution of any exports from, or imports to, the territory. The same basic data are required for the Romano-British period to establish how far, if at all, the pattern changed after the conquest. The speed at which Romanised goods arrived on sites within the territory, and the topographic context of the military sites, also demand close examination. This evidence, if collected in relation to further palaeoenvironmental investigations and the types of survey data already obtained from the Holme-on-Spalding-Moor area, will allow a fuller understanding of an area which possesses an exceptionally well preserved reservoir of information relating to both the Iron Age and Romano-British periods.

Acknowledgements

This paper has arisen out of the co-operative research in which I have been involved in the Holme-on-Spalding-Moor project. I am pleased to acknowledge the support for the project provided by the University of Durham, the Royal Archaeological Institute, the Society of Antiquaries of London, the Haverfield Bequest Fund and English Heritage. My ideas have been stimulated by discussion with those involved in the project, and Colin Haselgrove, who, together with Steve Willis and John Creighton, have commented upon a draft of this paper.

References

Breeze, D. and Dobson, B. (1985). Roman military deployment in North England. *Britannia* 16, 1-20.

Brewster, T.C.M. (1963). *The Excavation of Staple Howe.* East Riding Archaeological Research Committee, Scarborough.

Congreve, A.L. (1937). *A Roman and Saxon Site at Elmswell, East Yorkshire 1935-36,* Hull Museum Publications 193. Hull Museum, Hull.

Congreve, A.L. (1938). *A Roman and Saxon Site at Elmswell, East*

Yorkshire 1937, Hull Museum Publications 198. Hull Museum, Hull.
Cunliffe, B.W. (1978). *Iron Age Communities in Britain.* Routledge and Kegan Paul, London.
Dent, J.S. (1982). Cemeteries and settlement patterns of the Iron Age on the Yorkshire Wolds. *Proceedings of the Prehistoric Society* **48**, 437-57.
Dent, J.S. (1983). The impact of Roman rule on native society in the territory of the Parisi. *Britannia* **14**, 35-44.
Dent, J.S. (1987). *North Cave Excavations.* Humberside Archaeology Unit, Beverley.
Evans, J. (1985). Aspects of Later Roman Pottery Assemblages in Northern England. Ph.D. thesis, University of Bradford.
Frere, S.S. (1987). Roman Britain in 1986. *Britannia* **18**, 301-78.
Halkon, P. (1987). Aspects of the Romano-British Landscape around Holme on Spalding Moor, East Yorkshire. M.A. thesis, University of Durham.
Haselgrove, C.C. (1984). The later pre-Roman Iron Age between the Humber and the Tyne. In: *Settlement and Society in the Roman North* (ed. P. Wilson, R.F. Jones and D.M. Evans) pp. 9-26. School of Archaeological Sciences, University of Bradford.
Haselgrove, C.C. (1986). Central places in British Iron Age studies: a review and some problems. In: *Central Places, Archaeology and History* (ed. E. Grant) pp. 3-10. Department of Archaeology and Prehistory, University of Sheffield.
Hodder, I.R. (1982). *Symbols in Action: ethnoarchaeological studies of material culture.* Cambridge University Press, Cambridge.
May, J. (1976). The growth of settlements in the Later Iron Age in Lincolnshire. In: *Oppida: the beginnings of urbanisation in Barbarian Europe.* British Archaeological Reports (Supplementary Series) 11 (ed. B. Cunliffe and T. Rowley) pp. 163-80. British Archaeological Reports, Oxford.
Millett, M. (in press). *The Romanisation of Britain.* Cambridge University Press, Cambridge.
Millett, M. and Halkon, P. (1988). Landscape and economy: recent fieldwork and excavation around Holme on Spalding Moor. In: *Recent Research in Roman Yorkshire,* British Archaeological Reports (British Series) 193 (ed. J. Price and

P.R. Wilson) pp. 37-47. British Archaeological Reports, Oxford.
Millett, M. and McGrail, S. (1987). The archaeology of the Hasholme logboat. *Archaeological Journal* **144**, 69-155.
Ramm, H. (1984). Danes' Dyke, Flamborough. *Archaeological Journal* **141**, 37-9.
Selkirk, A. (1987). Garton Station. *Current Archaeology* **103**, 234-7.
Stead, I.M. (1968). An Iron Age hillfort at Grimthorpe, Yorkshire, England. *Proceedings of the Prehistoric Society* **34**, 148-90.
Stead, I.M. (1979). *The Arras Culture*. Yorkshire Philosophical Society, York.
Swan, V.G. (1984). *The Pottery Kilns of Roman Britain*. Royal Commission on Historical Monuments, London.
Wacher, J. (1975). *The Towns of Roman Britain*. Batsford, London.

26

The Humber and its people during the medieval period

G.C. Knowles

Early conflicts

At the start of the medieval period the Humber featured prominently, if briefly, in the history of England when on 18 September 1066 the combined forces of Harold Hadrada, King of Norway, and Earl Tostig sailed up the estuary in a fleet of 300 ships and disembarked at Riccall on the River Ouse (Fig. 26.1). This was the second hostile fleet to enter the Humber in that year. An earlier force of 60 ships led by Tostig had ravaged the territory on the south bank of the river before suffering defeat by the Lindsey Militia, a feudal force loyal to King Harold of England. If Lindsey owed nominal loyalty to the *de facto* King of England, from the Humber northwards considerable disaffection existed. It was Hadrada's aim to exploit this circumstance and the Humber and Ouse brought his forces swiftly to within easy distance of York, a city whose crucial importance with regard to the military control of northern England was long established. York's accessibility by boat from the North Sea must have been an important factor in it becoming the centre of an Anglo-Scandinavian kingdom in the tenth century, and no doubt the feeling of independence from the

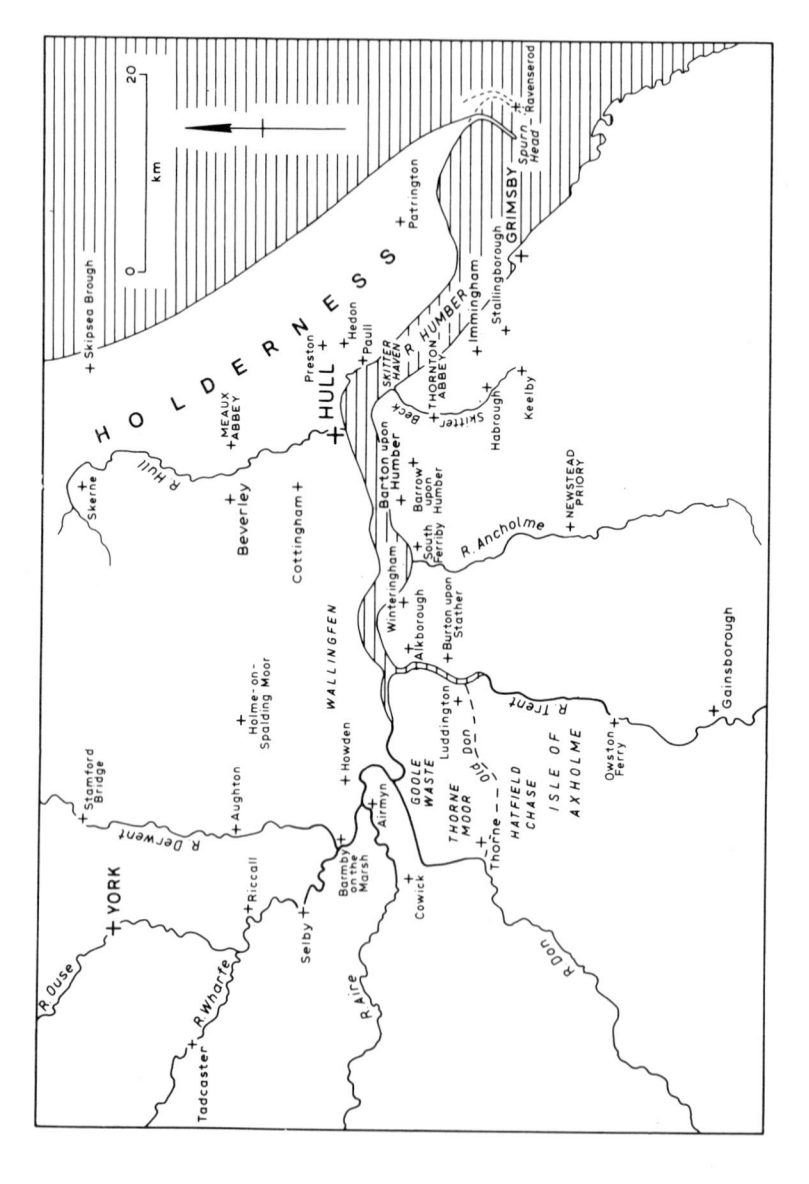

Fig. 26.1. Location map.

politics of southern England which was evident north of the Humber in the mid eleventh century was in part due to the strong links with Scandinavia which still existed.

York was taken easily by the invaders in 1066 but serious tactical errors brought defeat at Stamford Bridge, and Hadrada and Tostig paid for their failure with their lives (Stenton 1971). The battle of Stamford Bridge marked the effective end of two centuries of strife between England and Scandinavia, but allegiancies north of the Humber did not change overnight, and the region was apparently no more willing to accept William I than it had been to acknowledge Harold as King of England.

In 1069 Swein Estrithson, King of Denmark, sent a force to make good his claim to the English throne. Making their first landfall on the Kent coast, the 240 ships of the Danish fleet made their way northwards along the coast, being repulsed wherever they came in contact with local forces. Eventually the fleet took refuge in the Humber, where it was safe from immediate attack by forces loyal to William and was able to link up with rebellious English. Again York fell to invaders, but fearing the approach of William's army, the Danes withdrew to the Isle of Axholme, whose surrounding rivers and marshes evidently offered superior tactical advantages to a waterborne force. In due course William did approach, from the south, and the Danes crossed from Axholme to the north bank of the Ouse, from where they again entered York. Instead of an immediate frontal attack, William started to devastate the countryside in a wide area around the city, with such effect that the Danes feared being isolated and sought terms. The Scandinavians were given a cash payment and permitted to return to the Isle of Axholme during the winter of 1069/70 before returning home, while William continued his subjugation of northern England - his infamous 'Harrying of the North'.

In 1070 Swein Estrithson himself crossed to England and, notwithstanding their treaty with William, he joined the Danes still in the Humber and started a campaign in the East Midlands in conjunction with various factions of the disaffected English, notable among whom was the Lincolnshire thegn Hereward. By the summer, however, Swein came to terms with William and left the Humber (Stenton 1971).

The incursions of the second half of the eleventh century were the end of an episode which had lasted for 200 years. Throughout that period the estuary had been of the greatest benefit to the Scandinavians; it provided them with immediate and safe access to a large area of the interior of the country at a sufficient distance from the seat of English royal power for serious trouble to be caused before an adequate response could be organised. However, it was largely the invaders' inability fully to exploit these strategic opportunities which enabled the Conqueror ultimately to establish his control of northern England.

The Humber as a frontier

As the political and military threat from Scandinavia declined, other features of the Humber assumed greater relative significance. For some time the river continued to mark the divide between the politically more stable south of England and the unreliable north, which had been devastated by a series of savage campaigns. Following his success against Swein at York in 1070, William's continued brutal subjugation of the north of England appears to have caused widespread suffering and destruction. The Domesday survey of 1086 recorded extensive areas of waste ground in Yorkshire. Although the Conquerer's 'Harrying of the North' is often regarded as the cause of this (Brooks 1966), it may be too simple an explanation for all the waste recorded in the North. What is very clear from an analysis of the Domesday Book, however, is that whereas Lincolnshire manors had greatly increased in value, and therefore presumably in prosperity, between 1066 and 1086, north of the Humber there had been a correspondingly sharp drop in value, with many manors recorded as waste and complete settlements temporarily abandoned. Indeed, by 1086 Lincolnshire appears as one of the richest parts of the country. William's arrangements for the feudal settlement of Yorkshire are further evidence that he regarded the territory north of the Humber as a frontier area with a capacity for rebellion; the confiscated estates of Earls Tostig and Morcar he retained under his own control, while other manors and estates were awarded to a small number of trusted Norman lords.

On both sides of the Humber military control of key points remained a matter of great concern well into the twelfth century, and the locations chosen for the construction of motte-and-bailey castles in the region are revealing. On the south bank they are found still at Barrow upon Humber, a little way up the River Trent at Owston Ferry, and there is evidence for a castle of some description at Barton-upon-Humber, while on the north bank they were built on the River Derwent at Aughton, at Preston and at Skipsea Brough on the Holderness coast. The common feature possessed by all but one of these sites is easy accessibility by water, allowing comparatively rapid communication over long distances, but most were also located at major river crossing points and at sites which offered some commercial opportunities as ports.

It would be easy to allow accounts of invasion fleets, punitive expeditions and devastation to give a very distorted impression of life in the region in the eleventh century, and here again the Domesday Book can provide some valuable information. While the Humber served as a highway to those travelling by water, it was a considerable obstacle to others, and the establishment of formal ferry services in certain places was a matter worthy of note in the Domesday survey because of the income which was generated for the local lord. Domesday records ferries at Grimsby, Barton-upon-Humber, South Ferriby and Winteringham.

It is perhaps significant that none of the ferries listed was on the devastated north side of the Humber. Two ferries were recorded at South Ferriby in 1086, a matter which might seem confusing. However, as late as the eighteenth century the River Ancholme crossing at South Ferriby is known to have been notoriously unpleasant, and it seems reasonable to suppose that one of the eleventh century ferries there operated on the Humber while the other enabled travellers to cross the Ancholme in its tidal, undrained and unbridged condition. Perhaps a similar explanation could also be found for the two ferries at Grimsby which are also recorded in the Domesday survey. The provision of reliable ferries at key points was of vital importance to the Crown as well as to others, and when a royal charter was granted by Edward II in 1316 to the developing town of Kingston upon Hull, among the rights and privileges bestowed was the obligation to operate a ferry crossing of the Humber in perpetuity.

The growth of settlements

The Domesday Book contains frustratingly little evidence concerning the existence of ports in the area in the eleventh century. There are references to tolls being taken at Grimsby, Barton-upon-Humber and South Ferriby; in the latter two places the tolls related to bread, fish and hides, a useful indication of the commodities being produced locally in sufficient quantities to allow some proportion to be exported. Another indication of growing commercial activity by 1086 is the mention in Domesday of markets; these are recorded at Barton-upon-Humber and at Burton upon Stather, and in both places markets may have come into being as a result of trade passing in and out of the settlement by water. In the late eleventh century the dominant settlements on the south bank of the Humber were clearly Barton-upon-Humber and Grimsby. Few contemporary settlements on the north bank of the river seem to have been able to match Barton or Grimsby as centres of commerce, although by this time Beverley was beginning to develop its position as a manufacturing centre and as a port.

That Beverley was already a town of some importance by the eleventh century and was able to carry on trade with other places via the River Hull is certain. The town is mentioned rather briefly by the Domesday survey, not because it was of no importance but because a charter of privileges granted to the Minster by William I freed the town from geld. From an early date Beverley thrived as a centre for industry and trade, and by the early twelfth century the town held three fairs a year. A series of medieval charters, starting in the twelfth century, granted, confirmed and extended the rights and privileges of the borough; in 1377 Beverley still had about twice the population of Hull and was the eleventh largest town in England (Miller *et al.* 1982).

Tanning was one of its industries, but the town was famous for the production of woollen cloth, much of which was bought by London merchants. Raw wool was collected in Beverley from the East Riding and from other parts of Yorkshire, and all the processes required to complete the manufacture of woollen cloth were carried out there. Recent excavations by the Humberside Archaeological Unit in the Eastgate and Walkergate areas have revealed such evidence for clothmaking activity, including the remains of teasels, used to raise the nap on cloth, and other plant remains such as the seed heads of dyer's rocket and roots of madder, both used for dyeing (Hughes 1985, Evans this volume). Beverley continued to flourish through the thirteenth century, but towards the end of the fourteenth century it was beginning to be eclipsed as a port by Hull and as a wool town by other centres in the West Riding of Yorkshire.

While Beverley rose to prominence on the north side of the Humber as the port for the East Riding, on the south bank Grimsby's proximity to the North Sea undoubtedly gave it a commercial advantage over Barton. Grimsby achieved borough status as early as 1201, but the natural harbour relied on the flow of water from two rather modest streams to keep it scoured, and silting and congestion brought the port into serious decline towards the end of the Middle Ages (Ambler this volume). Further inland important settlements such as Gainsborough on the Trent, and Selby and York on the Ouse, were to have major significance as ports throughout the Middle Ages. The rise of Hull and problems of navigation on the Ouse caused York to decline as a place receiving seagoing ships towards the end of the medieval period, although a considerable traffic in barges and lighters continued long after. The other ports on the Trent and Ouse remained successful until great increases in the size of commercial ships made navigation of the rivers difficult for all but the smaller modern vessels.

If political and military events during the eleventh century had been disastrous for the area north of the Humber, it is clear that within rather less than 100 years the whole region was not only recovering but thriving. As trade began to develop by way of the Humber, those existing riverside settlements which were on well-drained land and had good access to the estuary, perhaps by short creeks, were the first to be able to benefit from, and exploit, the increase in trade. In addition to the places already mentioned it is apparent that some mercantile activity took place during the Middle Ages from Immingham, Skitter Haven, Patrington, Paull, Alkborough and an as yet unidentified port referred to in 1326 as "Brumemuth' (Hayfield and Slater 1984). The volume of trade passing through these places is likely to have been small, but it may have been sustained over several centuries and brought a steady, if modest, income to those involved.

As places with natural features capable of being developed easily as ports started to prosper, other riverside sites were selected for development by landlords anxious not to be left behind. Thus it was that a number of new settlements were created with the intention of bringing new ports into existence and benefiting from the prosperity of the twelfth and thirteenth centuries. In the early twelfth century the abbot of St Mary's, York, founded the most westerly of these settlements at the mouth of the River Aire. Given the name 'Airmyn', the settlement was placed on the river bank at one end of the parish of Snaith, and a map believed to have been compiled about 1407 shows the port with a small watchtower or lighthouse overlooking the river (Beresford 1986). Further east it has been suggested that Winteringham shows evidence of planned medieval development of a pre-existing settlement (D. Neave pers. comm.). The date of this venture is not known, but it would seem that an attempt was made to encourage the use of Winteringham's small haven which opens into the western end of the Humber estuary. Today both Airmyn and Winteringham remain only as villages and the attempt to develop them as ports evidently failed. Their lack of success, other than as rural communities, may have been because both were too far from the North Sea and perhaps lacked good communications with a sufficiently large hinterland. The ports which sprang up as new towns around the eastern half of the Humber were more successful.

The abbey of Meaux had been founded in the Hull valley in 1125. The abbey held the manor of Myton, where it had a grange, located at the eastern end of the parish of Hessle, by the mouth of the River Hull. In earlier centuries this area may have been regarded as too low-lying for a large permanent settlement based upon an agricultural economy. Commercially, however, the site had many advantages, and during the second half of the twelfth century a small seaport had started to develop there. Meaux Abbey's production of wool undoubtedly provided a major impetus for the foundation of Wyke, as the town was at first known. In 1193 the wool contributed by the Cistercian houses of Yorkshire towards the ransom of Richard I was collected there, and the port ranked sixth in England in 1203-5 when a tax was raised among merchants. In 1279 a weekly market and an annual fair were granted; in 1293 Edward I acquired the town from Meaux and it was renamed Kingston upon Hull. The town received its Royal Charter in 1296 and was of great strategic value to Edward as a secure supply base in his operations against the Scots. Under royal patronage the port developed rapidly during the next century and its more favourable position enabled trade to be won progressively from Beverley, whose importance as a port, although not as a market town and a centre in other respects, consequently declined. Perhaps the growth of Kingston upon Hull also led to the failure of Barton-upon-Humber to develop as a major port towards the end of the medieval period; Barton remained prosperous, however, as two fine medieval churches bear witness.

Hedon, another new town development, was in existence by 1142. Situated again in the corner of an older parish (Preston), the new port was intended to make use of a small creek opening into the Humber about four miles downstream from the mouth of the River Hull. Founded apparently by the Aumales, lords of Holderness, Hedon had its first Royal Charter by 1170 and the venture initially enjoyed great success. The natural watercourse was deepened and extended to make basins in which ships could be berthed, three churches and three hospitals were provided, a market was held twice weekly and there was an annual fair. For a century or more Hedon must have repaid amply those who had invested in its foundation. Its proximity to the North Sea would have been an advantage, but confined access to its wharves may have become a problem as the size and number of ships increased. More particularly, the town began to suffer from competition in trade with other Humber ports. Kingston upon Hull had come into existence later than Hedon and initially developed more slowly, but by 1280 the men of Hedon were complaining of unfair competition from Hull (Boyle 1895).

For a time, however, an even greater threat to the trade of Hedon had come from Ravenserod, a settlement which grew up on a medieval predecessor of Spurn Point (de Boer 1978). Like Hedon, Ravenserod was sponsored by the Earls of Aumale and it came into being at an unknown date during the early thirteenth century. Perhaps used first by fishermen, the town appears to have developed rapidly on a spit of land which emerged from the sea, and its convenient position led to it being used extensively by merchant ships. Soon Grimsby and Hedon started to suffer loss in trade to Ravenserod, and its rivals claimed that the port's success was due to the unlawful exacting of tolls from shipping, and perhaps other acts of dubious legality. By 1250 Ravenserod was holding a weekly market and an annual fair, and in 1299 the town obtained a borough charter which further extended its rights and privileges. Five years later the new borough was able to send representatives to Edward I's Parliament. Ravenserod's decline was as sudden as its rise; the tidal processes which had enabled the town to come into being reversed their effect during the first half of the fourteenth century and houses started to be lost to the sea. In 1346 it was said that two-thirds of the town had been destroyed, and two decades later Ravenserod had ceased to exist (Boyle 1889).

Religious houses

It is difficult to say much concerning the Humber region in the Middle Ages without mention of its monasteries. A consistent feature of the majority of the more significant religious houses is their ready access to the Humber by way of its tributaries. At first sight the rural monasteries appear to have been endowed with locations in remote corners of parishes where great effort was needed to drain and cultivate land which had previously been unproductive or, at best, of marginal value. To an extent no doubt this impression is correct, but it is surely no accident how often these situations placed the houses beside navigable waterways which could be used subsequently to communicate readily with the outside world. The earlier foundations of St Mary's, York, and Selby Abbey, although not in remote locations, made considerable use of their wharves alongside the River Ouse, and at Selby the remains of a warehouse, perhaps of twelfth century date, survive near the river (Duckham 1967). The bishops of Durham, as lords of Howdenshire, established a palace at Howden alongside an imposing minster church. Howden in the Middle Ages stood on the River Derwent, near its confluence with the Ouse, and for both long and short distance travel by water in all directions the town was very conveniently placed.

It has already been mentioned that the town and port of Hull owed its early foundation to the abbey of Meaux. Myton was not the only grange the monks held in the Hull valley; they stretched as far north as Skerne, and since the most practical method of reaching outlying properties through the carrs was by boat, a series of channels was created linking the estates with the River Hull. This was done in the late twelfth and early thirteenth centuries and had the secondary effect of helping to drain some parts of the valley (Sheppard 1958). In the

Ancholme valley similar use was probably made of the river, and drainage works were perhaps started by the communities at Thornholme and Newstead Priories. Also in northern Lincolnshire, Thornton Abbey could be reached from the Humber by way of Skitter Haven, and the headwaters of the Skitter Beck pass close to other religious houses at Newhouse and Nun Coton. Another monastery located within easy reach of an arterial waterway was Axholme Priory at Owston Ferry, on the River Trent.

Drainage schemes

During the twelfth century both religious and secular owners of low-lying land started to improve its productivity by draining and embanking. Simple sluices were positioned at the outfall of new drains, and in due course banks raised on neighbouring properties became joined to make a more effective defence against flooding. Thus there is evidence that during the thirteenth century a limited amount of reclamation took place along the estuarine margins of southern Holderness and along the lower reaches of the River Ouse (Sheppard 1966). Although parts of Wallingfen had dried sufficiently to allow some summer grazing and peat-cutting, serious drainage of large areas of low ground had to wait until after the medieval period, and there is little evidence of further reclamation being undertaken during the fourteenth and fifteenth centuries (Sheppard 1966). That the early banks were insufficient to withstand much more than normal tides was demonstrated in 1265 when it is recorded that there was extensive flooding of the Humber and the water reached as far inland as Cottingham. During the following two or three centuries drainage work seems to have been confined mainly to the consolidation and minor refinement of earlier achievements (Sheppard 1958).

In the area surrounding the Isle of Axholme the present course of the River Don north of Thorne has been shown to be artificial (Gaunt 1975). The date of this diversion is uncertain, but there is evidence that by 1344 the waterway had been in existence for some time and it may represent an earlier medieval scheme by the Crown or a religious house to drain part of the Hatfield Chase area (Gaunt 1987). Another river diversion was undertaken during late medieval times when the lower reaches of the Derwent were given their present course west of Barmby on the Marsh, and in 1413 the abbot of Selby authorised the cutting of the Mere Dyke east from Luddington to bring the eastern branch of the Don more quickly to the River Trent (Gaunt 1987). These examples serve to show that ambitious drainage works began at an earlier date than is generally appreciated, and that Vermuyden's scheme in the seventeenth century was continuing a tradition, not beginning one.

Economic activity

The Domesday reference to tolls on fish, bread and hides demanded at Barton and South Ferriby is tantalisingly brief, but at least it provides an indication that at least in part the prosperity of the region was based on agriculture, both the rearing of animals and cultivation of the soil. More directly associated with the Humber and its tributaries was fishing. Fisheries and places where eels were taken are recorded at many places in the Domesday Book. On the south side of the Humber there was a concentration of fisheries around the Isle of Axholme, and smaller numbers were found on the Humber itself and in the Rivers Trent and Ancholme; on the north side fisheries were recorded in the valleys of the Hull and Derwent. It is hard to imagine, however, that no fish were taken from the River Ouse or from the sea during the eleventh century, and we therefore have to accept that the evidence of the Domesday survey is incomplete. Indeed, fishing, and it must have been sea-fishing, was one of the enterprises undertaken by the men of Ravenserod in the thirteenth century, and it is therefore likely that men in places like Grimsby were taking fish from the sea 200 years earlier. Eels were frequently taken as a by-product of the operation of watermills, and other river fish were caught in elaborate traps which were permanent structures built across the river bed. Stakes and woven wattles made fish traps a considerable hazard to navigation, and a number of merchant ships and their cargoes were lost on the River Ouse during the fourteenth century; some loss of life was suffered also. There was a long-running dispute during the fifteenth century between the Corporation of York and proprietors of 'fishgarths' on the Ouse, and not until well into the sixteenth century was the river freed of this hazard to navigation (Duckham 1967).

Salt is known to have been produced in considerable quantities during the medieval period on the Lincolnshire coast (Owen 1984) and, although some of the output certainly passed inland by road, a proportion was probably traded further afield by way of the Humber. Although the main concentration of saltern sites occurs in the strip of coastal marshland running south from Grimsby, some salt seems to have been produced beside the Humber. Again using the evidence of the Domesday survey, we know of salt being produced at Habrough, Stallingbrough and Keelby during the eleventh century. However, we have no knowledge of salt being produced on the north side of the Humber during the Middle Ages.

Chalk and Jurassic limestone are the only stones occurring locally which may be used for building purposes, but every medieval church in the area contains evidence of large quantities of freestone transported over considerable distances. Again, it is inconceivable that stone was brought from quarries such as Tadcaster to towns and villages near the Humber other than by water. The difficulty of obtaining good building stone in sufficient quantities was eventually alleviated by the manufacture of brick, for which considerable quantities of clay existed locally, the alluvial deposits of the Humber and its tributaries being particularly suitable for this purpose. Substantial use was made of brick; this can still be seen today in Holy Trinity Church, Hull, where it was used *c.* 1300-20, in the vault of the nave of Beverley Minster, built between 1308 and 1349, in the gatehouse of Thornton Abbey, begun in 1382 and at Beverley North Bar built in 1409. Millions of bricks were also made to build the town walls of Hull, starting in the fourteenth century.

The same raw material was used by the medieval pottery industry in the Humber region. Because of similarity in designs, technique and material, the products of local kilns have been given the generic term 'Humber Ware'. Individual sites for the manufacture of medieval pottery in the area have so far been identified at Cowick (Wilson and Hurst 1965), Holme-on-Spalding-Moor (Mayes and Hayfield 1980, Halkon this volume) and recently in Beverley (Humberside Archaeology Unit 1986, Williams and Fairbank 1987, Evans this volume). Medieval tile kilns have also been identified at Meaux Abbey (Eames 1961) and again recently at Beverley. Whereas there is reason to think that bricks, because of their bulk, were made close to the site where they were intended to be used, the impression gained for medieval pottery is that it was traded widely over the region (Hayfield and Slater 1984), and again the waterways are the obvious route by which the products of local pottery kilns were transported.

An interesting sidelight on the brick, tile and pottery making industries locally has been revealed recently by Beresford (1986). A map, dating from about 1407 and showing 'Inclesmore', the area now known as Goole Waste and Thorne Moor, was evidently drawn up to help validate a landowner's rights in an area which was of considerable financial value. A series of associated documents reveals that the peat of Inclesmore was being exploited on a considerable scale by late medieval times and sections of the moor were being leased by various interests wishing to cut peat for fuel. Again the product was being removed from the site by water and much was clearly travelling up the River Ouse to York. The brickyards at Hull are also known to have been using Inclesmore peat, and the proximity of this major source of fuel to the Cowick potteries makes it likely that the kilns there were fired with peat as well as the coal noted by the excavator. Seen in this light the location of the medieval kilns at Beverley, Meaux and Holme-on-Spalding-Moor, close to potential sources of peat fuel, take on additional significance.

There is much more which could be said about all aspects of the Humber during the medieval period which lack of space prevents. Nothing has been said, for example, of the importance of the Humber and its waterways to the lead-producing areas of Derbyshire and the Pennines, and much more should be said about the production of wool both in Lincolnshire and the East Riding of Yorkshire. It would be difficult to exaggerate the influence the Humber exerted on the social, political and economic development of this region during the Middle Ages and it makes a fascinating theme for future historical, archaeological and geographical studies.

References

Beresford, M.W. (1986). Inclesmoor, West Riding of Yorkshire, circa 1407. In: *Local Maps and Plans from Medieval England* (ed. R.A. Skelton and P.D.A. Harvey) pp. 147-61. Clarendon,

Oxford.

Boyle, J.R. (1889). *The Lost Towns of the Humber.* A. Brown and Sons, Hull.

Boyle, J.R. (1895). *The Early History of the Town and Port of Hedon.* A. Brown and Sons, Hull.

Brooks, F.W. (1966). *Domesday Book and the East Riding.* East Yorkshire Local History Society, York.

de Boer, G. (1978). Holderness and its coastal features. In: *North Humberside Introductory Themes* (ed. D.G. Symes) pp. 69-76. Department of Geography, University of Hull.

Duckham, B.F. (1967). *The Yorkshire Ouse.* David and Charles, Newton Abbot.

Eames, E.E. (1961). A thirteenth-century tile kiln site at North Grange, Meaux. *Medieval Archaeology* 5, 137-68.

Gaunt, G.D. (1975). The artificial nature of the River Don north of Thorne, Yorkshire. *Yorkshire Archaeological Journal* 47, 15-21.

Gaunt, G.D. (1987). The geology and landscape development of the region around Thorne Moors. In: *Thorne Moors Papers* (ed. M. Limbert) p. 21. Doncaster Naturalists Society, Doncaster.

Hayfield, C. and Slater, T. (1984). *The Medieval Town of Hedon,* Humberside Heritage Publication No. 7. Humberside County Council, Hull.

Hughes, J. (1985). *The Archaeology of the Medieval Cloth Industry in Beverley.* Humberside Archaeology Unit, Beverley.

Humberside Archaeology Unit (1986). *Beck View Tilery, Beverley,* Information Sheet No. 13. Humberside Archaeology Unit, Beverley.

Mayes, P. and Hayfield, C. (1980). A late medieval pottery kiln at Holme on Spalding Moor. *East Riding Archaeologist* 6, 99-113.

Miller, K., Robinson, J., English, B. and Hall, I. (1982). *Beverley: an archaeological and architectural study.* HMSO, London.

Owen, A.E.B. (1984). Salt, sea banks and medieval settlement on the Lindsey Coast. In: *A Prospect of Lincolnshire* (ed. N. Field and A. White) pp. 46-59. N. Field and A. White, County Offices, Lincoln.

Sheppard, J.A. (1958). *The Draining of the Hull Valley.* East Yorkshire Local History Society, York.

Sheppard, J.A. (1966). *The Draining of the Marshlands of South Holderness and the Vale of York*. East Yorkshire Local History Society, York.

Stenton, F.M. (1971). *Anglo-Saxon England*. Oxford University Press, Oxford.

Williams, A. and Fairbank, J. (1987). *Medieval Humberside, 1066-1485*. Humberside Archaeology Unit, Beverley.

Wilson, D.M. and Hurst, D.G. (1965). Medieval Britain in 1962 and 1963. *Medieval Archaeology* 8, 297.

27

Rural population and land use in Humberside from the sixteenth to early nineteenth centuries

D. Neave and S. Neave

Agriculture

The administrative county of Humberside can be divided into four broad farming regions. First there is the Lincolnshire Marsh to the southeast and the similar area of Holderness to the northeast, second the chalk and limestone uplands of the Yorkshire and Lincolnshire Wolds and Lincoln Edge, third the low-lying Vales of York, Trent and Ancholme, and finally the fenland of the Isle of Axholme (Thirsk 1967). In the period before the major agricultural changes of the later eighteenth century each of these regions - marshland, upland, vale and fenland - had a distinctive farming pattern (Thirsk 1957, Harris 1961).

Holderness and the Lincolnshire Marsh were famed in the post-medieval period for the grazing of cattle and sheep, with locally bred animals being joined by large numbers from the Wolds and further afield. The landscape and land use was diverse; in both areas considerable enclosure took place during the sixteenth, seventeenth and early eighteenth centuries, but nevertheless there were still common arable fields around a number of settlements in 1750. The typical village had two large open arable fields and the principal crops were wheat, beans and barley.

The parishes of the Wolds were more uniform in character, for although a few smaller townships (chiefly those depopulated in the Middle Ages) had been enclosed, the general character was one of vast expanses of treeless open arable fields, sheep walks and rabbit warrens. By the mid eighteenth century three-quarters of the uplands still had to be enclosed. Most Wolds villages had two or three arable fields and the main crops were wheat and barley, with the latter of major importance on the highest parts of the Wolds. Farmers kept some cattle but the important stock were sheep, and during the seventeenth and early eighteenth century the size of flocks and area of pasture increased. Rabbits, bred commercially, may have been more numerous than sheep in this area, and it has been calculated that in the mid eighteenth century warrens covered as much as 15 000 acres in the East Riding, chiefly on the Wolds and the sands and gravels of the Vales of York and Pickering (Harris 1968). South of the Humber the sandy land on the western side of the Vale of Ancholme was particularly suitable for warrens and there were at least twelve to the north and west of Brigg, where fur-dressing had become a major industry by the eighteenth century (Doughty 1965).

In the Vales of York, Trent and Ancholme a major part of the arable land had been enclosed by the early eighteenth century. North of the Humber there still remained large areas of poorly drained common pasture. Holme Moor covered some 7000 acres and the adjoining commons of Bishopsoil and Wallingfen occupied together a further 9000 acres. In the Vale of York wheat and rye were the principal crops and large numbers of cattle, sheep and horses were grazed on the commons. Stock were considered more profitable than crops in the north Lincolnshire vales, where wheat, peas and barley, rather than rye, were the main crops.

The Isle of Axholme, covering over 50 000 acres, was an area of predominantly pastoral farming based on vast areas of unstinted common which provided rich summer grazing, peat and wildfowl. Within the manor of Epworth there were 14 000 acres of common, and within Crowle manor almost 4000 acres. Arable land was confined to the higher ground around the settlements where barley, wheat, peas, hemp and flax were grown in open fields (Thirsk 1953).

In addition to the considerable amount of enclosure of arable land for pasture that took place chiefly in the lowlands of Humberside, the major landuse changes in the seventeenth and early eighteenth centuries were brought about by drainage and reclamation. Early in the seventeenth century nearly 2500 acres of marshland were reclaimed along the south Humberside coast, and on the north side of the Humber during the eighteenth century Sunk Island and Cherry Cobb Sands were reclaimed (Thirsk 1957, Harris 1961, Sheppard 1966). Various drainage schemes were implemented by landowners along the Ancholme and Hull valleys in the seventeenth century, but they had only a limited impact on land use in these areas, unlike the massive undertaking of the Dutch drainage engineer Vermuyden in the Isle of Axholme and Hatfield Chase. Here, during 1626-8, he diverted the main rivers of the area, the Don, Torne and Idle, and other existing watercourses along new man-made channels so they would discharge continuously into the Trent and Ouse (Cory 1985). Not all agreed about the success of the scheme, but in time much of the grazing land of the Isle was converted to arable, and new crops such as rape and coleseed were introduced. At the end of the eighteenth century the soil of the Isle was described as 'among the finest in England' (Thirsk 1953 p. 19).

During the second half of the eighteenth century the major landuse change in Humberside took place on the uplands. This was brought about by the enclosure of most of the remaining common fields by Act of Parliament (Russell and Russell 1982, 1987, English 1985). Parliamentary enclosure also had an important but more limited impact on the lowlands. Figure 27.1 shows the division between places in Humberside that were enclosed by private agreement and those that had at least some of their open arable fields or common grazing lands enclosed by Act of Parliament. Much of the non-parliamentary enclosure took place before 1726, the date of the first parliamentary enclosure Act in Humberside. This Act confirmed an award that had already been made for enclosure at Fangfoss in the Vale of York. In the East Riding between 1726 and 1810 almost 70 000 acres were enclosed in Holderness, 45 000 acres in the Vale of York and over 200 000 acres on the Wolds (Harris 1961). Proportionately less of south Humberside was affected by parliamentary enclosure, where it generally took place later. Over two-thirds of the north Humberside enclosure awards were signed before 1800, in contrast to south Humberside where less than half were signed by this date (Table 27.1).

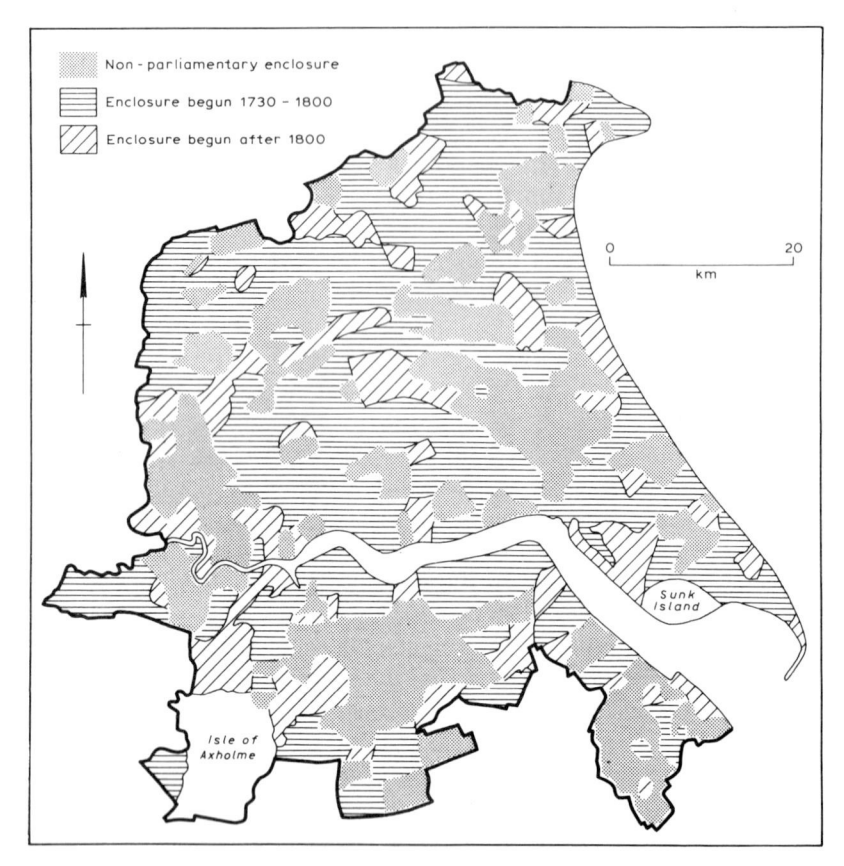

Fig. 27.1. Enclosure in Humberside.

In those places which had extensive areas of common lands enclosed under an Act of Parliament, the impact on the landscape was immense. New farmsteads were built away from the village, shelter belts and hedges planted and wide 'enclosure' roads laid out. Rabbit warrens disappeared, and on the Wolds vast acreages of grassland were ploughed out and planted with oats and wheat. Turnips, which had been grown in open fields, became more important and by the 1780s had become the basis for the continuation of the traditional Wolds dependence on corn and sheep. Change was less dramatic in the lowlands except where improved drainage was combined with enclosure, as in the Hull and Ancholme valleys from the 1760s and in

Table 27.1. The timing of enclosure 1720-1859: Humberside enclosure awards.

Decade	North Humberside	South Humberside	Total
1720-29	3	0	3
1730-394	4	1	5
1740-493	3	0	3
1750-59	11	0	11
1760-69	24	3	27
1770-79	46	10	56
1780-89	12	1	13
1790-99	16	5	21
1800-09	13	11	24
1810-19	13	2	15
1820-29	9	3	12
1830-39	5	4	9
1840-49	9	3	12
1850-59	5	2	7
Total	173	45	218

Sources: Russell and Russell (1982, 1987), English (1985).

the Vale of York with the enclosing and draining of the vast commons of Bishopsoil and Wallingfen in 1767-77 and 1777-82 respectively (Thirsk 1957, Sheppard 1958, 1966).

Little enclosure took place in the Isle of Axholme before 1800. In the southern part of the Isle in the nineteenth century the opposition of the large numbers of small proprietors, many of whom had farms of from 5 to 20 acres, prevented the enclosure of the arable open fields (Thirsk 1957). Around Haxey, Epworth and Belton there survives today a considerable acreage of arable land which is farmed in strips, although it is held in severalty (Loughlin and Miller 1979).

Manufacturing industry

Manufacturing industry played little part in the changing land use of rural Humberside before the mid nineteenth century. In 1812 Henry Strickland, referring to the East Riding, wrote: 'Fortunately for this district, it is as nearly as possible exempt from manufactories, ... it may indeed be looked upon as purely agricultural; perhaps there is not another in the kingdom of equal extent more completely of that description' (Strickland 1812 p. 284). This comment is true for the whole of the area of the present administrative county of Humberside. Although crops and grazing were the principal resources, lime, marl and relatively poor-quality building stones were also obtained from the land. Various attempts were made to find coal at Broughton near Brigg in the late seventeenth century, and at Warter, Everingham and Market Weighton during the eighteenth century, but all of them were unsuccessful (Jackson 1870, Neave 1973).

Non-agricultural employment, which was concentrated in the towns and larger 'open' villages, was largely confined to crafts and retail trades, and the small-scale processing of agricultural products, chiefly represented by tanning, maltsting and corn-milling. Most villages had one or two weavers and various unsuccessful attempts were made to re-establish a textile industry in the region. In the late seventeenth century the Winn family introduced linen weaving at the village of Appleby in south Humberside, and by 1752 there was a large linen factory there. This factory was seemingly short-lived, but there were still weavers in the village in the 1840s (Dudley 1932-4). Linen and hemp weaving developed most extensively in the Isle of Axholme, and in the early 1780s John Wesley noted the existence of four establishments for spinning and weaving at Epworth (Curnock 1938). In East Yorkshire the emphasis was initially on woollen weaving. In the mid 1760s Sir George Strickland set up a woollen manufactory at Boynton near Bridlington which in its heyday employed over 150 workers. Men worked the looms, and women and children spun the yarn. By 1769, however, there were less than a dozen employees. A more ambitious scheme was that initiated by Sir Christopher Sykes in the 1780s when he helped establish a carpet mill at Wansford; in 1793 it was said to be employing 400 hands. Another large-scale woollen manufactory was built in 1792 at the nearby Bell Mills, south of Driffield (Allison 1970). Both ventures failed in the early nineteenth century.

The stimulus for the building of the woollen factories at Wansford and Driffield, and the limited industrial development that took place elsewhere in rural Humberside about this time, came from the improvements in water communications, particularly the Driffield Navigation (1767) and Market Weighton Navigation (1772) schemes

(Duckham 1972, Noble this volume). The latter led to the discovery of excellent brick-making clay where the canal met the Cave causeway - the main routeway to the West Riding from Hull - and here the industrial village of Newport grew up, based on the making and transporting of bricks and tiles.

Population and settlement

Newport was the only completely new settlement to emerge in Humberside between the Middle Ages and the early nineteenth century, but many other settlements underwent considerable changes in both appearance and population (Allison 1976). Before the first national census of 1801 the sources for the population history of rural settlements in the present administrative area of Humberside differ between those parishes which lie in the Diocese of Lincoln and those in the Diocese of York. For south Humberside the post-medieval sources are earlier and more extensive, commencing with returns of households in 1563 which survive for the parishes to the east of the Ancholme (Hodgett 1975). For all parishes here, numbers of communicants (taken to be everyone over 16) exist for 1603 and similar details are available for most parishes in 1676 (Foster 1926, Whiteman 1986). Between these dates listings of the adult males of most settlements exist in the Protestation Returns for 1642 (Webster 1984). More reliable as indicators of population change and more comprehensive are the numbers of families stated in the periodic returns which incumbents made to the Bishop of Lincoln in the years 1705-23 and 1788-92 (Cole 1913, Lincolnshire Archives Office Speculum H 1788-92). For north Humberside parishes there are no reliable sources for estimating population change before the late seventeenth century. For all settlements there are reliable Hearth Tax Returns for the 1670s and at the same period there are communicant figures for the majority of parishes in 1676 (Purdy 1975, Whiteman 1986). Similarly, for most parishes numbers of families are given in the visitation returns made by incumbents to Archbishop Herring in 1743 and Archbishop Drummond in 1764 (Ollard and Walker 1928-9, Borthwick Institute York Bp.V.1764/Ret.).

Maps showing the density of population in Lincolnshire in 1563 and 1801 are available in Thirsk (1957) and a population density map

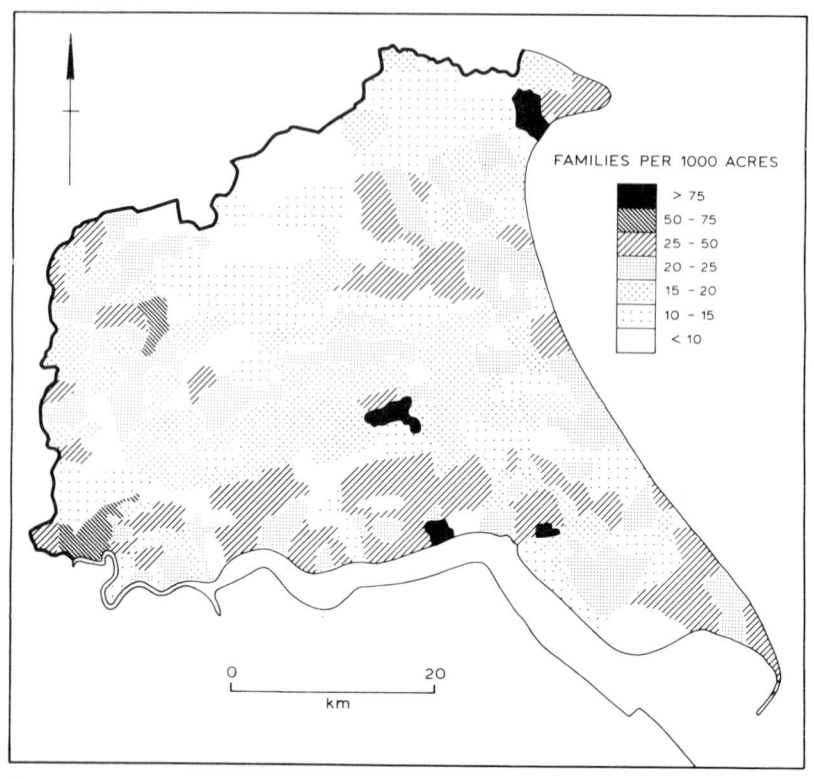

Fig. 27.2. Density of population in north Humberside in 1672.

of the East Riding for 1743 appears in Harris (1961). Figures 27.2 and 27.3 illustrate the density of population in townships in north Humberside using the Hearth Tax Returns of 1672 and in parishes in south Humberside using returns of families around 1705. Generally the region was sparsely populated; outside the market towns there were few parishes with over 25 households or families per 1000 acres. The large unenclosed parishes on the Wolds and ill-drained lowlands must have appeared empty and inhospitable to the traveller. Defoe writing in the 1720s noted that the middle of the East Riding 'is very thin of towns, and consequently of people' (Woodward 1985 p. 54), and in 1764 a Wolds clergyman commented on how 'thinly are our would (*sic*) villages peopled' (Borthwick Institute York Bp.V.1764/Ret. Weaverthorpe).

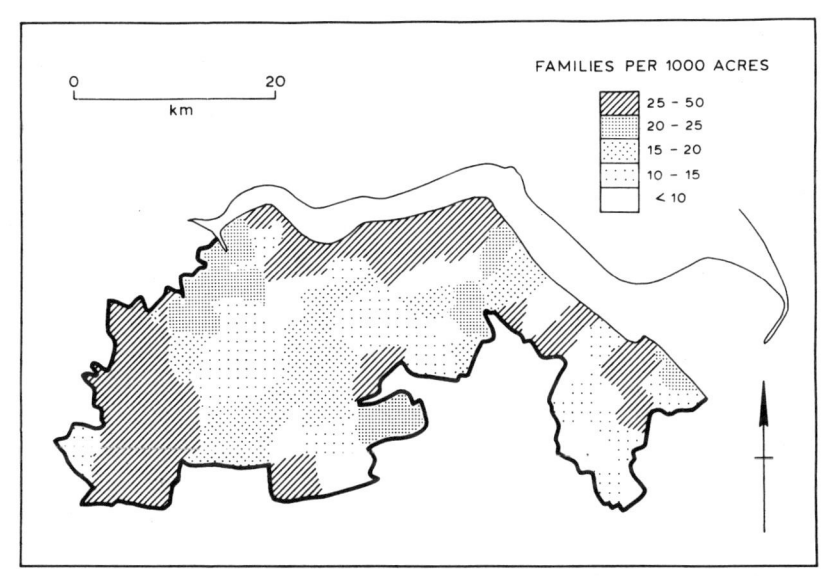

Fig. 27.3. Density of population in south Humberside in 1705.

The sparseness of population on the Wolds in the late seventeenth century is emphasised by the heaviest concentration there of townships with less than 20 families per 1000 acres. Parts of Holderness and the Vale of York were more populous, but not in the poorly drained areas such as the Hull valley and the commons of the southern Vale. Groups of townships to the north and west of Hull, in south Holderness and around Howden had the highest population densities. In south Humberside the most populous area was the Isle of Axholme. The southern Isle, both before and after drainage in the mid seventeenth century, had been an area which had attracted immigrants because of its plentiful common land. In the forty years between 1590 and 1630 a hundred additional cottages were built in the manor of Epworth, and in 1675 it was noted that 'The libertic the common people have of graveing in the common is that which drawes multitudes of the poorer sort from all the counties adjacent to come and inhabite in this Isle' (John Ryland's Library, Manchester University, Ryland Charters 2550a). Except for the string of villages along the south bank of the Humber from Alkborough to East Halton, the rest of south Humberside was thinly populated in the early eighteenth century. This was particularly the case on the edges of the Lincolnshire Wolds and Marsh to the west and south of Grimsby, and in the Vale of Ancholme.

Figures 27.2 and 27.3 give the density and distribution of the population of Humberside at a time of population stagnation both locally and nationally. The various population sources outlined above show that although the distribution pattern altered little, the actual population of the area and the size of individual settlements underwent marked fluctuations between the mid sixteenth and early nineteenth centuries. Information on population change can be gained by converting to an approximate settlement population the various details of families, oath takers, households and communicants by using the generally accepted multipliers of 4.5 for families/households, 1.66 for communicants and 2.8 for adult males (Drake 1982). Eighteen parishes with reliable figures have been selected to indicate the general pattern of population change in south Humberside (Table 27.2). Larger samples relating to only two sets of returns indicate that these parishes were typical of the area as a whole. The drop in population in the late seventeenth and early eighteenth centuries which these figures show is borne out by the more limited figures available for north Humberside (Table 27.3).

The pattern of population change in Humberside outlined by these limited statistics corresponds broadly to the national situation (Wrigley and Schofield 1981, Clay 1984). It is widely accepted that the population of England had a marked rise in the later sixteenth century followed by a more limited increase after 1600 to a peak in the 1640s. This can be attributed to a great increase in the birth rate and a limited decline in the death rate. Then followed a period of slight decline until the last decade of the seventeenth century when the population began to rise again, although suffering a further setback in the 1720s. Upward movement returned in the next decade and continued throughout the rest of the century with particularly high growth rates from the 1770s.

Humberside parish registers provide evidence of the various mortality crises which contributed to the death rate from the end of the sixteenth century. On both sides of the Humber from the 1580s to the 1660s many settlements were severely affected by epidemics, including the plague (Maddock 1897, Brears 1940, Shrewsbury 1970). With the demise of the plague other diseases,

Table 27.2. Population change for eighteen rural parishes in south Humberside, 1563-1801.

1563	998 households	4491 estimated population
1603	3501 communicants	5812 estimated population
1642	2247 adult males	6292 estimated population
1676	3042 communicants	5049 estimated population
1705-23	1102 families	4959 estimated population
1801	1233 families	5378 actual population

Table 27.3. Population change in forty rural parishes in north Humberside, 1672-1801.

1672	2392 households	11 840 estimated population
1743	2017 families	9984 estimated population
1764	2000 families	9900 estimated population
1801	2454 families	12 144 actual population

particularly smallpox, influenza and unspecified 'fevers', took its place and Humberside, along with much of the country, was severely affected by a number of epidemics in 1657-8, 1679-81, 1719-20 and 1728-9 (from a sample of north Humberside parish registers in Humberside County Record Office, Beverley). Burials exceeded baptisms in many Humberside parishes during the late seventeenth and early eighteenth centuries, and this was clearly a factor in the general population decline.

In many cases specific population trends in individual settlements owed much to the structure of local land ownership and agricultural change. 'Closed' townships with a single, or one dominant, landowner generally exhibited the most substantial population falls in the seventeenth and early eighteenth century, particularly where enclosure had taken place. For example, Bradley near Grimsby, enclosed early in the seventeenth century, had 32 households in 1563 but only 11 families in the 1720s, while nearby Aylesby, enclosed by 1664, experienced a decrease from 45 households to only 14 families over the same period (Johnson 1961-2). Routh in north Humberside, enclosed around 1685, had a drop from 45 households in 1672 to 22 families in 1743, and between the same years Burnby, enclosed by private agreement in 1731, had a decrease from 30 households to 17 families (Borthwick Institute York Ter.I. Routh 1685, Humberside

County Record Office DDAN/239).

Among the few places in south Humberside to undergo a marked decline in population later in the eighteenth century was the marshland parish of Stallingborough to the northwest of Grimsby, which throughout the period 1562-1723 was the most populous parish in the Wapentake of Bradley-Haverstoe. The number of families in the parish dropped from around 120 in the early 1720s to only 66 in 1788-92. It is probable that this decline occurred soon after the enclosure of the arable fields in 1736-7. Extensive earthworks survive to show the position of many of the houses that were abandoned at this time (Everson 1981, Lincolnshire Archives Office Speculum H 1788-92).

In Humberside post-1760 parliamentary enclosure usually contributed to an increase rather than decrease in population, especially when areas of common land were taken into arable cultivation. Two-thirds of the north Humberside sample parishes which recorded an increase in population between 1764 and 1801 had their open fields enclosed in the years 1760-98 (English 1985). For example, at Holme-on-Spalding-Moor, where 7000 acres of land were enclosed in 1773-7, the population rose from 622 in 1773 to 919 in 1789 (British Library Add. Mss. 40132/12). Winteringham in south Humberside, which was enclosed under Acts of 1763 and 1795, had a rise in numbers of families from 80 in the 1720s to 130 in 1788-92, and to 150 in 1801 (Neave 1984). Such increases were, however, not confined to enclosed parishes, for at Middleton-on-the-Wolds (enclosed 1803-5) the number of families rose from 36 in 1764 to 64 in 1801, and during the same period the number of families at Seaton Ross in the Vale of York (enclosed 1811-14) increased from 60 to 86. These rises were a prelude to the much greater and more generally experienced increases in rural population during the first half of the nineteenth century, discussed in the following chapter.

References

Allison, K.J. (1970). *East Riding Water-Mills.* East Yorkshire Local History Society, York.
Allison, K.J. (1976). *The East Riding of Yorkshire Landscape.* Hodder and Stoughton, London.

Brears, C. (1940). *Lincolnshire in the 17th and 18th Centuries.* A. Brown, London.
Clay, C.G.A. (1984). *Economic Expansion and Social Change: England 1500-1700. Vol. 1. People, land and towns.* Cambridge University Press, Cambridge.
Cole, R.E.G. (1913). *Speculum Dioceseos Lincolniensis.* Lincoln Record Society, Lincoln.
Cory, V. (1985). *Hatfield and Axholme.* Providence Press, Ely.
Curnock, N. (ed.) (1938). *The Journal of John Wesley, Vol. 6.* Epworth Press, London.
Doughty, P.S. (1965). The rabbit in Lincolnshire, a short history. *Journal of the Scunthorpe Museum Society* 2, 15-23.
Drake, M. (1982). *Population Studies from Parish Registers.* Local Population Studies, Matlock.
Duckham, B.F. (1972). *The Inland Waterways of East Yorkshire 1700-1900.* East Yorkshire Local History Society, York.
Dudley, H.E. (1932-4). Linen weaving at Appleby. *Lincolnshire Magazine* 1, 246.
English, B. (1985). *Yorkshire Enclosure Awards,* Studies in Regional and Local History 5, University of Hull.
Everson, P. (1981). Stallingborough - earthwork survey. *Lincolnshire History and Archaeology* 16, 32.
Foster, C.W. (1926). *The State of the Church,* Lincoln Record Society 23, Lincoln.
Harris, A. (1961). *The Rural Landscape of the East Riding of Yorkshire 1700-1850.* Oxford University Press, London.
Harris, A. (1968). The rabbit warrens of East Yorkshire in the eighteenth and nineteenth centuries. *Yorkshire Archaeological Journal* 42, 429-43.
Hodgett, G.A.J. (1975). *Tudor Lincolnshire,* History of Lincolnshire 6. History of Lincolnshire Committee, Lincoln.
Jackson, C. (ed.) (1870). *The Diary of Abraham de la Pryme.* Surtees Society, Durham.
Johnson, S.A. (1961-2). Some aspects of enclosure and changing agricultural landscapes in Lindsey from the sixteenth to the nineteenth century. *Lincolnshire Architectural and Archaeological Society Reports and Papers* 9, 140.
Loughlin, N. and Miller, K.R. (1979). *A Survey of Archaeological Sites in Humberside.* Humberside Libraries and Amenities,

Hull.

Maddock, H.E. (1897). Parish registers of south Holderness. *Transactions of the East Riding Antiquarian Society* **5**, 1-34.

Neave, D. (1973). The search for coal in the East Riding in the 18th century. *Yorkshire Archaeological Journal* **45**, 194-7.

Neave, D. (ed.) (1984). *Winteringham 1650-1760*. Winteringham Workers' Educational Association Branch, Winteringham.

Ollard, S.L. and Walker, P.C. (eds) (1928-9). *Archbishop Herring's Visitation Returns 1743,* Yorkshire Archaeological Society Record Series, vols 71, 72, 75. Yorkshire Archaeological Society, Leeds.

Purdy, J.D. (1975). The Hearth Tax Returns for Yorkshire. M.Phil. thesis, University of Leeds.

Russell, E. and Russell, R.C. (1982). *Landscape Changes in South Humberside.* Humberside Leisure Services, Hull.

Russell, E. and Russell, R.C. (1987). *Parliamentary Enclosure and New Lincolnshire Landscapes,* Lincolnshire History Series 10. Lincolnshire Recreational Services, Lincoln.

Sheppard, J.A. (1958). *The Draining of the Hull Valley.* East Yorkshire Local History Society, York.

Sheppard, J.A. (1966). *The Draining of the Marshlands of South Holderness and the Vale of York.* East Yorkshire Local History Society, York.

Shrewsbury, J.F.D. (1970). *A History of Bubonic Plague in the British Isles.* Cambridge University Press, Cambridge.

Strickland, H.E. (1812). *A General View of the Agriculture of the East Riding of Yorkshire.* London.

Thirsk, J. (1953). The Isle of Axholme before Vermuyden. *Agricultural History Review* **1**, 16-28.

Thirsk, J. (1957). *English Peasant Farming: the agrarian history of Lincolnshire from Tudor to recent times.* Routledge and Kegan Paul, London.

Thirsk, J. (1967). *The Agrarian History of England and Wales, Vol. 6, 1500-1640.* Cambridge University Press, Cambridge.

Webster, W.F. (ed.) (1984). *Protestation Returns 1641-2 - Lincolnshire.* Nottingham.

Whiteman, A. (ed.) (1986). *The Compton Census of 1676: a critical edition.* Oxford University Press for the British Academy, London.

Woodward, D. (1985). *Descriptions of East Yorkshire: Leland to Defoe.* East Yorkshire Local History Society, Beverley.
Wrigley, E.A. and Schofield, R.S. (1981). *The Population History of England 1541-1871.* Edward Arnold, London.

28
Population change and settlement geography in the Humber region, 1801 to present
M.T. Wild

Introduction

In this chapter the Humber region is defined as the territory bounded by a line first running westwards and southwestwards from Atwick on the East Yorkshire coast to Airmyn near the confluence of the Ouse and Aire, then turning eastwards to cross Lindsey from Eastoft in the west to Humberston at the southern entrance of the Humber estuary. This area is more symmetric than the new administrative county of Humberside and is more tidily arranged around its dominating natural focus. The study commences in 1801, the date of the first national census and publication of population counts at parish and township level.

Regional population growth

The 1801 census enumerated less than 100 000 people living in the Humber region, and of these, more than one-quarter inhabited the growing city of Hull. Yet, although this part of England had made great progress in agricultural development, especially land reclamation and improvement, capitalisation of farming and Parliamentary enclosures (Harris 1961, Allison 1976, Neave and Neave this volume), its population density was only 109 persons per square mile (Table 28.1). This was well below the average figure of 152 for England and Wales, and was also exceeded by several highly rural farming counties, including Devon, Wiltshire and Herefordshire.

Over the next 60 years the pace of population growth in the Humber region generally approximated the national trend (Table 28.1), exceeding it during 1801-11, 1831-41 and 1841-51, but falling behind during other decades. Population numbers rose from 97 290 to 229 411 (Table 28.2), an increase which was sustained by high birthrates rather than any net inflow of people. Until the onset of a vigorous era of industrialisation and port development after 1861, the region had contributed little to the Industrial Revolution and, compared with other parts of northern England, was becoming something of an economic backwater. In 1861 only 25% of the working adult population were engaged in manufacturing and mining, a proportion which was well below the England and Wales figure of 34% (Her Majesty's Stationery Office 1863).

Heavy investment in railways, accelerated expansion of the Humber ports (North this volume) and development of the North Lincolnshire iron industry (Pocock this volume) dramatically changed the situation, bringing a sharp increase in employment opportunities and large, if very localised, inflows of people (Wright 1982). During the period 1861-1931, while the population of England and Wales increased by 98%, that of the Humber region grew by 175%, and by 1931 its population density had risen above the national level (Table 28.1).

The Humber region, although containing more 'new' industry than 'old', did not escape the economic depressions of the inter-war years. With many people joining the drift from the North of England to the South and Midlands, the migration flow altered once again, and the regional population growth rate after 1931 dipped below the national trend for the first time since 1851-61 (Table 28.1). During the half-century 1931-81, the Humber region saw a modest 20% population increase, nearly two-thirds of this coming during the post-war boom of the 1950s and 60s when there was some appreciable industrial expansion along both banks of the Humber (Lewis and Jones 1970). Since then, however, there has been a relentless reduction of the

Table 28.1. Population change in the Humber region and England and Wales, 1801-1981.

Intercensal rates of population change

Intercensal decade	1 Humber region (%)	2 England & Wales (%)	Difference (1 minus 2) (%)
1801-11	18.3	14.0	+4.3
1811-21	16.1	18.1	-2.0
1821-31	13.0	15.8	-2.8
1831-41	16.6	14.3	+2.5
1841-51	19.0	12.6	+6.4
1851-61	9.5	11.9	-2.4
1861-71	18.6	13.2	+5.4
1871-81	19.1	14.7	+4.4
1881-91	20.0	11.6	+8.4
1891-1901	17.1	12.2	+4.9
1901-11	16.7	10.9	+5.8
1911-21	7.5	5.0	+2.5
1921-31	9.6	5.5	+4.1
1931-51 (Average)	7.0	9.5	-2.5
1951-61	6.3	5.5	+0.8
1961-71	4.9	5.7	-0.8
1971-81	1.0	0.8	+0.2

Population Density (Persons per square mile)

Intercensal decade	1 Humber region	2 England & Wales	Difference (1 minus 2)
1801	109	152	-43
1811	129	174	-45
1821	149	206	-55
1831	169	238	-69
1841	197	273	-76
1851	234	307	-73
1861	256	344	-88
1871	304	389	-85
1881	375	445	-70
1891	438	497	-59
1901	513	558	-45
1911	598	618	-20
1921	643	649	-6
1931	705	685	+20
1951	754	750	+4
1961	801	791	+10
1971	841	836	+5
1981	848	843	+5

Source: Census Reports 1801-1981.

industrial base, particularly the traditional port-orientated manufacturing trades (North this volume). The resulting decline in industrial

Table 28.2. Population change in the Humber region, 1801-1981.

	Population of rural parishes	Population of urban centres	Total population	% of total population living in urban centres
1801	64 289	33 010	97 290	33.9
1811	70 318	44 791	115 109	38.9
1821	81 183	52 490	133 673	39.3
1831	79 964	71 032	150 996	47.0
1841	88 393	87 723	176 116	49.8
1851	98 412	111 176	209 588	53.0
1861	94 265	135 146	229 411	58.9
1871	94 523	177 662	272 185	65.3
1881	90 383	245 003	335 386	73.1
1891	88 890	303 627	392 517	77.4
1901	88 829	370 862	459 691	80.7
1911	79 198	456 424	535 622	85.2
1921	84 624	491 102	575 726	85.3
1931	88 601	542 259	630 860	86.0
1951	93 431	581 554	674 985	86.2
1961	92 274	624 938	717 212	87.1
1971	90 014	662 646	752 660	88.0
1981	84 915	674 194	759 109	88.8

Source: Census Reports 1801-1981.

employment has not been adequately matched by growth in the service sector, which has lagged behind that in most other parts of the country.

Transformation from an agricultural to a predominantly industrial area, and progression from a rather sparsely settled backwater to a quite heavily populated part of the country playing an integral role in the national economy, are two major themes in the nineteenth and twentieth century development of the Humber region. The rest of this chapter will examine their impact on the patterns of settlement and population change. For this purpose two series of maps are presented, and it is necessary now to clarify a few points concerning their construction.

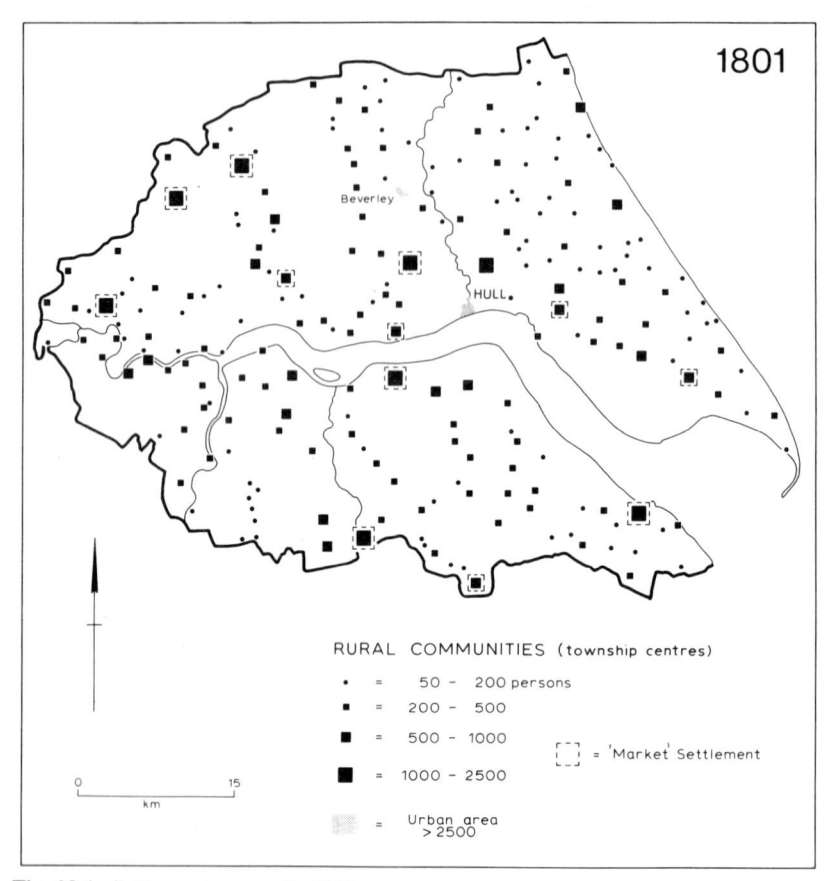

Fig. 28.1. Settlement pattern in 1801.

The settlement pattern maps

The smallest areas for which population counts are available in the nineteenth century census reports are the 'townships'. With few exceptions in the Humber region, these had a single focus of population, normally a village, but it could be a hamlet or, at the other end of the size scale, an urban centre. The symbols on these maps (Figs 28.1 and 28.2) are positioned to represent these settlement foci or 'township centres'. The following six categories should be noted:
1. Settlement foci in townships with fewer than 50 inhabitants. These are too small to be villages and, therefore, are not shown

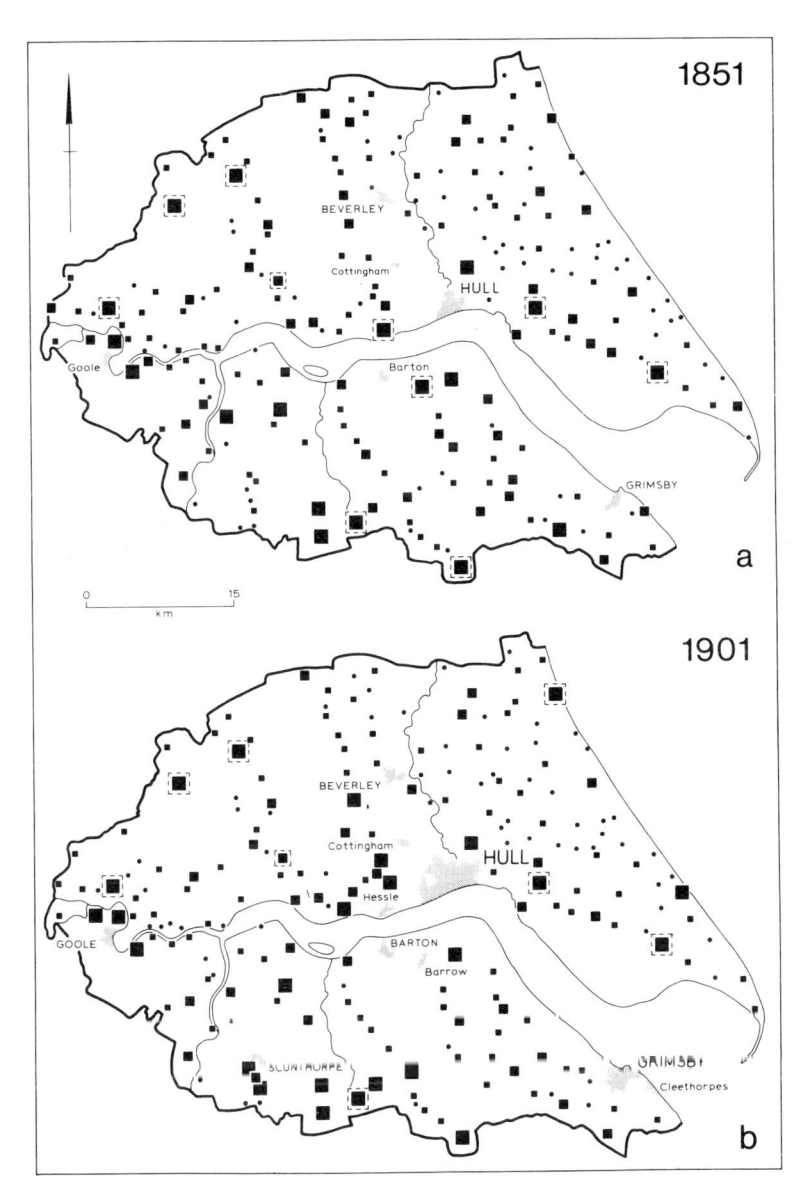

Population change and settlement geography 393

Fig. 28.2. (a) Settlement pattern in 1851; (b) settlement pattern in 1901. For key see Figure 28.1.

on the maps. At no time during the nineteenth century did they number more than 5% of the region's 240 township centres.
2. Small villages, in townships with 50-200 inhabitants. In 1801 there were 106 of these in the region and they were easily the commonest type of community. By 1901, however, their numbers had dwindled to 69.
3. Medium-sized villages, in townships with 200-500 inhabitants.
4. Large villages, in townships with 500-1000 inhabitants.
5. 'Rururban' settlements in the 1000-2500 range. On the 1801 map (Fig. 28.1) these were small countryside market towns like Market Weighton, Howden and Caistor. Later they included growing industrial settlements and dormitory communities.
6. Urban centres with township populations above 2500. This figure was used by Law (1967) to define true urban settlements in his study of urban population growth in England and Wales. He argued that places with less than 2500 inhabitants, although they may contain some industry and services, normally offered a rural rather than an urban way of life. It should be noted, however, that certain previous chapters in this volume (e.g. Ambler, Noble) have used the term 'town' when referring to some settlements which, although containing a market or other commercial function, had a population of below 2500.

After 1901, census compilers discontinued presenting population counts for township areas and instead employed a new framework of civil parishes. This framework, with a few boundary alterations, has remained in use to the present day. In the Humber region most of these parishes were devised simply from an existing township. The others were created through amalgamating two, three or occasionally four townships. The maps for 1951 and 1981 (Fig. 28.3), being based on civil parishes, are therefore not strictly comparable with the earlier maps. However, in the context of the twentieth century, the settlements are represented in a more meaningful way. The method of showing urban areas is unchanged, but the rural communities are divided only into expanded settlements in parishes whose populations have doubled since 1901, and less developed settlements, mostly traditional agricultural villages, where the demographic trend has not been so rapid.

Apart from the 1801 map, where the outlines of Hull and Beverley are based on the town plans of Hargrave (1791) and Wood

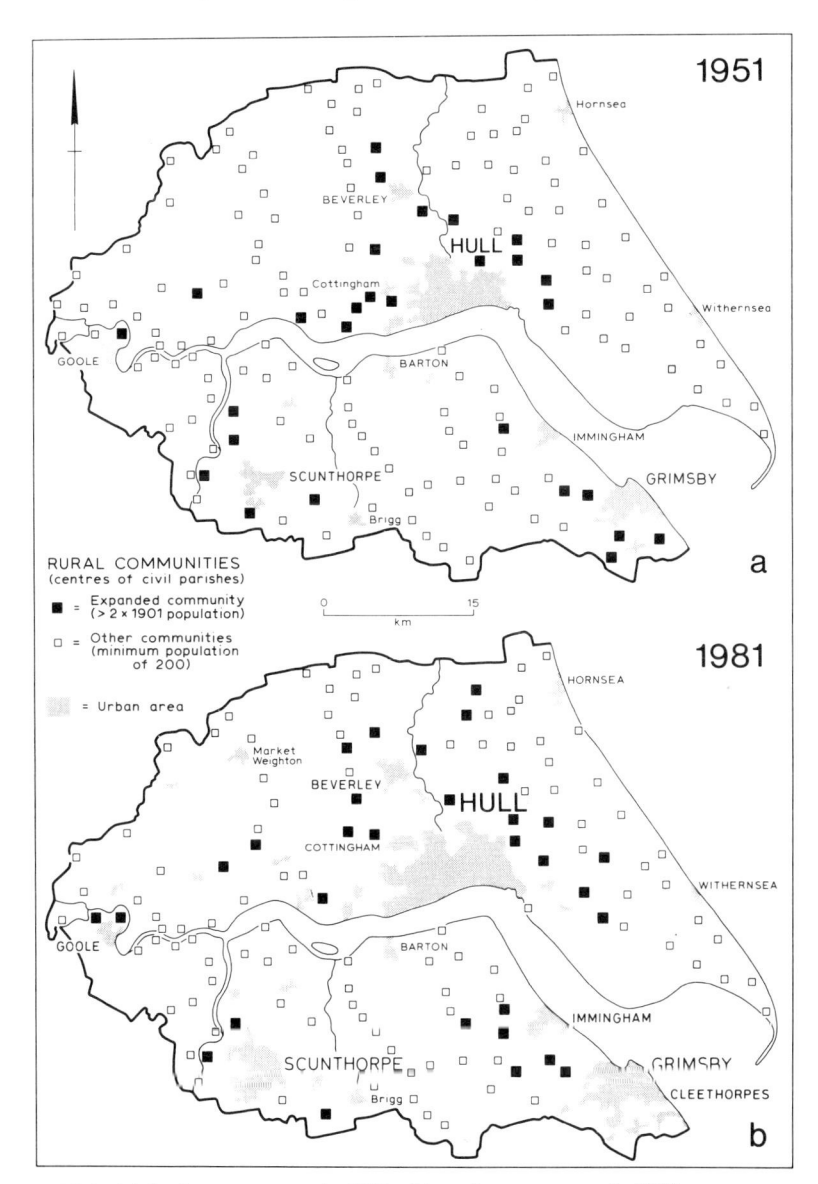

Fig. 28.3. (a) Settlement pattern in 1951; (b) settlement pattern in 1981.

(1828) respectively, the configurations of urban areas have been drawn from appropriate Ordnance Survey maps. These are the relevant sheets of the First Edition series surveyed here in the mid nineteenth century, the Third Edition (1905), the 'New Popular' Edition (1947) and the modern 1:50 000 Second Series (1974).

The population-change maps

The statistical areas employed in these maps (Figs 28.4 and 28.5) are the 165 civil parishes which make up the Humber region. These presented no problems for 1901-51 and 1951-81, since each census published population counts for each of these units. For 1801-51 and 1851-1901, however, only township figures are available. Where necessary these have therefore been added together to conform with the full area of a civil parish.

The maps use proportional-sized squares to indicate the actual amounts of population change. Three types of local trend can be identified: rapid population growth, exceeding an average of 10% per decade (shading), moderate growth, averaging between 0% and 10% per decade (stippling), and decline (blank).

The settlement pattern in 1801

At the beginning of the nineteenth century the Humber region was predominantly rural, with urban areas (Hull and Beverley) accommodating less than one-third of the population. More than 200 villages appear in Figure 28.1. Their distribution, however, was very uneven. On the one hand there were tracts of countryside, notably the dry chalklands and the flat, often waterlogged, reclaimed marshlands of Sunk Island, the Humberhead Levels and parts of the Hull and Ancholme valleys, that were occupied only by isolated farmsteads. On the other hand one can see four major alignments of township centres. Particularly prominent are the two lines of villages taking advantage of the springs and good farmland on the edges of the chalk Wolds (Gleave 1962), one following the west-facing scarp slope right across the region from Londesborough in the north to Caistor in the south, and the other running along the eastern side of the Wolds

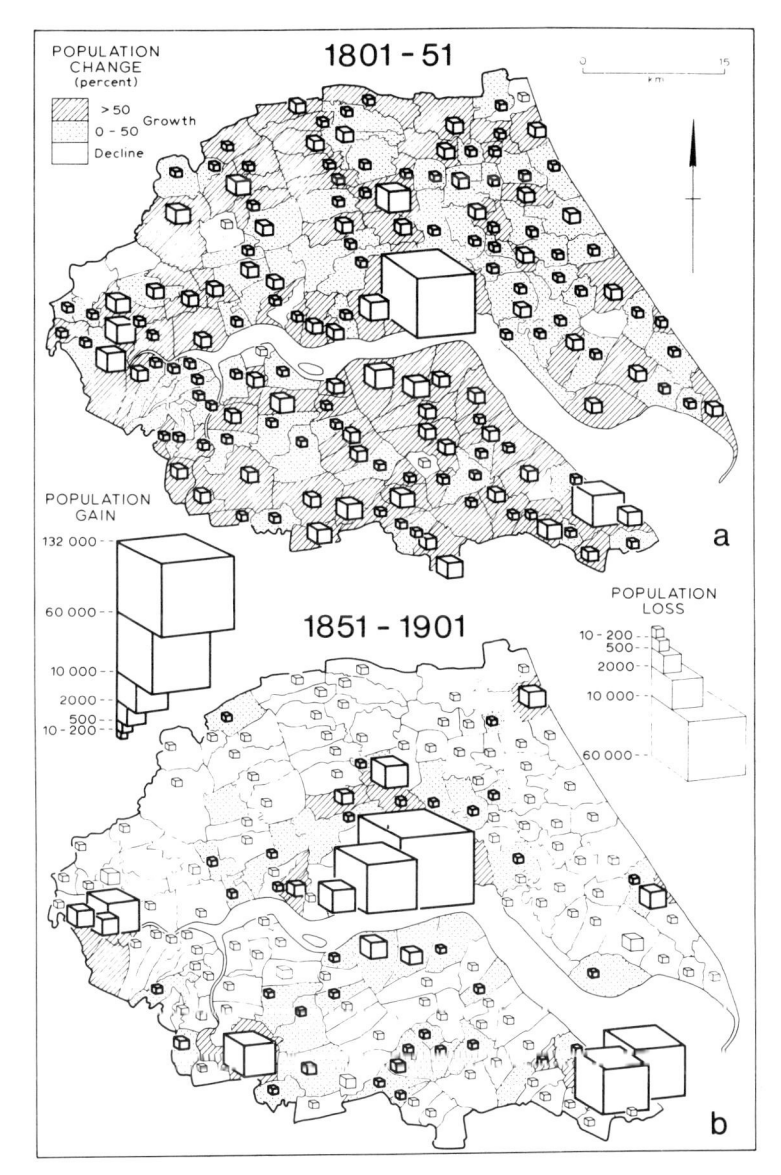

Fig. 28.4. (a) Population change, 1801-51; (b) population change, 1851-1901.

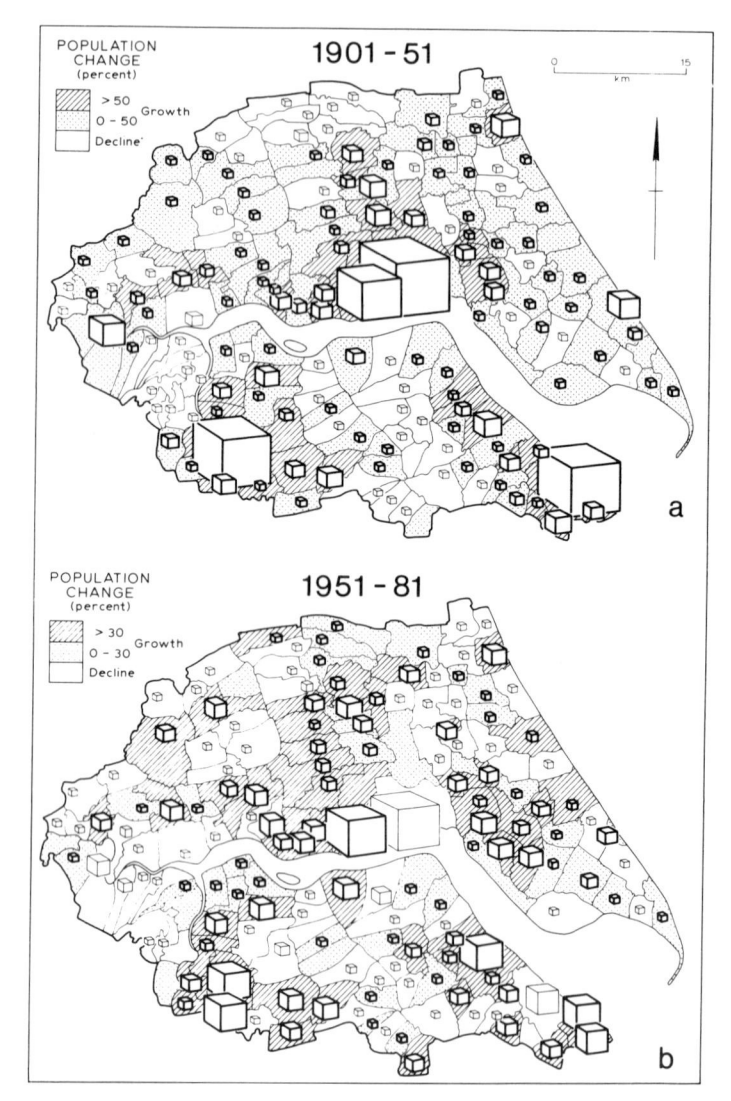

Fig. 28.5. (a) Population change, 1901-51; (b) population change, 1951-81. The cubes, representing net increases or decreases, are drawn to the same scale as in the key of Figure 28.4.

from Middleton to Laceby. The two other lines of villages can be seen occupying 'drypoint' sites along both banks of the Humber and the Ouse.

Changes in settlement pattern and population distribution

1801-51
During 1801-51 the numbers of people living in the Humber region increased from 97 290 to 209 588 (Table 28.2). Nearly half of this increase belonged to Hull, while 16 600 came from gains in Beverley and the emergent urban settlements of Grimsby, Goole, Barton and Cottingham. However, this period also witnessed sizeable and widespread rural population growth (Fig. 28.4a). Indeed, only 9 of the 165 parish areas experienced any decrease, and as many as 85 had gains of more than 10% per decade. In 1801 there had been 27 township centres with populations greater than 500; by 1851 the number had increased to 61 (cf. Figs 28.1 and 28.2a). The Humber region, therefore, was a part of lowland England where the parliamentary enclosure movement, the diminution in numbers of small farmers and the application of 'new husbandry' did not lead immediately to rural depopulation. Until the second half of the nineteenth century, farming here was labour-intensive. Consequently, agricultural employment was generally quite easy to find and, while much of the work was poorly paid and insecure (Hammond and Hammond 1911), its availability did much to curb migration from village to urban centre.

The population-change map for this period (Fig. 28.4a) shows a confused pattern, with all parts of the region containing a mixture of different trends. Parishes with fast population growth, others with moderate performances and a few with a declining trend are distributed close together without any clear geographical regularity. A similar situation was noticed by Mills (1959) in a study of rural settlement in Kesteven, in which he concluded that very often differences in the population trends of rural communities reflected local variations in landholding structures and settlement policies. He made a fundamental distinction between 'open' and 'closed' villages. In the former, land was worked by several freeholding farmers who, for their own labour needs and also to provide opportunities for speculative cottage construction, encouraged newcomers to settle and thereby augment local population growth. In a 'closed' village, however, land was either held by a small group of large landowners or run as an estate owned by a single wealthy family. Here the settlement of newcomers was actively discouraged, mainly because there was little or no competition for local labour; at times when gentlemen farmers and estate squires did require additional workers, they usually found it more practical to recruit people from nearby 'open' communities rather than run the expense of building new residential accommodation. Typical examples of 'open' villages in the Humber region are Ulceby on the Lincolnshire Wolds, Middleton on the Yorkshire Wolds, Keyingham in Holderness and Swinefleet on the southern bank of the Ouse. During 1801-51 their populations grew by 154%, 127%, 87% and 82% respectively; these were appreciably larger increases than occurred in 'closed' villages such as Bishop Burton (37%), Everingham (30%) and Brocklesby (29%).

1851-1901
This period brought rapid industrialisation to the Humber region and more than a doubling of population from just over 200 000 to not far short of half a million (Table 28.2). This was achieved wholly by a massive increase in numbers of urban dwellers who, by the end of Queen Victoria's reign, accounted for as much as 82% of the regional population. Indeed, it is worth comparing this proportion with Law's (1967) lower figure of 78% representing the level of demographic urbanisation in England and Wales in 1901. For the first time, the Humber region, although still containing extensive rural spaces, could be described as an urbanised part of the country. The urban centres shown in the settlement map for 1901 (Fig. 28.2b) varied greatly in size, function and age. Hull, with 244 200 citizens, still dominated, but its share of the region's urban population had fallen from 88% to 65%. Four new centres, the seaside resort of Cleethorpes, the iron and steel town of Scunthorpe and the part-industrial and part-dormitory communities of Hessle and Barrow upon Humber, had joined the growing list of urban settlements.

While witnessing very rapid urbanisation, the period 1851-1901 brought a reversal of the region's rural population trend. The large majority of rural parishes experienced nineteenth century population peaks at sometime between 1841 and 1871, followed by losses at each subsequent census (Table 28.2). Rural depopulation was a widespread feature of the late nineteenth and early twentieth century English countryside (Saville 1957), but it was particularly strong in the Humber region. Here the 1850s, 60s and 70s saw the transition from a labour-intensive agricultural economy to capital-intensive, mechanised 'high farming'. This was accompanied by a long-lasting decline in farm labour and a drift of young men, women and families away from their villages in search of other sources of work (Olney 1979). Many of them moved into the region's growing urban centres, but thousands migrated further afield to other parts of the country or overseas.

The extent of rural depopulation during 1851-1901 can be gauged in Figure 28.4b. Nearly two-thirds of the rural parishes suffered population losses, some eventually having less inhabitants at the beginning of the twentieth century than they had a hundred years earlier. A few, however, did experience substantial increases. These were the small seaside resorts of Hornsea and Withernsea, and a dozen parishes situated close to a major urban centre. Around Hull, extending along the railway axes westwards to Brough and northwards to Beverley, a group of shaded areas is observable on the map, representing the earliest conversions of farming villages into dormitory settlements.

1901-51

Although the population growth rate slowed considerably, the period 1901-51 saw a further addition of 215 000 people to the region. Hull, despite passing the 300 000 mark in 1931, accounted for only 26% of this increase (during the preceding half-century it had accounted for 64%). The two large towns of Grimsby and Scunthorpe together accounted for 42%, which was a substantially greater share. The remainder came from a quite diffuse pattern of population growth, involving the fourteen other urban centres and several favourably situated rural settlements.

As Figure 28.5a shows, the apparent recovery in the rural demographic trend was by no means general throughout the region. Nearly one-third of the parishes, mostly in the remoter parts, continued to suffer population decline as farming employment contracted further, but other parishes, where local industry had developed (Watts 1964) or a dormitory function had been acquired, enjoyed regeneration of population growth. Such revival of rural population growth could only be localised in its geographical occurrence, hence the diagonally-shaded parishes are nearly all concentrated in the Hull area and around Grimsby, Scunthorpe and the new port of Immingham.

1951-81
During this shorter period the population of the Humber region grew by 84 124, more than half of this increase belonging to the first of the three decades and only 6449 coming during the last (Table 28.2). However, notwithstanding the continued slackening of the growth rate, there were extensive changes in the geographical distribution of population (cf. Figs 28.3a and b). Dominating these changes were the shifts of large numbers of people from the two largest urban centres, Hull and Grimsby, outwards into their widening belts of dormitory settlements. The population of Hull had in fact been falling ever since 1931, when the city had recorded its peak of 313 649. Between then and 1951 the decline amounted to less than 10 000, but thereafter the city experienced much heavier depopulation, with losses totalling 26 605 during 1951-81. Grimsby's peak of 97 955 came later, in 1961; by 1981 the figure here had fallen to 92 596.

The population losses in Hull and Grimsby (and, one can note, Goole also) were representative of an intensifying nationwide population redistribution from large industrial towns and cities to much smaller and environmentally more attractive settlements within convenient daily-travel distance. Hull's 'sphere of dispersal' exerts a major impact on the 1951-81 population change map (Fig. 28.5b). Noticeably, the belt of fast-growth parishes is at its broadest to the west and north of the city, where there are good communications and, on the edges of the Yorkshire Wolds, attractive undulating topography. To the east of Hull the belt is only easily identifiable in the area between Bilton, Keyingham and Roos, where cheap land prices encouraged considerable housing development during the 1960s and 70s. Grimsby's influence on the 1951-81 map is much more localised and is complicated by the proximity of Cleethorpes and Immingham. However, included within a belt of fast population growth stretching from South Killingholme to Humberston are several expanding dormitory settlements (Fig. 28.3b).

Beyond the commuting areas of Hull and Grimsby, a small group of fast-growth parishes can be seen around Scunthorpe (Fig. 28.5b) where there is an interesting mixture of outlying industrial and dormitory settlements. Elsewhere, parishes of this type are few and far between. Indeed, in the remoter parts of the region, including large tracts of Holderness, the flatlands on either side of the Ouse, and the Ancholme valley, the picture is only of sustained rural depopulation. Many villagers here are experiencing not only further contraction of agricultural employment, but also decline of such basic needs as village schools, shops and bus services.

The settlement pattern today

Today almost nine out of every ten people in the Humber region live in urban communities. If we still use Law's (1967) statistical definition, there were as many as thirty such communities in 1981, thirteen more than in 1951. All the new urban communities were primarily dormitory settlements and had developed through residential growth around former villages and small country towns. This diffuse urbanisation, together with the accelerated physical extension of Hull, Grimsby, Scunthorpe and other established urban areas, has greatly enlarged the quantity of urban land use, with a consequent substantial loss of rural space. Nevertheless, the region today contains well over a hundred villages, many still keeping their rustic agricultural character and experiencing little development other than the modernisation and gentrification of existing buildings. However, Figure 28.3b shows several other villages in the urbanising fringes of Hull, Grimsby, Scunthorpe, and now even Beverley, Goole and Immingham, that have expanded rapidly during recent decades and may soon see their populations passing the 2500 rural-urban threshold.

In 1979 Humberside's first Structure Plan was approved (Humberside County Council 1979), in which a major aspect of policy was the use of planning controls to steer future housing development and population expansion into existing urban settlements and a list of over fifty selected 'growth villages'. In these designated settlements new residential development is encouraged, but it must be 'in character with its surroundings' and has to conform to the needs of conserving good quality farmland and protecting attractive rural scenery. Hopefully, therefore, while rural suburbanisation will undoubtedly be a continuing process within Humberside, there will be far less of the type of poorly controlled settlement sprawl that did so much damage to the region's environment during the second and third quarters of this century.

References

Allison, K.J. (1976). *The East Riding of Yorkshire Landscape.* Hodder and Stoughton, London.

Gleave, M.B. (1962). Dispersed and nucleated settlement in the Yorkshire Wolds, 1770-1850. *Transactions of the Institute of British Geographers* **30**, 105-18.

Hammond, J.L. and Hammond, B. (1911). *The Village Labourer 1760-1832: a study of the Government of England before the Reform Bill.* Longman, London.

Hargrave, J. (1791). *Plan of the Town of Kingston upon Hull.* Hull.

Harris, A. (1961). *The Rural Landscape of the East Riding of Yorkshire 1700-1850.* Oxford University Press, London.

Her Majesty's Stationery Office (1863). *Census of England and Wales for the Year 1861. Population Tables. Vol. 2. Ages, Civil Condition, Occupations and Birth-Places of the People.* HMSO, London.

Humberside County Council (1979). *Humberside Structure Plan: policies approved.* Humberside County Council, Beverley.

Law, C.M. (1967). The growth of urban population in England and Wales, 1801-1911. *Transactions of the Institute of British Geographers* **41**, 125-44.

Lewis, P. and Jones, P.N. (1970). *The Humberside Region.* David and Charles, Newton Abbot.

Mills, D.R. (1959). The Poor Laws and the distribution of population, *c.* 1600-1860, with special reference to Lincolnshire. *Transactions of the Institute of British Geographers* **26**, 185-95.

Olney, R.J. (1979). *Rural Society and County Government in Nineteenth-Century Lincolnshire.* History of Lincolnshire Committee for the Society for Lincolnshire History and Archaeology, Lincoln.

Saville, J. (1957). *Rural Depopulation in England and Wales, 1851-1951*. Routledge, London.

Watts, H.D. (1964). The Industrial Geography of Rural East Yorkshire. M.A. thesis, University of Hull.

Wood, J. (1828). *Plan of Beverley*. Beverley.

Wright, N.R. (1982). *Lincolnshire Towns and Industry, 1700-1914*. History of Lincolnshire Committee for the Society for Lincolnshire History and Archaeology, Lincoln.

29
The history of the Humber crossing
J. North

Introduction

The Humber has been one of Britain's principal commercial waterways since medieval times. Its east coast position encouraged short-sea trading links with western and northern Europe, and navigable tributaries such as the Ouse and Trent, later augmented by canals, provided effective inland waterway links with the industrialising North and Midlands of England. These locational advantages, plus the presence of a deep, navigable channel and an abundance of flat land alongside the estuary, have been the basis for the third largest shipping complex in the UK, which today accounts for over 10% of Britain's total sea-borne trade (Jones and North 1987).

For land transport, however, the Humber presents a major physical obstacle. It penetrates eastern England for 62 km between Spurn Point and Trent Falls, varying in width from 2.5 km between Hessle and Barton to almost 9 km further downstream. From the mid nineteenth century, when first rail and subsequently road transport became dominant, the Humber's negative role assumed particular significance. The north and south banks of the estuary were isolated from one another both physically and psychologically, and their economies developed separately; the only regular links across the estuary were maintained by ferries, often subject to delays or cancellations during adverse tidal conditions. Since that time, some local interests sought a permanent, direct estuarine crossing. However, none of the proposed rail or road crossing schemes was successful until 1972, when construction of the Humber road bridge began. This chapter traces the history of the Humber crossing issue, showing why the bridge project was so long delayed and why support for a permanent crossing, even at a local level, has never been unanimous.

Ferry crossings

To overcome the physical obstacle of the Humber, it was necessary to provide ferries from an early date. The Roman Ermine Street, linking London to York via Lincoln, crossed the Humber by a ford or ferry between Winteringham and Brough (Whitwell 1970), and ferries proliferated along the Humber, Trent and Ouse during the medieval period (Ingram 1969). As Hull's status as a port grew, ferries across the Humber became especially important, providing a direct link to the agricultural county of Lincolnshire and a shorter route to London. By the late eighteenth century the Hull-Barton and Barton-Hessle crossings had become the most important, but their efficiency was often criticized; journeys were hazardous and uncertain, as some notable travellers have testified (Defoe 1948 ed.).

In 1832 a rival Hull-New Holland steam ferry was established, which offered a more frequent and much faster crossing. By 1846 it was claimed that 70 000 passengers travelled via New Holland annually, and mail and coach services had transferred to link with the new route. The New Holland ferry was acquired by the Great Grimsby & Sheffield Junction Railway (GG&SJ) in 1845 and was served by a branch from the company's Grimsby-Gainsborough main line. When the GG&SJ amalgamated with others to form the Manchester, Sheffield & Lincolnshire Railway (MS&L) in 1846, the new company sought to develop the ferry along with its railways south of the Humber, and the other ferries gradually fell into disuse (Harris 1961).

The campaign for a Humber rail crossing, 1840-1914

The campaign for a permanent estuarine crossing originated between 1830 and 1850. Railway development offered Hull, then unrivalled as the leading Humber port, the prospect of extending its hinterland still further and of realising the ambition to become a major coal exporting port. However, railway development also raised the threat of competition to Hull from rival ports no longer handicapped by their inferior inland waterway connections (Ingram 1969). By 1850 railways had reached both Hull and its potential Humber rivals, Grimsby and Goole. These smaller ports gained a mileage advantage over Hull for the growing Midlands industrial traffic. Hull's southward connections were poor, with market boats and the unreliable Humber ferry providing the only regular links to the south bank of the estuary. The 'Railway Mania' of 1845-6 had therefore inevitably stimulated several ambitious but unsuccessful locally inspired projects designed to improve links between Hull and the Midlands (North 1978).

Firm proposals for a Humber rail crossing emerged soon after the initial railway amalgamations north of the estuary. These had culminated in 1854 with the formation of the North Eastern Railway (NER), which immediately established a monopoly over all rail approaches to Hull. So began a period marked by bitter relations between Hull merchants and the NER which lasted until the monopoly was broken in 1885 (Brooke 1972). From 1854-85 the NER's traffic policies were vigorously opposed in Hull. Local merchants feared competition from Northeast ports, especially Hartlepool where the NER effectively controlled both railways and docks. The company seemingly discriminated against Hull by charging on tonnages rather than distance for goods movements between industrial Yorkshire and Hartlepool and Hull, thus denying the latter its natural locational advantage. Meanwhile, the MS&L and Lancashire & Yorkshire (L&Y) Railways were actively promoting trade via Grimsby and Goole, and the MS&L had acquired the New Holland ferry. Hull merchants therefore sought independent rail outlets and instigated several schemes which incorporated plans for bridging or tunnelling the Humber.

Plans for a Humber rail bridge were formally discussed by Hull Chamber of Commerce in 1855 but no further action was taken. A decade later, however, proposals for 'a lofty viaduct, about a mile and a half in length' between Hessle and Barton were included in the Hull, Lancashire & Midland Counties Railway scheme (North 1978). This aimed to give Hull more direct access to the Yorkshire coalfield via the MS&L system south of the estuary (Fig. 29.1). The scheme was short-lived, however, because the crucial financial support anticipated from Hull merchants and the MS&L did not materialize. A similar fate befell plans for another rail bridge published in 1867 (Hull Corporation Archives 1867 Box 109 *Papers relating to bridges*).

In sharp contrast, the Hull, South & West Junction Railway project of 1872-3 attracted widespread local subscriptions. Promoted at the height of the feud between Hull and the NER, it proposed to link Hull with the MS&L at Brigg to create a shorter route to London and to improve access to the expanding Yorkshire, Derbyshire and Nottinghamshire coalfields. John Fowler, the eminent railway engineer, produced plans for a £340 000 tunnel under the river between Barton and Hessle (Fig. 29.2).

The Hull, South & West Junction Railway Bill, backed by a petition of 10 000 local signatures, was submitted to Parliament in 1873. It was approved by a House of Commons Select Committee but subsequently rejected by a Committee in the House of Lords, reportedly by a single vote. Suggestions that Fowler's scheme was rejected solely on engineering grounds are seemingly refuted by evidence from the respective Committee proceedings and from MS&L company records. The NER apparently procured the downfall of the tunnel project by inducing the MS&L, which had remained neutral throughout the Commons examination, to oppose the Bill in the Lords in return for the granting of 'running powers' over NER lines to and from Hull (see evidence of J. Fowler Esq., 11 July 1873, House of Lords Select Committee Records Vol. 23; an agreement giving MS&L 'running powers' into Hull over NER lines was signed on 11 July 1873 - see British Transport Historical Records MSL/1/13, Manchester, Sheffield & Lincolnshire Railway Minutes of Directors Meetings, for 13 June (Minute 3130b), 27 June (3154) and 18 July 1873 (3180)).

The opening of the coal-carrying Hull & Barnsley Railway (H&BR) and its associated dock at Hull in 1885 gave the port its long-awaited independent rail outlet. Meanwhile, the Hull & Lincoln

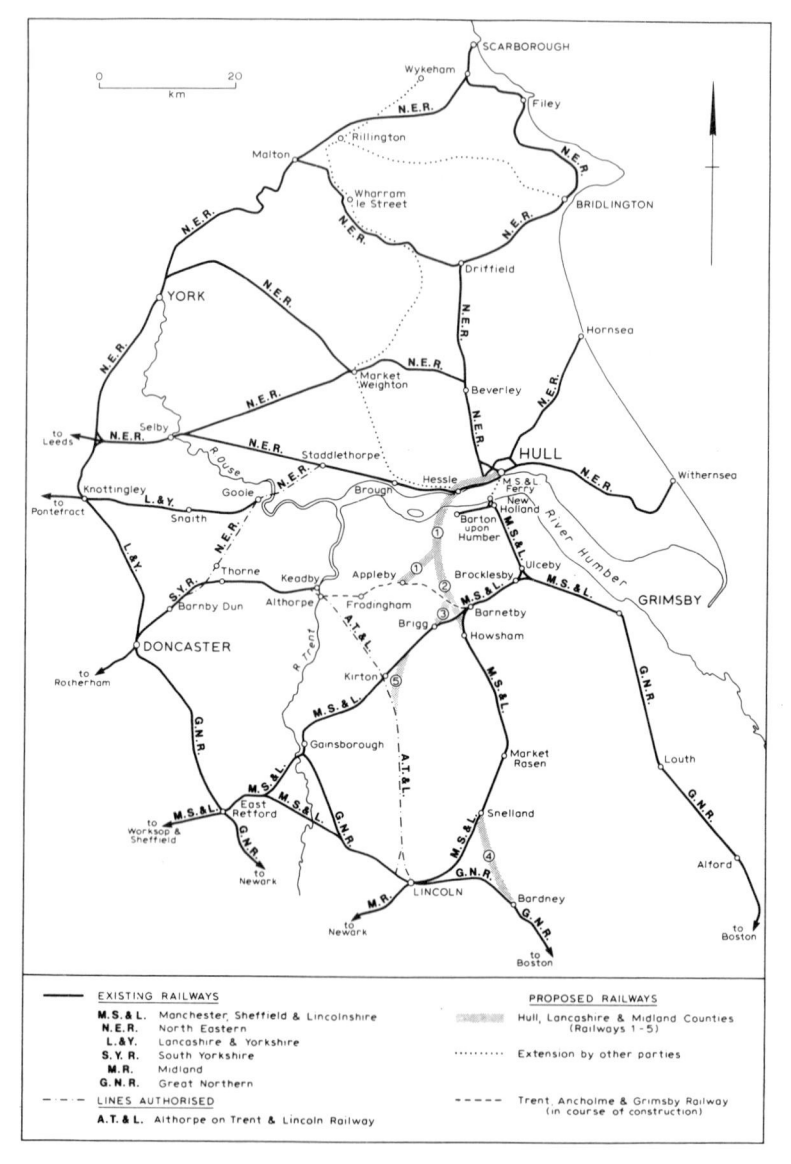

Fig. 29.1. The Hull, Lancashire & Midland Counties Railway, 1865.

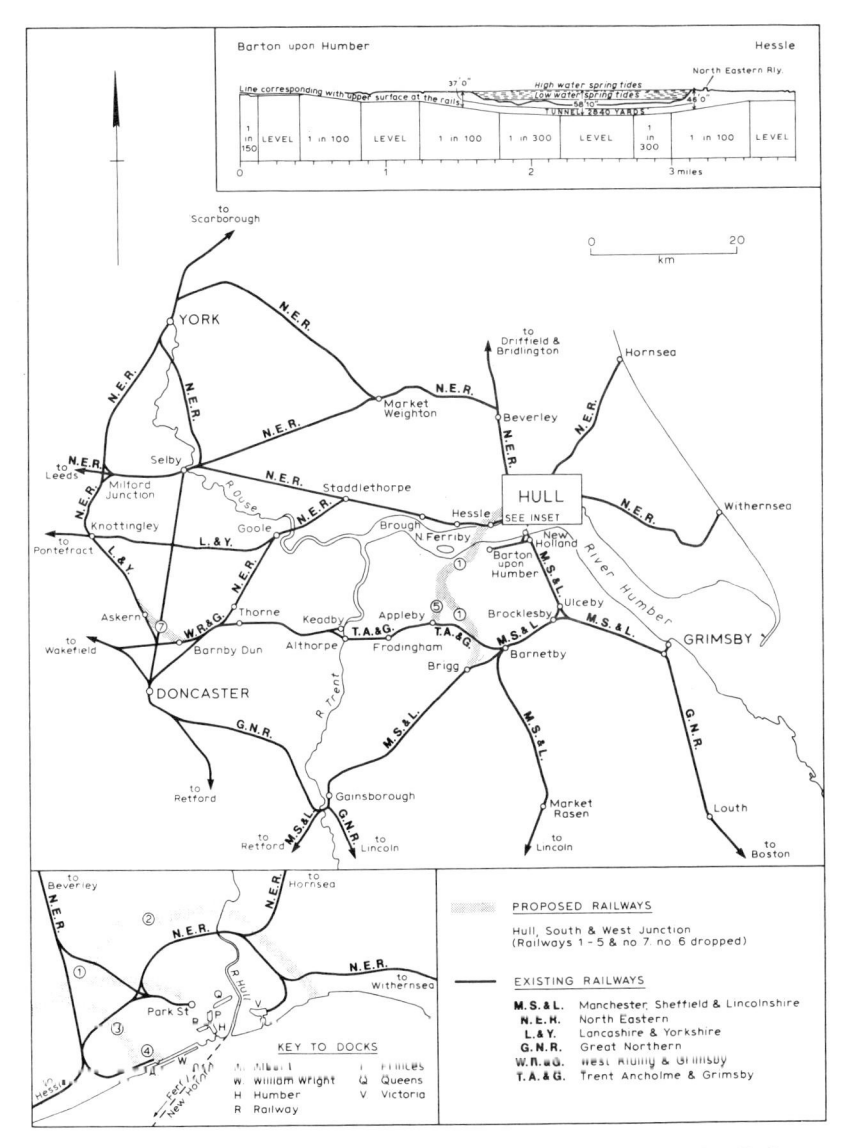

Fig. 29.2. Map and section of the proposed Hull, South & West Junction Railway, 1872-3, showing John Fowler's proposed Humber rail tunnel.

Railway of 1882-3 proposed a link from the new H&BR at Anlaby, just west of Hull, to a junction with the Great Northern (GNR) and other railways at Lincoln, with a multiple-span bridge costing £532 000 linking Hessle and Barton (Fig. 29.3). However, the Hull & Lincoln Railway Bill encountered fierce and overwhelming opposition in Parliament in 1883, both from the NER and MS&L, and particularly from shipping and river navigation interests representing Goole and other inland ports. Goole shipowners argued that the erection of thirty-six bridge piers in the notoriously unstable Humber would impair the navigable channel, threatening their port's existence.

Two main factors accounted for the failure of the various Humber rail crossing schemes. First, engineering evidence given by their respective promoters failed to overcome the objections raised by highly influential shipping and river navigation interests. Second, and probably more significant, the MS&L chose to honour working arrangements made with the NER; without MS&L support, plans for independent lines across the Humber had little prospect of success.

After 1885 interest in a Humber rail crossing waned, although it revived briefly between 1910 and 1913 when the Great Central Railway (GCR) built railways and a massive dock at Immingham to cater for increasing coal exports from south Yorkshire and Nottinghamshire. When the crossing issue re-emerged during the 1920s, the case for a rail link had been seriously weakened following amalgamation of the NER, GCR, GNR and others to form the London & North Eastern Railway (LNER), which thus gained control of all railways on both banks of the Humber and also the New Holland ferry. Hull interests therefore turned their attention to the promotion of schemes for a road crossing (North 1978).

A road crossing 'in the national interest', 1929-65

The next crucial phase in the crossing campaign occurred between 1929 and 1931. Hull Corporation, conscious of the increasing inadequacy of the Humber ferry, commissioned Sir Douglas Fox & Partners to 'advise upon the most suitable economic method and geographical position for transport communication between the East Riding of Yorkshire and North Lincolnshire in the vicinity of Hull.' Their report (Fox 1930) favoured construction of a road

The history of the Humber crossing

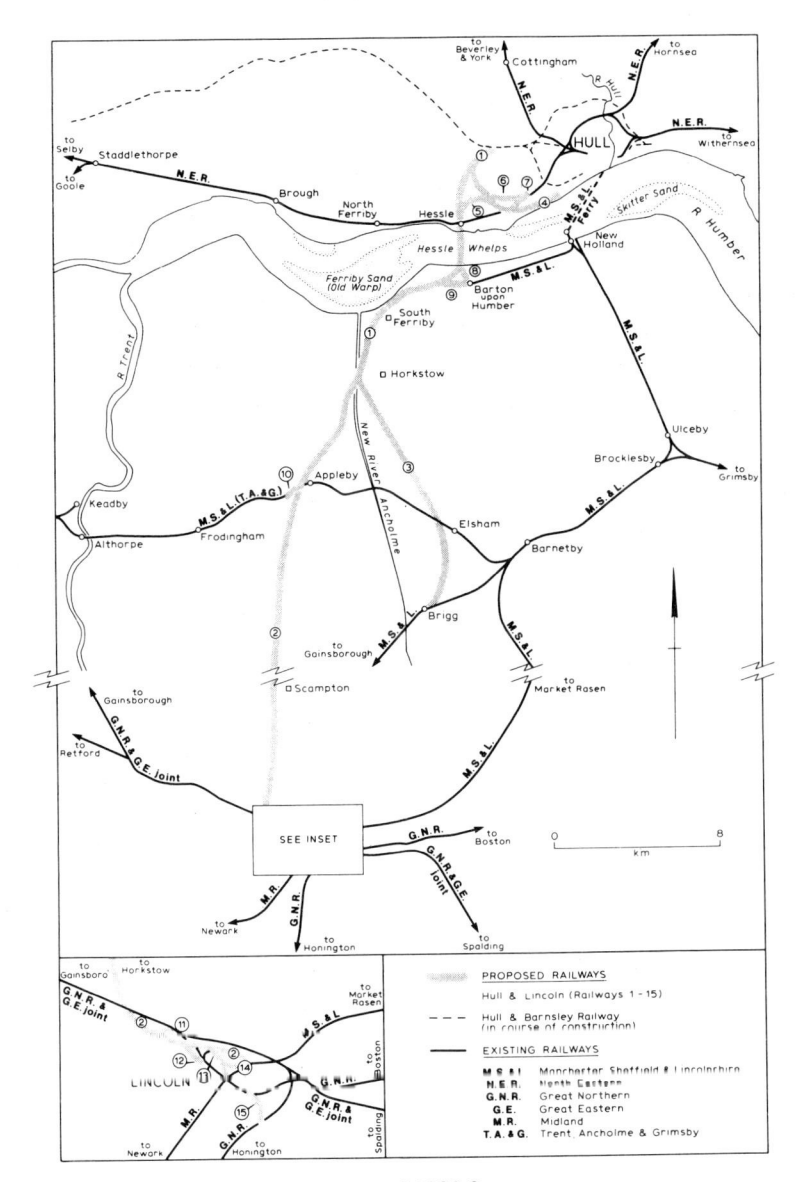

Fig. 29.3. The Hull & Lincoln Railway of 1882-3.

Fig. 29.4. Artist's impression of Sir Douglas Fox & Partners' design for a Humber road bridge, 1930.

bridge between Hessle and Barton on economic, engineering and environmental grounds, and included designs for a bridge with a main cantilever section spanning the entire navigable channel plus some twenty-two smaller spans (Fig. 29.4). The Ministry of Transport promised a 75% grant towards a Humber bridge to help relieve unemployment, and a Bill was submitted to Parliament. Shipping and river navigation interests again opposed the project, but Professor A.H. Gibson, a leading hydrologist, convinced the examining Committee that the bridge piers would not profoundly affect the Humber channel (House of Commons Records of Select Committee on Private Bills, Group F, 6-7 May 1931). However, the mounting national financial crisis of 1931 forced withdrawal of the promised loan and the scheme was shelved.

The 1931 Humber Bridge Bill was significant for contrasting reasons. It confirmed the engineering feasibility of a bridge, and seriously undermined opposition from river interests. Unfortunately, the decision by the promoting local authorities, led by Hull Corporation, to base their case for a Humber bridge on its potential significance as part of a direct national trunk route linking London with northeast England was undoubtedly a grave error. This argument was based upon a geographical misconception; the most direct route between these two areas clearly passed some distance west of the Humber estuary (Appleton 1966). For the next 35 years successive Governments rightly argued that a Humber bridge would serve regional rather than national interests, and was therefore a lower priority than crossings for the Severn, Forth and Mersey estuaries. The Humber crossing issue progressed little between 1931 and 1955, although Ralph Freeman did publish new designs for a single-span suspension bridge in 1935, which seemed likely to remove any remaining objections from navigation interests. Meanwhile, the estimated cost of a bridge rose from £2.5 million in 1935 to £13 million by 1955.

In 1955 there seemed little immediate prospect of building a bridge. Nevertheless, Hull Corporation persuaded neighbouring county and local authorities to promote a Parliamentary Bill to obtain the necessary legal and financial powers. The Humber Bridge Act (1959) established a Bridge Board with powers to build a bridge, issue bonds and collect tolls. Membership of the Board was dominated by Hull Corporation, although the Lincolnshire and East Riding County Councils and other local authorities were also represented.

Government attitudes towards a bridge were unchanged during the early 1960s. Indeed, a Technical Report for the Ministry of Transport (Scott & Wilson, Kirkpatrick & Partners 1965) concluded that separate east-west motorways, with new high-level crossings of the Ouse and Trent, would best serve the principal traffic flows to and from the north and south banks respectively, and that a Humber bridge was therefore unjustifiable. The only possible alternative was a bridge financed by the local authorities themselves. Hull Corporation, concerned by the tendency for major new industrial development to be located south of the estuary in the Grimsby-Immingham area, sought to initiate a scheme. However, the south bank councils, recognising their stronger bargaining position, considered east-west and other road improvements a much higher priority (Bowman 1966, Ward 1967). Without Government aid, a bridge was therefore unlikely to succeed.

Events since 1965

Within five years, a unique and short-lived combination of economic, demographic and political circumstances produced a dramatic turn of events. Regional planning became dominant against a background of economic boom, population growth and forecasts of a much larger

UK population by the 1980s (Simon 1987). The boundaries of the new Yorkshire and Humberside Economic Planning Council were drawn to include both banks of the estuary within a single unit. This council saw completion of a Humber bridge and the east-west routes for north and south Humberside as 'essential elements in the region's development' (Yorkshire and Humberside Economic Planning Council 1966). Leading national planners now favoured diversion of future UK industrial growth towards deep-water estuaries, where raw materials for capital-intensive industries such as oil refining and chemicals could be assembled and processed cheaply (James *et al.* 1961). The Government's 'think tank', the Central Unit for Environmental Planning, saw Humberside as an ideal reception area for anticipated population and industrial growth. Its 'Humberside feasibility study' (Central Unit for Environmental Planning 1969) envisaged growth in Humberside's population from under one million to over three million, proposed a new city of 750 000 inhabitants for south Humberside and recommended completion of a bridge and east-west roads by 1976. A bridge was considered essential to overcome the 'divisive effect of the estuary' and to promote complementary development of the hitherto separate sub-regional economies on either bank. These factors were instrumental in changing Government opinion in favour of a bridge, but further impetus was provided by factors of political expediency; the Minister of Transport promised a Humber bridge during the crucial Hull North parliamentary by-election campaign of 1966 (Crossman 1977).

The Government now accepted the need for a bridge, but still considered it of local rather than national importance and refused to fund it directly from the trunk road programme. Eventually, in 1971 the Ministry of Transport offered to loan 75% of the then estimated £26 million cost of a bridge; the Humber Bridge Board had to borrow the remaining 25% on the commercial market. Repayments were to be over 60 years with an initial 13 year period of grace, the monies being raised from tolls. Construction began in 1972, but a combination of bad weather, labour disputes and technical problems with the foundations of the south pier delayed completion until 1981, almost five years behind schedule. The urgency of the bridge project was increased by the creation of the new administrative county of Humberside in 1974; without a permanent physical link across the estuary, the county appeared likely to remain an artificial region despite its common estuarine focus (North et al. 1987).

Meanwhile, the favourable national economic and demographic trends of the 1960s had disappeared. The concept of Maritime Industrial Development Areas was shelved. High inflation and interest rates sent capital costs and loan charges for the bridge soaring. Final capital costs reached £97.2 million, and the total bridge debt, including loan charges, on opening was £138.1 million. Unfortunately, recession and de-industrialisation on Humberside, notably in the steel and fishing industries, had brought drastic revision of earlier, wildly overoptimistic forecasts for bridge traffic. Initial estimates of 31 000 vehicles per day published in 1971 had been reduced to only 4000-10 000 by 1981 (North 1987). Finally, the east-west M62 and M180 motorways, with their toll-free Ouse and Trent crossings respectively, were well established inter-regional routeways by the time the Humber Bridge opened, leaving the latter to perform an essentially local function (Fig. 29.5). Critics immediately labelled the bridge 'a white elephant' and the 'bridge from nowhere to nowhere'. Others saw it as an essential element of regional infrastructure which could enhance prospects for future development on Humberside (Kershaw 1980, North 1981). However, faced with the 60 year repayment period and forecasts of limited bridge usage, the Humber Bridge Board was forced to set initial tolls at a high level, ranging from £1 for cars to £7.50 for the largest heavy goods vehicles (North 1988).

The opening of the bridge transformed pre-existing spatial relationships on Humberside, and changed the points of ingress for traffic moving between the north and south banks of the estuary. Hull is now a mere 48 km from Grimsby and only 34 km from Scunthorpe. For journeys between northeast and southeast Humberside, distance and time savings offset toll charges, although these savings diminish rapidly for trips with origins and/or destinations west of the A15-A164 axis. A physical barrier has therefore in certain respects been replaced by an economic one.

Conclusions

Support for a Humber crossing, both nationally and locally, has never been unanimous. Government approval for the Humber Bridge in

418   *Humber Perspectives*

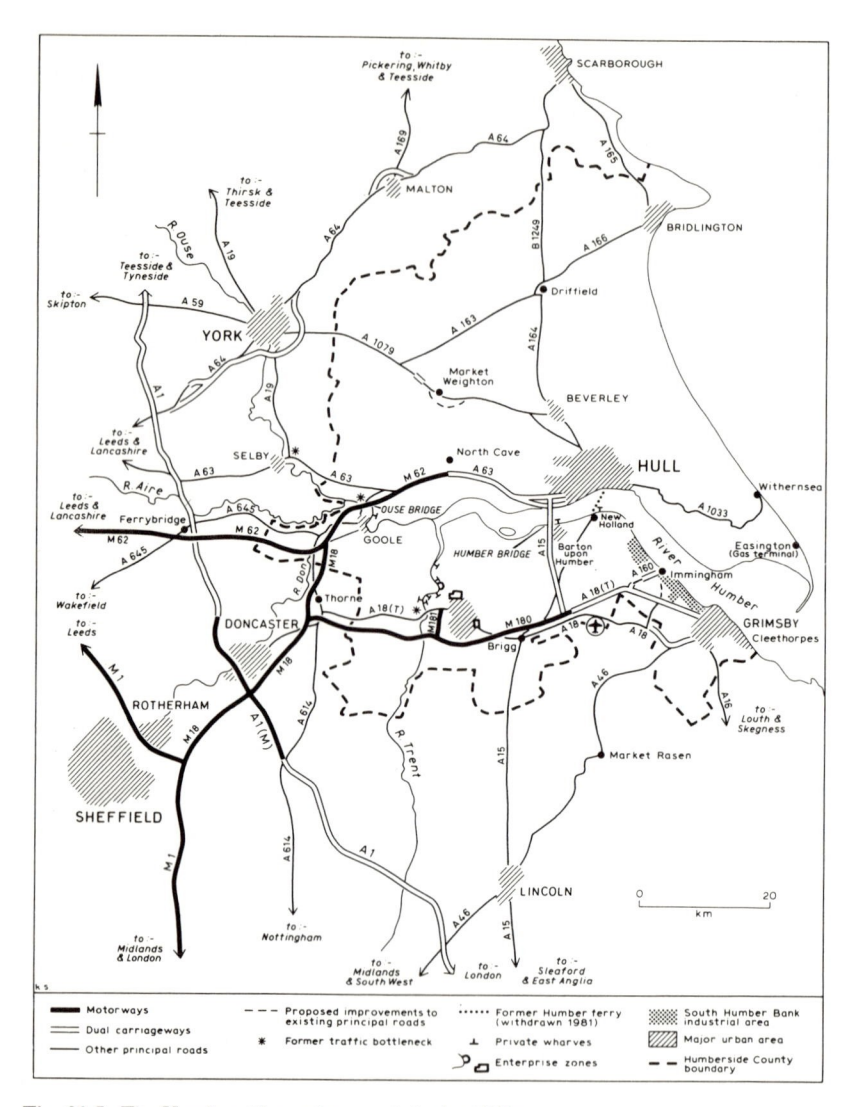

Fig. 29.5. The Humberside road network in the 1980s.

1971 was tempered by refusal to fund it from the trunk road programme. Locally, all the major initiatives, both for rail and road crossings, stemmed from Hull industrial and mercantile interests. With the largest population and widest range of industrial and service activities on Humberside, Hull always stood to gain most from an estuarine crossing. This factor undoubtedly explains the adoption of attitudes ranging from indifference to outright opposition by south bank authorities. Yet perhaps an equally strong motivating force for Hull interests was the threat of competition. Between 1840 and 1914 the threat from potential rival ports was uppermost; from 1945 onwards it was the fear that Hull could become isolated from the new focus of capital-intensive industrial activities in the Grimsby-Immingham area.

Since the general public of Hull have never expressed any great enthusiasm for a crossing, critics have concluded that the opening of the bridge represented a triumph for an influential minority on Humberside. However, this oversimplification neglects the many less quantifiable and indirect benefits accruing from the bridge, for example, time savings for personnel and delivery vehicles, an enlarged potential market and opportunities for rationalisation in the business sector, plus access to a wider range of commercial, retailing and recreational activities for the general public. Unfortunately, the harsh economic baptism and infancy of the bridge have simply fuelled the controversy surrounding it. Despite high tolls, low traffic levels have brought mounting bridge debts (in excess of £300 million at the end of 1988), with little likelihood of reversing the upward trend given current traffic forecasts.

In January 1988 bridge tolls were raised to the maximum levels permitted under the original Parliamentary order, £1.50 for cars and £8 for the largest heavy goods vehicles. By that time traffic flows exceeded 4 million crossings per year, with over 80% of journeys being made by private cars. However, the income from tolls, which amounted to £7.4 million in 1988, was more than offset by annual expenditure, including interest charges on loans, of more than £30 million. The bridge faced a mounting crisis of progressively escalating debt, with no prospect of meeting the 60 year repayment deadline. Following urgent discussions with the Government, and despite considerable opposition from local road haulage interests, a further increase in bridge tolls came into force in August 1989. Tolls for private cars were increased to £1.60 per crossing, but rates for the largest heavy goods vehicles soared to £10.90. It has been suggested that the Government may now consider writing off sufficient of the outstanding bridge debt to enable total repayment by the year 2042. Such an agreement is still by no means certain however. Without Government intervention the bridge debt will increase by a further £35 million in 1989 alone. Even with Government intervention, there is little prospect of a reduction in toll levels, which would still have to rise in line with inflation to ensure repayment of the outstanding balance.

References

Appleton, J.H. (1966). Let's get the Humber Bridge plan into perspective. *Voice of Yorkshire & Humberside Industry, August,* 17-19.
Bowman, S. (1966). Roads come first for South Humberside. *Voice of Yorkshire & Humberside Industry, April,* 25.
Brooke, D. (1972). The struggle between Hull and the North Eastern Railway, 1854-80. *Journal of Transport History New Series* **1,** 228-9.
Central Unit for Environmental Planning (1969). *Humberside: a feasibility study.* HMSO, London.
Crossman, R. (1977). *The Diaries of a Cabinet Minister: Volume III, Secretary of State for Social Services, 1968-70.* H. Hamilton, London.
Defoe, D. (1948). *A Tour through England and Wales.* Everyman Edition, London.
Fox, Sir Douglas & Partners (1930). *Transport Communication across the Humber estuary.* Sir Douglas Fox & Partners, London.
Harris, A. (1961). The Humber Ferries and the rise of New Holland, 1800-1860. *East Midland Geographer* **15,** 11-19.
Ingram, M.E. (1969). Communications. In: *History of Yorkshire, East Riding, Victoria County History* (ed. K.J. Allison) pp. 387-9. Oxford University Press, London.
James, J., Scott, S.F. and Willatts, E.C. (1961). Land use and the changing power industry in England and Wales.

Geographical Journal **127**, 286-309.
Jones, P.N. and North, J. (1987). Ports and wharves. In: *Humberside in the Eighties* (ed. D.G. Symes) pp. 97-112. Department of Geography, University of Hull.
Kershaw, R. (1980). Not such a white elephant. *The Times* 11 November.
North, J. (1978). The Humber crossing: an unfinished saga. In: *North Humberside Introductory Themes* (ed. D.G. Symes) pp. 51-61. Department of Geography, University of Hull.
North, J. (1981). The Humber Bridge: a bridge of opportunity? *Transport* **2**, 27-8.
North, J. (1987). Transport. In: *Humberside in the Eighties* (ed. D.G. Symes) pp. 79-96. Department of Geography, University of Hull.
North, J. (1988). The Humber Bridge - lame duck or golden goose? In: *A Dynamic Estuary: man, nature and the Humber* (ed. N.V. Jones) pp. 113-31. Hull University Press, Hull.
North, J., Spooner, D.J. and Symes, D.G. (1987). Humberside: an introductory profile. In: *Humberside in the Eighties* (ed. D.G. Symes) pp. 1-8. Department of Geography, University of Hull.
Scott & Wilson, Kirkpatrick & Partners (1965). *Improved Road Communications between Kingston upon Hull and the Great North Road.* Scott & Wilson, Kirkpatrick & Partners, London.
Simon, D. (1987). Spanning muddy waters: the Humber Bridge and regional development. *Regional Studies* **21**, 25-36.
Ward, F.W. (1967). Bridging both banks. *Voice of Yorkshire & Humberside Industry, October,* 32.
Whitwell, J.B. (1970). *Roman Lincolnshire,* History of Lincolnshire Volume 2. Lincolnshire Local History Society, Lincoln.
Yorkshire and Humberside Economic Planning Council (1966). *A Review of Yorkshire and Humberside.* HMSO, London.

30
Development of the Humber region during the nineteenth and twentieth centuries
J. North

Introduction

Recent descriptions of the Humber region still emphasise its 'spacious' and 'uncongested' character, noting how the sinuous nature of the deep-water channel in the strongly tidal estuary has led to a staggering of port development on the south and north banks, and thus a 'discontinuous' pattern of related industrial activities separated by 'extensive empty spaces' (North *et al.* 1987). The apparent immaturity of the urban system is also stressed. North of the Humber the system is dominated by the greater Hull urban area (population 1981, 330 323), accounting for nearly two-thirds of the north Humberside population. South of the river the Grimsby and Cleethorpes (140 552) and Scunthorpe (67 016) urban areas are two rather less dominant centres. To many observers, therefore, Humberside is essentially an agricultural region with an industrial and commercial facade. This impression persists despite a comparatively vigorous era of port and industrial development, especially from 1860 onwards. This chapter examines both the nature and the geographical impact of these developments, and should be seen alongside Wild's (this volume) discussion of population change and settlement geography.

The late eighteenth and early nineteenth centuries

The comparative neglect of the Humber region as a focus for industrial development during the late eighteenth and early nineteenth centuries can be explained by lack of suitable resources. The low relief and sluggish drainage offered little scope for developing water-powered industries, while the lack of accessible coal precluded the extensive industrialisation which typified the traditional nineteenth century industrial regions of Britain (Lewis and Jones 1970). Instead, import of raw materials and export of finished products, chiefly for the Lancashire and West Yorkshire textile industries, provided the stimulus for accelerated growth of port traffic. Many of the raw materials originated from northern Europe, and Hull, with its long-established mercantile connections in Baltic ports, became a natural focus for this traffic (Bellamy 1988). Until the 1770s port activity here was confined to the lower reaches of the River Hull, which afforded a sheltered harbour. By 1774, however, severe congestion at the wharves and quays alongside the river prompted plans for constructing the town's first enclosed dock. Between 1778 and 1829 three docks (Queen's, Humber and Prince's) were opened, following the line of the city's former medieval fortifications between the Hull and Humber frontages (Fig. 30.1). This 'Town Docks' complex, together with the lower River Hull, became the focus of commercial activity in Hull. By the 1820s, however, Hull faced the threat of competition for traffic, following the establishment of Goole as a canal terminus and transhipment port by the Aire & Calder Navigation Company (Porteous this volume).

Inevitably, Hull also became a focus for industries using imported raw materials or processing local agricultural resources. During the late eighteenth century, sites flanking the River Hull became congested with numerous small industrial premises. Seed crushing (reflecting the longstanding trading connections with North European countries, then important sources of linseed), flour milling, saw milling and rendering whale blubber to oil were all prominent. Some of these activities provided the basis for the subsequent development of related industries, including the manufacture of pigments, paint and

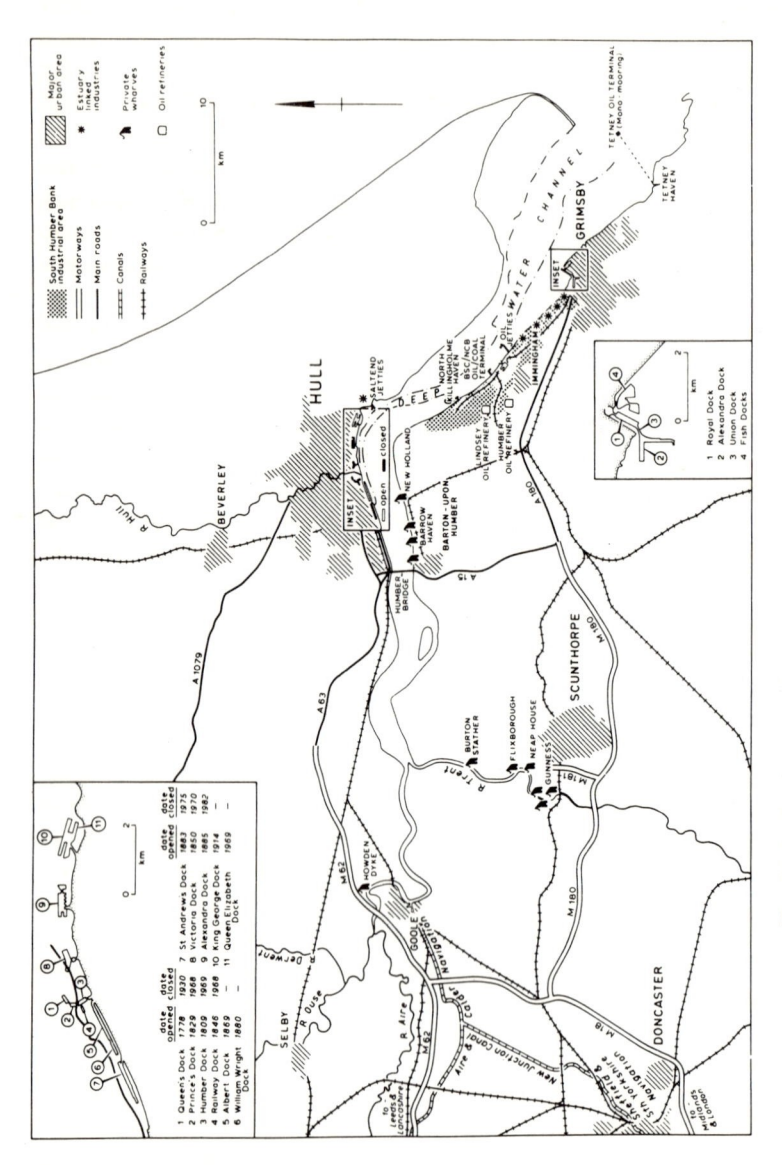

Fig. 30.1. Humber ports and wharves (from Jones and North 1987).

chemicals (Bellamy 1971). However, these developments merely reinforced the preceding emphasis upon developing overseas trade links, rather than on the establishment of closer connections with the rest of Britain. Cotton manufacture was also introduced into the port during the 1820s, employing over 2000 people by the middle of the century, and in the 1840s Isaac Reckitt took over an old starch works, his staff numbering 51 by 1851 (Bellamy 1988). The 1840s also saw the development of the Humber fishing industry, when fishing smacks from Brixham, Devon transferred their base of operation to Hull and Grimsby to be close to the rich new North Sea grounds (Symes 1978), again emphasising external rather than internal associations. Even with the railway developments of the 1840s and 50s, the Humber region remained geographically remote from the main centres of economic activity, and internally, the estuary itself was still a physical and psychological barrier (North 1978, 1988). Before 1860 only the concentration of port-related industries at Hull, the canal port complex at Goole and the infant port and fishing developments at Grimsby disturbed the essentially rural character of the Humber region.

1860-1914

With only one notable exception, the vigorous era of industrialisation and port development between 1860 and 1914 reinforced the established geographical pattern within the Humber region. Railway developments heralded an era of traffic growth and dock development at both Hull and Grimsby, and competition between these ports and Goole intensified as each sought to establish itself as the principal outlet for growing coal exports from the expanding Yorkshire, Derbyshire and Nottinghamshire coalfield. At Hull five additional docks were opened between 1850 and 1885; these extended along the Humber frontage both upstream (Albert, William Wright and St Andrew's Docks) and downstream (Victoria and Alexandra Docks) from the original port nucleus (Fig. 30.1). Alexandra Dock, built by the Hull & Barnsley Railway & Dock Company in 1885, marked the culmination of Hull's fight to establish an independent rail access to the port (North this volume), and offered the prospect of developing coal export traffic. St Andrew's Dock, opened in 1883, reflected the rapid growth of the Hull fishing fleet from 1860 onwards, although actual fish landings at the port were still relatively small due to the practice of shipping catches direct to Billingsgate market in London by carrier vessels in a system known as 'fleeting'. Meanwhile, at Grimsby the Manchester, Sheffield & Lincolnshire Railway Company had been instrumental in the construction of the Royal Dock (1852), and encouraged the growth of the fishing industry following the opening of No.1 Fish Dock in 1857 (Fig. 30.1). A second fish dock was opened in 1878 and a further commercial dock (Alexandra Dock) in 1880. Grimsby's population grew from 9000 in 1851 to 40 000 by 1880. Timber imports from Scandinavia and the Baltic countries became a staple traffic as the port flourished, but it was undoubtedly the fishing industry which gave Grimsby its unique character (Gillett 1970, Ambler this volume).

Dock developments and the growth of the fishing industry at both Hull and Grimsby naturally resulted in additional industrial and housing developments. In Hull the riverside industrial area was extended progressively northwards towards Stoneferry. Other firms established plants on land immediately behind the newer docks along the Humber frontage, particularly west of the River Hull, initiating the crosswise component of the emerging inverted T-shaped pattern of industrial activity within the city. Oil seed crushing, paint manufacture, marine engineering and shipbuilding were important growth industries. Other new developments included the refining of cod liver oil and the manufacture of industrial belting. The Hessle Road district, adjacent to St Andrew's Dock, soon became a closely knit community intimately associated with the fortunes of the fishing industry and a host of ancillary activities such as ice and net manufacture. By 1900 it was estimated that 10 000 people in Hull were directly employed in the fishing industry, 3500 as trawlermen and the rest in ancillary activities (Bellamy 1971). In Grimsby housing and ancillary industries soon occupied most available land around the fish docks. Poor quality housing extended to the New Clee area between Grimsby and Cleethorpes; here population increased from 2000 in 1871 to 11 000 in 1881, most families being dependent on the fishing industry. By 1890, however, problems of over-fishing in the North Sea grounds led trawlermen from both ports to seek more extensive but far-distant sources off Iceland, the White Sea and Newfoundland.

The rapid development of the North Lincolnshire iron industry around Scunthorpe from 1859 onwards introduced a new element into the geographical pattern of industrial activity. The principal location factor was the lean (20-30% iron content) Frodingham ironstone, while the completion of the Keadby rail bridge across the River Trent in 1864 allowed coal and coke to be imported from South Yorkshire. Six ironworks were established between 1864 and 1876; these original works were progressively expanded and a further plant, the geographically separate Normanby Park works, was opened in 1912 (Pocock this volume). Steel-making began at Scunthorpe in 1890. The rapid development of the industry was paralleled by the growth of urban settlement. At the time of the ore discovery in 1859, the population of the five townships (Scunthorpe, Crosby, Frodingham, Brumby and Ashby) in the Scunthorpe district was 1300, but by 1914 the figure had risen to 25 000, nearly all of whom were dependent on the steel industry (Pocock 1981).

By 1900 the Humber ports, especially Hull, were experiencing increasing pressure on capacity. Coal exports via Hull had increased from 507 000 tonnes in 1874 to over one million tonnes per year during the 1890s. Total traffic had grown from two million tonnes per year in 1870 to over four million tonnes by 1900. Employment in the docks and allied occupations had doubled between 1881 and 1901 to reach 21 000. Hull's trade also reflected the growing diversification of the UK economy, with a decline in textile exports and growth in general merchandise. To cope with growing traffic, King George Dock was opened in 1914; its scale (water area 21 ha) and location (6 km downstream from the port nucleus) reflected the need to accommodate ocean-going vessels of up to 25 000 DWT. Meanwhile, industrial development in Hull had begun to extend along Hedon Road, immediately behind the newer and larger eastern docks.

However, the most significant development of this period occurred south of the Humber, with the construction of a major new dock where the deep water channel swung close to the bank at Immingham, 4 km north of Grimsby. Immingham Dock, opened in 1911, was built on a grand scale by the Great Central Railway, originally to handle coal exports from the Yorkshire, Derbyshire and Nottinghamshire coalfield. From the outset large vessels were planned for, the massive entrance lock (256 m long x 27 m wide x 10 m deep) providing access to and from the 20 ha compact dock at all states of the tide (Jones and North 1987). East and west jetties were built at the dock entrance; these reached out directly into the deep-water channel, enabling vessels of 30 000 DWT to be handled. Extensive rail facilities were also provided. Although the decline of the coal trade after the First World War impeded growth - indeed, Immingham was labelled a 'white elephant' between 1919 and 1939 - the existence of this excellently appointed but under-utilised dock with deep-water access was to become the key to the post-1945 industrial development of the south Humber bank. Outside the main port areas estuarine industrial activities included brick and tile-making along the south bank of the Humber, especially at Barton and Killingholme, using local clays. Barton had also become a centre dominated by cycle manufacture, which employed 500 in 1911.

The inter-war years

Although the Humber region had comparatively few traditional heavy industries, it did suffer high unemployment during the economic depression of the inter-war years. However, because its problems were less severe than those of South Wales and Durham, it was excluded from the initial list of Special Areas receiving assistance (Lawless and Brown 1986). Unfortunately, neither did it share in the growth of new light industries between the wars. Electricity from the national grid, and growing use of road transport, favoured sites divorced from traditional locational requirements, but access to large urban centres such as London, Birmingham and Manchester, which offered substantial markets and agglomeration benefits, also became key influences. The Humber region, with poor external road links, therefore once again stayed remote from these rapidly growing centres of industrial and commercial expansion. Some Hull firms diversified into new production; T.J. Smith & Nephew Ltd added medical goods and toiletries to its surgical dressings, and Reckitt & Sons entered the pharmaceuticals field, but shipbuilding declined dramatically. The fishing industry still dominated the economy of Grimsby.

Within the region, however, one important trend was evident between 1919 and 1939. Large industrial concerns became attracted to extensive flat sites alongside the Humber estuary. At Saltend, east of Hull, a large chemicals plant producing alcohol, acetone and acetic acid was developed during the 1920s, with raw materials imported via jetties capable of accommodating 40 000 DWT tankers. Today the Saltend plant of BP Chemicals is the largest producer of acetic acid in Western Europe, with a continuing large-scale investment programme. Two further developments occurred to the west of Hull; at Brough a Leeds firm opened a factory during the 1920s specialising initially in the construction of naval aircraft, while nearby at Melton, Capper Pass Limited opened a plant smelting non-ferrous metals in 1936. Today the Brough factory, now part of British Aerospace, employs over 4500, while Capper Pass, now a subsidiary of the RTZ International mining conglomerate, has seen a doubling of capacity since 1945 and currently employs 800 people. A cement works was also opened at Melton. However, these plants appeared in the 1930s as islands of industrial activity within a rural landscape. Indeed, the expansion of horticulture under glass was a notable feature in the area west of Hull between 1919 and 1939.

Meanwhile, the Scunthorpe steel plants had become major producers of cheap crude steel and semi-finished products, exploiting cost advantages arising from a cheap and reliable source of ironstone and from the technical efficiency achievable from fully integrated plants (Lewis and Jones 1970). Scunthorpe's contribution to national steel output grew from 3% to 10% during the inter-war period (Pocock this volume).

1945-70

The Humber region was again omitted from the list of UK Development Areas which operated from 1945 to 1960 (Spooner 1987). However, despite the lack of Government aid, the 1950s witnessed a new phase of industrialisation which modified the pre-existing geographical pattern. The isolated stretch of the south Humber bank between Grimsby and Immingham became a new focus of industrial activity. Abundant, cheap, flat land, access to Immingham Dock and opportunities for direct discharge of effluent into the estuary proved attractive to dynamic, highly capitalised chemical and allied industries processing imported raw materials. The area was subsequently earmarked as suitable for 'special' industries involving hazardous processes (North and Spooner 1987). Several major companies, including BTP (now Tioxide), Fisons (now Norsk-Hydro), Laporte (now SCM Corporation), Courtaulds, Ciba-Geigy and ICI, bought up extensive sites, but only developed part of the land, reserving the remainder as a land 'bank'. This produced a discontinuous industrial zone, with large installations sited amid green fields.

A second phase of industrialisation, this time exploiting the advantages of the deep-water estuary in addition to the other site factors, occurred in the late 1960s with the opening of two major oil refineries at South Killingholme, near Immingham. Since the refineries are not adjacent to the Humber frontage, as this was already occupied by other activities, they are supplied with crude oil piped from the Tetney mono-buoy river terminal south of Cleethorpes (Fig. 30.1). Partly loaded 250 000 DWT tankers can berth at Tetney, and the Killingholme refineries now produce nearly 20% of total UK output.

Government reports of the late 1960s recognised the Humber region's potential to accommodate substantial industrial and urban development. The Humberside Feasibility Study (Central Unit for Environmental Planning 1969) referred to 'the area's great potential value to the country', while the Hunt Committee on Intermediate Areas (1969) concluded 'on the face of it, the area seemed suited to the kind of maritime industrial development that has taken place since the war in Holland at Europoort and in France at Fos'. Further optimism was provided by Government approval for construction of east-west motorways linking each bank of the estuary into the national motorway system, and by sanctioning of the Humber Bridge, which was seen by many as a key investment in breaking down the traditional pattern of separation, both physical and psychological, between north and south Humberside and in initiating complementary, rather than competing, economic development (North this volume). Britain's closer economic ties with Europe encouraged visions of capitalising on the Humber's geographical position. Additionally, it was hoped that the region could participate significantly in the planned exploitation of oil and gas from the North Sea.

However, this optimism was accompanied by the recognition of mounting problems in certain localities, notably Hull and Goole.

Despite some successes, for example the establishment of the Imperial typewriter factory in 1954, Hull had failed to attract sufficient industrial development by outside firms. The city had received Government financial assistance as a Development District between 1958 and 1966, but lost this status when the larger Development Areas were introduced in 1966. By 1968 new trading patterns and advances in shipping technology were adversely affecting the port of Hull. Some bulk traffics, notably petroleum imports and coal exports, were lost to Immingham, where the new generation of oil supertankers and large bulk mineral carriers was able to berth at new, purpose-built facilities. Another factor was the decline of the 'overside' trade, whereby goods were discharged from ships in dock to smaller inland waterway craft. Some vessels now by-passed Hull and headed directly for small, private riverside wharves located on the Humber, the lower Ouse and especially on the lower Trent (Fig. 30.1), where a particular concentration occurred between Gunness and Burton Stather (Jones and North 1987). Thus the fullest exploitation of the Humber as a navigable waterway did not necessarily conform to the rigidities of cargo handling facilities located in the main ports. Closure of the older Town Docks, shedding of surplus port labour and job losses in related activities such as the railways were inevitable consequences adding to Hull's problems. By the late 1960s Immingham had become the leading Humber port in terms of volume of traffic handled. Hull was, however, successful in developing unitized (Lift on-Lift off and Roll on-Roll off) traffics, and a purpose-built facility, Queen Elizabeth Dock, was opened in 1969 to cater for these traffics. Unitised cargoes now account for 58% of total traffic through Hull docks.

Meanwhile, Scunthorpe's steel industry was on the verge of significant change. From 1960 onwards the discovery of vast overseas deposits of rich iron ores made imported supplies cheaper than local ores. Nationally, the optimum location for steel production shifted to coastal plants, where large ore carriers could discharge at specialised deep-water terminals (Warren 1984). Scunthorpe therefore became less competitive than coastal plants in South Wales and on Teesside, a situation accentuated by its retention of open hearth furnaces when its rivals had switched to more efficient LD converters. Although Scunthorpe was selected as one of the British Steel Corporation's five major producing centres in 1969, the huge capital investments in the so-called 'Anchor' modernisation project were accompanied by a switch to the use of foreign ores imported via Immingham, and by the first planned reduction in the workforce from 20 000 to 16 500.

The Humber region since 1970

Since 1970 the economic situation in the Humber area has worsened and the region has failed to capitalise on its promising position. External factors have contributed substantially to this situation. Slower UK population growth and deteriorating national economic performance forced the abandonment of grandiose schemes for large-scale urban and industrial development. Rising fuel costs, the introduction of 200 mile exclusion zones, notably by Iceland, and subsequent limitations on catches by UK vessels in European waters under the European Common Fisheries Policy led to the dramatic collapse of the Humber distant water fishing industry. Between 1970 and 1984 landings by Hull vessels slumped from 197 000 tonnes to a mere 8500 tonnes; at Grimsby, with a lesser dependence on distant water fishing, the decline was longer delayed, but UK vessel landings fell from 166 000 tonnes in 1970 to just 24 200 tonnes in 1983 (Symes 1987a). Ironically, landings by Icelandic vessels are now crucial to the survival of Hull and Grimsby as major fish-landing ports. Meanwhile, problems of over-capacity in both the European and UK steel industries accelerated planned cutbacks at Scunthorpe, where over 10 000 steel jobs have been lost since 1978. With its unhealthy dependence on this single industry, Scunthorpe immediately became a 'crisis locality' in need of special assistance to attract alternative job opportunities.

Unfortunately, the changes in Government regional policy of 1977 and 1982, which raised Hull, Grimsby and Scunthorpe from Intermediate Area to full Development Area status, came too late to enable Humberside to obtain a significant share of mobile manufacturing industry. The situation has been made worse by the loss of Development Area status to all but the Scunthorpe Travel to Work Area since 1984, in line with Government de-emphasis on regional policy and increasing aid to inner urban areas and individual industrial sectors (Spooner 1987). Enterprise Zones have been established in Scunthorpe with some success in attracting new employment opportunities. Internally, the delayed completion of the Humber Bridge, and its mounting financial crisis, plus continuing political controversy over the necessity for the administrative county of Humberside which was set up in 1974, have added to the area's problems. Neither did the Humber region escape the general decline in manufacturing employment; important losses included the closure of the Imperial typewriter factory in Hull and Dixon's papermill at Grimsby.

Throughout the twentieth century, however, Humberside's agricultural industry has remained a 'strong, efficient, innovative and expanding sector of the regional economy . . . generating sufficient employment opportunities both upstream and downstream of farm production' (Symes 1987b p. 9); 49% of the region's farmland falls within Grades 1 and 2 of the MAFF Agricultural Land Classification, and 95% within the first three grades (Humberside County Council 1987, Ellis this volume). The enclosures of the period 1750-1820 (Neave and Neave this volume) laid the basis for the present pattern of dispersed farmsteads set within large fields. Average farm size in Humberside (80 ha) is substantially higher than that for England and Wales (59 ha); although many holdings are under 20 ha, they are often intensive livestock or horticultural units. On the freely drained rendzinas and brown earths of the Yorkshire and Lincolnshire Wolds, large-scale arable farming, chiefly cereal growing, predominates. In sharp contrast, more intensive farming, including pigs, poultry and horticulture, is characteristic of the more poorly drained gley soils of Holderness and the Lincolnshire Marsh. Around the head of the Humber estuary, man-made warp soils provide much Grade 1 quality land farmed for arable crops and field vegetables (Ellis this volume). Industries processing field vegetables and other local agricultural products have also provided considerable employment, particularly in Grimsby. However, even the prosperous agricultural industry faces some future uncertainty over measures designed to curb surplus grain production in the European Community.

Thus agriculture is arguably the strongest and most sustainable element in the Humber region's economy, and undoubtedly the dominant landscape feature. Port and industrial developments over the past two centuries have resulted in a discontinuous pattern of activities located on the estuary margins and at Scunthorpe, separated

Table 30.1. Humber estuary: total traffic 1987 (000 tonnes).

Port	Dry bulk	Liquid bulk	Container Roll on/Roll off	Semi-bulk	Conventional	Total
Hull	786	1235	3330	175	123	5650
Goole	489	66	216	877	119	1766
Grimsby and Immingham	7958	19 104	3598	1363	222	32 244
River Hull & Humber wharves	1673	5509	-	149	2	7333
River Ouse wharves	552	5	-	483	-	1039
River Trent wharves	2356	72	-	922	1	3351
Total Humber	13 814	25 991	7143	3969	466	51 383

Source: British Ports Federation (1988). Note: totals may not add up due to rounding.

by extensive empty spaces. This industrial and commercial facade is dominated by a backcloth of prosperous agriculture. In the 1960s the spacious, uncongested character of the region was seen as a prime asset, yet anticipated development did not occur. In addition to the external influences discussed earlier, it is clear that the remoteness and isolation of the Humber region from the principal centres of UK population and economic activity before the motorway developments of the late 1970s did inhibit growth, while media portrayal of Hull and Grimsby as centres of 'fish and ships' presented negative images to potential developers. The ports and wharves of the Humber estuary handled over 51 million tonnes of cargo in 1987 (Table 30.1), equivalent to 11.3% of the total trade of British seaports. Total traffic through the Humber has risen at an average rate of 5.5% per annum since 1982, compared with the UK figure of 2.2% annual growth over the same period. Indeed, a major study (Coopers & Lybrand Associates 1987) has recently identified sufficient market demand for a further deep-water port development at Killingholme in south Humberside. Nevertheless, the lasting impression is still of a hitherto underdeveloped estuarine region on the edge of the national space.

References

Bellamy, J.M. (1971). *The Trade and Shipping of Nineteenth Century Hull*. East Yorkshire Local History Society, York.
Bellamy, J.M. (1988). The Humber estuary and industrial development: (A) Historical. In: *A Dynamic Estuary: man, nature and the Humber* (ed. N.V. Jones) pp. 132-50. Hull University Press, Hull.
British Ports Federation (1988). *Port Statistics, 1987*. British Ports Federation, London.
Central Unit for Environmental Planning (1969). *Humberside: a feasibility study*. HMSO, London.
Coopers & Lybrand Associates (1987). *Killingholme Port Development Potential*. Coopers & Lybrand, Leeds.
Gillett, E. (1970). *A History of Grimsby*. Oxford University Press for the University of Hull, Oxford.
Hunt Committee (1969). *The Intermediate Areas*, Cmnd 3998. HMSO, London.

Humberside County Council (1987). *Humberside Facts and Figures: 1986.* Economic Development Unit, Humberside County Council, Beverley.

Jones, P.N. and North, J. (1987). Ports and wharves. In: *Humberside in the Eighties* (ed. D.G. Symes) pp. 97-111. Department of Geography, University of Hull.

Lawless, P. and Brown, F. (1986). *Urban Growth and Change in Britain: an introduction.* Harper & Row, London.

Lewis, P. and Jones, P.N. (1970). *The Humberside Region.* David & Charles, Newton Abbot.

North, J. (1978). The Humber crossing: an unfinished saga. In: *North Humberside Introductory Themes* (ed. D.G. Symes) pp. 51-61. Department of Geography, University of Hull.

North, J. (1988). The Humber Bridge - lame duck or golden goose? In: *A Dynamic Estuary: man, nature and the Humber* (ed. N.V. Jones) pp. 113-31. Hull University Press, Hull.

North, J. and Spooner, D.J. (1987). Land for industry. In: *Humberside in the Eighties* (ed. D.G. Symes) pp. 67-78. Department of Geography, University of Hull.

North, J., Spooner, D.J. and Symes, D.G. (1987). Humberside: an introductory profile. In: *Humberside in the Eighties* (ed. D.G. Symes) pp. 1-8. Department of Geography, University of Hull.

Pocock, D.C.D. (1981). The urban response, 1859-1918. In: *An Industrial Island: a history of Scunthorpe* (ed. M.E. Armstrong) pp. 55-66. Scunthorpe Borough Museum and Art Gallery, Scunthorpe.

Spooner, D.J. (1987). Regional policy and Humberside. In: *Humberside in the Eighties* (ed. D.G. Symes) pp. 133-47. Department of Geography, University of Hull.

Symes, D.G. (1978). The Humber fishing industry - end of an era? In: *North Humberside Introductory Themes* (ed. D.G. Symes) pp. 43-50. Department of Geography, University of Hull.

Symes, D.G. (1987a). The fishing industry. In: *Humberside in the Eighties* (ed. D.G. Symes) pp. 23-32. Department of Geography, University of Hull.

Symes, D.G. (1987b). Agriculture. In: *Humberside in the Eighties* (ed. D.G. Symes) pp. 9-22. Department of Geography, University of Hull.

Warren, K. (1984). Iron and steel. *Geography* **69**, 147-50.

INDEX

agriculture 6, 25, 29, 32, 34, 51, 90-1, 150, 152, 213, 245, 302, 368, 373, 433, 435
Aire, River 321, 364, 388
Airmyn 364, 388
Alkborough 165, 363, 381
alluvium 5, 25, 33, 105, 134, 149, 200-1, 203-4, 206-8, 334
Ancholme, River 63, 115-16, 119, 128, 195, 294, 361, 368, 379
  valley 16, 21, 33, 119, 134, 367, 373-6, 382, 396, 403
Anglian Stage 23
Anglo-Saxon period 78, 200, 219
animal husbandry 206-7
Anlaby 412
Appleby 115, 294, 378
archaeology 2, 4-5, 56, 71-2, 74, 76, 78, 81-2, 85, 89, 143, 147, 213, 219, 224-5, 274, 281, 348
  maritime 2, 4, 71, 109, 120
Arras culture 216
Ashby 337-9, 427
Atwick 76, 388
Aughton 361
Aylesby 383

Barmby on the Marsh 368
Barmston 90, 104
Barnetby 333
Barrow Haven 218
  upon Humber 296, 299, 361, 400
Barton-upon-Humber 5, 232, 293-7, 299, 302-3, 361-3, 365, 368, 399, 406-7, 409, 412, 414, 428
Basement Till 19, 21-2
Belton 296, 299, 377
Beverley 5, 83, 102, 200-1, 224, 269-71, 273-7, 279-81, 283-4, 286-8, 290-1, 297, 309, 312, 315, 362-3, 365, 369-70, 394, 396, 399, 401, 403
Bilton 402
Bishop Burton 400

boatbuilding 109, 122, 125, 127
Bonby 294
Bottesford 302-3
boulder clay 18, 134
  see also till
Boynton 378
Bradley 220, 244, 383
Brandesburton 79, 93, 104-5
Brantingham 150
brewing 286
brickmaking 269, 274-5, 302, 325, 370, 379, 428
Bridlington 2, 233, 290, 378
Brigantes 179, 350-1
Brigg 5, 76, 79, 84, 115-16, 120, 140, 294-7, 299-300, 302-3, 374, 378, 409
  'raft' 116, 118, 120-1
Brigham 105
Brigsley 220
Brocklesby 400
Bronze Age 4, 51, 80, 91, 98, 106, 111, 142, 173, 215, 218
bronze working 217
Broomfleet 154, 158, 168
Brough 21, 56, 60, 77-8, 81, 127, 154, 163, 165-7, 173, 183-4, 191, 194-5, 204, 208, 350, 401, 407, 429
Broughton 297, 299, 378
Brumby 337, 339-40, 342, 427
Burnby 383
Bursea 147, 149-50, 153-4
Burton Agnes 104-7
Burton upon Stather 165, 293-6, 362, 431

Caistor 394, 396
Calder, River 112
canal 309, 313, 316-18, 321-2, 324, 326-8, 330, 334, 379, 406, 423, 425
carr 91-2, 102, 142-3, 269, 340, 366
census 289, 396, 401

national census 6, 379, 388
chalk 14-16, 18-19, 21, 23-4, 32, 45, 48-51, 58-60, 90, 199, 220, 280, 302, 369, 373, 396
Cleethorpes 5, 65, 213-15, 218-19, 224, 227, 233, 235, 242-4, 246, 296, 302, 400, 402, 422, 426, 430
climate 29, 43, 46, 48, 50, 214, 216
climatic change 25, 90
clothmaking 362
Civil War 251, 284
coppicing 91, 152
Corieltauvi 182, 185, 192, 348
corn milling 260, 286, 300, 378
Cottingham 200, 367, 399
cotton spinning 260
coversands 24
Cowick 369
crannogs 83, 91
Cretaceous 16, 18
Crimean War 290
Crosby 337, 342, 427
Crowle 296, 299, 303, 374
cryoturbation 24, 32
cultivation 35-6, 104, 142-3, 216, 270, 368, 384

Danes' Dyke 76, 350
deforestation 34, 90, 98
    see also forest clearance, woodland clearance
deglaciation 59, 95-6
dendrochronology 118, 275
depopulation 6, 266, 399, 401-3
Derwent, River 321, 361, 366, 368
    valley 112, 368
Devensian 18, 24, 44, 58-60, 94-6, 98-9, 102, 142, 172
Dimlington Stadial 18-19, 21-4, 32, 44, 58-9, 62, 89-90, 95, 99, 102, 199
Don, River 113, 321, 367-8, 375
Doncaster 19, 234, 299
Donna Nook 64
Dragonby 150, 183-6, 189, 191-3, 195, 197

drainage 4, 30, 33-9, 51, 89-90, 102, 104, 106-7, 142, 149-50, 160, 162, 172, 178, 206, 269-70, 280, 322, 334, 367-8, 375-6, 381, 423
Driffield 2, 5, 83, 313, 315, 317, 378
    see also Great Driffield
Dutch River 322
dyeing 269, 275, 277, 363

Easington 18, 21
East Ferry 115
East Halton 295, 381
    Skitter 219
Eastoft 388
East Riding 2, 71, 74, 78, 80-1, 83, 284, 286-8, 313, 316, 362-3, 370, 374-5, 377, 380, 412
East Yorkshire 71, 82-3, 104, 163, 200, 291, 297, 348-9, 351, 353, 378, 388
economy 207, 230, 234, 245, 274, 283-4, 295, 299-300, 312, 317, 348, 364, 391, 401, 427-8, 433
Elloughton 15
employment 302, 337, 378, 389, 391, 399, 401, 403, 427, 433
enclosure 373-4, 383-4, 389, 399, 433
engineering 236, 260, 426
epidemics 307, 382-3
Epworth 296, 299, 374, 377-8, 381
Ermine Street 5, 189, 191, 193, 195, 407
erosion, coastal 89-90
    soil 34-5, 90-2, 134
Escrick 19
eskers 93
Etton 83
European (Economic) Community 52, 241, 433
Everingham 378, 400
exports 240, 274, 317-18, 328, 330, 354, 425, 427, 431

fair 230, 233, 274, 284-5, 293-4, 299, 307, 311, 362, 364-5
Fangfoss 375
farming 51, 92, 218, 230, 294, 313,

Index

373-4, 389, 399, 401, 433
   arable 32, 35, 38-9, 50, 52, 433
farmland 149, 243, 396, 403, 433
Faxfleet 4, 127, 154, 158-63, 165-8, 195
fen 161, 200-1, 216
Ferriby 73-4, 79, 82, 84, 121, 139
   see also North Ferriby, South Ferriby
   boats 1, 4, 71, 118, 122-3, 127, 131-2, 143, 218
   ferry 235, 293-4, 296, 361, 407-8, 412
First World War 262, 327-8, 428
fishing 160, 205, 227, 234-5, 241, 290, 368, 417, 425-6, 428, 432
fish processing 260
Flamborough Head 14, 21, 77, 350
Flandrian 25, 48, 59-60, 172, 199, 200
   see also Holocene
flooding 36, 64, 105, 149, 162, 325, 367
flour milling 423
forest 44, 48, 50-1, 140, 143
   clearance 35, 50, 92, 200-1, 214
   see also deforestation, woodland clearance
Foulness, River 4, 147, 149, 154, 165, 350
Freshney, River 214, 218, 229, 236
fulling 269-70, 275, 277

Gainsborough 2, 115, 299, 363, 407
Garton 353
gelifluction 23-4, 32
geology 2-3, 18, 29, 71
glacial deposits 16, 25, 44, 102, 199
glaciation 18, 19, 58
glass making 161
Goole 6, 234, 321-2, 324-30, 399, 402-3, 408, 412, 423, 425, 430
   Waste 370
Goxhill 294, 299
   Haven 218
Gransmoor 105
grassland 32, 39, 49-50, 140, 270, 376
grazing 36, 50, 200, 207-8, 241, 367, 373-5, 378
Great Coates 220, 229, 244
Great Driffield 309, 312-13, 318
   see also Driffield
Great Wold Valley 48
Grimsby 5, 13, 65, 213-21, 223-5, 227, 229-36, 238, 240-5, 296, 299, 302, 361-3, 365, 368-9, 382-4, 399, 401-3, 407-8, 415, 417, 419, 422, 425-9, 432-3, 435
Gunness 333-4, 431

Habrough 369
Halsham 111
Hatfield Chase 367, 375
   Moor 39
Haxey 296, 299, 303, 377
Hayton 183
Healing 220
Hedon 315, 317, 365
Hessle 22, 60, 72, 364, 400, 406-7, 409, 412, 414
High Hunsley 14
hinterland 238, 269, 317, 364, 408
Holderness 4, 13-14, 16, 18, 21-2, 24, 34-6, 38, 44-6, 48, 50-2, 59, 76-7, 79, 83, 89-95, 98-9, 102, 109, 139, 142, 361, 367, 373, 375, 381, 400, 403, 433
Holme-on-Spalding-Moor 4, 123, 147-9, 155, 160-1, 165, 353-4, 369-70, 384
Holocene 25, 48, 50, 90, 94-5, 98, 199
   see also Flandrian
Holton le Clay 219
Hornsea 21, 112, 307, 401
   Mere 44, 89-90
horticulture 429, 433
housing 241-2, 254-8 262-7, 275, 280, 291, 328, 338-9, 402-3, 426
Howden 234, 311, 318, 322, 366, 381, 394
   Dyke 318, 329
Hoxnian 22, 44

Hull 5, 60, 64, 82, 110, 155, 165, 200-1, 204, 207-8, 221, 224, 234-5, 250-6, 258-66, 273-4, 284, 286-7, 290, 295, 297, 299, 307, 309, 313, 315-18, 324, 326, 362-3, 365-6, 369-70, 379, 381, 388, 394, 396, 399-403, 407-9, 412, 417, 419, 422-3, 425-33, 435
  see also Kingston upon Hull
  River 5, 13, 25, 90, 102, 110, 199, 201, 205-8, 252, 254-5, 259-60, 269, 274, 286, 362, 364-6, 423, 426
  valley 4-5, 25, 51, 102, 104-6, 162, 199, 201, 204, 269, 274, 364, 366, 368, 375-6, 381, 396
Humber basin 4, 109-10, 128, 148, 199
  Bridge 56, 58, 60-2, 417, 430, 433
  estuary 2-3, 54, 58, 63, 119, 128, 133, 149, 160, 174, 199, 203-4, 213, 219, 322, 264, 388, 414, 428, 433, 435
  foreshore 1, 4, 131, 158, 254
  Gap 19, 21, 172
  Lake Humber 19, 21, 149, 172
  region 1-2, 4, 6, 18, 29, 43-4, 46, 52, 77, 85, 162, 366, 369, 388-9, 391-2, 394, 396, 399-403, 422-3, 425, 428-30, 433, 435
Humberhead Levels 34-5, 134, 140, 396
Humberside 1-2, 39, 163, 246, 291, 293-4, 296, 299-300, 302-3, 373-5, 377-84, 388, 403-4, 416-17, 419, 422, 430, 432-3, 435
Humberston 214, 219, 223, 233, 244, 302-3, 388, 402

ice age 4, 44, 46
ice sheet 19, 22, 44, 89-90, 95, 99, 102, 199
Idle, River 375
Ilfordian 22
Immingham 5, 55, 63-5, 240, 295, 302, 334, 337, 363, 402-3, 412, 415, 419, 427-32
imports 318, 329-30, 354, 426, 431
industrialisation 289, 389, 400, 423, 425, 429-30
Industrial Revolution 250-1, 253, 260, 389
industry 147, 150-1, 154, 241, 274, 277, 279-80, 286, 290-1, 302-3, 317-18, 332-3, 336, 362, 374, 377-8, 401, 423, 427, 432-3
Ipswichian 21, 44, 58-9
Irby-on-Humber 219
Iron Age 5-6, 51, 78, 80, 83, 91, 98, 125, 150, 152, 162, 183, 191, 204, 216, 218, 347-50, 353-4
iron manufacturing (working) 150, 152, 217, 350
ironstone 332-4, 337, 339-40, 342, 427, 429
Isle of Axholme 16, 19, 33, 38, 296, 299, 303, 359, 367-8, 373-5, 377-8, 381

Jurassic 16

Keadby 333, 427
Keelby 369
Kesteven 399
kettle-holes 25, 89
Keyingham 21, 400, 402
Killingholme 402, 428, 430, 435
Kingston upon Hull 13, 361, 364-5
  see also Hull
Kirmington 22, 44, 182-6, 189, 191-3, 195
Kirton in Lindsey 293-4, 296, 299

Laceby 214, 219-20, 229, 231, 294, 399
lake dwellings 83, 104
leather working 260, 277
Leconfield 106, 200
Leven Carrs 102, 106
limestone 16, 32, 369, 373
Lincoln 179, 182, 221, 223-4, 294, 379, 407, 412

Edge 16, 32, 38, 119, 184, 300, 333, 373
Lincolnshire 2, 22, 24, 154, 206, 221, 223, 235, 238, 297, 300, 347, 359-60, 367, 369-70, 374, 379, 407, 412
  Marsh 13-14, 16, 21-2, 38, 44, 46, 213, 373, 382, 433
  Wolds 13-16, 19, 22, 32, 44, 58, 119, 172, 182, 184, 213, 218-19, 300, 373, 382, 400, 433
Lindsey 388
Loch Lomond Stadial 24, 32, 46, 95-7
Lockington 104
logboat 76, 109, 111-13, 115-16, 118, 123, 128, 149
  Hasholme logboat 84, 117-18, 123, 150, 160, 165
Londesborough 396
loess 23-4
Luddington 368

Mablethorpe 2
maltsting 286, 378
Malton 14, 77, 112, 309, 315-16, 318, 350
manufacturing 254, 260, 317, 362, 377, 389, 390, 433
market 233, 284, 293-4, 296-7, 299, 307, 309, 311-13, 318, 325, 329, 335, 362, 364-5, 394
  town 5, 235, 293, 299-300, 307-10, 312-13, 315-16, 318, 322, 365, 380, 394
marketing 235, 284, 293, 295, 299, 307, 318
Market Rasen 2
Market Weighton 5, 16, 22, 310-11, 315-18, 378, 394
marl 16, 33, 91, 134, 378
marsh 51, 89, 102, 104, 160, 214, 216, 270, 359, 375
  land 51, 104, 135, 149, 269, 369, 373, 384, 396
Meaux 364, 366, 370
medieval period 5, 89, 220-1, 227, 250, 357, 363, 365, 367, 369-70, 407

Melton 74, 132, 429
mere 25, 34, 48, 51-2, 89-90, 93-5, 97-8, 102, 104-5, 109, 112
Mesolithic 104, 128
Messingham 299
Middle Ages 149, 231, 233, 251, 274, 288, 293-6, 363, 366, 369-70, 374, 379
Middleton-on-the-Wolds 384, 399-400
morainic ridge 21, 172, 215
motorway 329, 343, 415, 417, 430, 435
mudflats 119-20, 127, 135, 138, 143, 173

Napoleonic Wars 286, 290, 299
navigation 56, 317, 321, 363, 368-9, 412, 414-15
Neolithic 5, 83, 92, 98
New Holland 407-8, 412
Newport 154, 379
Norman Conquest 270, 273, 275
North Cave 150, 348
North Ferriby 4, 13, 15, 21, 60, 72-3, 78-9, 109, 120-1, 131, 134, 139-40, 172, 184
  see also Ferriby
North Frodingham 107
North Sea 13, 18-19, 21, 23, 56, 58, 90, 213, 241, 357, 363-5, 425-6, 430
North Yorkshire 7

oil refining 303, 416
  seed crushing (extracting) 254, 260, 426
Old Winteringham 178, 182, 184-6, 189, 191-5, 197
Ouse, River 13, 36, 54, 59-60, 112, 234, 316, 318, 321-2, 324, 328-9, 357, 359, 363, 366-8, 370, 375, 388, 399-400, 403, 406-7, 415, 417, 431
Owston Ferry 295, 299, 361, 367

paint making (manufacture) 260, 426
Palaeolithic 77
Parisi 166, 179, 183, 192, 349-51, 353-4
Patrington 307, 312, 315, 317, 363
Paull 363
peat 25, 34, 39, 72-3, 90-2, 94, 97, 106-7, 118, 133-4, 138-40, 142, 150, 152, 161, 172-3, 199-200, 234, 370, 374
permafrost 23-4
Petuaria 78, 81, 208, 352
plague 284, 382
Pliocene 44
Pocklington 2, 5, 310, 315, 317-18
population 6, 227, 236, 238, 241-2, 244-6, 250-2, 254, 256, 258, 283, 286-9, 291, 294, 302, 307-9, 325, 328, 330, 337, 379-84, 388-9, 391-2, 394, 396, 399-403, 415-16, 419, 422, 426-7, 432, 435
pottery making (manufacture, production) 152-5, 195, 370
potting 269, 275
prehistory 105, 173, 177, 213
Preston 361, 365

quarrying 4, 90, 106, 302
Quaternary 3, 18, 23-4, 44, 54, 58, 60

radiocarbon 18, 46, 80, 92, 95, 97-8, 104, 111-13, 115, 118-19, 121, 132, 139, 215, 272
railway 238, 242, 258, 260, 290, 326-7, 329-30, 333-4, 340, 389, 401, 407-9, 412, 425, 431
Read's Island 62
reclamation 35, 62, 104, 273, 367, 375, 388
Redcliff 5, 74, 78, 84, 172-5, 177-9, 184, 186, 192-4, 197, 350
relief 3, 13, 24, 29-30, 37-8, 423
religious houses 221, 280, 366-7
Riccall 357
Riplingham 81
Roman army 5, 179, 182, 194

Empire 174, 179, 194
period 78, 154, 186, 201, 203-4, 206, 208, 218, 349-50
Romanisation 6, 348, 350-1, 353
Romano-British period 5-6, 152, 162, 219, 347, 354
Roos 46, 50-1, 76, 95, 111, 142, 402
rope making 302
Routh 102, 104, 106-7, 269, 383
Rudston 78, 83

Saltfleet 233
saltmarsh 51, 138, 142-3, 149, 200, 206-7
Sancton 81
saw milling 423
Scartho 217, 219-20, 244
Scotter 115
Scunthorpe 6, 128, 150, 152, 302, 332, 336-40, 342-3, 400-3, 417, 422, 427, 429, 431-3
sea level 16, 22, 25, 59-61, 63-6, 102, 119-20, 134, 139-40, 149, 162, 172, 199, 203-4
Seaton Ross 384
Second World War 74, 78-9, 203, 240, 245, 261, 266, 328
seed crushing 423
Selby 2, 5, 309, 315-18, 321-2, 324, 363, 366
Sewerby 21-3
shipbuilding 254, 290, 426, 428
shipping 65, 168, 253-4, 317, 322, 328-9, 365, 406, 412, 414, 431
Shiptonthorpe 350
Skerne 104-6, 366
Skipsea 91, 94, 104, 361
Till 21-3, 89, 213
Withow Mere 4, 90-5, 98-9, 105
Skitter Haven 363, 367
Point 59, 62
slum-clearance 258, 262, 264-6
smelting 152, 333-5, 338, 429
Snaith 364
soil 24, 29-30, 32-5, 37-9, 43, 48, 50-1, 95, 97-8, 142, 147, 149-50, 158, 200-1, 270, 368, 375

South Cave 152, 318
South Ferriby 13, 21, 72-3, 128, 134, 172, 184-6, 191-5, 361-2, 368
South Yorkshire 7, 165, 427
Sproatley 48
Spurn Bight 62, 65
   Point 13, 56, 58, 60-1, 64, 105, 138, 365, 406
Stallingborough 233, 369, 384
Stamford Bridge 183, 359
steelmaking 336-7, 427
sugar refining 254
Sunk Island 34, 36, 51, 62, 375, 396
Sutton 59, 200, 204, 207
Sutton Common 7
Swanland 208
Swinefleet 400

tanning 269, 274-5, 277, 286, 289, 302, 318, 362, 378
Tertiary 15, 18
Tetney 233, 430
Thealby 293
Thorne 2, 322, 342, 367
   Moor 39, 142, 370
Tickton 102, 200, 269
tile making 269, 274-5, 302, 370, 428
till 18-19, 21, 24-5, 33, 45, 59-60, 72, 89-90, 92, 95-7, 134, 138, 140, 172, 199-201, 203-4, 207-8, 216, 220
Torne, River 375
trade 166, 168, 213, 230, 233-5, 238, 253, 274, 286, 293-5, 297, 299-300, 302, 312-13, 315, 317-18, 326, 328, 350, 362-3, 365, 406, 425, 427-8, 431, 435
trading 150, 251, 273, 284, 311-12, 315-16, 318, 326, 328, 406, 431
transport 165, 206, 307, 312, 327, 330, 334, 347, 350, 406, 412, 428
Trent, River 13, 36, 54, 59-60, 113, 115, 231, 234, 294, 299, 322, 324, 329, 333-4, 361, 363, 367-8, 375, 406-7, 415, 417, 427, 431

valley 24, 33, 373-4

Ulceby 400
Ulrome 90, 104
urbanisation 309, 400, 403

vegetation 3, 24-5, 29-30, 34, 44-6, 48, 51-2, 135, 143
Viking army 272

Walkington 82
Wallingfen 149, 367, 374, 377
Waltham 220, 302
Wansford 104-5, 378
warp 72, 134
   soils 34, 36, 433
warping 25, 36-7
Warter 378
waterways 5, 105, 152, 313, 318, 366, 370, 406, 408
Watton 104, 106
Wawne 200, 204
weaving 378
Welton 72-3, 84
West Riding 317-18, 321, 325-6, 363, 379
wetland 4, 7, 43, 52, 90-2, 94, 98, 104, 107, 111, 142, 200-1, 252, 270, 277
Wharfe, River 321
Willow Garth 34, 48, 51
Windermere Interstadial 46, 95-6
Winteringham 296-7, 299, 361, 364, 384, 407
Winterton 165, 192, 195, 297, 299
Withernsea 112, 401
   Till 21, 89
Wolds 16, 19, 21-3, 32, 34-5, 37-9, 51, 74, 104, 195, 274, 348, 373-6, 380-1, 396
   see also Lincolnshire Wolds, Yorkshire Wolds
Wolstonian 19
woodland 34, 46, 48, 50, 52, 89, 92, 95, 98, 142, 152, 214, 270
   clearance 34-5, 348
   see also deforestation, forest

clearance

York 155, 166, 183, 220, 250, 272-4, 287, 307, 309, 315, 350-1, 357, 359, 363-4, 366, 368, 370, 379, 407
    Vale of York 13-14, 16, 18-22, 24, 33, 35, 39, 44, 51, 60, 160, 321, 347-8, 350, 373-5, 377, 381, 384
Yorkshire 234, 238, 242, 273-4, 322, 333, 347-8, 350, 360, 362, 364, 408-9, 412
    Wolds 13-16, 18-19, 32, 34-5, 38, 44, 46, 48, 58, 102, 107, 172-3, 216, 348, 350, 373, 400, 402, 433